The Janáček
Compendium

The Boydell Composer Compendium Series

The aim of the Composer Compendium series is to provide up-to-date reference works on major composers and their music that can both provide instant information and act as a gateway to further reading. The authors are all leading authorities on the composers in question who have been given the remit not only to assemble and present already existing data but also, where appropriate, to make personal interpretations, to introduce new facts and arguments and to shed light on the many discourses surrounding the chosen musicians from their lifetime up to the present day.

The core of each volume is a dictionary section with entries for people, institutions and places connected with the composer; musical, analytical and historical terminology of particular relevance to them; significant events in the reception history of their music; the genres in which they composed; individual compositions or groups of compositions – in short, anyone and anything judged to be pertinent. Entries in the dictionary section are carefully cross-referenced to each other and also to a very comprehensive bibliography section at the end of the volume. Between the dictionary and the bibliography there is a work list based on the latest information, and the volume is prefaced by a concise biography of the composer. Numerous music examples and illustrations are included. By means of this simple formula, the series aims to provide handbooks of wide and durable interest responding to the needs of scholars, performers and music-lovers alike.

Michael Talbot
Series editor

Proposals are welcomed and should be sent in the first instance to the publisher at the address below. All submissions will receive prompt and informed consideration.

Boydell & Brewer, PO Box 9, Woodbridge, Suffolk, IP12 3DF
email: editorial@boydell.co.uk

Previous volumes in this series:

The Vivaldi Compendium, Michael Talbot, 2011
Also available in paperback
The Rameau Compendium, Graham Sadler, 2014
Also available in paperback

Frontispiece: Janáček in the front garden of his home in Brno. Photograph by his pupil Mirko Hanák, 1925, signed by Janáček.

The Janáček Compendium

Nigel Simeone

THE BOYDELL PRESS

First published 2019
The Boydell Press, Woodbridge

ISBN 978 1 78327 337 9

The Boydell Press is an imprint of Boydell & Brewer Ltd
PO Box 9, Woodbridge, Suffolk IP12 3DF, UK
and of Boydell & Brewer Inc.
668 Mt Hope Avenue, Rochester, NY 14620–2731, USA
website: www.boydellandbrewer.com

A catalogue record for this book is available
from the British Library

In Memoriam
JOHN TYRRELL
(1942–2018)

Contents

Illustrations

Frontispiece: Janáček in the front garden of his home in Brno. Photograph by his pupil Mirko Hanák, 1925, signed by Janáček (author's collection).   iv

1. Brno: The Beseda House (Besední dům) and Hotel Slavia, looking east along Solniční (formerly U solnice / Salzamtgasse). Postcard dated 1916 (author's collection).   18

2. The auditorium of the Brno National Theatre (now the Mahen Theatre) where the world premieres of all Janáček's operas from *Káťa Kabanová* to *From the House of the Dead* took place (author's collection).   23

3. Janáček's funeral procession at the Brno National Theatre (now the Mahen Theatre), 15 August 1928 (Janáček Archive, Moravian Museum, reproduced with permission).   77

4. Jaroslav Kvapil with the Beseda brněska chorus and the orchestra of the Brno National Theatre on stage in the Stadion Hall where the *Glagolitic Mass* was given its premiere by the same forces in December 1927. This photograph was taken in March 1928 before a performance of Handel's *Judas Maccabeus* (Janáček Archive, Moravian Museum, reproduced with premission).   81

5. *Gott erhalte den Kaiser!* Autograph manuscript of Janáček's unpublished arrangement (Janáček Archive, Moravian Museum, reproduced with permission).   83

6. *Ukvalská lidová poezie v písních* [*Hukvaldy Folk Poetry in Songs*], first edition, published by A. Píša, Brno, 1899 (author's collection).   94

7. Hukvaldy, 'Birthplace of the master Dr Leoš Janáček', including views of the castle, the church and the schoolhouse where Janáček was born. Postcard dated 1934 (author's collection).   95

8. Ondřej Sekora: 'When Leoš Janáček returned from the Prague *Excursion to the Moon*', cartoon in *Hudební rozhledy*, 15 December 1926 (author's collection).   98

9. Announcement for the concert of Janáček's music at the Wigmore Hall, London, on 6 May 1926 (Wigmore Hall Archives, reproduced with permission).   133

10. J. L. Budin (pseud. Jan Löwenbach) and Dr Desiderius (pseud. Hugo Boettinger): 'Leoš Janáček' from *Muzikantské dušičky* [*Musical Souls*], published by A. Srdce, Prague, 1922 (author's collection).   134

11. The Music Pavilion at Luhačovice designed by Dušan Jurkovič. Postcard from 1910 (author's collection).   135

12. Membership card for the Moravian Teachers' Choir (PSMU) using the design made specially for the choir by Alfons Mucha in 1911 (author's collection).   152

13. Janáček and Alfons Mucha in Luhačovice, 1922 (Janáček Archive, Moravian Museum, reproduced with permission).   154

The author and publisher are grateful to all the institutions and individuals listed for permission to reproduce the materials in which they hold copyright. Every effort has been made to trace the copyright holders; apologies are offered for any omission, and the publisher will be pleased to add any necessary acknowledgement in subsequent editions.

Abbreviations

b.: born
Brno NT: Brno National Theatre
d.: died
HMUB: Hudební matice Umělecké besedy
ISCM: International Society for Contemporary Music
JAMU: Janáčkova Akademie Múzických Umění v Brně (Janáček Academy of
    Music and Performing Arts in Brno)
KMS: Klub moravských skladatelů (Moravian Composers' Club)
KPU: Klub přátel umění v Brně (Club of the Friends of Art in Brno)
Prague NT: Prague National Theatre
PSMU: Pěvecké sdružení moravských učitelů (Moravian Teachers' Choral
    Society)
SMH: Spolek pro moderní hudbu (Society for Modern Music)
SNKLHU: Státní nakladatelství krásné litertatury, hudby a uměni
SO: Symphony Orchestra
UE: Universal Edition, Vienna
VSMU: Vachův sbor moravských učitelek (Vach Choir of Moravian Woman
    Teachers)

For bibliographical abbreviations, see Bibliography.

Introduction

Ninety years after his death, Leoš Janáček has become a permanent feature of the international operatic repertoire. In Brno and Prague, there has been a strong performing tradition since the 1920s, and German-speaking houses took up Janáček early on, thanks to conductors such as Otto Klemperer and Erich Kleiber. Starting in the 1950s, British opera audiences have been able to experience Janáček performances of the highest quality, thanks to the superlative advocacy of Charles Mackerras, followed by the likes of Richard Armstrong, Mark Elder, Andrew Davis and Simon Rattle. According to statistics on operabase.com, during the seasons 2013–14 to 2017–18 there were 1,212 performances (271 productions) of Janáček's operas in the world's opera houses, putting him between Britten and Gounod in the league table of most performed opera composers. The most popular opera remains *Jenůfa* (361 performances), closely followed by *The Cunning Little Vixen* (336).

All the major operas have appeared fairly regularly on British stages, with memorable productions at English National Opera, Welsh National Opera, Scottish Opera, Opera North and Glyndebourne. *Jenůfa*, *Káťa Kabanová* and *The Cunning Little Vixen* appear most often. Between 1964 and 2007, Sadler's Wells/ ENO had no fewer than three different productions of *The Makropulos Affair* (all conducted by Mackerras), which was also successfully staged at Glyndebourne. *Fate* and *The Excursions of Mr Brouček* have been performed in recent years by Opera North, and longer ago at English National Opera. Between 1975 and 1982, Welsh National Opera put on five of the operas conducted by Richard Armstrong and directed by David Pountney, with Elisabeth Söderström in *Káťa* and *Makropulos*. In the last season (2017–18), *From the House of the Dead* was not only revived by Welsh National Opera (one of Pountney's most inspired productions) but was given for the first time at the Royal Opera House, Covent Garden, using John Tyrrell's new edition of the score. Further new Janáček productions are planned there in the coming seasons.

In the United States, San Francisco Opera, Chicago Lyric Opera and the Metropolitan Opera in New York have all staged Janáček fairly regularly, as has Opera Australia in Sydney. In Europe, from Berlin to Barcelona, new productions continue to proliferate. At the National Theatre in Brno, Janáček's flame burns as brightly as ever: as I write, the 2018 Janáček Festival there is about to stage all of the operas, including *Šárka* and *The Beginning of a Romance*. All the operas have been recorded, some of them several times.

Janáček's concert works have fared just as well. There are currently more than forty different recordings of the *Sinfonietta* available, with *Taras Bulba*, the Violin Sonata, the two String Quartets and the *Glagolitic Mass* not far behind. The future looks promising for Janáček, not least because several young Czech conductors, including Jakub Hrůša, Tomáš Netopil and Tomáš Hanus (all pupils of Jiří Bělohlávek), have demonstrated an outstanding flair for his music, as have Czech instrumentalists such as the Pavel Haas Quartet.

This healthy picture of a composer who has come to be cherished by performers and audiences around the world makes *The Janáček Compendium* a book that will, I hope, not only be of interest to Czech specialists but also to music lovers and opera goers who want to learn more about aspects of the composer and his music. With this in mind, the dictionary has entries on all the operas, including synopses as well as introductions to their composition and performance history.

There are several outstanding books on Janáček in English, among them Jaroslav Vogel's pioneering life and works (*Leoš Janáček: A Biography*, revised edition 1981), John Tyrrell's two-volume biography (*Janáček: Years of a Life*, 2006 and 2007) and Tyrrell's other books, including *Káťa Kabanová* (1982), *Janáček's Operas: A Documentary Account* (1992), *Intimate Letters: Leoš Janáček and Kamila Stösslová* (1994) and *My Life With Janáček: The Memoirs of Zdenka Janáčková* (1998). I had the great pleasure of collaborating with Tyrrell and Alena Němcová on *Janáček's Works* (1997). Other important work in English includes the collection of Janáček's writings translated and edited by Mirka Zemanová: *Janáček's Uncollected Essays on Music* (1989). All of these have been of great help in compiling the *Compendium*. But I have also drawn extensively from the Czech literature on Janáček, including the first volume (the only volume published) of Vladimír Helfert's biography (1939), and numerous books and articles by his successors, including Ludvík Kundera, Bohumír Štědroň, Theodora Straková, Svatava Přibáňová, Alena Němcová, Jarmila Procházková, Libuše Janáčková and Jiří Zahrádka. Editorial work on Janáček's music (by many of the same scholars) has also yielded precious material: the introductions to volumes of the Complete Critical Edition of Janáček's works are often a mine of information, as are introductions to other critical-practical editions, particularly those edited by Tyrrell and Zahrádka.

Janáček research has been made a great deal easier thanks to the internet. The German-language online Janáček encyclopedia compiled by Jakob Knaus of the Leoš Janáček Gesellschaft in Zurich is a very useful resource (www. leos-janacek.org), and there have been exciting recent developments in the Czech Republic. Of these, the most important is the online *Korespondence Leoše Janáčka* (www.musicologica.cz/korespondencejanacek), edited by Jiří Zahrádka and others. This includes transcriptions of all of Janáček's correspondence held in the Janáček Archive of the Moravian Museum in Brno and is a priceless collection of primary source material. I have also delved into the press from Janáček's time, thanks to the availability online of Czech newspapers, especially the Brno daily *Lidové noviny* (accessed through www.digitalniknihovna.cz/mzk). The Czech online music encyclopedia *Český hudební slovník osob a institucí* (www.ceskyhudebnislovnik.cz) has been a valuable source of information (though not yet complete) and is the online successor to the indispensable *Československý hudební slovník* (2 vols., 1963 and 1965). I have aimed to include entries in the *Compendium* for places and people that Janáček knew in the city of Brno, and for these the *Encyklopedie dějin města Brna* has proved very helpful (encyklopedie.brna.cz). The recently launched website www.leosjanacek.eu includes details of all aspects of Janáček's life and work, compiled and maintained by Jiří Zahrádka and Šárka Zahrádková, and profusely illustrated with photographs.

The Janáček Compendium aims to shed light on specific musical works, and on other aspects of Janáček's professional activities (conductor, teacher, journalist, theorist and ethnographer), as well as particular features of his musical language. Along with entries on all the major works and many of the lesser ones, the Dictionary includes locations and institutions with

connections to Janáček, and significant personalities such as conductors,
pianists, composers, writers and critics. He was a teacher for over half a
century and a number of his pupils have entries, as do friends, collaborators
and publishers. With very few exceptions, I have excluded living musicians, as
the Dictionary is essentially historical in nature. The exceptions are a handful
of scholars whose work has enriched our knowledge of Janáček and shed new
light on his life and work.

Many friends and colleagues have helped in the preparation of this book.
In the Czech Republic these include Jiří Zahrádka and Šárka Zahrádková, Jan
Špaček, Jarmila Procházková and Alena Němcová, all of whom have been
generous with their time, their knowledge, their hospitality, or all three. Eva
Velická of Bärenreiter Prague has always been helpful. Tomáš Mařík in Prague
has supplied me with regular parcels of books from his *antikvariát* and has
kindly acquired material from other Czech booksellers on my behalf, including
many unusual items. In Brno, I was lucky enough to be able to purchase
Eduard Milén's large pastel portrait of František Neumann, who conducted
the world premieres of four Janáček operas: *Káťa Kabanová*, *The Cunning Little
Vixen*, *The Makropulos Affair* and *Šárka* (see plate 14, p. 157). Neumann's steady
gaze has watched over much of this project, and the picture is a tangible link
with an artist and a subject who were both close to Janáček.

Heinz Stolba of Universal Edition, Vienna, has been exceptionally generous
with scores, many of them not generally available and all of them gratefully
received. In England, Mark Audus, a friend of many years' standing as well as
a formidable Janáček scholar, has offered support, advice and humour. Cathy
Mackerras very kindly gave me a number of books on Janáček that had belonged
to her father. Jim Friedman has always offered thoughtful suggestions and sage
insights. Jan Smaczny, though he may not have realised it at the time, sowed
the seeds of this project during a conversation before *The Makropulos Affair* at
the Proms in August 2016. Patrick Lambert not only shared his knowledge
and enthusiasm but also kindly made copies of his extraordinary collection of
rare early Janáček recordings. Others to whom I owe thanks for various acts
of kindness and encouragement connected with this book include Tom Alban,
John Allison, Marius Carney, Jakub Hrůša, Sophie Redfern, John Snelson and
Emily Woolf.

My own discovery of Janáček began when I was a teenager, not only
with recordings but also with three live performances that made a lasting
impression: the *Glagolitic Mass* in 1970 (conducted by the young Andrew Davis),
The Cunning Little Vixen in 1972 (at Deutsche Oper am Rhein in Düsseldorf)
and *Káťa Kabanová* in 1973 (at the London Coliseum, conducted by Mackerras).
Once I got to university, adolescent enthusiasm for Janáček developed into
scholarly curiosity as well, and it was while I was a student that I first met John
Tyrrell. Subsequently I had the privilege of working with him on two books,
one of which (*Janáček's Works*) is often referred to in the Dictionary, and the
other (*Charles Mackerras*) was about a musician whose Janáček performances
inspired us both. For four decades, John shared his encyclopedic knowledge
and was the most loyal and generous of friends. In August and early September
2018 he read all the entries in the Dictionary and his comments were, as always,
illuminating and exceptionally helpful. The manuscript of the *Compendium*
was dedicated to him. John died on 4 October 2018 while the book was being

prepared for publication, and it is with sorrow that I now dedicate it to his memory, with love and gratitude for his friendship and his wisdom.

My grateful thanks are due to PhDr Jiří Zahrádka, head of the Janáček Archive of the Moravian Museum, for kind permission to reproduce manuscripts and photographs in the collection, for being so ready to answer questions and for providing unfailingly helpful answers.

At Boydell and Brewer, warm thanks go to Michael Middeke and Megan Milan, who have both been attentive and encouraging throughout. Ian Brooke was the most helpful and careful copy editor and Nick Bingham was a model of efficiency in preparing this book for publication. Thanks of a more personal kind go to Jasmine, my wife, for her constant support – and for sharing an inspiring week with me in Brno at the start of this project.

Nigel Simeone
Rushden, Northamptonshire
October 2018

Biography

Leoš Janáček was born on 3 July 1854 in Hukvaldy, a village 30 km (18 miles) south of Ostrava in Moravia. Hukvaldy was named after the medieval castle that overlooks it (the reason it was sometimes known as 'Pod Hukvaldy', below Hukvaldy), but the castle itself had been allowed to become a romantic ruin after a fire in 1820. Janáček's father Jiří was the village schoolmaster, and Janáček was born in the schoolhouse, 'in a room where one window looked on to the church, and the other on to the brewery', as he later recalled. Leo Eugen, the names with which he was baptised on 4 July 1854, the day after he was born, was the ninth child of Amalie (née Grulichová) and Jiří Janáček – who not only served as the village teacher but also its parish organist. The family had moved to Hukvaldy in 1848 and were well respected in the village, but only just got by financially as the schoolmaster in Hukvaldy was one of the worst-paid posts in the Moravian school system. Jiří was a talented musician: Janáček later remembered being taught Beethoven piano sonatas by him, and if the regime was strict and unforgiving, it was recalled with gratitude. At the age of eleven, Janáček became a chorister at the Augustinian Monastery in Old Brno.

At the time of Janáček's birth, Bohemia and Moravia were the *Kronländer* (Crown Lands) in the far northwest of the Habsburg Empire. Since the thirteenth century, there had been a large ethnic German minority in Moravia, mostly concentrated in the cities of Brno and Olomouc. In 1867, the year after Janáček started school in Brno, the Austro-Hungarian Compromise came as a blow to proponents of Czech self-rule: while Hungarian autonomy was recognised, the Czechs – the third largest group in the Empire numerically – were overlooked, and attempts to forge a similar agreement for Czech lands failed. On the one hand, this led to a hardening of attitudes towards the ruling monarchy in Vienna, but on the other, this period saw a flourishing of the Czech language and education, and the rediscovery of traditional culture, including folksong. At the Augustinian Monastery, Janáček's education was in the hands of a remarkable group of priests, including the composer Pavel Křížkovský and the scientist Gregor Mendel, the father of genetics. Under Abbot Cyril Napp, the Monastery was a centre of liberal thinking (and regarded with suspicion by the church authorities). Roughly half the priests were ethnic Germans and the others ethnic Czechs, several of them committed Czech nationalists. Napp died the year after Janáček arrived, and Mendel succeeded him as Abbot. The most important musical influence on Janáček at school was Křížkovský, whose conducting he particularly admired and whose choruses (especially his settings of folk texts from František Sušil's collection) helped to inspire Janáček's earliest compositions. When Křížkovský left for Olomouc in 1872, Janáček, still in his teens, succeeded him as director of the choir at the Monastery. He attended the Teachers' Institute, where he was soon teaching, and in 1873 he was appointed conductor of the Svatopluk choral society, for which he wrote his first compositions, choruses on Sušil's folk texts.

Set for a teaching career, Janáček spent 1874–5 at the Prague Organ School, where he was fortunate to have František Skuherský as his composition teacher. Janáček did not have the money to enjoy the cultural delights of Prague, though he did attend the concert in April 1875 at which Smetana's *Vltava* had its world premiere, the only time he saw Smetana. During his Prague year, Janáček put his energies into composition and returned to Brno with a dozen or so works that show him starting to develop a solid technique. In 1876 he became conductor of the Brno Beseda, the most important choral society in the city, with which he performed major choral-orchestral works, including the Mozart Requiem and Beethoven's *Missa solemnis*, as well as his own early orchestral compositions. He also started giving piano lessons to Zdenka Schulzová, the teenage daughter of Emilian Schulz, director of the Teachers' Institute. Zdenka and Janáček were very close by the time he went to Leipzig and Vienna in 1879–80, and when he came back from these further studies (nowhere near as useful as his time in Prague had been) they were married. On their honeymoon in Bohemia, they visited Dvořák, who was increasingly regarded by Janáček as his mentor. Janáček and Zdenka remained together for nearly fifty years, though theirs was a marriage marked by tragedy (both their children died) and by Janáček's entanglements with three women in particular: Kamila Urválková, Gabriela Horvátová and Kamila Stösslová (all three of them, incidentally, also married).

In the 1880s, Janáček made a name for himself as a trenchant critic of the Brno National Theatre, established in 1884. A week after it opened, Janáček founded the journal *Hudební listy* (financed by the Brno Beseda), and for the next four years his reviews and articles returned time and again to the need for standards to be raised, to improve the orchestra, to train young singers and to present an imaginative repertoire. Janáček had extensive exposure to opera during his years at *Hudební listy*, but he refused to attend the German theatre on principle, so he experienced no Wagner performances at the time (though he did write an analysis of *Tristan und Isolde*). With this kind of immersion in opera, it is no surprise that in 1887 Janáček decided to try his hand at one of his own. He chose Julius Zeyer's libretto for *Šárka*, but on asking for permission he was expressly forbidden to use it by the author (who had originally intended it for Dvořák). With typical single-mindedness, Janáček set it anyway, completing the orchestration of two acts in 1888. There the work lay for the next thirty years; when Janáček returned to *Šárka* in 1918, he realised that it had in embryo some elements of his mature operas and it was eventually produced in Brno in 1925.

It was from the mid-1880s onwards that Janáček's interest in folk music began to intensify and he started the systematic collection of Moravian folksongs and folk dances. In 1886 he added teaching at the Czech Gymnasium (grammar school) to his workload at the Teachers' Institute (which was in the same building). The Gymnasium's director from 1888 was the ethnographer and linguist František Bartoš. Together, Bartoš and Janáček published their first collection of Moravian folksongs in 1890, by which time Janáček had started to make a serious study of the folk musicians in the villages near Hukvaldy, collecting tunes that he soon arranged for orchestra as the *Valachian Dances* (published in 1890) which were later incorporated into the *Lachian Dances*. It was folksong and dance arrangements that provided much of the material for his next two stage works: the ballet *Rákoš Rákoczy*, given at the Prague National Theatre in the summer of 1891, and *The Beginning of a Romance*, a one-act opera based on a short story by Gabriela Preissová, which Janáček himself conducted at the Brno National Theatre in 1894.

In the same year, Janáček started another opera based on Preissová, this time on her play *Její pastorkyňa*. It was to take him the best part of a decade (with a

long break between the first and second acts) but in January 1904 *Jenůfa* had its triumphant Brno premiere. The most important piece written while *Jenůfa* was put to one side after Act I was *Amarus* (1896–7), a work that Dvořák told Janáček marked a decisive step forward in his musical development. In the summer of 1903, Janáček spent time in the spa town of Luhačovice, where he met Kamila Urválková. Her story was to inspire *Fate*, the opera he started by the end of that year, just before the premiere of *Jenůfa*. Often regarded as Janáček's operatic problem child on account of its shaky dramatic structure, *Fate* has a magnificent score, with a handling of short musical motifs that pointed the way forward to his later operas. The fruitless negotiations to put *Fate* on the stage (it was not produced during his lifetime) didn't discourage Janáček from embarking on a new operatic project in 1908: *The Excursion of Mr Brouček to the Moon*, based on Svatopluk Čech's novel of the same name. Largely due to problems with librettists (eight of them in all, including the composer), it was to be ten years before this was completed, and then Janáček decided to revise it as the first part of an operatic diptych to create *The Excursions of Mr Brouček*. This was another innovative design: two operas in one, combining whimsical comedy with deeply felt patriotism.

When Janáček turned sixty on 3 July 1914, he could look back on plenty of solid achievement: four decades of teaching, years of dedicated and productive work on the collection and classification of Moravian folksongs, and a big local success with *Jenůfa* in 1904 (with revivals in 1906 and 1911). He had become a central figure in Brno's musical, educational and cultural life, not only as a composer and teacher but also as an occasional contributor of aphoristic articles in the local newspaper, *Lidové noviny*. Some of Janáček's music had been published: *Jenůfa* and *In the Mists* by the Club of the Friends of Art in Brno, which also printed *The Fiddler's Child* to celebrate his sixtieth birthday. Local firms published other pieces, including *On the Overgrown Path* (Arnošt Píša in Brno) and the little *Bouquet of Moravian Folksongs* collected by František Bartoš and Janáček which was first issued in 1890 (Emil Šolc in Telč). Janáček's largest scholarly work, his vast study and collection of *Moravian Folksongs Newly Collected* with Bartoš, was published by the Czech Academy in Prague in 1901.

Even so, wider recognition continued to elude him and Prague performances were few and far between: apart from the production of *Rákoš Rákoczy* in 1891 (quickly forgotten), František Neumann included *Jealousy* in a concert with the Czech Philharmonic in 1906, and *Amarus* was given in October 1912, but his operas remained unperformed outside his home town. A long article about Janáček (by his former pupil Jan Kunc) appeared in the Prague journal *Hudební revue* in 1911, but Janáček's reputation was still largely confined to Brno. *Fate*, the opera composed straight after *Jenůfa*, came agonisingly close to being produced at the Vinohrady Theatre in Prague, but plans fell through. Meanwhile, *The Excursion of Mr Brouček to the Moon* was in a state of limbo, its music largely finished but hobbled by an incoherent libretto that would take a few more years to sort out. In terms of his stylistic development, Janáček had started to show extraordinary boldness of invention in the choruses he wrote on poems of Petr Bezruč (*Halfar the Schoolmaster*, *Maryčka Magdónova* and *The Seventy Thousand*). *In the Mists*, his most overtly Impressionist piano work, was probably inspired by his first hearing of Debussy's music in 1912, while the slightly earlier pieces of *On the Overgrown Path* were miniatures of Schumann-like concentration and intimacy. Brno was the second city in the Czech provinces of the Habsburg (Austrian) Empire, but its population at the time was around 125,000, similar to the present-day population of Eastbourne in England. Prague was not only four times the size, but also boasted a very fine opera company at the National Theatre, an excellent second house at the German Theatre (where Zemlinsky became chief conductor in 1911) and an outstanding orchestra in the Czech Philharmonic.

Clearly, it was in Prague that Janáček needed to make his mark and finally he did. The Prague premiere of *Jenůfa* in May 1916 was an unqualified success. Max Brod went to see it (on the recommendation of Josef Suk, who had been at a dress rehearsal) and he urged Emil Hertzka at Universal Edition to sign up Janáček at once (Hertzka took his advice). Brod also made the German translation which brought wider success to the opera within a few years. The Kostelnička in the Prague premiere was the Croatian singer Gabriela Horvátová and Janáček became utterly besotted with her. Mrs Janáčková watched their relationship unfold with considerable bitterness, not least because she took an instant dislike to Horvátová. For two years, Janáček went to Prague at every opportunity to spend time with Horvátová, but by mid-1918 things had cooled, not least because Janáček had met someone at Luhačovice in the summer of 1917 who was to change the course of his composing career: the second Kamila in his life – Kamila Stösslová – like Kamila Urválková before her, a young married mother.

The success of *Jenůfa* in 1916 gave Janáček a new-found confidence as he started his next operatic project, *Káťa Kabanová*, based on Ostrovsky's play *The Thunderstorm*. Kamila Stösslová was at the front of his mind when he wrote the opera, and Káťa was his musical embodiment of her (though, unlike Káťa, Kamila was happily married). Kamila also inspired the slightly earlier *The Diary of One Who Disappeared* (1917–19), in which the gypsy woman Zefka (the solo mezzo-soprano) was modelled on her. When Mrs Janáčková first met Kamila in 1917, she described her as 'a second edition of Horvátová' in terms of her appearance; but, as Zdenka grudgingly admitted, she was also somebody with whom one could have a friendly conversation.

Janáček's non-operatic works from this time include the 'Slavonic Rhapsody' *Taras Bulba* (1915–18) and the 'Legend' for soloists, chorus and orchestra *The Eternal Gospel* (1917), both pieces notable for their visionary grandeur and with a level of inventiveness showing that Janáček's new self-confidence reached well beyond the opera house. Janáček's creativity was not only fuelled by his love (mostly one-sided) for Kamila but also by the emergence of the independent Czechoslovak Republic, proclaimed on 28 October 1918. The first President, Tomáš Garrigue Masaryk, was a fellow Moravian, and the composer described him (in the dedications of *Brouček* and *The Ballad of Blaník*) as the 'liberator of the Czech nation'. In this context the Violin Sonata is another interesting work: it was started in September 1914 as first reports came through of successful Russian advances in the earliest days of World War I. As a pro-Russian Pan-Slavist, Janáček was heartened by this news, even though the Russian troops were on the 'wrong' side: Bohemia and Moravia were part of the Habsburg Empire, which was a German ally, and the vast majority of Czech soldiers fought on the German side, against the Russians. A small number – animated by Masaryk who was in exile in London – joined the Czech Legions who fought with the Allies (Janáček's chorus *The Czech Legion* is about one of these fighting in eastern France).

Káťa Kabanová was the first Janáček premiere to be conducted in Brno by František Neumann, who had been appointed Head of Opera at the Brno National Theatre in 1919 with Janáček's enthusiastic support. Neumann had conducted a new production of *Jenůfa* in his first season, but *Káťa* in 1921 was the first time composer and conductor worked closely on a new work. Following its success, Neumann went on to give the world premieres of *The Cunning Little Vixen* and *The Makropulos Affair*, as well as the belated premiere of *Šárka*. A pattern began to emerge that was very different from the prolonged battle over *Jenůfa*: after receiving their premieres in Brno, Janáček's later operas were quickly taken up in Prague, all conducted by Otakar Ostrčil.

Janáček's seventieth birthday was a marked contrast to his sixtieth. The respected Brno composer of 1914 was, by 1924, one of the leading figures in Czech music. Among the many concerts given to celebrate his seventieth birthday, the gala event in the Smetana Hall on 8 December 1924 was the highlight: the performers included the Czech Philharmonic and Václav Talich, President Masaryk was there, and the composer was invited to spend the interval in the President's box, where they spoke for fifteen minutes. Talich conducted *The Fiddler's Child* and *Taras Bulba*, and the other works on the programme included *The Eternal Gospel* conducted by Jaroslav Křička and three of Janáček's most innovative choruses sung by the Prague Teachers' Choral Society under Metod Doležil.

The Violin Sonata had been performed in Brno and Prague, and at the 1923 ISCM Festival in Salzburg. Janáček was soon inspired to write more chamber music: in October 1923, the Czech Quartet (whose second violinist was the composer Josef Suk) asked Janáček for a new work and the result was the First String Quartet, given its premiere in Janáček's seventieth birthday year, as was the wind sextet *Youth*. The *Concertino* for piano and chamber ensemble followed in 1925, and the *Capriccio* was written a year later. In May 1926, Janáček visited London for a concert of his music at the Wigmore Hall, organised by Rosa Newmarch. The timing was unfortunate (his visit took place during the General Strike, so there were no printed programmes and very few reviews) but, even so, Janáček was grateful for the invitation and dedicated his next orchestral work, the *Sinfonietta*, to Newmarch. This had its first performance on 26 June 1926, by the Czech Philharmonic under Talich, and it was quickly taken up by Otto Klemperer, who conducted it in Wiesbaden and New York before a triumphant performance in Berlin in September 1927 (by his own account, the best performance Janáček ever heard of the work). In December 1927, the *Glagolitic Mass* was given for the first time in Brno, and repeated (after revisions) in Prague the following April. As with the later operas, Universal Edition quickly published the vocal score, but the work took a little longer to establish itself outside Czechoslovakia: Alexander Zemlinsky gave the first German performance in 1929.

The *Glagolitic Mass* was a work that Janáček described privately to Kamila Stösslová as a nuptial Mass for their imaginary wedding. By late 1927 they had grown closer and she had started to reciprocate in a small way some of his feelings for her: in July that year – after a decade of intense friendship and even more fevered fantasies – they had their first kiss. Before then Janáček had Kamila firmly in mind when writing the central female characters of *The Cunning Little Vixen* (1922–3) and *The Makropulos Affair* (1923–5). In his last opera, *From the House of the Dead*, the Tartar boy Aljeja, a part written for a mezzo-soprano, was also a role inspired by Kamila. As Janáček was revising *From the House of the Dead* in 1928, he composed his most overt love song to Kamila: the Second String Quartet, eventually subtitled 'Intimate Letters', though his first thought had been to call it 'Love Letters'. The long-suffering Mrs Janáčková was immensely hurt by Janáček's coldness towards her during these last years, as he imagined himself growing ever closer to Kamila, but she remained loyal and provided him with the stability he needed to compose: however wounded she was by his behaviour, she never doubted his genius. Kamila was with Janáček when he died at a sanatorium in Moravská Ostrava on 12 August 1928: Zdenka never had the chance to be at her husband's bedside as she was only told after he had died. She rushed from Brno and had a meeting with Kamila that can only have been excruciating. Kamila returned to her home in Písek and Zdenka got on with making the arrangements for her husband's funeral, held in the National Theatre in Brno, with the final scene of *The Cunning Little Vixen* performed at the composer's request. Kamila died young in 1935, while Zdenka lived until 1938.

Revered in Brno after his death, with the operas never out of the repertoire and his pupil Břetislav Bakala conducting Janáček's music regularly on Brno Radio (including the first performance of *Fate* in 1934), it was to be many more years before Janáček was fully valued and understood outside Czech lands. In the United States, the *New York Times* critic Olin Downes (who had interviewed Janáček in 1924) was more or less a lone voice in recognising the bold and brilliant originality of Janáček's music. The situation in Germany was more complicated: Brod and some progressive critics were enthusiastic, and Berlin welcomed Janáček's operas. However, some critics complained about what they considered his patchwork approach to composition and the savage simplicity of his ideas. There was a nationalist undercurrent too: when *Jenůfa* and *Káťa Kabanová* were staged in Cologne during Janáček's lifetime (both conducted by Klemperer), local critics asked why German novelties were not being presented instead. On the basis of the few large works that were performed in Britain (the *Sinfonietta*, *Taras Bulba* and the *Glagolitic Mass*, all pioneered by Henry Wood), critical voices there were quick to pounce on the impracticality of the music, with the suggestion that Janáček was a misguided crank, toiling away in a Moravian backwater with a musical language that was a thing of fits and starts, and disjointed fragments. The critic Ernest Newman was at a loss to find anything good to say about Janáček, and he wasn't alone. When *Káťa Kabanová* finally reached the London stage in 1951, conducted by Charles Mackerras (then a young staff conductor at Sadler's Wells), reactions to the music were mixed. It was only in the 1960s that the critical tide began to turn. Janáček is now acknowledged as a singular genius, and one of the most significant musical figures of the first half of the twentieth century – but that kind of recognition was a long time coming.

Dictionary

Note for Readers

The main entries for Janáček's works are under the English translations established in *Janáček's Works* (JAWO), with cross-references from Czech titles. In general these are well known, but readers looking for *Osud* should look under *Fate*, and for *Mládí* under *Youth*. Definite and indefinite articles are ignored, so *The Cunning Little Vixen* (I/9) appears under the letter C, *The Danube* (IV/36) under D and so on. The numbering of works (in parentheses) is according to the classification in JAWO and all Janáček's compositions, grouped in their JAWO categories, are given in the List of Musical Works that follows the Dictionary. Institutions, clubs and societies have been placed under the city where they operated, so the Club of the Friends of Art (Klub přátel umění) is under 'Brno: Club of the Friends of Art in Brno' and the Society for Modern Music (Spolek pro moderní hudbu) is under 'Prague: Society for Modern Music'. References to the Bibliography are given in italics at the end of each entry using a system similar to that in earlier volumes in this series. Cross-references to other entries are followed by an asterisk. References to 'Janáček's autobiography' are to: Adolf Veselý (ed.), *Leoš Janáček: Pohled do života i díla* [Leoš Janáček: a view of the life and works] (Prague: Fr. Borový, 1924), which has a text almost entirely written by the composer.

1. X. 1905 (*From the street 1 October 1905*) [1. X. 1905 (*Z ulice dne 1. října 1905*)], sometimes known as Janáček's 'Piano Sonata' (VIII/19).   Composed between 2 October 1905 and the first performance (27 January 1906), the title refers to events in Brno on 1–2 October 1905. The German population of Brno organised a rally ('Volkstag') protesting against the establishment of a Czech university, the Czechs retaliated with their own mass meeting and violent clashes ensued. On 2 October 1905 the police and army were ordered to break up the demonstration outside the Beseda House where the Czechs, including Janáček, were holding their protest. When the army went in, František Pavlík* was fatally wounded by a bayonet. A plaque on the wall of the Beseda House marks the occasion and the date, indicating that Janáček should have called his work '2. X. 1905'. The first performance was given by Ludmila Tučková in the KPU club rooms in the Brno Beseda on 27 January 1906. According to Jan Kunc, Janáček destroyed the third movement at the rehearsal. After Tučková played the work a second time in Prague, Janáček threw the remaining two movements into the River Vltava, but the prudent Tučková had made a copy and in 1924 she was able to play the piece to Janáček. Her manuscript was used as the printer's copy for the first edition, issued by HMUB in 1924. The first edition has an inscription explaining the work's inspiration, without mentioning that Janáček had been present:

> The white marble steps of the Besední *dům* in Brno. A simple worker, František Pavlík, fell there, stained with blood. He only came to demonstrate his enthusiasm for higher education and was killed by cruel murderers. Leoš Janáček, in memory of a worker bayonetted during demonstrations for the university in Brno.

In Janáček's autobiography the work is called 'From the street (1. X. 1905), sonata in three movements', but the word 'sonata' does not appear on the first edition, which was authorised by Janáček. Vogel wrote that 'in places the work sounds more like the piano score of a symphony', and concluded that it had 'more importance as an idea rather than a composition'. But this is to overlook the tight motivic organisation (the theme of the second movement is derived from part of the opening of the first) and the dramatic use of piano sonority. *JAWO, JYL1, VogJan.*

70,000   See *The Seventy Thousand* (IV/36)

Album for Kamila Stösslová [*Památník pro Kamilu Stösslovou*] (including pieces listed in VIII/33).   An autograph book in which Janáček wrote intimate messages to Kamila Stösslová* between 2 October 1927 and 10 August 1928. The entries from October 1927 to June 1928 were made during Janáček's visits to Písek. Entries in August 1928 date from his last visit to Hukvaldy. Many of the entries include short pieces for keyboard, amounting to thirteen pieces in all. 'I am waiting for you' and 'The golden ring' are Janáček's last compositions, written between 5 and 8 August 1928. The final entry is dated 10 August, the day he was moved to the sanatorium in Ostrava where he died on 12 August.

This intensely personal document was used to establish Janáček's last wishes during the court case to settle his estate. On the recto of the leaf containing the start of 'I am waiting for you' there is a signed and witnessed codicil to Janáček's will, dated 5 August 1928, in which he left Stösslová the interest from two bequests and the royalties from *Kát'a Kabanová, The Diary of One Who Disappeared, From the House of the Dead* and 'our Quartet (No. 2)'. This was contested by Janáček's widow, but after three years of legal wrangling the court decided in Stösslová's favour on 14 October 1931. The court retained the album until further legal action saw its return to Stösslová in February 1934, without the leaf containing the codicil, which was kept in the court files. Stösslová died in 1935. In October 1939, Vladimír Helfert acquired the Album (and all Janáček's letters to Stösslová) from a pawnbroker in Prague. In 1994 a facsimile and transcription was published by the Moravian Museum with a commentary by Jarmila Procházková. *JAWO, ProPam.*

Amarus for soloists, mixed chorus and orchestra (III/6).   Composed in 1896–7 and revised in 1901 and 1906, *Amarus* represents a significant landmark in Janáček's development as a composer, particularly in its use of orchestral ostinatos and tenor writing that has parallels with the vocal style of the operas from *Jenůfa* onwards. Scored for solo tenor, solo baritone, mixed chorus and orchestra, *Amarus* sets Jaroslav Vrchlický's poem of the same name published in 1881. In the same year that Janáček wrote this work, Josef Bohuslav Foerster composed a setting of the same poem as a melodrama for reciter and piano. Janáček sent *Amarus* to Dvořák, who replied on 21 May 1897, noting a 'real step forward', praising the harmony, but wanting 'more melody'. When Vrchlický* saw the score he wrote to Janáček expressing his pleasure that the composer had 'found in my poem *Amarus* something suitable for setting to music' and telling him that the Czech Academy had awarded Janáček 200 florins for the work, on the recommendation of Zdeněk Fibich and Emanuel Chvála.

The first performance of any part of *Amarus* was in Brno on 20 March 1898, when the Epilogue (fifth movement) was given in the same concert as the premiere of Dvořák's *The Wild Dove*, both conducted by Janáček. The first four movements of *Amarus* were given in Kroměříž on 2 December 1900, with the Moravan choral society. Janáček remembered this performance decades later and wrote about it on 2 June 1928 to Eugen Třasoň (conductor of Moravan at the time): 'Witnesses are still living who heard how wretchedly it turned out. Let us hope you will fare better.' In the same letter, Janáček also described where he imagined the setting for *Amarus*: 'The Queen's Monastery in Brno. The long, cool corridors, the silence and the golden sun shining into the shady garden loud with birdsong, the high arches of the church and the almost invisible picture of the Madonna. Close by hangs the silver eternal lamp and Amarus's silent steps disturb the mute twilight. My youth is in the work. How could it have been otherwise?' The first complete performance was in Brno on 25 February 1912, conducted by Ferdinand Vach* with Stanislav Tauber* as the tenor soloist. Eight months later it was well received in Prague (6 October 1912), and after the concert Vilém Zemánek* asked Janáček to write a new piece for the Czech Philharmonic (the result was *The Fiddler's Child**, completed in 1913).

In 1897 Janáček described the process of composing *Amarus* in 'How Ideas Came About' (XV/313; English translation in *Janáček's Uncollected Essays on Music*). A vocal score was published by HMUB in 1938. A critical edition appeared as SKV B/1 (2000). *JAWO, JYL1, LJLD2, LJLR, VysAma, VogJan, ZemEss.*

Ančerl, Karel (b. Tučapy, South Bohemia, 11 April 1908; d. Toronto, Canada, 3 July 1973), Czech conductor. Ančerl studied with Pavel Dědeček at the Prague Conservatory and later with Hermann Scherchen and Václav Talich. He worked at the Liberated Theatre (Osvobozené divadlo) in Prague with Jaroslav Ježek (1931–3) and joined Czech Radio in 1933. On 6 November 1934 he directed a concert of chamber works by Janáček, including *The Diary of One Who Disappeared*, *Nursery Rhymes* and *Capriccio* (with Otakar Hollmann*). For Czech Radio he conducted the *Concertino* (with Walter Susskind and Rudolf Firkušný) and a rare broadcast of *Rákoš Rákoczy*. With the Czech Philharmonic he conducted *The Fiddler's Child* (8 April 1936). He was imprisoned at Theresienstadt concentration camp in 1942 with his family and in 1944 they were transported to Auschwitz-Birkenau extermination camp. Ančerl's wife, son and father all perished, as did his friend Pavel Haas*. From 1950 to 1968 Ančerl was chief conductor of the Czech Philharmonic, and he often performed the three Janáček works with which he became most closely associated: he gave the first of many performances of the *Sinfonietta** with the orchestra on 1 March 1954 and recorded it for Supraphon in January 1961 (it was also on the programme for his sixtieth birthday concert with the Czech Philharmonic on 5 June 1968); his recording of the *Glagolitic Mass** was made a few months later, in May 1961; *Taras Bulba** was performed at the Prague Spring in May 1958 and Ančerl's recording was made in April 1963. These magnificent recordings did much to bring Janáček's works to an international audience. *KarAnč.*

Augustinian Monastery, Old Brno   See Brno: Augustinian Monastery, Old Brno

Authorised copies   Janáček's usual working method was to write an autograph manuscript that he would give to one of his copyists in order for them to produce an authorised fair copy. He then made autograph revisions and additions on the authorised copy, often making extensive changes to produce a final version of the work. This manuscript would then be used for performance (for example, as a conducting score) or as a printer's copy for publication. The authorised copies of Janáček are thus of particular importance, since they frequently present the definitive versions of his works. For a number of works, more than one authorised copy survives. Janáček began this practice in the late 1880s, and entrusted the work to a small group of trusted copyists, most of them orchestral musicians at the Brno NT. His first regular copyist was the oboist Josef Stross*, and those who worked for him in later years included the flautist Václav Sedláček* and the trombonist Jaroslav Kulhánek*, both players in the Brno NT orchestra. From time to time, Janáček employed former pupils as copyists, including Břetislav Bakala* (vocal score of *Káťa Kabanová*) and Gustav Homola (full score of *Káťa Kabanová*; *The Diary of One Who Disappeared*). *JAWO.*

Autograph manuscripts The vast majority of Janáček's surviving autograph manuscripts are preserved in the Janáček Archive of the Moravian Museum in Brno. Broadly they comprise sketches and fragments, partial manuscripts, complete working drafts and fair copies. Most of them are written in ink, on various types of conventional manuscript paper, but in the last years of his life, Janáček abandoned ruled music paper in favour of hand-drawn staves written on plain sheets of paper. The autograph manuscripts of the *Glagolitic Mass** and *From the House of the Dead** are among the major works written in this way. Janáček's fair copies generally date from early in his career. His sketches range from the famously indecipherable single page for *Jenůfa** to substantial continuity drafts. Important as they are, Janáček's autographs – particularly those of his major works – usually amounted to a provisional stage in the composition process, the final revisions being added by the composer on the authorised copies prepared by a small group of trusted copyists who were able to decipher Janáček's unruly handwriting and on which he then made further revisions. (For examples of Janáček's handwriting published in facsimile, see Facsimiles*.) *JAWO.*

Axman, Emil (b. Rataje near Kroměříž, 3 June 1887; d. Prague, 25 January 1949), Czech composer. Axman's connection with Janáček came through his work as Secretary of the SMH in Prague (1920–7). On 3 July 1924, he sent Janáček seventieth birthday greetings: 'I rejoice that your work, for so long unperformed and unfairly judged, is now receiving the enthusiastic reception that it deserves all over the world. But I like even more that you are one of those for whom the music of your homeland provides such nourishment. You feed on these native springs and from them grows a work of art that stands like a tall, shining tree, planted fearlessly against the winds into Czech soil. That's right: a work that has its roots at home, but whose top is at the summit of European music.' *ČSHS, ČHS, JAWO, KLJ.*

Bakala, Břetislav (b. Fryšták near Zlín, 12 February 1897; d. Brno, 1 April 1958), Czech conductor. Born in the same small town as Jaroslav Kvapil*, Bakala began studies at the Brno Organ School in 1912, when Janáček taught him composition. He graduated in 1915. The Brno Conservatory opened in September 1919, with Janáček as its director. František Neumann* taught conducting and one of his first pupils was Bakala, who also studied the piano with Vilém Kurz and composition with Janáček. In 1920 Bakala became a

pianist and staff conductor at the Brno NT and also attended Janáček's Master School in Composition. The following year, Janáček asked Bakala to arrange the vocal score of *Káťa Kabanová**. Janáček was well disposed towards Bakala and allowed him to rummage through the painted chest where he kept his manuscripts. Bakala unearthed several early orchestral works and also came across the much more recent *The Diary of One Who Disappeared**. He was the pianist in the first performance of the *Diary* (18 April 1921), and on the day *Káťa Kabanová* had its premiere, Janáček inscribed a copy of the *Diary* to Bakala: 'For digging it out of the chest – a souvenir. L. Janáček, Brno, 23 November 1921.'

In February 1925, Janáček heard Bakala – an inexperienced conductor at the time – rehearsing the *Lachian Dances* at the Brno Opera. He wrote to Kamila Stösslová: 'I was present at a rehearsal in the theatre and saw how the conductor there was burrowing like a gimlet into the score – and didn't see the players. That's bad! It sends everyone to sleep.' A few months later, on 20 August 1925, Janáček wrote in much more generous terms to Emil Hertzka*: 'The young conductor Břetislav Bakala works at the local National Theatre – he's the one who did the vocal scores [of *Káťa* and *Vixen*] for me. Everything that's been given here is really his work. The conductor Neumann simply goes to the desk – and conducts. Preparing the soloists, chorus and so on is Bakala's job. He's worked for six years at the local theatre, but has done little conducting. He understands my operatic works – tempos – outstandingly.'

After nine months as an organist at Philadelphia Cathedral, Bakala returned in May 1926 to become a pianist and conductor for Brno Radio. Between 1929 and 1931 he worked at the Brno NT, conducting the world premiere of *From the House of the Dead** (12 April 1930), but his future lay in radio. For Brno Radio he conducted *The Beginning of a Romance** in 1931 and the world premiere of *Fate** in 1934. Bakala became principal conductor of the Brno Radio SO on 1 October 1937, and Janáček's music was at the core of his repertoire for the next twenty years. After Bakala's death, Rudolf Pečman wrote that 'during his tenure at Brno Radio and the Brno State Philharmonic, Břetislav Bakala created an authentic Janáček performing style.' Read alongside Janáček's assessment of Bakala's interpretative insights when preparing his operas, Pečman's claim deserves to be taken seriously. In a broadcast of 9 May 1941, Bakala conducted extracts from the original version of *Jenůfa*, which started with *Jealousy* and was followed by three scenes, including the end of the opera, all in Janáček's original orchestration. Shortly afterwards, Bakala wrote: 'I recently conducted several scenes from *Jenůfa* on Brno Radio without the retouchings. This reinforced my belief that it is possible to bring *Jenůfa* to life without any modifications. Janáček's orchestra just needs a good string section.' Between 1946 and 1957 Bakala conducted eight Janáček operas for Brno Radio: *The Beginning of a Romance, Šárka, Jenůfa, Fate, The Excursions of Mr Brouček, Káťa Kabanová, The Cunning Little Vixen* and *The Makropulos Affair*. These broadcasts were described by Charles Mackerras as a 'great milestone ... a real treasure' and several have been published by CRQ Editions. These radio recordings of the operas embody what is arguably the Brno Janáček tradition at its most authentic, led by a musician who studied with the composer and who was closer to Janáček than any conductor at the Brno Opera after František Neumann. Bakala also conducted almost all of Janáček's orchestral and choral music, and appeared as a pianist, including in a broadcast of *The Diary of One Who Disappeared* on 11 August 1953. On 2 May 1948, he conducted the first performance of Chlubna's completion of *The Danube**. Bakala made a number of commercial recordings of Janáček's music (see Recordings before 1960*).

As well as making the vocal scores of *Káťa* and *Vixen* for Janáček, Bakala also arranged *Youth* for solo piano and *Taras Bulba* for piano duet (both published by HMUB in 1925). *DucBak, JanBak, SimBak.*

Bakešová, Lucie, née Wanklová (b. Blansko, 26 December 1853; d. Brno, 2 April 1935), Czech folksong collector. Janáček and Bakešová first collaborated in a concert of folk music on 21 February 1889 at the Brno Beseda given in conjunction with Vesna, where Bakešová taught dance. This concert included the first performance of the *Valachian Dances* (VI/4) and probably Janáček's arrangement of *The Little Queens* (IV/20). With Xavera Běhálková and others, they collaborated on the *Folk Dances in Moravia** (VIII/10) published in 1891 and 1893, for which Bakešová provided descriptions of the dances. In 1895 she worked with Janáček on the Moravian contribution to the Prague Czecho-Slavonic Ethnographic Exhibition*, providing names of folk musicians, arranging costumes and discussing the logistics of getting so many people to Prague for the 'Moravian Days' that August. Janáček's relations with Bakešová had often been strained during preparations for the Exhibition and in 1905, when he was asked to form a working party for folksong in Moravia, he did not include her name, much to Bakešová's irritation. She later campaigned for humanitarian causes and women's rights. With her son, the surgeon Jaroslav Bakeš, she established a 'House of Consolation' ('Dům útěchy') for the care of cancer patients that later became the Masaryk Memorial Cancer Institute in Brno. One of its buildings, the Bakešová Pavilion, is named after her. *EDMB, JYL1, KLJ, ProNar.*

26 balad lidových   See Folk Ballads

The Ballad of Blaník [*Ballada Blanická*; *Balada Blanická*] for orchestra (VI/16). Probably composed in September–October 1919 and certainly complete by early 1920. Motivated by a desire to celebrate Czechoslovak independence, the manuscript has a dedication 'to the liberator, T. G. Masaryk'. The programme is based on a poem by Jaroslav Vrchlický*, though, as Vogel has observed, its epic subject matter is rather too expansive for a short orchestral work. Vrchlický's poem describes Jíra, a young man, walking on Blaník Hill one Good Friday, recalling the legend of St Václav and the Knights of Blaník, sleeping but ready to rise up to defend the Czech nation in times of peril. The side of the hill suddenly opens. Jíra is amazed by the heroic sight that confronts him and the rock crashes shut behind him (a moment of dramatic potential which Janáček ignores entirely in his tone poem). Jíra falls asleep and wakes to see the same figures with their swords now miraculously turned into ploughshares: the weapons of war transformed into implements of peace. On his way home, Jíra catches his own reflection while drinking from a stream and sees that he has become an old man. He returns to his village unrecognised by anyone save the skylark that sings above him. It is easy to see why this poem appealed to Janáček, with its clear relevance to national reawakening. Janáček's musical material is rich in possibilities, based on three main ideas: a folk-like theme to represent

Jíra, a sustained melody of a religious character, and a broad theme on harps and horns to evoke the Knights of Blaník. His development of these themes is occasionally short-winded and Vogel's conclusion is that *The Ballad of Blaník* is 'one of Janáček's interesting experiments rather than one of his key works'.

The first performance was in Brno on 21 March 1920 (with the title *The Knights of Blaník*), conducted by František Neumann*, in a concert to celebrate President Masaryk's seventieth birthday. It was given in Prague on 18 September 1921 by the Šak Philharmonic under Neumann, and Max Brod* reviewed it in the *Prager Abendblatt* (21 September 1921): 'In harmony with Vrchlický's text, Janáček presents a doom-laden picture of an enchanted mountain amid the intoxicating fragrances of the forest. The impression of opaque, shimmering colours is undisturbed by any false pathos. The basic motif gradually escalates into a warlike assault – but one that is free of the sounds of triumph. After a long wait, there is hope of redemption and this is revealed in the distance, in a phantom twilight. Then the symphonic poem returns to its original rustic tone, simply and with affecting melancholy.' The score was published in 1958, edited by Bakala. A critical edition with a more authentic text was published as SKVEJ D/8 (2003). *JAWO, ProBal, VogJan.*

Bartoš, František (b. Mladcová u Zlína, 16 March 1837; d. Mladcová u Zlína, 11 June 1906), Czech philologist and folksong collector. After school in Olomouc and studies at the University of Vienna, Bartoš taught in Strážnice, Olomouc, Těšín, and at the Slavonic (First Czech) Gymnasium in Brno, where he was appointed in 1869. When the Vesna Society opened Brno's first Czech girls' school in 1886, Bartoš served as its administrator. In 1888 he became director of the Czech Gymnasium in Old Brno, where Janáček taught. It was while they were colleagues there that Bartoš and Janáček started to collaborate on folk music collections, including three editions of the *Bouquet of Moravian Folksongs* (1890, 1892, 1901), and they both served on the Moravian committee for the Ethnographic Exhibition in Prague (1895). Their most important collaboration was the monumental collection of more than 2,000 songs and dances published as *Moravian Folksongs Newly Collected* (Prague: Czech Academy, 1901). Janáček's role in these projects included notating folk tunes and writing about the musical aspects of the songs. Bartoš was an ideal partner: a vastly experienced ethnographer with decades of experience as a folksong collector (see Folksong Editions*). Bartoš was also a linguist, and his *Dictionary of Moravian Dialect* was published by the Czech Academy in 1906. *EDMB, FraBar, JAWO, JYL1.*

Bartošová [–Lavická], Fedora (b. Vyškov, 24 June 1884; d. Brno, 30 November 1941), Czech poet. Bartošová attended the Vesna Girls' School, and from 1899 to 1903 she was a pupil at the Women Teachers' Institute in Brno. She was a near neighbour of the Janáčeks (then living at Klášterní No. 2) and became a close friend of Olga Janáčková. In late 1903, Bartošová took up a teaching post in Sudoměřice near Strážnice and it was there that she wrote most of the libretto of *Fate*. Janáček sent his initial ideas in November–December 1903, and by 21 December she had a draft prepared. Back in Brno for Christmas, she discussed the libretto with Janáček and revisions followed. They talked about further changes at a meeting in Luhačovice on 11–12 May 1904 but subsequent revisions to the libretto were made by Janáček. Bartošová moved from Sudoměřice to Židenice and in 1916 she married Josef Lavický. She later settled in Bratislava, from where she wrote to Mrs Janáčková on 15 March 1934 about the broadcast of *Fate* (on 13 March): 'Thirty years old – but it's still beautiful! ... How I worked at that time! When I left for Sudoměřice, I always had new ideas with me from my holidays, and a desire to work. And I was sorry when the composer was sometimes angry – and he revised his work again and again, on the advice of various friends. And there it rested for years. Dear Lady, it's been thirty years! And now I'm fifty – I can't deny it. ... I wonder what the master would make of his work today?' *EDMB, JODA, KLJ.*

Beginning of a Romance, The [*Počátek románu*], romantic opera in one act after the short story by Gabriela Preissová (I/3). Early in 1891, Gabriela Preissová* gave Janáček permission to set her story *The Beginning of a Romance*, which had been inspired by a painting with the same title by Jaroslav Věšín (1861–1915). This had been exhibited in Brno in 1885 and Janáček owned a print of it. Janáček asked František Rypáček (1853–1917), a teacher who used the pseudonym Jaroslav Tichý, to versify Preissová's story. On 13 May 1891, Preissová asked the poet Vladimír Šťastný for his opinion of Tichý's libretto, adding: 'God grant that this little opera of Mr Janáček's will succeed – our *first* Moravian opera!' Janáček began composing on 15 May 1891 and completed a first draft by 2 July. Revision and orchestration were completed by December. Janáček originally conceived the work as a Singspiel, with spoken dialogue, then tried setting the spoken passages as melodrama before eventually setting them to music. Janáček made further changes in 1892, when he played the opera to two conductors at the Prague NT, Adolf Čech and Mořic Anger (who had recently conducted *Rákoš Rákoczy**). Anger's report to František Adolf Šubert (administrator of the theatre) was damning: 'It is a pendant to *Rákoš Rákoczy* and *I cannot recommend this mixture of Moravian and Slovácko songs for performance because it is a manifest failure*. Stylistically it is not an opera and never can be.' Šubert told Janáček on 2 May 1892 that the opera would not be accepted in Prague. Janáček had also submitted it to the theatre in Brno, and on 10 February 1894 it was eventually put on at the Brno NT conducted by Janáček himself (the only time he conducted an opera). Karel Sázavský reviewed it in *Morvaská orlice* (13 February 1894): 'Not only has the composer written a work in the spirit of folk music and Moravian music, but he has also directly, and most effectively, used several folksongs whose texts fitted the action of the opera'. He added that Janáček received a 'warm reception'.

Janáček later became dissatisfied with the work, telling Max Brod that he had destroyed it (in fact, he had only torn out some numbers). In his autobiography Janáček called it 'an empty comedy', and that 'it was tasteless of me to force folksongs into it'. For the revival at the 1958 Janáček Festival in Brno, the score was reconstructed from surviving orchestral parts. Dilia printed a full score and vocal score in 1978 for hire only. To date, no score of *The Beginning of a Romance* has been put on sale. A complete recording, conducted by František Jílek*, was made by Brno Radio and issued on CD by Multisonic. *JAWO, JODA.*

SYNOPSIS

Poluška, a peasant girl, waits in a forest for Baron Adolf, son of Count Halužanský, the lord of the manor. The Baron has charmed Poluška so much that she has forgotten about her sweetheart, Tonka. She gazes at a portrait of the Baron, who then arrives as arranged and flatters Poluška. They are spotted by the gamekeeper Mudroch, Poluška's godfather, who watches in alarm as the Baron takes Poluška in his arms. After returning from the forest, Poluška meets Tonka, but finds that she no longer appreciates his charms. Tonka is puzzled by her behaviour and reproaches her. Meanwhile, the Baron meets Countess Irma, whom he has known since her childhood, and is enchanted by her beauty. He no longer gives any thought to Poluška. Mudroch tells Poluška's family about her relationship with the Baron. When Poluška returns, she is forced to confess to her angry parents. She makes no attempt to deny it, and shows them the portrait of the Baron. Her father decides to ask the old Count about a possible marriage between Poluška and the Baron, but the Count will not consider any relationship between his son and a humble village girl. Everything ends happily when Poluška is reunited with Tonka and arrangements are made for their wedding.

Běhálková, Františka Xavera (b. Tovačov, 23 October 1853; d. Tovačov, 28 April 1907), Czech folksong collector. Běhálková worked in the Tovačov region of Central Moravia, where she gathered a large number of folksongs and dances. Ten of the dances she collected in Haná were published in Janáček's *Folk Dances in Moravia** (VIII/10) as Nos. 1–5, 7–11 and 16. Janáček and Běhálková appeared together at a concert in the Brno Beseda on 7 January 1891 under the auspices of the Vesna Society: Janáček conducted four of his *Valachian Dances* and Běhálková gave 'excellent descriptions of the Haná dances' (according to a report in *Moravské listy*), which were performed as piano duets by Antonína Nikodemová and Anna Kumpoštová, two students from the Organ School. Twelve of the dance tunes Běhálková collected in the Haná region were used by Janáček in *Rákoš Rákoczy**. In 1895 she prepared the music performed by folk musicians from Tovačov for the Ethnographic Exhibition in Prague, and her collection of folk costumes, embroidery, ceramics and furniture formed the basis of the Haná display. *JAWO, JYL1, KLJ, ProNar, ProZáz.*

Bezruč, Petr [pseud. for Vladimír Vašek] (b. Opava, 15 September 1867; d. Olomouc, 17 February 1958), Czech poet. In 1889 Bezruč became an employee of the post office in Brno, working as a clerk and later as an inspector and director of the postal service, before retiring in 1927. In 1903 the nationalist newspaper *Čas* published a slim volume of poems entitled *Slezské číslo* [*Silesian Number*], in which Bezruč is only identified as the poet at the end of the volume. It was republished in 1909 as *Silesian Songs*. Janáček owned a copy of *Slezské číslo* and wanted to set *Maryčka Magdónova*. In October 1906, he wrote to Olga Vašková, secretary of the Brno Russian Circle: 'Is [Bezruč] really your brother? Please would he give me the right to compose a piece on *Maryčka Magdónova*? [Karel] Moor didn't get it right. Perhaps I can do better.' Bezruč gave permission for Janáček to set any of his poems and the composer set to work immediately on *Halfar the Schoolmaster**, completing it by 24 October 1906, before turning to *Maryčka Magdónova**. He composed two different settings of this poem, in November 1906 and March 1907. In 1909 Janáček composed a setting of Bezruč's *The Seventy Thousand**, making extensive revisions to it in 1912. The musical sketches for this chorus are written in the margins of his copy of *Slezské číslo* (illustrated in *JAWO*, p. 140).

Janáček's three Bezruč choruses are stirring and musically complex settings of poems that give an unflinchingly stark depiction of life in Moravian Silesia (the region to the north-west of Hukvaldy) and the fight for the Czech language (notably in *Halfar*). Before these choruses, Janáček had usually set folk texts; here he took up the challenge of setting poetry that resonated strongly with his own feelings about Czech national identity. They are some of the first works in which Janáček identified explicitly with the quest for Czech independence, and they show his choral writing at its most ambitious. *JAWO, JYL1, KleBez, VogJan.*

Bím, Hynek (b. Lomnice nad Popelkou, 5 March 1874; d. Tišnov, 30 December 1958), Czech folksong collector.   Bím studied with Janáček at the Teachers' Institute in Brno, graduating in 1892. He started to collect folksongs in Ivančice in 1893 and soon expanded his activities to other nearby locations. When Janáček saw the several hundred songs Bím had collected, he invited him to contribute to the collection that was eventually published as *Moravian Folksongs Newly Collected* in 1901. In 1905 Janáček invited Bím to join the Working Committee for Moravian and Silesian folksongs, and Bím subsequently collected an astonishing total of almost 3,000 songs and dances (only Františka Kyselková* was more productive). Bím was a systematic collector, noting how songs were presented and how the repertoire of individual singers changed. Janáček sent him to collect songs in Valachia, and over a period of six years (1907–13) he found not only many new songs but also instrumental pieces. From 1909 to 1912, along with Kyselková, Bím used the phonograph* provided by Janáček. After 1912, Janáček and his two most experienced and musically expert collaborators reverted to transcriptions by ear and by hand. Bím contributed 174 songs to *Moravian Love Songs* (XIII/5), published between 1930 and 1936. His phonograph recordings made for Janáček between 1909 and 1912 have been published in *Vzaty do fonografu* (2012). *ProNar, ProVza, ProZáz.*

Bodanzky, Artur (b. Vienna, 16 December 1877; d. New York, 23 November 1939), Austrian-born conductor.   Bodanzky worked as Mahler's assistant at the Vienna Opera (1902–4). In 1915 he became head of German repertoire at the Metropolitan Opera in New York. He conducted the American premiere of *Jenůfa* on 6 December 1924, with Maria Jeritza as Jenůfa. Bodanzky also conducted the American premiere of the *Glagolitic Mass* at the Metropolitan Opera on 28 October 1930, with Edytha Fleischer (soprano), Karin Branzell (contralto), Dan Gridley (tenor), Friedrich Schorr (bass) and Louis Robert (organ), the chorus of the Society of the Friends of Music and the Metropolitan Opera orchestra. A review in the *Columbia Spectator* (28 October 1930) said the Mass 'went a long way to prove that dullness is a quality fast disappearing in modern music', while the *New Yorker* critic called it 'the liveliest Mass that I have ever heard'. *MetArc.*

Boettinger, Hugo   See **Images of Janáček** and **Löwenbach, Jan**

Bohemian Quartet   See **Czech Quartet**

Bouquet of Moravian Folksongs (53 songs)   See *Moravian Folk Poetry in Songs* (V/2)

Bouquet of Moravian Folksongs (XIII/1)   See **Folksong Editions**

Bouquet of Moravian, Slovak and Czech Folksongs (XIII/2)   See **Folksong Editions**

Brno: Augustinian Monastery, Old Brno [Augustiniánské opatství na Starém Brně].   The Augustinian Monastery in Old Brno (often referred to as the

'Queen's Monastery' after its foundation by Queen Eliška, widow of Václav II) played an essential role in Janáček's education. In 1865, at the age of eleven,

Janáček became a choral scholar at the Monastery and received a thorough musical grounding from Pavel Křížkovský*. In 1872 Janáček succeeded him as director of the choir. As well as its distinguished musical tradition, the Abbey was an important centre of Moravian intellectual life, led by two enlightened Abbots: Cyril Napp (1792–1867) and Gregor Mendel (1822–84). Napp was a historian and an early figure in the development of Czech nationalism. The most famous of the gifted scholars he attracted to the Abbey was his successor, Mendel, the founder of modern genetics, whose experiments took place in the Abbey grounds. According to Orel, Janáček conducted the music at Mendel's funeral on 9 January 1884. *Folia Mendeliana* (2010, No. 1, p. 63) stated that Křížkovský 'composed a Requiem which was directed by Janáček'. This was almost certainly the Requiem for male voices and organ published in *Cecilie* in 1878 (newspaper reports of the funeral list many of the guests present but have nothing useful to say about the music). *Amarus**, the *Sinfonietta** and the *March of the Bluebirds** (and, by extension, *Youth**) all have programmatic elements connected with Janáček's years at the Augustinian Monastery. *JYL1, OreMen, ZahFoo.*

Brno Beseda [Beseda brněnská], musical association founded in 1861, and also its Beseda House [Besední dům], inaugurated in 1873. The initial aim of the Beseda was to foster singing in Czech by its male-voice choir. The first choirmaster was Pavel Křížkovský (until 1864). With the appointment of Janáček as conductor of the Beseda in 1876, its programmes became more ambitious, the choir was enlarged and standards of performance improved markedly. The Beseda House designed by Theophil von Hansen (architect of the Musikverein in Vienna) was completed in 1873, and Janáček first appeared there with the Svatopluk Choral Society. Once he became choirmaster of the Brno Beseda, he was able to perform large-scale choral and orchestral works (see Conducting, Janáček's*). In 1879 the Beseda changed its name to the Philharmonic Society of the Brno Beseda, reflecting its evolution into a larger organisation. It established a music school in 1882, and between 1884 and 1888 published *Hudební listy*, edited by Janáček (see *Hudební listy**). After disputes with the management, Janáček resigned as conductor of the Beseda in 1888. During the years when Rudolf Reissig was conductor (1899–1918), Janáček's relationship with the Beseda was frosty, but improved when Ferdinand Vach* was appointed conductor (1919–20), and it gave the Brno premiere of *The Eternal Gospel** under Vach on 18 February 1919. In 1920 Janáček's pupil Jaroslav Kvapil* became conductor. *Amarus** was given in 1922, and a gala programme in 1924 included *Amarus**, *Our Father**, *Čarták on Soláň** and *The Eternal Gospel*. Kvapil conducted the Brno and Prague premieres of the *Glagolitic Mass** with the Brno Beseda choir in 1927 and 1928 (both performances attended by Janáček), and took the choir to sing the *Glagolitic Mass* at the Geneva ISCM Festival in 1929. As well as its own choral and orchestral concerts, the Beseda promoted chamber concerts. On 13 December 1924, the Czech Quartet gave the Brno premiere of the First String Quartet. An evening of songs on 26 October 1925 with Kvapil at the piano included *The Diary of One Who Disappeared** and the premiere of the first version of the *Nursery Rhymes** (V/16). The first performances of

1. Brno: The Beseda House (Besední dům) and Hotel Slavia, looking east along Solniční (formerly U solnice / Salzamtgasse). Postcard dated 1916.

the 'Intimate Letters' Quartet were given by the Moravian Quartet on 7 and 11 September 1928. Janáček's music was also performed in the Beseda House at concerts promoted by other organisations: *1. X. 1905* (27 January 1906) in the rooms of the KPU; the first complete performance of *Amarus* (25 February 1912); *Youth* (21 October 1924); the *Lachian Dances* (2 December 1924); the *Concertino* (16 February 1926); and the revised version of the *Nursery Rhymes* (25 April 1927).

As well as its concert hall, the Beseda was also a meeting place for cultural activities: societies with rooms there included the Czech Readers' Club (where the Brno Russian Circle met) and the KPU. The Beseda House was an important symbol of Moravian identity, and it was on the steps of the building that František Pavlík was killed during a demonstration on 2 January 1905 (see *1. X. 1905** and Pavlík, František*). The Beseda House is the present home of the Brno Philharmonic. Despite its handsome interior, the limited capacity (500 seats) and small stage make it less suitable for large-scale symphonic concerts. Construction is in progress (2018) on a brand-new concert hall (1,250 seats) on an adjacent site, with plans to link this via an overhead bridge to the Beseda House. *BajHud, BesDům, ČHS, FilSpo.*

Brno Central Cemetery [Ústřední hřbitov], Vídeňská No. 96. Brno Central Cemetery opened in November 1883 on a large site 3 km south of the city centre. The original design was by Alois Prastorfer, who was also the architect for the administrative buildings added in 1901–3 near the main entrance at Vídeňska No. 96. Two notable modernist buildings were added in the 1920s: the Ceremonial Hall built in 1925–6, designed by Bohuslav Fuchs and Josef Polášek; and the extraordinary crematorium completed in 1930, designed by Ernst Wiesner. Brno's Central Cemetery is the largest cemetery in the Czech Republic.

Janáček is buried in the 'Honorary Circle' (Čestný kruh), Section 25e, No. 64. Designed by Eduard Milén*, his tomb is a square column in white marble with uncompromisingly modern, geometric lines. On a panel, slightly offset to the right, there is music from *The Wandering Madman*. Though this reproduces Janáček's handwriting, the musical 'quotation' isn't strictly accurate, since it juxtaposes two phrases sung by the solo soprano in bars 138–9 and 144–5. Tagore's English translation of the passage reads: 'his body bent, and his heart in the dust, like a tree uprooted' (see Funeral, Janáček's*). Zdenka Janáčková, Vladimír Janáček and Olga Janáčková are buried in a family grave (Section 32, Nos. 144–5). Others buried in the Central Cemetery include Břetislav Bakala, Josef (Joža) Barvič, Gracian Černušák, Osvald Chlubna, Karel Elgart Sokol, Leoš Firkušný, Rudolf Firkušný, František Jílek, Václav Kaprál, Vítězslava Kaprálová, Pavel Křížkovský, František Kudláček, Jaroslav Kvapil, Františka Kyselková, Jiří Mahen, František Mareš, Gregor Mendel, Eduard Milén, Alois Mrštík, František Musil, Arne Novák, František Pavlík, Vilém Petřželka, Bohumír Štědroň, František Sušil, Vilém Tauský, Rudolf Těsnohlídek and Ferdinand Vach. *EDMB*

Brno: Club of the Friends of Art in Brno (KPU) [Klub přátel umění v Brně]. The KPU was founded on 14 January 1900, with the initial aim of fostering literature and visual art through lectures, exhibitions and publications. On 16 March 1902, Janáček gave a lecture under the auspices of the KPU on his teacher Pavel Křížkovský, one of the Club's first ventures into music. On 26 April 1904, the Club put on a concert of music by Janáček's pupil Jan Kunc*, and this prompted the formation of a music section on 8 January 1905, with Janáček on its committee. The music section quickly put on two concerts (19 and 26 February 1905), and John Tyrrell has suggested that Janáček may have drawn up the programmes (the first was on the growth of the Czech sonata and the second was called 'Spring Songs'). On 27 January 1906, the Club's concert of piano music played by Ludmila Tučková included the first performance of Janáček's *1. X. 1905**. A few months later, on 30 April 1906, the Club put on a Dvořák concert that included the String Quartets Op. 51 and 106 played by the Ševčík Quartet, with Janáček joining them on the harmonium in the *Bagatelles* Op. 47. On 5 December 1907, Janáček's *Folk Nocturnes** were given their first performance at a concert organised by the KPU. Three days earlier, it had resolved to start publishing music, and Janáček suggested that its first publication should be the vocal score of *Jenůfa**. The committee agreed (possibly unaware that the score would run to 281 pages), and even before the end of the year proofs began to arrive from the engravers in Leipzig. By March 1908, 600 copies had been printed, 300 of them reserved for members of the KPU. This was a significant moment for Janáček: his first operatic masterpiece was now in print thanks to the Club. A year later, in February 1909, Janáček was appointed Chairman of the Club at a meeting in the Hotel Slavia. He held the post for two years and was succeeded by František Veselý*. On 2 April 1909, the first performance of Janáček's Piano Trio after Tolstoy's *Kreutzer Sonata** (X/22) was given in a Club event in the Organ School to celebrate Tolstoy. Two other works by Janáček were published by the KPU: *In the Mists** in 1913 and *The Fiddler's Child** in 1914, issued to mark Janáček's sixtieth birthday. The KPU was disbanded in 1919, though a part of it was renamed the Graphic Artists' Club.

The KPU was a meeting place for the whole cultural community in Brno, and its members included the architect Dušan Jurkovič*, the artists Alfons Mucha*, Láďa Novák* and Stanislav Lolek*, and the writers Alois and Vilém Mrštík, and Karel Elgart Sokol. The list of musicians who belonged to the KPU reads like a Who's Who of Janáček's friends and pupils: Hynek Bím*, Pavel Dědeček*, Marie Dvořáková*, Bohumil Holub, Cyril Metoděj Hrazdira*, Jan Kunc*, Jaroslav Kvapil* and Ferdinand Vach*. For Janáček, the lasting importance of the KPU lay in its decision to publish *Jenůfa* and its subsequent promotion of the work (above all by František Veselý). In 1916 its efforts bore fruit when *Jenůfa* was given in Prague and the KPU sold its remaining copies to HMUB, with the original engraved plates. *GryKPU, JAWO, JYL1, JYL2, KunJan.*

Brno Conservatory [Konservatoř Brno], founded in 1919. The Brno Conservatory opened on 25 September 1919, with Janáček as director. It was the result of a merger between the Organ School, the music school of the Brno Beseda, and the music school of Vesna. It was initially housed in the Organ School building: the Chleborád villa on Smetanova that now houses the Janáček Archive. It moved in 1945 to its present location on the south side of Lužánky Park (a building that formerly housed the German Teachers' Institute). Jan Kunc* succeeded Janáček as director in September 1920 (when Janáček became professor of the Master School in Composition), remaining in the post until 1945. During its first fifty years, teachers at the Brno Conservatory included many of Janáček's friends and former pupils, among them Břetislav Bakala*, Josef Blatný, Gracian Černušák*, Bohumil Holub, Václav Kaprál, Jaroslav Kulhánek*, Ludvík Kundera*, Vilém Kurz, František Neumann*, Vilém Petrželka, Ludmila Tučková, Ferdinand Vach* and Ota Zítek*. *PetMaj, ZahFoo.*

Brno: Czech Gymnasium, Old Brno [Czech Gymnasium II]. The Czech Gymnasium, in the same building as the Teachers' Institute at Poříčí No. 5, was established in 1885. Berthold Žalud* was appointed to teach music but died in 1886 and Janáček took over his duties, teaching there until 1902. It may have been František Bartoš* (appointed director of the school in 1888) who persuaded Janáček to take on this commitment on top of his teaching at the Institute. He was required to teach choral singing for four hours each week, supplementing rehearsals with such theory and notation as was necessary. Janáček performed music by Haydn, Grieg, Liszt and Fibich, as well as his own works: on 17 March 1901, the Gymnasium choir gave the first known performance of *The Wild Duck* (IV/18), the chorus he had originally written for his friend Žalud's songbook in 1885. Under Bartoš's directorship the school expanded and in 1901 Janáček made two arrangements especially for the Gymnasium choir: Grieg's *Landkjending* (XII/3) and Liszt's *Missa pro organo* (XII/4), which suggest Janáček had established an impressive young choir by the time he retired in 1902. *JAWO, JYL1, ZahFoo.*

Brno: Moravian Composers' Club (KMS) [Klub moravských skladatelů]. The KMS had its origins in the Young Moravian Composers' Club (Klub mladých skladatelů moravských), established in 1920, which arranged the first performances of Janáček's *The Diary of One Who Disappeared** (18 April 1921) and the Sonata for Violin and Piano (22 April 1922). The KMS was officially founded on 19 June 1922, with Jaroslav Kvapil*, Ludvík Kundera* and Vilém Petrželka as its officers. Janáček served as its president until his death. From the start, its aim was to promote contemporary music from Moravia and beyond. On 4 December 1922, it presented a talk on quarter-tone music by Alois Hába followed by a performance of his String Quartet No. 2. On 2 March 1925, Bartók gave a concert (of his own music and Kodály), and the next day the Club put on an evening of Schoenberg introduced by Helfert and attended by the composer. Janáček performances included a concert on 2 December 1924, when František Neumann* conducted the Suite for strings, Prelude to *Šárka**, *Jealousy** and the *Lachian Dances** with the Brno NT orchestra in a programme that also included *Youth**. The Club presented the premieres of the *Concertino** with Ilona Štěpánová-Kurzova* on 16 February 1926, and the definitive version of the *Nursery Rhymes** on 25 April 1927. *ČHS, JAWO, VohKMS.*

Brno National Theatre (Brno NT) [Národní divadlo Brno, formerly Národní divadlo v Brně]. The Brno NT opened on 7 December 1884 with Smetana's *The Bartered Bride* in the Veveří Theatre, a renovated dance hall in the tavern 'U Marovských' on Veveří Street. Six days later, the first issue of *Hudební listy* appeared, dedicated to 'music and the art of the theatre' and edited by Janáček (see *Hudební listy**).

The Veveří Theatre was the location of the National Theatre until 1919, but it was small and cramped. Two of Janáček's operas received their premieres there: *The Beginning of a Romance* in 1894 and *Jenůfa* in 1904. Janáček was among those who argued that a larger and properly equipped theatre was needed. Various plans were drawn up for a replacement, including a striking design by Emil Králík for an opera house in Lužánky Park (the site favoured by Janáček, perhaps because it was a short walk from the Organ School), but nothing came of them. Janáček's most persistent plea in *Hudební listy* was for an improvement in the standard of the orchestra, and the provision of good instruments for the players. It was in 1919 that everything started to change for the better.

Thanks to the efforts of Janáček and members of the Družstvo (the management committee of the theatre), the company secured the use of the German City Theatre in Brno. From 1919 until 1965, almost all its performances took place in what is now known as the Mahen Theatre in Malinkovský Square. Designed by Ferdinand Fellner and Hermann Helmer, it had originally opened in 1882 as the Deutsches Stadttheater, when it was one of the first theatres in Europe to have full electric lighting, installed by Thomas Edison's assistant Francis Jehl. When it became the home of the Brno NT in 1919 it was known as the Theatre on the Ramparts (Divadlo na Hradbách). Under the Nazi occupation the name reverted to German City Theatre (1939–45), and from 1945 to 1965 it was called the Janáček Theatre. With the opening of the new Janáček Theatre on Rooseveltova in 1965, it was renamed the Mahen Theatre. Since 2010 the Reduta in Zelný trh has also become part of the National Theatre.

The move into a well-equipped and much more spacious theatre in 1919 coincided with the arrival of a new conductor as Head of Opera. Janáček had lobbied hard for the appointment of František Neumann*, who took up his post in 1919. The Neumann era coincided with Janáček's late operatic masterpieces. He was a gifted and determined advocate of Janáček's music, conducting the world premieres of *Káťa Kabanová, The Cunning Little Vixen, The Makropulos Affair* and *Šárka*. He died in 1929, but in his ten years in Brno standards had risen to a level unimaginable beforehand. The orchestra was enlarged and vastly improved with the hiring of good new players.

The following is a list of Janáček productions by the Brno NT during the composer's lifetime. World premieres are marked with a dagger (†). Performances from 1894 to 1916 were in the Veveří Theatre; those from 1919 onwards were in the Mahen Theatre. Abbreviations: c.: conductor; d. director; des.: designer.

10 February 1894: *The Beginning of a Romance*, c. Janáček, d. František Šípek†

21 January 1904: *Jenůfa*, c. Cyril Metoděj Hrazdira, d. Josef Mály†

6 October 1906: *Jenůfa*, c. Hrazdira, d. Eduard Aschenbrenner

31 January 1911: *Jenůfa*, c. Rudolf Pavlata, d. Malý

4 October 1916: *Jenůfa*, c. Josef Winkler, d. Karel Komarov, including two performances with Gabriela Horvátová as guest

23 August 1919: *Jenůfa*, c. František Neumann, d. Rudolf Walter

23 November 1921: *Káťa Kabanová*, c. Neumann, d. Vladimír Marek, des. Vladimír Hrska†

9 October 1924: *Jenůfa*, c. Neumann, d. Ota Zítek, des. Čeněk Jandl

16 October 1924: *Káťa Kabanová*, c. Neumann, d. Zítek, des. Jaroslav Provazník

6 November 1924: *The Cunning Little Vixen*, c. Neumann, d. Zítek, des. Eduard Milén†

11 November 1925: *Šárka*, c. Neumann, d. Zítek, des. Vlastislav Hofman†

15 May 1926: *The Excursion of Mr Brouček to the Moon* (Brno prem. of Part I of *The Excursions of Mr Brouček*), c. Neumann, d. Zítek, des. Josef Čapek

28 October 1926: *Jenůfa*, c. Neumann, d. Zítek

18 December 1926: *The Makropulos Affair*, c. Neumann, d. Zítek, des. Josef Čapek†

28 March 1928: *Káťa Kabanová*, c. Neumann, d. Zítek

[15 August 1928 (morning): Janáček's funeral, including the final scene from *The Cunning Little Vixen*, c. Neumann

15 August 1928 (evening): memorial performance of *Jenůfa*, c. Neumann]

The first new Brno production after Janáček's death was the posthumous premiere of *From the House of the Dead*. By then František Neumann had also died and his temporary successors were his pupils Břetislav Bakala* and Zdeněk Chalabala. In 1932 Milan Sachs took up the post (with Vilém Tauský* and Quido Arnoldi as assistant conductors), remaining until 1938, when the Nazi threat forced him to return to his native Croatia. Rafael Kubelík* was chief conductor from 1939 to 1941. After the war, Bohumír Liška and Robert Brock were the main Janáček conductors until the appointment in 1952 of František Jílek*, whose long tenure lasted until 1978. Jaroslav Vogel* and Charles Mackerras* both appeared as guest conductors. Following Jílek's retirement, the regular Janáček conductors were Jaroslav Kyzlink and Jan Zbavitel. In 2015 Marko Ivanović was appointed chief conductor. From the 1930s until the present day, the Brno NT has kept Janáček's operas in the repertoire, refreshing them regularly with new productions. The Janáček Festivals in 1958, 1978, 2004 and 2018 included performances of all the operas. *NDBrOA, PosFes, PřiLed ZahDiv.*

Brno Organ School [Varhanická škola]. On 29 November 1879, Janáček confided in a letter to Zdenka Schulzová that 'the idea of the Organ School in

2. The auditorium of the Brno National Theatre (now the Mahen Theatre) where the world premieres of all Janáček's operas from *Káta Kabanová* to *From the House of the Dead* took place.

Brno is one to which I have been devoted since my first years of independent thinking. I already took this idea with me to my studies in Prague and I see its realisation as one of my most important tasks.' In 1881 he was appointed director of the new Organ School, where he taught theory of music and musical form. The school also offered classes in organ, singing, history of music and liturgy. Emilian Schulz, Janáček's father-in-law, offered the new school premises in the Teachers' Institute, which he directed at the time, but there were soon disputes between Janáček and Schulz (the start of a lasting rift), and in 1886 the Organ School moved to premises at Starobrněsnká Street. It remained there until 1896, when it moved to the corner of Jakubská Street and Česká Street. There it stayed until the move into the Chleborád Villa. The Neo-Renaissance Chleborád Villa has stood on the corner of Smetanova (formerly Haberlerova) and Kounicova (formerly Giskrova) since 1891. Antonín Tebich designed it for the economist and politician František Ladislav Chleborád. In 1906 the Association for the Promotion of Church Music in Moravia (the organisation that had founded the Organ School) purchased the villa and established a permanent home for the school there.

The initial aim of the Organ School was to train organists, choirmasters and teachers, but by the 1890s the school had expanded greatly and was offering a much broader curriculum, including harmony (which Janáček taught himself), counterpoint, score-reading, piano and choral singing. By 1905 Janáček was able to describe it in its annual report as 'a school of composition: that is to say the highest discipline within the subject of music teaching'. Long-standing teachers included František Kolísek (liturgy), Marie Kuhlová (piano) and Maximilian Koblížek (organ). Those who joined the staff later included Pavel Dědeček* (violin), Marie Dvořáková* (piano), Bohumil Holub (organ) and Ludmila Tučková (organ and piano). Several former Janáček pupils taught briefly at the school, including Jaroslav Kvapil*, Vilém Petržela, Jan Kunc*, Josef Blatný, Břetislav Bakala* and Osvald Chlubna*. Other pupils included Josef Charvát, Gustav Homola, Cyril Metoděj Hrazdira* and Václav Kaprál. In 1919 the Organ School became part of the Brno Conservatory under Janáček's direction (see Brno Conservatory*). From 1920, Janáček's Master School in Composition*, established and administered by the Prague Conservatory, was also held in the Chleborád Villa. Today it houses the Janáček Archive. *JYL1, KunVar, ZahFoo, ZemJan.*

Brno Russian Circle [Ruský kroužek].   Fired with enthusiasm for all things Russian after returning from his visit to the country in 1896, Janáček co-founded the Brno Russian Circle in 1897. It met in the rooms of the Czech Readers' Club in the Beseda House. Janáček's daughter was also a member, and on 7 June 1899 she was one of the readers at the ceremony for the centenary of Pushkin's birth. Other members included Maria Nikolayevna Veveritsa (Olga's Russian teacher and author of the poem Janáček set in his *Elegy on the Death of my Daughter Olga**), František Veselý*, Ferdinand Jokl (from the Czech Gymnasium), František Mareš (director of Vesna) and the bookseller Joža Barvič. From 1909, Janáček was the chairman. Given the political sensitivity of the Russian language in a German-speaking empire, it is not surprising that the Russian Circle came under scrutiny from the Austrian authorities. After the outbreak of war in 1914, the Circle was seen as promoting sympathy for Russia instead of Austria-Hungary, and in February 1915 it was closed down and its archives searched (by then the archivist, Olga Vašková, Petr Bezruč's sister, had removed any potentially sensitive material). Janáček was questioned at police headquarters but no further action was taken. The Circle was revived in 1919 but closed in 1922. In 1905 Janáček read Gogol's *Taras Bulba* as a member of the Russian Circle and John Tyrrell has speculated that it may have been there that he also came across Tolstoy's *Kreutzer Sonata* and Zhukovsky's *Tale of Tsar Berendyey* (the inspiration for the *Fairy Tale**). *JYL1, JYL2, VrbRus.*

Brno: Svatopluk Society [Řemeslnická beseda Svatopluk]. Janáček's first conducting experience outside the Augustinian Monastery came in 1873, when he was appointed as an eighteen-year-old to conduct the male-voice choir of the Svatopluk Society, a group of artisans and craftsmen named after Svatopluk I, the ruler of the Great Moravian Empire in the late ninth century. At the Monastery, Janáček was used to working with experienced choristers who were good sight-readers and quick learners. Svatopluk was a very different proposition: a large group of amateurs whose enthusiasm usually outstripped their musical skills. Janáček relished the challenge, and the choir was soon being described as one of the best in Brno. Janáček conducted Svatopluk between March 1873 and 1876 (with a break from Autumn 1874 to Summer 1875 when he was studying in Prague). For Janáček the importance of this appointment was that he began his composing career by writing at least seven choruses for the Svatopluk choir. The first and most successful of these was *Ploughing* (IV/1), which was encored at its first performance (27 April 1873). Janáček was appointed choirmaster of the Brno Beseda in 1876 and his final appearance as Svatopluk's conductor was at a gala in honour of Dr Josef Illner (1839–94), the chairman of Svatopluk, who had first recognised Janáček's talent. *HelJan, JAWO, JYL1.*

Brno: Teachers' Institute [Slovanský ústav ku vzdělání učitelů].   From 1878 until 1948, the Teachers' Institute (officially the Slavonic Institute for Teacher Training) was situated in the building which has, since 1956, housed the Faculty of Architecture of the University of Technology at Poříčí No. 5, on the northern bank of the River Svratka. The Institute was established in 1869 as a result of the Schools Act, which put the training of teachers on a more formal footing. Janáček studied there from 1869 until 1872, when it was still housed in the Minorite Monastery on Minoritská Street. After completing his studies at the Prague Organ School, Janáček's first regular paid job in Brno was teaching music at the Institute, and he remained there until 1904.

In 1878 the Institute moved to premises at Poříčí No. 5. The foundation stone was laid on 15 July 1877 and Janáček composed a chorus to mark the occasion: the *Festive Chorus for Laying the Foundation Stone of the Teachers' Institute* (IV/12) was performed outdoors with the choir on a specially constructed platform. Just over a year later, when the building was ready, Janáček composed the *Festive Chorus for the Consecration of the New Building of the Imperial and Royal Slavonic Teachers' Institute in Brno* (IV/13), which he conducted at the ceremony on 15 September 1878. Other compositions have connections to the Institute: the choruses *You Cannot Escape your Fate* (IV/9) and *On the Ferry* (IV/15) survive in copies made by pupils, probably transcribed from what Janáček wrote on the blackboard. For a festival of Brno schools on 19 April 1896, Janáček composed

Lord, have mercy [*Hospodine!*] (III/5), and it was performed at the Institute. His arrangement of Haydn's *Gott erhalte den Kaiser** (XII/1) was almost certainly made for official use at the Institute (or perhaps for the Old Brno Czech Gymnasium, with which it shared premises). *Veni Sancte Spiritus* (II/13) has a bolder harmonic style, suggesting a date of around 1900.

Janáček's teaching load was formidable: he taught the piano (to classes), the organ to more advanced students, theory, history, folksong, pedagogy and choral singing (compulsory for all students). Janáček was also responsible for providing music for the Institute's church services and for special occasions. His repertoire with the singing classes ranged from Palestrina to Gounod and Brahms. It was at the Institute that Janáček met his future wife, Zdenka. Her father Emilian Schulz was the Institute's director, whose accommodation was at the back of the building and where Janáček went to teach Zdenka the piano. The original building from 1878 still stands, but there is now a later extension. To commemorate his long association with this location, a bronze and marble sculpture of Janáček by Zdeněk Makovský was unveiled in 2008. *EDMB, JYL1.*

Brno: Vesna, a women's educational society established in 1870, initially as a singing club. In 1886 Vesna opened the first Czech girls' school in Brno – co-founded by the teacher Eliška Machová – providing lessons in Czech, history, teaching, pedagogy and practical subjects, and becoming a leading institution in women's education. František Mareš (1862–1941) was appointed director of the school in 1888 and remained in the post until his retirement in 1918. One of the founders of the KPU and its chairman from 1900 to 1906, Mareš was also a member of the Brno theatre Družstvo and was instrumental in encouraging Dušan Jurkovič* to settle in Brno. He was a co-founder of the Brno Russian Circle* with Janáček in 1897. The Vesna Society built its first school on Údolní Street and later expanded it to include a building on the adjacent Jaselská Street, with decorative interiors designed by Jurkovič. The Vesna School fostered links with artists, writers and musicians, including Janáček. He gave lectures there, and several of his works were performed under its aegis. On 21 February 1889, at a 'Vesna Evening' in the Brno Beseda, *The Little Queens* (IV/20) and two of the *Valachian Dances* were performed for the first time. In January 1891, Janáček gave the first of a series of talks with Xavera Běhálková under the auspices of Vesna to introduce the *Folk Dances in Moravia** (VIII/10). František Rypáček [Jaroslav Tichý], who had previously written the libretto for *The Beginning of a Romance*, sent Janáček the poem for *Spring Song* (V/3) in December 1897, and the first version of the song was written by 6 March 1898, with a revised version in April 1905. The song is dedicated 'To the Brno Vesna Society'. Vesna was the goddess of spring in ancient Slav mythology, which is presumably why Tichý chose the subject. John Tyrrell has speculated that 'perhaps, too, with its unambitious tessitura and the repetitions minimizing the amount of rehearsal needed, it was originally intended for the girls at the Vesna School to sing'. On 18 December 1898, Janáček gave the first public performance of the *Hukvaldy Folk Poetry in Songs* (V/4) for the Vesna Society. Beforehand he gave an illustrated lecture on the different types of Moravian folksongs and their characteristic features. In 1902 he gave a lecture at the Vesna Society on Pavel Křížkovský. Janáček's daughter Olga attended classes in sewing, and Marie Stejskalová, the Janáčeks' housekeeper, attended school there for a year. Zdenka Janáčková joined the Vesna association in 1881, soon after her marriage.

On 12 September 1899, Eliška Machová founded the Brno Women's Shelter, providing accommodation for young women seeking work in Brno and it soon opened its doors to orphans and abandoned children. Though not part of Vesna, it was closely allied to it. Zdenka and Olga Janáčková were both supporters and Zdenka served on the committee. For the Slavonic Beseda on 10 January 1900 in aid of the Shelter, Janáček composed and conducted three orchestral dances (VI/11–13). On 15 June 1901, the first performance of *Our Father* was given at a fundraising event for the Women's Shelter, when it was performed as the musical accompaniment to a series of *tableaux vivants* inspired by paintings illustrating the Lord's Prayer. See *Our Father* (IV/29)*. *EDMB, JAWO, JYL1, MLWJ, ZahFoo.*

Brod, Max (b. Prague, 27 May 1884; d. Tel Aviv, 20 December 1968), Czech writer and translator. During Janáček's lifetime, Brod was one of the most energetic advocates of his music and Janáček's first biographer. He played a pivotal role in establishing Janáček's international reputation: in 1916 Brod drew *Jenůfa* to the attention of Emil Hertzka at UE, an intervention that led quickly to a contract being drawn up between composer and publisher. He was commissioned to make a German translation of *Jenůfa** and subsequently translated *The Diary of One Who Disappeared**, *Káťa Kabanová**, *The Cunning Little Vixen**, *The Makropulos Affair** and *From the House of the Dead**. In *Sternenhimmel: Musik- und Theaterleben* (Prague, 1923), Brod devoted the whole first section (pp. 17–77) to Janáček. In 1924 his pioneering biography was published in a Czech translation by Alfred Fuchs, and the following year the original German version was published in Vienna. As Charles Mackerras put it in his foreword to Susskind's *Janáček and Brod* (1985), 'Brod's translations provided the channel for the international recognition of Janáček's operas, because most of the important opera houses between the two world wars were German'. His literate and intelligent German translations led to early productions conducted by the likes of Klemperer* and Kleiber*, as well as the American premiere of *Jenůfa* at the Metropolitan Opera. Rudolf Firkušný* claimed that 'without Max Brod, Leoš Janáček's world reputation would not have arrived for many more years'.

The extensive correspondence between Janáček and Brod between 1916 and 1928 (Janáček's letters are in Czech and Brod's in German) was published as Vol. 9 of the *Korespondence Leoše Janáčka* (1953). Janáček quickly realised that Brod's interest in his work was one of selfless enthusiasm, and that he could be trusted. As Jan Racek put it in his preface to the 1953 edition of the correspondence, 'that is why Janáček is so open and candid, cordial and informative in these letters. Janáček often confides ideas in them which he did not express to his other Czech friends.' Though there were strong disagreements over Brod's choice of animal–human parallels and his proposed changes to the music of the *Vixen*, the letters remained robust but friendly. When Brod suggested adding a line of text at the end of the opera to explain that 'everything comes round again', Janáček pointed out that this was inherent in the music: 'the final scene with the little frog – there's no help for it – it's charming! Let it be!' With the German translation of *Makropulos*, Janáček considered Brod's translation to be too free and sent a list of fifty-two discrepancies on 2 January 1927. Brod conceded some of the composer's demands, though by then the vocal score was already in print.

Brod was also a composer. Most of his music is unpublished, though UE published *Four Songs* [Op. 10] for voice and piano in 1927 (settings of Goethe, Flaubert, Schiller and Psalm 126). Brod served as the literary executor of Franz Kafka (1883–1924). He ignored his friend's instructions that unpublished writings should be destroyed, and as a result *The Trial* and *The Castle* saw the light of day (in 1925 and 1926). His biography of Kafka was published in 1937. Brod fled Prague the day before German troops arrived in 1938, making his way via Romania to Tel Aviv in Israel, where he settled. *BroJan, GolMax, JODA, SusJan.*

Budin, J. L.   See Löwenbach, Jan

Bursík and Kohout, bookseller and publisher in Prague, active from 1884 until 1949.   Jaroslav Bursík and František Kohout established their business in 1884, specialising in publications on medicine and history. Their music catalogue was small but included some interesting titles. In 1889 Bursík and Kohout issued the posthumous first edition of Smetana's String Quartet No. 2. In 1890 the firm issued Janáček's *Valachian Dances* Op. 2 (VI/4), the first of his orchestral works to be published. *FELJ, JAWO, JYL1.*

Calma-Veselá, Marie [pseud. for Marie Veselá, née Hurychová] (b. Unhošť near Kladno, 8 September 1881; d. Prague, 7 April 1966). Czech singer and writer.   Marie Veselá, usually known by her pseudonym Marie Calma, was the second wife of František Veselý*, who developed the spa at Luhačovice in the early years of the twentieth century. Janáček met her at Luhačovice in 1908, the year she married Veselý. In 1958 she published an account of their first meeting: 'I got to know him in the house of Dr František Veselý where we were invited together. On the upright piano lay a vocal score of *Jenůfa* with the pages uncut, published by the KPU. Janáček cut open a few pages and sat down at the piano. "They say you sing nicely – so show us what you can do." He was surprised that I could sight-sing Jenůfa and the Kostelnička.' Calma-Veselá was an accomplished musician, a pianist and singer who had studied with Karel Kovařovic* and auditioned successfully for Felix Mottl at the Munich Court Opera. Under pressure from her parents, she declined the offer to sing there, turning instead to concert work and developing her career as a poet. In 1915–16 Calma-Veselá played a pivotal role in persuading Kovařovic to produce *Jenůfa* at the Prague NT. In her article 'On the battle for Janáček's *Jenůfa*' (*Listy Hudební matice*, Vol. 4, January 1925), she recalled that 'After I had sung Jenůfa's solos and also some of the Kostelnička's part, Kovařovic thawed. He liked some of the solos so much that we repeated them two or even three times. *Jenůfa* broke through!' But there was still work to be done: 'the worst wasn't over. Although Kovařovic promised that he would study *Jenůfa*, he didn't want to do this until he had obtained the composer's consent to make any essential revisions to the work in regard to orchestration, cuts, etc. On no account, however, did he want to negotiate over this with Janáček himself. Thus the role of intermediaries fell again to me and my husband.' This meeting with Kovařovic can be dated precisely, as Calma-Veselá wrote to Janáček on 9 December 1915, describing the private performance and Kovařovic's desire to make some 'small changes'. Eventually, in late December 1915, Janáček and Kovařovic met during the interval of Smetana's *Libuše*. Calma-Veselá had prepared the ground carefully: 'I must admit that I had told each composer only the nice things they had said about each other. In this way the rough edges were smoothed over. Janáček returned to his box satisfied and remarked to me in his terse way, "It's all settled!" He had no idea how much work and how many words had been needed for it to be settled.'

Despite Calma-Veselá's efforts to persuade Kovařovic to produce *Jenůfa*, she was not chosen to sing the role of Jenůfa, which was given to Kamila Ungrová. Calma-Veselá wrote to Janáček on 25 February 1916, 'My only disappointment is that you could not say, or did not know how to say, I want Mrs Veselá to sing Jenůfa because I feel that no one else would sing it like her.' Janáček responded to this reproach with sullen mulishness, and he failed to invite the Veselýs to the Prague premiere of *Jenůfa* on 26 May 1916, even though František Veselý had guaranteed to underwrite the first six performances if they were not sold out. After Calma-Veselá's article appeared in 1925, a chastened Janáček wrote to her on 31 January, saying that it 'illuminates so many of the incidents about which I didn't know', and placing the blame squarely on Kovařovic for not casting her: 'Perhaps you believe now that Kovařovic didn't want to allow you as Jenůfa for the premiere. He promised me a repeat performance, and didn't keep his promise.' The correspondence between Janáček, Marie Calma-Veselá and František Veselý was published as Vol. 8 of the *Korespondence Leoše Janáčka* (1951). Marie Calma-Veselá is not to be confused with Marie Veselá (1892–1969), the Viennese-trained soprano who created the title role in *Káťa Kabanová* (see Veselá, Marie*). *JAix, JODA, JYL2, KLJ.*

Čapek, Josef (b. Hronov, 23 March 1887; d. Bergen-Belsen concentration camp, April? 1945), Czech artist and writer, brother of Karel Čapek*. Josef Čapek worked as an editor and cartoonist at the Prague offices of *Lidové noviny* from 1921 until 1939. He designed the sets for the Prague premieres of *The Cunning Little Vixen** (1925) and *The Makropulos Affair** (1928), and for the Brno production of *The Excursion of Mr Brouček to the Moon** (1926). Zahrádka and Janáčková have both suggested that Čapek also designed the sets for the Brno premiere of *Makropulos* on 18 December 1926. While Janáček praised Čapek's sets for the Prague production of *The Cunning Little Vixen* (writing to Kamila Stösslová on 29 March 1925 that they were 'most effective'), he was less pleased with the sets for the Prague *Makropulos*. On 27 February 1928, he wrote to his wife that 'Čapek's sets weren't a success'.

Čapek often collaborated with his brother, Karel, most famously as co-authors of *The Life of Insects*, and though Karel Čapek introduced the word 'Robot' into the vocabulary in *RUR: Rossum's Universal Robots* (1920), he later explained that the idea had come from his brother. On 1 September 1939, Josef Čapek was arrested in Prague by the Gestapo and was imprisoned. On 25 February 1945, he was transported to Bergen-Belsen, where he died of typhus a few days before the camp was liberated in April 1945. *JODA, MarRob, PřiLed.*

Čapek, Karel (b. Malé Svatoňovice, 9 January 1890; d. Prague, 25 December 1938). Czech writer, brother of Josef Čapek*. In a letter to Max Brod on 22 August 1922, Janáček wrote: 'Do you know Čapek? *RUR*, *The Life of Insects*. His sister said something about a libretto.' Čapek's sister Helena Čapková worked in the offices of *Lidové noviny* in Brno and knew Janáček. It is not known if she suggested a particular play, but Janáček went to see *The Makropulos Affair* at the Vinohrady Theatre on 10 December 1922. He saw the play again in Brno on 19 January 1923, when he met Čapek for the first time (he took down a speech melody of Čapek talking about a sausage – in fact, his description of one of the actors). He was clearly taken with *Makropulos* and asked about the rights to the play in February 1923. Čapek was courteous but sceptical, writing on 27 February 1923: 'I have too high an opinion of music – and especially of yours – to be able to imagine it united with a *conversational*, fairly unpoetic and garrulous play such as my *Makropulos Affair*. I fear that you may have in mind something different and better than my play can really provide, apart from that 300-year-old character.' In private he was more forthright. His sister Helena recalled that 'Karel simply brushed it aside and grumbled: "That old crank! Soon he'll be setting the column in the local newspaper to music."' In fact, that's exactly what Janáček *was* doing, hard at work on *The Cunning Little Vixen*. On his summer holidays at Štrbské Pleso in Slovakia, he read *Makropulos* again and decided to go ahead with the project, though he still needed Čapek's permission. Čapek replied on 10 September 1923: 'you are free to make use of my piece ... and I give you the right to arrange my own text as you need. I would have liked to have given you something better to set than this particular play, but if you are drawn to it, you will certainly make something great from it, and with my whole heart I most fervently wish you much happiness.' Janáček agreed terms with Čapek's agent in October 1923 and wrote at once to Kamila Stösslová (on 13 October) to tell her about his newest project: 'I will compose a piece about a beautiful woman who is already 300 years old, and who does not want anyone.' Less than a month later, on 11 November, he started composing, during which time he seems to have had no contact with Čapek, but he invited him to the premiere on 18 December 1926. Helena Čapková recorded her brother's delighted reaction: 'He did it a hundred times better than I could ever have imagined!' (see *The Makropulos Affair**). *ČapMoj, JanLid, JODA.*

Capriccio for piano left hand, flute/piccolo, two trumpets, three trombones and tenor tuba (VI/12).   On 15 January 1926, Otakar Hollmann* wrote to Ludvík Kundera asking him to approach Janáček on his behalf for a new work for piano left hand. On 11 June 1926, he wrote to Janáček directly but received no reply. Janáček started a piece for piano left hand in the autumn of 1926 but had doubts about whether it would work. He wrote to Kamila Stösslová on 29 October 1926: 'I have written something for a pianist who only has his left hand. But I do not know how it will end. It's hard to dance when one only has one leg!' Hollmann read about the finished *Capriccio* in the *Prager Tagblatt* and wrote to Janáček (7 November 1926) asking whether he could give the first performance. Janáček told Hollmann that he would let him know when the score was copied but that Ilona Štěpánová-Kurzová* was also interested in playing the work. A few months later, Hollmann wrote again (12 May 1927) and this time Janáček sent him a copy of the score. On 6 February 1928, Hollmann played the work for Janáček at his home in Brno and the composer was impressed, telling Stösslová that 'the one-handed virtuoso came from Prague to see me. He'll play my piece nicely.' The first performance was given in Prague on 2 March 1928, with Hollmann accompanied by members of the Czech Philharmonic conducted by Jaroslav Řídký. Janáček was present and also attended several rehearsals in Prague (the premiere of the *Capriccio* coincided with the Prague production of *The Makropulos Affair*, which opened on 1 March). Janáček wrote to Hollmann on 5 March 1928 praising his playing and thanking him for taking on the work. Once Janáček was convinced that Hollmann would be capable of realising his work, he came to admire the pianist's personal courage. In early February, around the time Hollmann had visited Janáček in Brno, Janáček wrote to Stösslová calling the work 'Capriccio (Defiance [Vzdor])', which he later shortened to the informal title 'Defiance'. *Capriccio* was always the official title, and Janáček described the work as 'whimsical, all wilfulness and witticisms'. It is also one of the strangest instrumental ensembles that Janáček wrote for: one woodwind instrument (flute doubling piccolo), six brass instruments and one-handed piano soloist. Janáček's flair for unusual sonorities creates music of memorable oddness and, in the last movement, a sort of quirky nobility and exhilaration. The *Capriccio* was published by SNKLHU in 1953. A critical edition appeared as SKV E/5 (2002). *JAWO, ProCap.*

Čarták on Soláň [*Na Soláni Čarták*], cantata for tenor solo, male chorus and orchestra (III/7). Vilém Steinmann [Steinman] (1880–1962), conductor of the Orlice male-voice choir in Prostějov, visited Janáček in Brno towards the end of 1910 to request a new work for the choir's fiftieth anniversary in 1912. Janáček quickly finished a first version of the work and wrote to Steinmann on 21 March: 'It's done. But I'd like to put it to one side and have another look at it. There's a lot to do to it.' After making the changes he wanted, Janáček sent the score to Steinmann on 24 April. The work was dedicated 'To Orlice in Prostějov'. The first performance took place in Prostějov on 23 March 1912, with Steinmann conducting Orlice and the Band of the 8th Infantry Regiment from Brno. In 1920 Janáček made a thorough revision that involved a comprehensive metrical reorganisation of the music and rebarring it: the 1911 version comprises 241 bars, mostly in 6/16 time, while the 1920 version comprises 117 bars, mostly in 4/8 time (both are published in SKV B/3, so they can be compared). The revised version was first performed on 19 October 1924, with Stanislav Tauber* as the tenor soloist, the Brno Beseda chorus and the orchestra of the Brno NT conducted by Jaroslav Kvapil*. The poem came from a collection by Max Kurt, the pseudonym of Maxmilián Kunert (1877–1960). Kurt's poems are in the style of folk ballads and his subjects range from the Valachian countryside to the industrial upheaval of Ostrava. The location of a 'Čarták', a wooden shelter (i.e. an inn), on Soláň (861 m/2,824 ft) in the Beskydy Hills was real, and today there is a hotel on the site. In 1924 Kurt wrote to congratulate Janáček on his seventieth birthday, adding that 'It is a great source of pride in my life that the simple poem "Na Soláni Čarták" gave your genius some inspiration.'

Čarták on Soláň is rarely performed. Lasting around eight minutes and scored for double woodwind, four horns, percussion, harp and strings, it has a distinctive and rather dark character. Theodora Straková described it as 'an intimate and emotionally ardent nocturne'. A vocal score of the 1920 version was published in 1958 by SNKLHU. A critical edition of both versions was published in SKV B/3 (1981). *JAWO, KLJ, StrČar.*

Catalogues of Janáček's Works The earliest detailed listing of Janáček's works appeared as part of the profile of the composer by his pupil Jan Kunc* in *Hudební revue* (1911), and two later catalogues appeared in publications for his seventieth birthday, in Max Brod's *Leoš Janáček: Život a dílo* (pp. 73–6) and Adolf Veselý's *Leoš Janáček: Pohled do života i díla* (pp. 153–63); both included information provided by Janáček. Jan Racek's *Leoš Janáček: obraz života a díla* (1948, pp. 31–54) has a more detailed catalogue of works by Theodora Straková and Vítězslav Veselý and a catalogue of writings by Straková (pp. 55–61). Vladimír Telec's *Leoš Janáček 1854–1928: výběrová bibliografie* (1958) provides useful details of first editions. Bohumír Štědroň's *Dílo Leoše Janáčka* (1959) was the most thorough and detailed catalogue to date, and this was followed by Jaroslav Procházka's *Hudební dílo Leoše Janáčka* (1979) and the 'Catalogue of Works by Leoš Janáček' in the revised English edition of Vogel's biography (1981, pp. 397–415). Nigel Simeone's *The First Editions of Leoš Janáček* (1991) was the earliest descriptive bibliography of first editions. *Janáček's Works*, by Nigel Simeone, John Tyrrell and Alena Němcová (*JAWO*, 1997) is by far the most comprehensive catalogue of Janáček's music in any language and also includes an annotated catalogue of his writings by Straková. Its numbering has gradually been adopted by record companies, publishers and performing organisations. A summary version of *JAWO* in Czech and English can be consulted online at www.leosjanacek.eu. *BroJan, DLJ, FELJ, JANGES, JAWO, LEOJAN, ProHud, RacObr, TelJan, VesJan, VogJan.*

Čech, Svatopluk (b. Ostředek, 21 February 1846; d. Prague-Holešovice, 23 February 1908). Czech writer.   After graduating in law, Čech's earliest writings included historical epics such as *The Hussite on the Baltic* (1868) and *The Adamites* (1873), inspired by the Hussite Wars. In the allegorical epic *Slavie* (1884) he advocated a Pan-Slavic vision. Čech's two most famous novels are *The True Excursion of Mr Brouček to the Moon* (1888) and *The New Epoch-making Excursion of Mr Brouček, this time to the Fifteenth Century* (1889). The first considers the relationship of artists (represented by delightfully ludicrous moon-dwelling aesthetes) with wider society (exemplified, at its worst, by the obstinately philistine Mr Brouček). The second novel has at its heart the Hussite uprising about which Čech had often written before, with its implications for the liberation and resurgence of the Czech nation, a cause Čech held dear. These two satires went on to inspire the most grandly conceived of Janáček's operas (see *The Excursions of Mr Brouček**). Čech himself appears as an operatic character near the start of Janáček's 'Fifteenth Century' Excursion (vocal score pp. 178–182). Janáček had known the novels since they first appeared, and he printed a passage from the 'Moon' excursion in *Hudební listy* (1 February 1888) in which Brouček flees from a concert hall during a performance of *The Storm* by the Moon's leading composer. It could be that the operatic possibilities of the Brouček stories occurred to Janáček around this time, but it was not until after Čech's death that he took up the idea. Before then, in 1895, he had considered setting Čech's *Slave Songs* (*Písně otroka*, 1894) as a cantata (X1/4) but the idea got no further than some annotations in the margins of the book. In *The Excursions of Mr Brouček*, Janáček produced an operatic setting of Čech's novels that mirrored their preoccupations, retained their comic absurdity and celebrated their deeper underlying message. *JAWO, JODA, KLJ.*

Čelanský, Ludvík Vítězslav (b. Vienna, 17 July 1870; d. Prague, 27 October 1931), Czech composer and conductor.   In 1897 Čelanský completed his opera *Kamilla* and conducted it at the Prague NT on 23 October. The plot concerns a young woman who is wooed by a sensitive poet, Viktor, and a wealthy but uncouth neighbour. She chooses the neighbour but soon regrets her decision when Viktor renounces her. The Kamilla of the title and Viktor the jilted poet were closely based on real people: Kamila Urválková* and Čelanský himself. Their passionate affair had ended in acrimony (perhaps terminated by Urválková's parents) and Čelanský – by all accounts a man of strong emotions – wrote this one-act opera as a kind of revenge. It was Urválková telling Janáček about this opera at Luhačovice in 1903 that led directly to the composition of *Fate**. *Kamilla* ran for six performances in October and November 1897 at the Prague NT, and there were three further performances in 1898–9. Čelanský was assistant conductor at the Prague NT (1899–1900) but fell out with Kovařovic, the new music director. When orchestral players went on strike against Kovařovic in 1901, Čelanský formed a new orchestra made up of the striking musicians, and on 15 October 1901 the Czech Philharmonic gave its first concert as a fully independent organisation, conducted by Čelanský. In 1907 he became music director of the new Town Theatre in the Prague district of Královské Vinohrady, known as the Vinohrady Theatre. Janáček offered *Fate* to the theatre, apparently unaware that the character of Živný was partly based on its music director. If Čelanský realised, it didn't seem to worry him: he lobbied enthusiastically for *Fate* to be staged at the Vinohrady, telling an interviewer for *Národní obzor* (27 June 1913): 'Leoš Janáček belongs among the unrecognised composers. ... This is why his opera *Fate* was accepted even though at first glance it didn't look as if it would be a box-office success. Since the opera is very interesting *it was worth a try*. Six years ago the management of the Vinohrady Theatre agreed to stage the work on my recommendation. In my first year I could not proceed right away with the rehearsal of such a difficult opera.' Čelanský had a dispute with the Vinohrady Theatre in 1908 and left to take up a position at the Apollo Theatre in Paris, but he returned as the conductor at the Vinohrady in 1913. In the meantime, Janáček had taken out a lawsuit against the theatre for breaking its contract to stage *Fate*. Undeterred, Čelanský wrote to Janáček on 18 July 1913. He was keen to perform the opera but felt it necessary to spell out the financial reality to Janáček: 'You know that it was I myself who accepted your opera, as an example of a new artistic direction and of your own individuality. I was never led to this by any possible financial success in the theatre, and you cannot surely believe that the theatre could make any profits from the performance of your opera – rather the opposite. Just think how many rehearsals I will need if I want to give your opera even half decently.' He urged Janáček to drop the lawsuit and resubmit the work to the new administration. Janáček did not take this olive branch and, despite Čelanský's attempts at diplomacy (and his genuine desire to perform the opera), by March 1914 negotiations had broken down and Janáček withdrew the work. Janáček was his own worst enemy during this episode, choosing to reject the offer from a prominent Prague conductor to stage his newest opera. It remained unperformed in Janáček's lifetime. Čelanský was quixotic and irascible, but he was a gifted musician who deserves credit for his ultimately unsuccessful attempt to put on the first production of any Janáček opera in Prague. *ČHS, HolČes, JODA, KLJ, NDPrOA.*

Černušák, Gracian (b. Ptení near Prostějov, 19 December 1882; d. Brno, 13 October 1961), Czech writer and lexicographer. Černušák was educated in

Olomouc and in Kroměříž, where he was a student of Ferdinand Vach (he sang in the Kroměříž performance of *Amarus* on 2 December 1900 conducted by Janáček). He studied at the Charles University in Prague, in law and then in history and music (with Otakar Hostinský). He taught at the Business Academy in Hradec Králové from 1905 to 1918. After moving to Brno in 1918, he was appointed music critic of *Lidové noviny* and was invited by Janáček to teach music history at the Brno Conservatory. He was one of the most significant music critics in Brno during Janáček's later years, reviewing the world premieres of *Káťa Kabanová*, *The Cunning Little Vixen*, *The Makropulos Affair* and the *Glagolitic Mass* for *Lidové noviny*, and writing the paper's main obituary for Janáček. Černušák was also an important lexicographer: he was the editor of Part I of the *Pazdírkův hudební slovník naučný* (Brno, 1929) and co-editor with Helfert of Part II (the biographical section), a project that reached the letter M before the Nazi occupation forced its abandonment. After the war, Černušák worked with Bohumír Štědroň and Zdenko Nováček on the *Československý hudební slovník osob a institucí*, which remains the most comprehensive dictionary of Czech musicians. At a politically sensitive time, Černušák also contributed many entries to the 1954 edition of *Grove's Dictionary of Music and Musicians*. ČSHS.

Červinka, Vincenc (b. Kolín, 2 August 1877; d. Prague, 2 October 1942), Czech writer and translator.   In 1905 Červinka was sent as a reporter to St Petersburg by *Národní listy*, a newspaper for which he later worked as an editor. During World War I he was a member of the Czech resistance, and in July 1916 he was sentenced to death for treason and espionage. In July 1917, he was released as part of an amnesty and later wrote a memoir of his time in jail, *My Austrian Prison* (*Moje rakouské žaláře*), published in 1928. Alongside his work as a journalist, Červinka was a translator specialising in Russian literature, including works by Bulgakov, Chekhov, Dostoyevsky, Gorky, Tolstoy and Turgenev. It was his translation of Ostrovsky's *The Thunderstorm* (Prague: J. Otto, 1918) that brought him to Janáček's attention (see *Káťa Kabanová**). JAWO, JODA, TyrKat.

Česká legie   See *The Czech Legion* (IV/42)

Charpentier, Gustave (b. Dieuze, 25 June 1860; d. Paris, 18 February 1956), French composer.   Janáček's enthusiasm for Charpentier's *Louise* is well documented. In a lecture given at the Brno Organ School in 1909 he said: 'There was no real life in opera. This only began with Charpentier's *Louise* ... Charpentier took correct original types [of authentic street cries].' He first saw *Louise* in Prague on 21 May 1903 and it made a deep impression. When he started work on *Fate** at the end of the year, the impact of *Louise* is clear. Charpentier's opera is subtitled a *roman musical* ('musical novel'), while the subtitle of *Fate* is 'three scenes from a novel'. *Louise* certainly had an important influence on *Fate* in terms of its urban setting, its large cast of smaller characters, the complex multi-layered writing for chorus and the use of the viola d'amore (in the earlier versions of *Fate*), as well as the parallels between Louise's mother and Míla's mother. John Tyrrell has argued that *Louise* was 'the most important influence on Janáček's approach to the conventions of opera and on the formation of what we take today to be typical ingredients of Janáček's later operas'. Tyrrell further suggests that Louise's mother may have provided the model for Janáček's most formidable female anti-heroine, Kabanicha in *Káťa Kabanová*. Charpentier's use of waltzes presented Janáček with the model for a more metropolitan dance form than Czech folk dances, and this is apparent in the opening chorus of *Fate*, in *Brouček* and in *The Cunning Little Vixen*. While the musical language of *Louise* had little impact on Janáček, his getting to know this work marked, as Tyrrell put it, 'a turning-point in his operatic life'. *JYL1*.

Chlubna, Osvald (b. Brno, 22 July 1893; d. Brno, 30 October 1971). Czech composer. Chlubna studied at the Czech Technical School in Brno (1911–13) with the intention of becoming an engineer. He studied with Janáček at the Brno Organ School in 1914–15, and later in Janáček's Master School in Composition (1923–4). He worked at the Brno Conservatory (1919–35 and 1953–9), teaching harmony, orchestration and theory. At the same time he held an official post at the Cyril and Methodius Savings Bank in the magnificent art nouveau building that is currently the Hotel Grandezza, in Brno's Zelný trh.

Chlubna was a member of the Moravian Young Composers' Club (1920–2) and the KMS (1922–48), and on several occasions his compositions were included in the same programmes as Janáček premieres. In 1918 Janáček asked Chlubna to orchestrate Act III of *Šárka**, a task he completed by 25 August, when he handed it back to the composer for revisions. The most controversial of Chlubna's posthumous Janáček projects was his rescoring of *From the House of the Dead**, and his composition of a new ending in place of Janáček's original. He did this in collaboration with Břetislav Bakala*, who conducted the first performance at the Brno NT on 12 April 1930. It was not until John Tyrrell's edition of 2019 that all of Chlubna's alterations were finally excised from the work. Though Chlubna's version of *From the House of the Dead* is now considered misguided, his interventions were well intentioned; much the same can be said of Chlubna's realisation of *The Danube*, finished in 1948 (see *The Danube**). *ČSHS, EDMB, JAWO, ProDun, ZahŠár*.

Choruses for Male Voices These were an important aspect of Janáček's output throughout his career, above all because they were a medium in which he was able to experiment and in which he later extended the possibilities of writing for male voices. They were the form in which he began his career as a composer, writing choruses for Svatopluk between 1873 and 1876 (see Brno: Svatopluk Society*). They were also the means through which he was able to make powerful social commentary through his musical settings of Petr Bezruč (see *Halfar the Schoolmaster**, *Maryčka Magdónova** and *The Seventy Thousand**). His last choruses reveal his most daring work in the form, above all in *The Wandering Madman** (IV/43), but also in works such as *The Czech Legion** (IV/42) and *Our Flag** (IV/44). The influence of these later choruses can be heard in larger works such as the *Glagolitic Mass* and, especially, *From the House of the Dead*. Two other sets of male choruses are worthy of note. The *Four male-voice choruses* (IV/17) were composed in 1885. After rejection by a Prague publisher, they were issued in 1886 by Karl Winkler in Brno, with a dedication from Janáček 'to the esteemed master Antonín Dvořák' (see Dvořák, Antonín* for Dvořák's comments on these choruses). The other outstanding set was the *Four Moravian male-voice choruses* (IV/28), composed in 1900 (Nos. 1 and 3) and 1906 (Nos. 2 and 4). It was Nos. 1 and 3 that Janáček sent Ferdinand Vach and his PSMU in 1905, marking the start of a long and extremely productive relationship between the composer and this remarkable choir. The four choruses were together one of Janáček's earliest Prague publications, issued by Mojmír Urbánek in 1906. Two of them, 'Dež viš' ('If only you knew') and 'Klekánica' ('The Evening Witch'), were among his first works to be performed abroad, in Vienna, Munich and Paris in 1905–6 by the PSMU on tour. These two choruses show more harmonic and metrical freedom than any other works by Janáček from 1900, and his natural setting of the rhythms of the folk poetry was to be applied with striking success a few years later to Bezruč's poems. *JYL1, StrMuž, VogJan.*

Club of the Friends of Art in Brno   See Brno: Club of the Friends of Art in Brno

Comenius Iohannes Amos   See *Lullaby* (V/14)

Concertino for piano, two violins, viola, clarinet, horn and bassoon (VII/11).   Composed in 1925, the idea for the *Concertino* first came to Janáček as he walked back from a performance in Prague of *The Diary of One Who Disappeared* on 23 November 1924, in which the pianist was Jan Heřman*. The earliest sketch, dated 1 January 1925, is marked 'by the Vltava'. The work was completed in Hukvaldy on 15 April 1925, with further revisions by 29 April. The earliest of Sedláček's authorised copies has the title 'Piano Concerto' altered by Janáček to 'Piano Concertino', but Janáček also called the work 'Spring – Suite' on the autograph of the fourth movement. He wrote to Kamila Stösslová on 23 April 1925, 'I've written a piano concerto – *Spring*. There's a cricket, midges, a roebuck, a fierce torrent, yes, and a man!' A year later, Janáček wrote an open letter about the work for *Pult und Taktstock* (May–June 1927). The details of the programme had changed, but what remained was a suite-like piece about spring, filled with animals:

> First movement [Moderato]: It was in the spring, when we once blocked the entrance of a hedgehog's house in a linden tree. The hedgehog had lined a soft nest in that old tree. It was beside itself with anger! It just could not understand it. That is also why my horn persists with its sulky motif. Should the hedgehog stand on its hind legs and burst into a lament? No sooner had he put his snout out, than he had to roll up again.
>
> Second movement [Più mosso]: The squirrel chattered away as it jumped from the top of one tree to another. Later it moaned in a cage, like my clarinet, but turned around and danced to amuse the children.
>
> Third movement [Con moto]: The wide-open eyes of little owls and big owls stared insolently out from the strings of the piano, as did those of other grumbling night creatures.
>
> Fourth movement [Allegro]: Everything seems like the penny that one quarrels over in fairy tales. And the piano? Someone, surely, has to be in charge.

Janáček lists the principal motifs (three for each movement), and ends by describing the work as 'a small musical joke'. Though the *Concertino* is dedicated to Jan Heřman, Janáček did not give him the premiere. Ilona Štěpánová-Kurzová* lobbied hard to persuade Janáček that she should give the first performances, which she did with great success in Brno on 16 February 1926 and Prague on 20 February. Janáček told Rosa Newmarch (24 February 1926), that the *Concertino* was encored at both perfromances. It was published by HMUB in 1926 and a critical edition appeared as SKVEJ E/7 (2001). *DrlCon, JAWO, JYL2, ZemEss.*

Conducting, Janáček's   Janáček was very active as a conductor until around 1900, and his repertoire, especially as conductor of the Brno Beseda, included large-scale works such as Beethoven's *Missa solemnis*, Mozart's Requiem, and Dvořák's *Stabat Mater* and *Spectre's Bride*. He also conducted a number of orchestral pieces by Dvořák, including the world premiere of *The Wild Dove* Op. 110. The views of two well-informed eyewitnesses give a useful impression of Janáček's conducting. Karel Kovařovic* (at the start of his career as a conductor at the Brno NT) reviewed the concert given on 10 January 1886 for *Hudební listy*. It included Dvořák's *Hymnus* and Seventh Symphony. He praised 'the conductor's firm control', and his musical insights: 'The most subtle nuances and the smallest details of Dvořák's deeply felt work were given their fullest significance ... The magnitude of the performance should have far-reaching consequences, not only for local music but for Czech music in general.'

Pavel Dědeček* taught at the Brno Organ School during Janáček's directorship, and was leader of the orchestra at the Brno NT. He later became professor of conducting at the Prague Conservatory. In 1945 he wrote to Bohumír Štědroň about Janáček's conducting:

> He was, in my opinion, a conductor in the full sense of the word and not a mere composer-conductor. Janáček – a true conductor – second only to Karel Kovařovic, has so far not been fully appreciated. He was a great artist, who not only knew how to present large-scale works convincingly, both dynamically and rhythmically, but also had complete technical understanding of each work, which is surely one of the most important conditions for a successful orchestral ensemble and for the perfect balancing of the woodwind and brass, etc. During his later years, Janáček's health prevented him from conducting. Once, when I asked him, he replied in a joking way, 'I don't conduct because I have a bad heart.' ... Janáček the conductor was far superior to the usual class of composer-conductors who, in every respect, fail to match his ability.

Janáček's last appearance as a conductor was in 1909, when he took on a performance of Gounod's *Mors et vita*, replacing Ferdinand Vach who had fallen ill. Janáček resisted an offer from Kovařovic to conduct a gala performance of *Jenůfa* at the Prague NT in 1916. In later years, he was happy to leave his works in the hands of trusted conductors such as František Neumann*, Otakar Ostrčil*, Ferdinand Vach* and Václav Talich*.

The following list gives Janáček's known performances as a conductor. All were in Brno unless otherwise stated. Abbreviations: BB: Brno Beseda; SV: Svatopluk; CNK: Česká národní kapela [Czech National Orchestra]; NT: Brno National Theatre; NTO: Brno National Theatre Orchestra; OS: Brno Organ School; TI: Teachers' Institute Choir. First performances are indicated with a dagger.

27 April 1873 SV	Janáček: *Ploughing* (IV/1)†
5 July 1873 SV	Janáček: *War Song* [2] (IV/3)†
9 November 1873 SV	Janáček: *The fickleness of love* (IV/4)†
14 March 1874 SV	Janáček: *Ploughing* (IV/1); *Alone without comfort* [1] (IV/7)†
6 September 1874 SV	Janáček: *Ploughing* (IV/1), *War Song* [2] (IV/3), *The fickleness of love* (IV/4), *Alone without comfort* [1] (IV/7). Concert at Šlapanice, near Brno

23 January 1876 SV	Janáček: *True love* (IV/8)†
3 April 1876 BB	Janáček: *Vocal Elegy* (IV/10)†
13 May 1876 BB	Rubinstein: Piano Concerto No. 3, first movement
13 November 1876 BB	Janáček: *Death* (X/3)†
14 December 1876 BB	Mendelssohn: Psalm 95 Op. 46
22 April 1877 BB	Dvořák: Serenade in E major Op. 22; Skuherský: *Máj*; Bruch: Violin Concerto No. 1
15 July 1877 TI	Janáček: *Festive chorus* (IV/12)†
28 October 1877 BB	Janáček: *Festive chorus* (IV/12)
2 December 1877 BB	Janáček: Suite for strings (VI/2)†
14 April 1878 BB	Mozart: Requiem K626
19 May 1878 BB	Haydn: Symphony No. 97
15 September 1878 TI	Janáček: *Festive chorus* (IV/13)†
15 December 1878 BB	Janáček: *Idyll* (VI/3)†; Dvořák: 4 [unspecified] Slavonic Dances
2 April 1879 BB	Beethoven: *Missa solemnis* Op. 123
12 December 1880 BB	Janáček: *Autumn song* (IV/14)†; Dvořák: *Slavonic Rhapsody* Op. 45 No. 1; Smetana: *Vltava*
2 April 1882 BB	Dvořák: *Stabat mater*; Tchaikovsky: *Serenade for Strings*
18 March 1883 BB	Dvořák: Symphony No. 6; Smetana: *Vltava*; Brahms: *Schicksalslied* Op. 54
30 March 1884 BB	Dvořák: *Legends* Op. 59, Nos. 1–4; Saint-Saëns: *Danse macabre*
12 February 1885 BB	Dvořák: Nocturne in B major Op. 40; Liszt: *Mazeppa*
10 January 1886 BB	Dvořák: *Hymnus* Op. 30, Symphony No. 7
14 November 1886 BB	Janáček: *Four male-voice choruses* (IV/17), Nos. 2 and 3†; Smetana: *Vyšehrad*; Beethoven: Piano Concerto No. 1
27 November 1887 BB	Dvořák: *Legends* Op. 59, Nos. 6–10
29 April 1888 BB	Dvořák: *The Spectre's Bride* Op. 69
4 Janunary 1891 NTO	Janáček: *Valachian Dances* (VI/4): Starodávný II, Požehnaný, Kožich, Čeladenský
20 November 1892 NTO	Janáček: *Rákoš Rákoczy* I/2 (8 numbers)
7 May 1893 NTO	Dvořák: *My Home* Op. 62
10 February 1894 NT	Janáček: *The Beginning of a Romance* (I/3)†
13 May 1894	Janáček: *The sun has risen above that hill* (IV/23)†
11 April 1897 CNK	Dvořák: *The Water Goblin* Op. 107
20 March 1898 CNK	Dvořák: *The Wild Dove* Op. 110†; Janáček: *Amarus* (Epilogue)†
24 April 1898 TI	Janáček: *Festive chorus* (IV/25)†
7 June 1899 CNK	Glazunov: *Slavonic Festival* Op. 26a, at a concert organised by the Russian Circle to mark the centenary of Pushkin's birth
19 November 1899 CNK	Dvořák: *A Hero's Song* Op. 111
10 January 1900 CNK	Janáček: *Požehnaný* (VI/11)†, *Kozáček* (VI/12)†, *Serbian Reel* (VI/13)†, at a concert to mark the opening of the Women's Shelter in Brno

2 December 1900	Janáček: *Amarus* (without Epilogue)†. Concert at Kroměříž	
17 March 1901	Janáček: *The Wild Duck* (IV/18)†	
4 March 1909 OS	Gounod: *Mors et vita*. Janáček's last public appearance as a conductor, standing in for Ferdinand Vach	

JAWO, JYL1, LJLR, ProLeo, VDKS.

Conductors See individual entries for: Ančerl, Karel; Bakala, Břetislav; Bodanzky, Artur; Doležil, Metod; Gregor, Bohumil; Hrazdira, Cyril Metoděj; Jílek, František; Kleiber, Erich; Klemperer, Otto; Kovařovic, Karel; Krombholc, Jaroslav; Kubelík, Rafael; Kvapil, Jaroslav; Mackerras, Charles; Maixner, Vincenc; Neumann, František; Neumann, Václav; Nosek, Václav; Ostrčil, Otakar; Spilka, František; Steinberg, Hans Wilhelm [William]; Talich, Václav; Tauský, Vilém; Vach, Ferdinand; Vogel, Jaroslav; Wood, Henry; Zemlinsky, Alexander. See also **Brno National Theatre; Moravian Teachers' Choral Society; Prague National Theatre; Radio Broadcasts during Janáček's Lifetime; Recordings before 1960**

Copyists See **Authorised copies**; and entries on Jaroslav Kulhánek, Václav Sedláček and Josef Stross

Correspondence Janáček's correspondence is extensive, and substantial portions of it have been published. Most of his letters were written in Czech but he used German in his early love letters to Zdenka Schulzová (after their marriage he insisted they communicated in Czech) and in his business letters to UE in Vienna. Janáček wrote to Max Brod in Czech, but Brod replied in German. The first systematic attempt to publish Janáček's letters started in 1934 with Vol. 1 of the series 'Janáčkův archiv' (Janáček archive). After a long interruption, the series resumed in 1948. Altogether nine volumes appeared comprising letters to Artuš Rektorys, Otakar Ostrčil, F. S. Procházka, the other *Brouček* librettists, Gabriela Horvátová, Karel Kovařovic, Maria Calma-Veselá and František Veselý, and Max Brod (see Bibliography, *JAi–JAix*, for details). Further collections followed, of which the most extensive was the correspondence between Janáček and Kamila Stösslová in 1990 (ed. Přibáňová; English edition ed. Tyrrell, 1996). Of similar significance was the publication in 2007 of Janáček's correspondence with his wife and daughter, also edited by Přibáňová. The letters with Rosa Newmarch (ed. Fischmann, 1986) and with UE (ed. Hilmar, 1988) were particularly important in terms of Janáček's success outside Czech lands. Janáček's letters have appeared in many other publications, including a number in English in Tyrrell's *Janáček's Operas: A Documentary Account* (1992) and *Janáček: Years of a Life* (2006 and 2007).

In 2016 the website *Korespondence Leoše Janáčka* (*KLJ*, edited by Jiří Zahrádka* et al.) went online, comprising transcriptions of the letters in the collection of the Janáček Archive: around 14,000 items (over 95 per cent of Janáček's known correspondence), including many unpublished items. This comprehensive online archive can be consulted following a registration process, and access is protected by password. For each letter, a complete transcription is followed by explanatory notes and usually by an English summary. The URL is: www.musicologica.cz/korespondencejanacek. The database can be searched by name of correspondent, date and call number. *JAi–JAix, JYL1, JYL2, KLJ, PřiHad, PřiThe, TyrInt.*

Cowell, Henry (b. Menlo Park, California, 11 March 1897; d. Shady, New York, 10 December 1965), American composer. In 1926 Cowell was invited to Brno by the KMS. He gave a talk on 8 April 1926, and the next day gave a concert of his works. The review by Ludvík Kundera* in *Hudební rozhledy* (Vol. 2, No. 8, pp. 127–8) suggests that Cowell's performance was an evening of startling experimentation but little more. Janáček was present at the lecture and the concert, and he met Cowell. It is not known what Janáček made of Cowell's music, but Cowell regarded Janáček highly. On 3 August 1927, he wrote: 'I shall always remember with the greatest pleasure our meeting last year, and I consider that you are without doubt one of the very greatest of living composers.' Cowell returned to Brno two years later: a concert on 6 June 1929 included works by Cowell, Janáček, Petrželka and Kaprál played by the Moravian Quartet. On the same day, *Lidové noviny* published Cowell's article 'Folk song as a basis for new music', in which he wrote approvingly about Janáček's methods of folksong collection. Many of Cowell's later compositions were based on American folk music, but in a style that was far more conservative than his earlier works. *DrlCow, ZahCow.*

The Cunning Little Vixen [Příhody lišky Bystroušky, lit. The Adventures of Vixen Bystrouška], opera in three acts, with libretto by Janáček after Rudolf Těsnohlídek's story *Liška Bystrouška* published in *Lidové noviny* between April and June 1920 (I/9). Composed between 22 January 1922 and 10 October 1923, with revisions to the fanfares preceding the final scene made by 31 October 1924 during rehearsals for the premiere. Těsnohlídek's story with illustrations by Stanislav Lolek, appeared in instalments in *Lidové noviny* between 7 April and 23 June 1920 (see Lolek, Stanislav* and Těsnohlídek, Rudolf*). According to Janáček's housekeeper, Marie Stejskalová, she drew the composer's attention to the stories, and he kept a set of cuttings. He was still working on *Káťa Kabanová* when he gave an interview to Adolf Veselý, published in *Lidové noviny* on 15 May 1921, announcing his intention to make *The Cunning Little Vixen* his next opera. It was the depiction of animals that seems to have appealed to him most: 'People will act in it as well as speak, but like animals. Foxes, old and young, frogs, mosquitoes – but you know them from the book. It will be an opera and a pantomime [i.e. ballet] ... In my *Vixen* there will be dramatic action, stage action. And then there are the animals! For years I've listened to them, memorising their speech, and I'm at home with them.' Polygrafie, the Brno publishers of Těsnohlídek's story in book form, lost no time in associating it with the city's most famous composer: an advertisement that first appeared in *Divadelní šepty* on 4 June 1921 failed to mention Těsnohlídek's name, but announced the forthcoming opera: '*The Cunning Little Vixen*, with 192 illustrations by Stanislav Lolek, whose story will be told in music by Maestro L. Janáček, is available for 22 Kč.' This appeared several months before Janáček started work on the opera: according to dates on the autograph manuscript, it was composed between 22 January 1922 and 10 October 1923.

The libretto was drawn almost entirely from Těsnohlídek's story and, at Janáček's request, Těsnohlídek also wrote the words for the song 'Verunko!' in Act II. Three other songs are based on folk texts, including 'Běží liška k Táboru', sung by the fox cubs in Act III. Janáček's brilliant *coup de théâtre* – an inspired change to the original story – was to have the Vixen shot and killed by Harašta early in Act III, giving the work an intensely moving poignancy without sacrificing any of Těsnohlídek's humour. The closing pages of the story contain the same nostalgic musings by the Forester as the last scene of the opera, but in Těsnohlídek's original his thoughts are witnessed by the Vixen, surrounded by her cubs. The words of the Frog at the very end of the opera are taken directly from the last lines of spoken dialogue in Těsnohlídek's story.

The location of the story is in the forests near the village of Bílovice nad Svitavou, 10 km (6 miles) north of Brno in the valley of the River Svitava. Těsnohlídek often travelled to Bílovice and eventually settled there. Janáček also visited the area, particularly while he was composing *The Cunning Little Vixen*, and he observed a family of foxes there. A natural spring in Bílovice is today named the Studánka Leoše Janáčka, and another is named after Stanislav Lolek*. Janáček also drew on the inspiration of the woods around Hukvaldy, and sought expert advice on the life of foxes from locals there. His Hukvaldy friend Ludvík Jung wrote to Janáček on 26 January 1923: 'Fox (male and female). Reaches maturity in its second year. Comes into heat in January or February (earlier for the older vixens, later for the younger ones). Pregnancy lasts 60 days, with litters of five or six cubs … once a year.' As he did near Bílovice, Janáček tracked foxes in the woods near Hukvaldy to observe their behaviour, and the Hukvaldy connection with the work is commemorated by the bronze statue of the Vixen in the park below Hukvaldy Castle (see Hukvaldy*).

The first edition of the vocal score, arranged by Břetislav Bakala*, was published by UE on 30 July 1924, several months before the premiere. With Czech text only, this edition (182 pp.) lacks the horn fanfares that Janáček added during rehearsals for the premiere, given at the Brno NT on 6 November 1924, conducted by František Neumann*. The production was by Ota Zítek* with designs by Eduard Milén*, who also drew the front cover of the UE vocal score. The Brno cast included Arnold Flögl as the Forester, Hana Hrdličková as the Vixen and Božena Snopková as the Fox. The Prague premiere followed on 18 May 1925, conducted by Otakar Ostrčil*, with sets by Josef Čapek*. In time for this production, UE published a revised vocal score (183 pp.) that included the fanfares Janáček had added before the Brno premiere as well as Max Brod's German translation. The full orchestral score was only available on hire until 2010, when UE published a new critical edition by Jiří Zahrádka with performing suggestions by Charles Mackerras. A new edition of the vocal score was issued at the same time, and both included the English translation by Norman Tucker along with Brod's German translation.

The opera was slow to be taken up by companies outside Czechoslovakia. A production in Mainz opened on 13 February 1927 but otherwise the pre-war productions were almost all Czech (Liberec, Bratislava and Brno in 1934, Olomouc in 1935, Plzeň and Ostrava in 1936). In 1937 Václav Talich* conducted *Vixen* at the Prague NT in a version reorchestrated at his behest by František Škvor and Jaroslav Řídký. Apart from Mainz in 1927, the only non-Czech pre-war production was in Zagreb in February 1939. During the war, the opera was seen in Ostrava and Olomouc, and a new Brno production opened in 1947, but *Vixen* was still not established in the international repertoire. Productions in Leipzig (1951), Zurich (1955) and Cologne (1955) were followed on 30 May 1956 by the opening of Walter Felsenstein's production at the Komische Oper, Berlin, conducted by Václav Neumann*. This was astonishingly successful, with 218 performances given between 1956 and 1964. It was filmed for television in 1965 (later issued on DVD). This production was a major breakthrough for the opera. It was subsequently taken up by houses all over Europe. David Pountney's extremely successful production, with sets by Maria Björnsen, was first staged by Welsh National Opera in 1980 (conducted by Richard Armstrong and then Charles Mackerras) and by Scottish Opera (also in 1980). It was later seen in London at English National Opera (conducted by Mark Elder and Charles Mackerras). Simon Rattle made his Glyndebourne début conducting the 1977 revival of Jonathan Miller's production, and in 1990 he conducted the first production to be given at the Royal Opera House, Covent Garden (directed by Bill Bryden, with designs by William Dudley). In the United States, New York City Opera first gave Frank Corsaro's production, with sets by Maurice Sendak, on 9 April 1981, conducted by Michael Tilson Thomas. In 1995 Charles Mackerras* conducted a new production directed by Nicholas Hytner with designs by Bob Crowley at the Théâtre du Châtelet in Paris. Thanks to productions like these, the opera has gone from being something of a rarity to one of Janáček's most popular works, a position it has since consolidated. There have been a number of commercial recordings. The first was made by Supraphon in 1957, conducted by Václav Neumann. A second Supraphon recording, conducted by Bohumil Gregor with Prague NT forces, was made in 1971–2. Václav Neumann recorded the work again for Supraphon in 1979–80 and Charles Mackerras made his Decca recording in 1981. An English-language version conducted by Simon Rattle was issued by EMI (later Chandos). Versions on DVD include Neumann (Berlin, 1965) and Mackerras (Paris, 1995). A 1953 Brno Radio recording under Břetislav Bakala was released on LP by Panton and has subsequently been reissued by CRQ Editions. It is of particular interest given Bakala's close association with Janáček and his preparation of the vocal score.

Janáček's *Vixen* is his most radiant and evocative operatic score, as well as one of his most concise. With its extended passages of orchestral music and vocal writing notable for its sensuous beauty (especially in the love duet between the Vixen and the Fox and in the Forester's final scene), it occupies a special place in his output. This was recognised by Milan Kundera*: in his collection of essays published in English as *Encounter* (New York: Harper, 2010), Kundera calls *Vixen* 'the most nostalgic opera' and comments on its 'very intensely lyrical atmosphere'. Kundera ends his essay by encapsulating the mood of the opera: 'Elegiac nostalgia: the sublime, eternal subject of music and poetry. But the nostalgia that Janáček unveils in *The Cunning Little Vixen* is a far cry from theatrical gestures bemoaning times gone by. This nostalgia is terribly real, it is to be found where no one looks for it: in the quiet talk of two old men at an inn; in the death of a poor animal; in the love of a schoolteacher on his knees before a sunflower.'

The final scene of the opera was chosen by Janáček to be performed at his own funeral, held at the Brno NT on 15 August 1928, when it was sung by Arnold Flögl and conducted by František Neumann (see Funeral, Janáček's*). In July 2010, the same scene was chosen by Charles Mackerras for his funeral. Including some of the most luminous music Janáček ever wrote, this scene was memorably described by Milan Kundera as 'the exaltation of a long-gone springtime'. *JAWO, JODA, KunMůj, KunVar, SusJan, ZahVix.*

SYNOPSIS

Act I, Scene 1: A forest clearing in the summer. The Badger dozes in the heat of the afternoon, bothered by flies. The Dragonfly dances. The Forester pauses for a nap on his way home. While he sleeps, the Cricket and the Caterpillar give a concert. The young Vixen Bystrouška explores the forest for the first time. When the Forester wakes, he captures her.

Act I, Scene 2: The yard of the Forester's lodge. Afternoon sun. Autumn. Vixen Bystrouška discusses romance with the Forester's Dog and defends herself against the taunting of the Forester's children. She is tied up as a punishment and falls asleep. She dreams of freedom in the forest and of her sexual awakening. Outraged by the treatment of the Hens by the domineering Cockerel, she becomes a feminist. But the Hens' conservatism is too much for her, and she tricks them into coming closer before killing them all. She escapes.

Act II, Scene 1: The Badger's sett in the forest. Late afternoon. The Vixen returns to the forest and evicts the Badger in order to move into his home.

Act II, Scene 2: A room in Pásek's inn. The Forester is drinking with the Priest and the Schoolmaster. They tease the Schoolmaster about his unrequited love for the gypsy girl Terynka. The Forester leaves after he is goaded about the Vixen's escape, and he sets off in pursuit of her.

Act II, Scene 3: The forest, later the same evening. Moonlight. The Schoolmaster, wandering home unsteadily in the snow, mistakes the Vixen for Terynka. Meanwhile, the Priest reminisces about a girl he once loved, watched by the Vixen. They are startled by the Forester, who shoots at the Vixen but misses.

Act II, Scene 4: The Vixen's burrow. A moonlit night in the summer. The Vixen meets a handsome Fox and tells him about her life. They fall in love and mate, scandalising the birds in the forest. The Vixen realises that she is pregnant, and they marry. All the forest creatures celebrate.

Act III, Scene 1: On the edge of the forest. Autumn, noon, under a clear sky. Harašta, a poacher, is caught stealing a hare by the Forester. Harašta announces that he is on his way to see Terynka and that they are going to be married. The Forester uses the hare to set a trap for the Vixen, who arrives with the Fox and their brood of fox cubs. They quickly spot the trap, and talk amorously as they watch their cubs at play. Harašta returns and the Vixen taunts him. In a rage, he shoots her and she falls lifeless to the ground.

Act III, Scene 2: The garden of Pásek's inn. It is unusually still. The Schoolmaster and Forester are drinking together. Both miss the Priest, who has moved away, and the Schoolmaster is depressed about Terynka's marriage to Harašta. The Forester reflects on old age and sets off for the forest in nostalgic mood.

Act III, Scene 3: A forest clearing as in Act I. The sun shining after a shower. The Forester muses on the glories of nature and on the passing of time. He falls asleep. Forest creatures appear, including a vixen cub who resembles a younger version of the Vixen. The Forester tries to catch her, but instead catches a Frog. His gun falls to the ground and the Forester surrenders to the beauty of the forest.

Čvanová, Alexandra (b. Odessa, Ukraine, 25 April 1897; d. Jihlava, 20 March 1939), Ukrainian soprano. Čvanová joined the Brno NT in 1926, making her debut on 25 February as Tatiana in *Eugene Onegin*. On 18 December 1926, she created the role of Emilia Marty in the world premiere of *The Makropulos Affair**, for which she was warmly praised by Janáček. She sang in the world premiere of the *Glagolitic Mass** on 5 December 1927, and at Janáček's funeral on 15 August 1928. Later roles in Brno included Jenůfa (1933 and 1937), as well as the title roles in Dvořák's *Rusalka* and Shostakovich's *Katerina Ismailova*. She created the role of Amaranta in Pavel Haas's *The Charlatan* in 1938. Čvanová died in a car accident near Jihlava in 1939, aged 41. *VěžZpí.*

The Czech Legion [*Česká legie*], chorus for male voices (IV/42). Composed between 15 and 18 November 1918, this chorus for male voices is a setting of a poem published anonymously in *Národní listy* in early November 1918. The author was Antonín Horák, and many editions appeared to honour the contribution of the Czech Legion in France in 1918, and to celebrate the foundation of the Czechoslovak Republic on 28 October 1918 (Horák's poem is dedicated 'In memory of 28 October 1918'). The connection was a close one, as the Czech Legion had been founded by Tomáš Garrigue Masaryk* to provide Slavic resistance to German and Austrian forces. Horák's poem lists towns from which the members of the Czech Legion came, urging them to fight at Chemin des Dames alongside the French. It ends with an 'Epitaph for the fallen', a threnody to those who died and a plea that this must never happen again. Vogel points out that the Czech Legion 'never fought at the poet's chosen locale' (the Chemin des Dames), and in fact they saw combat some 80 km (50 miles) further east, near Vouziers. With such a stirring text, it is no surprise that Janáček's setting is one of his most dramatic choruses for male voices. The first performance was given on 26 September 1920 in Kroměříž, by the PSMU under Ferdinand Vach*. Plans for publication by HMUB in 1922 came to nothing and *The Czech Legion* was first published in 2011 in SKV C/2. A supplement includes passages cut by Janáček. *JAWO, StrMuž, VogJan.*

Czech Philharmonic See individual entries for: Ančerl, Karel; Čelanský, Ludvík Vítězslav; Kubelík, Rafael; Mackerras, Charles; Talich, Václav; Zemánek, Vilém. See also: **Radio Broadcasts during Janáček's Lifetime and Supraphon Record Company**

Czech Quartet [Bohemian Quartet], string quartet. This distinguished ensemble commissioned and gave the premiere of Janáček's String Quartet No. 1. It was founded in 1892 by Karel Hoffmann, Josef Suk* and Oskar Nedbal (all pupils of Antonín Bennewitz at the Prague Conservatory) and Otakar Berger (a pupil of Hanuš Wihan). Wihan replaced Berger in 1894 when the latter died prematurely, and Jiří Herold replaced Nedbal as the viola player in 1906. Wihan retired in 1914 and was replaced by Ladislav Zelenka. The ensemble that Janáček knew comprised Hoffmann, Suk, Herold and Zelenka. Hoffmann gave the Prague premiere of Janáček's Violin Sonata on 16 December 1922 and Suk had long admired Janáček's music: he first met the composer at the dress rehearsal for *Jenůfa* at the Prague NT in 1916, and all four members of the quartet attended a rehearsal of *Jenůfa* in Vienna in 1918. In October 1923, Janáček visited Prague and wrote to Zdenka on 13 October: 'I did a good thing. The Czech Quartet has asked me to write something for them.' This is the only reference Janáček made to the commissioning of the work, and no written request survives. By 28 October 1923, he had a draft of the whole work and made revisions in 1924. The Czech Quartet gave the first performance in Prague on 17 October 1924, at a concert of the SMH attended by Janáček (see String Quartet No. 1*). Josef Suk later recalled Janáček's visit to a rehearsal on 15 October: 'He was very curious what we would make of it. His excitement increased from movement to movement, then he began to embrace us and finally said: "We will play that ending twice as fast – we must defend enslaved womanhood." After the rehearsal he walked with me around the Kinský Gardens, moved, and said, "Now I see how many people and how many composers you've made happy."' The dedication 'To the Czech Quartet' appears on the autograph manuscript and on the first edition, which was edited anonymously by Josef Suk. Given his involvement in the premiere, it is fair to assume that his additions (mostly tempo and expression markings) reflect the Czech Quartet's performances. The Czech Quartet disbanded in 1934. It did not record Janáček's String Quartet No. 1 but the work's earliest recording was made in 1941 by the Ondříček Quartet, which worked with Suk in 1932. *CobCyc, ČSHS JYL2, KvěSuk, TyrInt.*

The Danube [Dunaj], symphony for orchestra (IX/7).   According to Janáček's autobiography, the idea for *The Danube* came to him in 1923, with 'a misty picture of the embankment at Bratislava', a city Janáček visited on 23 March to see the Slovak premiere of *Káťa Kabanová*. He finished the second movement (the first to be composed) by 18 June, and continued sporadically until at least 27 July 1925, when he wrote to his wife that he had finished the third movement. By May that year he had, according to his pupil Osvald Chlubna, written a draft of all four movements and that he planned to finish the symphony after taking a river trip down the Danube. This never happened, though Janáček planned it in some detail and wanted to take Kamila Stösslová* with him. There is only occasional evidence for work on *The Danube* after July 1925, but it was a project Janáček never completely abandoned. On 2 October 1924, he wrote in his autobiography that 'the work is growing in me of its own accord – because it has sunk its roots into my mind. *Káťa Kabanová, The Wandering Madman*, the suite *Youth*: none of these will smother the future *Danube*. Nor will it be smothered by *The Makropulos Affair*. On the contrary, it's swelling and taking its nourishment from all this, unnoticed.' While Janáček's intentions were clear enough, the reality was that composing three operas, the *Sinfonietta*, the *Glagolitic Mass* and other works did indeed 'smother' his work on *The Danube* – there was simply not enough time to finish it. Otakar Ostrčil* asked Janáček for permission to perform the work with the Czech Philharmonic, but Janáček told him he was in 'no hurry' to finish it. Though *The Danube* remained unfinished, Janáček gave every indication that he wanted to complete it and he took the manuscript with him on what turned out to be his last visit to Hukvaldy in August 1928. There is a reference to it as late as 5 August (a week before he died) in the *Album for Kamila Stösslová**.

The Danube includes music originally intended for other works. The first movement uses material rejected from Act III of *The Cunning Little Vixen** and the third movement uses ideas originally written for Act II of *The Makropulos Affair**. In a letter to his wife of 27 July 1925, Janáček noted that he had 'finished the revisions to Act II [of *Makropulos*]. And I have done one movement from the symphony. So there was lots of work.' The inclusion of a solo soprano in the sketches for the third movement (and in the Faltus and Štědroň realisation) suggests a link with an operatic project, and the wordless soprano passages in *The Danube* were originally meant for Emilia Marty to sing as vocal exercises backstage in *Makropulos*, now repurposed to become what John Tyrrell calls 'a voice of nature, such as the offstage wordless choruses in *Káťa Kabanová* and *The Cunning Little Vixen*'. The manuscript of the opening movement shows an explicit connection between *The Danube* and *Vixen*: it reads 'Symf. I' and underneath this 'III. jed.' [i.e. Act III] has been scratched out. In fact, pp. 4–13 of the manuscript were removed wholesale from the opera (the original page numbering is still visible), where it was intended as music to cover the scene change in Act III. Janáček outlined some of the work's programme in his autobiography but it remains confusing. He kept two poems from *Lidové noviny* with the manuscript: 'Utonulá' [The Drowned Woman] by Pavla Křičková and 'Lola' by Alexander Insarov. As John Tyrrell explained: 'here the problems proliferate. Is the second movement to be associated, as Janáček suggested in his autobiography, with 'Lola'? ... If so, why into the score of this movement did he write sections of the text from a second poem, 'The Drowned Woman' ... about a young woman who, bathing in a pool, finds herself being spied on by a young man and, in her shame, drowns herself? What is the significance of the Danube itself, and of Janáček's wish to take a trip from Bratislava to Belgrade?' To add to the complication, Janáček imagined Kamila Stösslová at the heart of his symphony. He wrote in her *Album* on 5 August 1928: 'Darling little wave, so soft, don't run away! I want to take you into my heart. ... I won't ever catch you. On you the Danube will grow!' Janáček then quotes five short passages, the first headed 'The little waves of my darling Kamila' and the second 'The Danube'. The entire genesis of *The Danube* is wrapped up with Kamila, and this might explain why Janáček was still trying to finish it at the time of his death.

Janáček left sketches for all four movements. In 1948 Osvald Chlubna* finished the realisation of *The Danube* on which he had been working since 1932. It was performed by the Brno Radio SO under Břetislav Bakala* on 2 May 1948. Bakala conducted it again during the Janáček centenary year on 14 April 1954 (issued on CD by Multisonic). In 1985 Otakar Trhlík asked Leoš Faltus and Miloš Štědroň* to produce a new realisation that kept as close as possible to Janáček's original score. This was performed on 2 October 1985 by Trhlík and the Janáček Philharmonic of Ostrava at the Brno Festival. The British premiere was given at Leeds Town Hall on 6 June 1987 by the Royal Liverpool Philharmonic under Charles Mackerras*. This realisation appeared in its final form as SKV H/3. *JAWO, ProDun, TyrCh2, VesJan.*

Dědeček, Pavel (b. Prague-Smíchov, 27 December 1885; d. Prague, 23 November 1954), Czech violinist and conductor.   Dědeček studied the violin at the Prague Conservatory with Ferdinand Lachner, a close friend of Dvořák who gave the premiere of the 'Dumky' Trio with Dvořák and Hanuš Wihan in 1891, shortly before embarking with them on an extensive chamber music tour. Between 1908 and 1912, Dědeček led the orchestra of the Brno NT and taught at the Brno Organ School. He took part in the first performance of Janáček's Piano Trio and his recollections provide the most substantial contemporary account of this lost work (see Piano Trio*). Dědeček later taught conducting at the Prague

Conservatory, where his pupils included Karel Ančerl*, Bohumil Gregor*, Rafael Kubelík*, Václav Neumann*, Václav Nosek* and Václav Smetáček. As well as his recollections of the Piano Trio, Dědeček also wrote a memoir of Janáček as a conductor (see Conducting, Janáček's*). *ČHS, LJLR, WinJan, ZahDiv.*

Dedications by Janáček Janáček's dedications on published editions include two in memory of his daughter Olga (*Jenůfa* and the *Elegy in memory of my daughter Olga*), but otherwise they are unpredictable. For example, there are no dedications to conductors who championed his operas and orchestral works (such as František Neumann or Otakar Ostrčil), but there is one to a conductor who didn't organise a promised premiere (Vilém Zemánek). Choral conductors fared better (with works dedicated to Ferdinand Vach and František Spilka), as did various choirs, choral societies and singing groups. Dr Jaroslav Elgart treated Janáček for rheumatism in 1912–13 (as well as being an enthusiastic supporter of his music) and was dedicatee of the *Fairy Tale*. The *March of the Bluebirds* was dedicated to Janáček's copyist, the flautist Václav Sedláček; other instrumentalists were dedicatees of the String Quartet No. 1 (Czech Quartet) and *Concertino* (Jan Heřman), as were those associated with folk music in Hukvaldy, including Marie Jungová (*Valachian Dances*). Two singers, Růžena Maturová and Anna Ondříčková, were dedicatees on two volumes of *Moravian Folk Poetry through Songs*; more surprisingly, so were two Archbishops of Olomouc: Theodor Kohn (specifically for his support of the Brno Organ School on Janáček's harmony book *On the Composition of Chords and their Connections*) and Leopold Prečan (*Glagolitic Mass*). Dvořák was the dedicatee of Janáček's *Four male-voice choruses* (IV/17). President Masaryk was the eventual dedicatee of *The Excursions of Mr Brouček* and *The Ballad of Blaník*. Others included the Serbian musician Miloje Milojević (*Reminiscence* for piano) and Rosa Newmarch (*Sinfonietta*). The twenty-year-old František Pavlík, killed while demonstrating for the establishment of a Czech university in Brno, was memorialised in the inscription for *1. X. 1905*. *Taras Bulba* was retrospectively dedicated 'To our troops' (the Czech armed forces) in an article published in 1923 (XV/247). Other dedications – all of them more personal – are to be found on unpublished sources: the *Theme and Variations* (VIII/6) to his fiancée Zdenka Schulzová (in a letter to Zdenka), *The Excursion of Mr Brouček to the Moon* to Gabriela Horvátová (on the unpublished proofs of the vocal score, see *The Excursions of Mr Brouček*), the song 'Uncertainty' ['Neijstota'] (No. 28 of *Moravian Folk Poetry in Songs*, V/2) to Olga Janáčková on the autograph manuscript (dated 5 October 1896), and two works for Kamila Stösslová (*Káťa Kabanová* in a letter and inscribed score, and the String Quartet No. 2 on the autograph manuscript).

Dedications to Janáček Works dedicated to Janáček include original compositions by Cyril Hrazdira* (*Nálady a Rozmary*, 1908), Jaroslav Kvapil* (*100 Slováckých písní*, 1917), Vítězslav Novák* (*Písničky na slova lidové poesie moravské*, Set II, Op. 17) and Erwin Schulhoff (Duo for Violin and Cello, 1926). *Zpěvy moravských kopaničářů*, a collection of folksongs from the Kopanice region of south-east Moravia compiled by Josef Černík (1880–1969), was dedicated to Janáček, as was a poem by Stanislav Kovanda (1878–1954). Hrazdira, Kvapil and Černík had all been Janáček pupils at the Organ School, and Kovanda attended the Czech Gymnasium while Janáček was teaching there. Kovanda's poem ('Verses from Brno, 28. 1. 1904') was published in the magazine *Neděle* (Vol. 1,

1904, No. 6, p. 73) and dedicated to Janáček a week after the premiere of *Jenůfa*. Two of Kovanda's other poems were published in *Lumír*. He wrote to Janáček in November 1904 to say that one of them was dedicated to Janáček, though there is no printed dedication. In April 1905, he wrote to Janáček thanking the composer for his kind words about another poem and recommending that Janáček should read Oscar Wilde's *Salome*, as Kovanda thought it would make an excellent opera libretto (Richard Strauss's *Salome* was first performed nine months later, in December 1905).

Demänovská Freedom Cave [Demänovská jaskyňa slobody], cave system in the Liptovský Mikuláš region of Slovakia.   This spectacular cave was discovered on 3 August 1921 by Alois Král*, Janáček's former pupil at the Teachers' Institute. Král wrote to Janáček about the cave on 14 June 1922, describing 'the majestic beauty of the stone walls, the rocky fortresses ... the carpets of magnificent flora' and 'a gigantic dome and fairy-tale chambers', and he invited his old teacher to visit the cave with him. Král subsequently sent minutely detailed directions (on 31 July 1922). Janáček arrived in Liptovský Mikuláš on 7 August 1922 and spent the afternoon at the cave, astonished and enchanted by the spectacular formations of domes, stalactites and stalagmites, and stones in an array of colours. In 'Springs', an article in *Lidové noviny* published on 8 September 1922 and dedicated to Král, Janáček described his impressions: 'When the curtains of eternal night were lifted – thanks to the painstaking work of Alois Král – oh, what amazement! Can it be that in the darkness there grew this work of beauty, flushed with pink?' Janáček was particularly taken with the sounds: 'the chords of the stalagmites covered in hoarfrost', the 'groan of a falling fragment' and 'the sounds of water, from a single drop to a torrent'. The caves were also visited by Rudolf Těsnohlídek*, who published an illustrated guide entitled *Demänová* in 1926. By the time this guide appeared, Král had named some of the notable features of the cave: the Jurkovič Hallway (after Dušan Jurkovič*), the Těsnohlídek Pool, the Masaryk Hall (after President Masaryk) and the Janáček Dome, which is the natural masterpiece of the cave, dominated by columns and a gigantic stone chandelier in pink and orange. *JYL2, TěsDem.*

Desiderius, Dr   See Images of Janáček and Löwenbach, Jan

The Diary of One Who Disappeared [Zápisník zmizelého], song cycle for tenor, alto, three female voices and piano (V/12).   During a visit to Luhačovice* in July 1917, Janáček met Kamila Stösslová* for the first time. The earliest work to be written as a result of their encounter was *The Diary of One Who Disappeared*. Janáček had kept the cuttings of the anonymous poems about a gypsy girl published in *Lidové noviny* on 14 and 21 May 1916 headed 'From the writings of a self-taught man'. Janáček wrote to Stösslová on 10 August 1917 after his return from Luhačovice, telling her that 'in the afternoons I come up with a number of motifs for those lovely verses about that gypsy love. Perhaps a nice musical romance will come out of it – and a tiny bit of the Luhačovice mood.' Janáček's reference to 'those lovely verses' suggests that he may have discussed them with Kamila during their walks in Luhačovice. By the time he sent this letter, he had already made a start on the *Diary*: the earliest date on the sketches is the day before, 9 August 1917 (on No. 3). Janáček wrote to Stösslová on 22 August to say that he would have the work finished soon, but that was unduly optimistic. It is interesting to note that in his first draft of the *Diary*, Zefka is a soprano rather than an alto. At Christmas 1917 (24 December), Janáček wrote

to Kamila that 'I always thought about you in that work. You were that Žofka [Zefka].' Other projects (including *The Excursions of Mr Brouček*) intervened, and when Janáček looked at the *Diary* a few months later he told Stösslová (on 2 September 1918) that he was unhappy with it, adding that it was 'a pity that my gypsy girl cannot be called something like Kamilka'. On 11 March 1919, he announced to Stösslová that the *Diary* was 'finished'. In fact, the autograph has a completion date of 6 June 1919 and Janáček continued to revise it for several months. He wrote to his brother Karel on 5 October 1919: 'I am finishing my life's work, although it is not in the shape that I would wish it to be.' Janáček put the *Diary* in the painted chest where he kept his manuscripts. According to Audebert Koreček, Břetislav Bakala 'found *The Diary of One Who Disappeared* in the chest. It had lain there for more than a year.' Bakala and Jaroslav Lecian 'rehearsed several of the songs from the *Diary* and on a Sunday afternoon they paid Maestro Janáček a visit and sang the songs to him. Janáček made some changes there and then. The *Diary* was then published in its definitive form and Janáček presented Bakala with a copy with the dedication "For digging it out of the chest – a souvenir. L. Janáček, Brno 23 November 1921."' Though some aspects of this story sound too good to be true, Jiří Zahrádka has pointed out that in 1920 Janáček was engrossed in intensive work on *Káťa Kabanová*', so 'Bakala really could have found the score "lying there for more than a year" some time early in 1921'.

The first performance was given at the Reduta in Brno at a concert of the Young Moravian Composers' Club on 18 April 1921. The tenor was Karel Zavřel (1891–1963), a graduate of the Brno Organ School and member of the Brno NT company. Zefka was sung by Ludmila Kvapilová-Kudláčková and the pianist was Břetislav Bakala. More performances soon followed. Zavřel performed it in Berlin on 21 September 1922 (with Felix Petyrek as the pianist), and Mischa-Léon gave the British premiere at the Wigmore Hall in London on 22 October 1922, repeating it in Paris on 15 December 1922 (both with Harold Craxton as the pianist).

The *Diary* is an unorthodox song cycle in terms of its scoring, its structure and its theatrical features. Comprising twenty-two numbers in all, Nos. 1–8 and 14–22 are sung by the tenor; No. 9 is sung by the alto and tenor with three female voices (offstage), No. 10 by alto with female voices, and No. 11 by tenor and alto. No. 13 is an Intermezzo for solo piano. The cycle includes several stage directions. The whole work is directed to be performed 'on a half-darkened stage', in other words, under dimmed lights. A footnote to No. 8 states that 'while the song is being sung, the alto soloist should enter inconspicuously', and in No. 9 the three female voices are marked 'almost inaudibly offstage'. At bar 56 of No. 11, the alto is instructed to leave the stage inconspicuously. Throughout the work, Janáček is careful to indicate how long the breaks between songs should be. Some are marked to be performed 'without pause', while others have a 'longer pause'. The dramatic character of Janáček's conception of the *Diary* led to a staged production during his lifetime, in Ljubljana on 27 October 1926. On 16 February 1928, Karel Veverka, director of the theatre in Plzeň, asked Janáček for an orchestral version to be used in a staged production. Janáček seems to have replied enthusiastically, as Veverka thanked him on 18 February 1928 and the local press reported that Janáček had written (in a letter that does not survive): 'I like your idea of a stage performance. So let's do it.' Busy with other projects, Janáček gave the matter no more thought, but in 1943 Ota Zítek* and Václav Sedláček* made their orchestral version of the *Diary*, first performed at the theatre in Plzeň on 26 June 1943.

After HMUB failed to send anyone to the premiere, Janáček chose Pazdírek to publish the work. Once the composer had corrected the proofs in late July 1921 (during a stay in Luhačovice), the firm put the score on sale in September 1921. The front cover has a woodcut of an embracing couple surrounded by birds, trees and hills designed by the folk artist Ferdiš Duša (1888–1958). The female figure is a stylised likeness of Kamila Stösslová, in accordance with Janáček's wishes. On 30 April 1921, he wrote to her: 'I wanted to have your head with your hair let down as the cover picture for the *Diary*.' Two critical editions have appeared in recent years, edited by Alena Němcová (SKVEJ E/4, 2004) and Jiří Zahrádka (Bärenreiter, 2016).

The identity of the poet remained a mystery until the 1990s, when Ozef Kalda was shown to be the author (see Kalda, Ozef [Josef]*), and Janáček may have believed the texts to be folk poems. What mattered was the strong connection he found between the poems and his growing love for Stösslová. He told her, on 8 June 1927, that 'you're the gypsy with the child in *The Diary of One Who Disappeared*'. Janáček left the royalties of the *Diary* to Stösslová in his will, underlining its connection to the start of their relationship. *JAWO, NěmZap TyrInt, VohKMS, ZahZap.*

Doležil, Metod (b. Kunčice pod Ondřejníkem, 15 October 1885; d. Prague, 10 October 1971), Czech conductor. Doležil attended school in Olomouc (1896–1900) and at the Teachers' Institute in Kroměříž, where he was taught by Ferdinand Vach*. He later studied composition with Vítězslav Novák* at the Prague Conservatory. On 6 April 1921, Doležil and his Prague Women Teachers' Choral Society choir gave the first performance of *Kašpar Rucký**. Janáček wrote to Max Brod on 12 April: 'I was afraid they wouldn't be able to do it and it would be real caterwauling. But it went well.' From 1922 to 1956, Doležil was conductor of the male-voice Prague Teachers' Choral Society, and on 8 December 1924, at Janáček's seventieth birthday concert attended by President Masaryk, Doležil conducted the choir in *Maryčka Magdónova**, *The Seventy Thousand** and *The Wandering Madman**. Doležil also performed Janáček's choruses on the choir's overseas tours, and in January 1929 they sang *The Seventy Thousand* in Boston and New York. *JAWO, JYL2, KLJ, MetDol.*

Downes, Olin (b. Evanston, Illinois, 27 January 1886; d. New York City, 22 August 1955), American critic. Downes was the first American writer on music to recognise Janáček's individuality and wrote several articles about his music in the *New York Times*, for which he was music critic from 1924 to 1955. Downes visited Janáček in Brno in June 1924, and extracts from their conversation appeared in the *New York Times* on 13 July in Downes's article 'The Music of Janáček, composer of *Jenůfa* to be heard at Metropolitan'. Downes quoted extensively from Janáček on folk music and human speech (see Speech melodies*). He asked Janáček which composers had influenced him most ('None'), which he most admired ('Chopin and Dvořák'), and which operas he preferred. 'He had heard Mussorgsky's *Boris Godunov* for the first time a year ago and admired it very much. This opera, and Charpentier's *Louise*. But he was tiring of *Louise*.' As for Wagner: 'No. It is not only that he is too symphonic ... but his system of motives is at once too detailed and too inelastic.' Downes asked: 'Do you like *Pelléas et Mélisande*?' to which Janáček gave an interesting response: 'To a certain point, but there is too little *melos*. It is too much speech and too little song. Melody cannot be replaced in music, and I prefer a better balance of symphonic style and musical diction than Debussy believed in. In certain places in my operas the orchestra takes a musical phrase from the singers and explains it. The phrase is absolutely truthful, and the instruments, in such instances, carry out its implications as no human voice could. Opera must be an organic whole, based equally upon truthful declamation and upon the song which the composer must evolve from his own creative spirit.' One work that made a particular impact on Downes in Prague was *The Seventy Thousand*: '[It] shows a composer of very true and strong dramatic power ... This chorus expresses the anguish of 70,000 Czech miners who found themselves for a period under the domination of Germany on the one side and Poland on the other, in Silesia. ... It is a superb composition, and as sung by the splendid amateur choir of [Prague] school teachers which Metod Doležil directs with enthusiasm and mastery, made an overwhelming effect. ... As the climax approaches there are cross-rhythms, and an inspired use of the highest and hardest register of the tenors – an effect of intense and incoherent excitement. "We will live! We will live!" That cry had a force, suddenness and certainty as if it had been flung, with one explosion of feeling, on paper.' *NYT*.

Dunaj See *The Danube* (IX/7)

Dvořák, Antonín (b. Nelahozeves, near Prague, 8 September 1841; d. Prague, 1 May 1904), Czech composer. Dvořák was a decisive influence on Janáček's early development as a composer, nurturing his interest in Pan-Slavism, serving as a model in terms of employing traditional Czech dances and inspiring Janáček to explore particular genres: it's no accident that soon after Janáček conducted Dvořák's *Serenade for Strings* in 1877, he composed his own Suite (VI/2) and *Idyll* (VI/3) for string orchestra. Janáček's *Valachian Dances* (VI/4) were clearly modelled after Dvořák's *Slavonic Dances*. The exact date of their first meeting is uncertain, but it was probably while Janáček was at the Prague Organ School in 1874–5. Janáček certainly heard Dvořák's organ improvisations at St Vojtěch's church at that time. In Janáček's autobiography, he mentions an expedition from Prague with Dvořák in 1877. Dvořák first heard Janáček's music on 15 December 1878, at a concert in Brno which included four *Slavonic Dances* and the premiere of Janáček's *Idyll**. In January 1880, Dvořák was in Brno to conduct his Fifth Symphony and *Slavonic Rhapsody* No. 2, a concert Janáček attended with Zdenka Schulzová. On their honeymoon in July 1881, Janáček and Zdenka visited Dvořák in Prague. In July 1883, Janáček spent ten days with Dvořák's family at Vysoká and then spent the rest of August with Dvořák at his flat in Prague.

Though Janáček sought Dvořák's advice on several works, the *Four male-voice choruses* (IV/17) were sent only once they were published in August 1886, with a dedication 'to the esteemed master Antonín Dvořák in token of unbounded respect by Leoš Janáček'. Dvořák wrote a gracious reply, thanking Janáček for the dedication and adding: 'I was taken aback in many places, especially as far as your *modulations* were concerned, and wasn't sure what to make of it all. ... But after I had played them through once, twice, three times, my ear got used to it ... what emanates from them above all is a *true Slavonic spirit.*' In November 1887, Janáček consulted Dvořák about *Šárka** and on 20 April 1888, Dvořák came to Brno for a performance of *The Spectre's Bride* conducted by Janáček. On 8 May 1897, Dvořák conducted a concert of his own works in Brno: the 'New World' Symphony, *The Noon Witch*, *The Golden Spinning Wheel* and the *Carnival* Overture. On his copy of the programme, Janáček wrote 'magnificent' beside the Largo of the Symphony. A few days later, Janáček sent *Amarus** to Dvořák for his comments and advice. Dvořák sent an encouraging reply: 'You've made a substantial step forward in every respect. The piece is interesting, particularly from the harmonic point of view. I would only like more *melody* ... don't be scared of it.' Their last meeting was at a rehearsal for Dvořák's *Armida* at the Prague NT in March 1904. It went badly, and as Janáček recalled in a 1911 tribute to Dvořák (XV/201), he had 'never seen Dr Antonín Dvořák so irritated'.

Janáček conducted many works by Dvořák at the Brno Beseda (see Conducting, Janáček's*), and Dvořák was frequently the subject of Janáček's writings. His most detailed discussion of Dvořák's works is in 'Currents in Czech music' (XV/152–3, 152–4 and 156), a group of articles published in *Hlídka* in 1897–8. Dvořák's four Erben-inspired tone poems (*The Water Goblin*, *The Noon Witch*, *The Golden Spinning Wheel* and *The Wild Dove*) are analysed in depth, with extensive music examples. Janáček's plans for a dictionary of Dvořák's themes never came to fruition. In his 1911 tribute, Janáček wrote: 'Do you know what it is like when someone takes the words out of your mouth before you speak them? This is how I always felt in Dvořák's company. His personality and his works are interchangeable for me.' *JYL1, ZemEss.*

Dvořáková, Marie (b. Mělník, 6 September 1887; d. Brno, 25 November 1953), Czech pianist. Dvořáková studied at the Prague Conservatory with Josef Jiránek and in Vienna with Theodor Leschetitzky. She began teaching at the Brno Organ School in 1911, where her pupils included Josef Blatný and Břetislav Bakala*. She was a member of the KPU and served on its committee in 1912 and 1913. Dvořáková gave two Janáček premieres. On 5 March 1911, she played *Six Folksongs sung by Eva Gabel** (V/9), sung by L. Vytopilová, and on 7 December 1913, she gave the premiere of *In the Mists** in Kroměříž. Janáček was not present, but his friend Jaroslav Elgart wrote an enthusiastic letter the next day: 'I was struck with the impressionism of the piano writing. ... Miss Dvořáková played with extraordinary delicacy – and perhaps it is significant that the audience's applause was as enthusiastic as it was for Chopin and Smetana.' A few weeks later, Dvořáková played *In the Mists* at an Organ School concert in the Lužánky Hall (24 January 1914), attended by Janáček. It's fitting that Dvořáková gave the first performances of this most Impressionist of Janáček's piano works: two years earlier, at an Organ School concert on 28 January 1912, she had played Debussy's *Reflets dans l'eau* and John Tyrrell has suggested that '*In the Mists* with its rather greater sophistication than the *Overgrown Path* pieces and in particular its more pianistic texture' may have been Janáček's response to Debussy. *JYL1, JYL2, KLJ, KunVar.*

Dwellings, Janáček's Four of Janáček's dwellings survive: the schoolhouse in Hukvaldy where he was born and lived until the age of eleven; the house in Hukvaldy which he purchased in 1921; the Augustinian Monastery in Brno where he spent his school years; and the house in the grounds of the Brno Organ School which was his Brno home from 1910 until his death. The house where Janáček and his family lived from 1882 until 1910 was demolished when the area was redeveloped in 1918.

1. *The schoolhouse in Hukvaldy.* Janáček was born in the schoolhouse in Hukvaldy and lived there until he was eleven. The building was altered in 1877 and 1908, but a plaque incorporating a profile in bronze by the sculptor Augustin Handzel (1896–1952) above the words 'The Genius of Czech Music' commemorates Janáček's birth there. It was unveiled at a celebration attended by the composer in July 1926.

2. *The cottage in Hukvaldy.* The house in which Janáček spent much of his time away from Brno in later years is now the Leoš Janáček Memorial (Památník Leoše Janáčka). Janáček's sister-in-law Marie [Máša] sold it to him on 31 December 1921. Early in 1928, Janáček set about renovating and extending the house, and on 6 February his letter to Kamila Stösslová included a drawing showing the new upstairs room that 'will be for you'. He visited on 21–24 May to inspect building work and by early June the rebuilding was complete, in good time for her visit in August 1928 (see Hukvaldy* and Stösslová, Kamila*).

3. *The Augustinian Monastery, Old Brno.* Situated on the north side of Mendlovo náměstí (Mendel Square), this was where Janáček went to school when he arrived from Hukvaldy in 1865 (see Brno: Augustinian Monastery*). For many years he also lived in this part of the city. In 1881–2 he was at Měšťanská No. 46 (now Křížová), which was demolished. From 1882 until 1910 he lived at Klášterní náměstí No. 2, the home where he composed *Jenůfa* and where his daughter Olga died. Neither the building nor the street survives: they were absorbed into what is now Mendel Square when the area was redeveloped around 1918.

4. *The house in the grounds of the Organ School.* On 2 July 1910, Janáček and his wife moved into the newly built house in the garden of the Brno Organ School at Smetanova No. 14, which was Janáček's Brno home until his death. It is now the Leoš Janáček Memorial (Památník Leoše Janáčka) of the Moravian Museum and is open to the public. The house, modestly proportioned and fitted with electric lighting, was designed by Alois Horák. Janáček's study faced west, and it was in this room, away from the noise of the city, that Janáček composed during the most productive years of his life. Between the windows of Janáček's study was the painted chest in which he kept his manuscripts, decorated in folk style for the Janáčeks by Anežka Uprková (1874–1959), the wife of the artist Joža Uprka. Marie Stejskalová watched Uprková at work: 'The flowers and apples seemed to grow by themselves beneath her touch. She painted the chest so beautifully that you couldn't take your eyes off it.' According to Přibáňová, Zdenka Janáčková died in this study, beneath the photograph of her daughter Olga, on 17 February 1938.

For a time after Janáček's pursuit of Gabriela Horvátová*, Zdenka required Janáček to sleep in a room in the Organ School rather than in the house, though she later allowed him to return. *ProVol, PřiPam, ZahFoo.*

Dyk, Viktor (b. Pšovka u Mělníka, 31 December 1877; d. Lopud, near Dubrovnik, Croatia, 14 May 1931), Czech writer. Dyk studied law at the Charles University in Prague, and as well as writing poetry and plays he was active as a vigorous proponent of Czech independence. He was also a Janáček enthusiast and wrote in *Lidové noviny* on 15 June 1916: 'Enough Wagner! After [*Die Walküre*], Janáček's *Jenůfa* has deep roots, and hopefully lasting ones.' Having read this, Janáček tracked down its author to ask for his help with rewriting the libretto of *The Excursion of Mr Brouček to the Moon*. By this time, Dyk was already under surveillance from the Austrian police for his known secessionist views. Between June and November 1916, Dyk was in regular contact with Janáček, either by letter or at meetings. The detailed revisions Dyk made to the 'Moon' Excursion are documented thoroughly by John Tyrrell (in *JODA*), who quotes extensively from Dyk's correspondence with Janáček and his 'Memoir of Leoš Janáček' published in *Lumír* (10 October 1928). Dyk's revisions marked a crucial step forward in the gestation of *Brouček*, and this is reflected in the credit on the vocal score of *The Excursions of Mr Brouček**: 'Libretto after Svatopluk Čech: the first part written by V. Dyk, the second by Fr. S. Procházka.' On 20 November 1916, nine days after sending his last revision to Janáček, Dyk was arrested for high treason. He was implicated in the 'Štěpánek affair', a round-up of prominent members of the Czech resistance. Dyk was imprisoned in Vienna and released on 27 May 1917 for lack of evidence. In 1920 he was elected to the Czechoslovak Parliament and became a member of the Senate in 1925. He was also a highly respected chess player. He died of heart failure while swimming off the island of Lopud in Croatia. *JAv, JODA, JYL2.*

Editions, Critical and Scholarly   The first attempt at a critical edition of any work by Janáček was Vladimír Helfert's 1934 revised vocal score of *Jenůfa* (HMUB), in which Kovařovic's reworkings and retouchings were clearly differentiated from Janáček's original. Also issued by HMUB, Otakar Šourek's revised scores of the two String Quartets (1945 and 1949) included editorial notes, and his 1947 edition of *Taras Bulba* aimed to clarify ambiguities and correct errors in the original (1927) score, drawing on sources including Sedláček's authorised copy. It was during the 1950s and 1960s that experienced Janáček conductors turned their attention to editorial problems in the operas, including Charles Mackerras* for *Káťa Kabanová* and Rafael Kubelík* for *From the House of the Dead*, but apart from Kubelík's revised vocal score of the latter (published in 1964), nothing appeared in print at the time.

Discussions about a critical edition of Janáček's music and writings began in 1965, and the *Complete Critical Edition of the Works of Leoš Janáček* (*Souborné kritické vydání děl Leoše Janáčka*, abbreviated to SKV) started publication in 1978 with the solo piano works (F/I), jointly published by Editio Supraphon and Bärenreiter, Kassel. The editorial board comprised scholars based in Brno, and the editorial guidelines were devised by Burghauser and Milan Šolc (published in 1979 as *Leoš Janáček: Edicni zasady a smernice*). From the outset there was criticism of the editorial guidelines of SKV, particularly the use of an unorthodox style of time signatures (of a sort not used by Janáček) and the introduction of key signatures where the composer employed none. These guidelines have evolved as the edition has progressed, and the most recent volume (*Fate*, 2016) uses conventional time signatures. Bärenreiter has also issued a number of works in practical editions derived from SKV with new prefaces and sometimes incorporating revisions to the note text.

Presumably to speed up publication of the edition, a parallel series started to appear in 2001 from Editio Janáček in Brno, using the same editorial guidelines (these Brno volumes are designated below as SKVEJ). This Brno series adopted numbering that was intended to complement the volumes in the Bärenreiter series, though two volume numbers (E/4 and E/5) were used twice. Editio Janáček is also responsible for Series I of the edition, devoted to the composer's writings. The first opera to appear in SKV was *Fate* in 2016, but a prospectus for the edition published in 1990 noted that 'Universal-Edition Wien is expected to become the publishing partner of Supraphon and Bärenreiter … in issuing Janáček's musico-dramatic scores'. Since then, UE has published critical-practical editions of most of the operas and other works including the *Sinfonietta* (discussed below), but these are completely unconnected to SKV.

The following is a list of the volumes of the complete edition published to date (2018) by Bärenreiter/Supraphon (SKV) and Editio Janáček (SKVEJ), according to the work groups used by the publishers: A: Stage Works; B: Choral-Orchestral Works; C: Choruses; D: Orchestral Works; E: Chamber Works; F: Keyboard Works; G: Arrangements of Folksongs and Dances; H: Arrangements, Fragments and Miscellaneous; I: Writings; J: Liturgical Works.

SKV A/5: *Fate*, ed. Jiří Zahrádka; introduction by Jiří Zahrádka (Kassel: Bärenreiter, 2016) [I/5]

SKVEJ A/11: Operatic Fragments, ed. Miloš Štědroň and Veronika Vejvodová; introduction by Veronika Vejvodová (Brno: Editio Janáček, 2010) [*Paní mincmistrová* IX/3; *Živá mrtvola* IX/6; *Schluck und Jau* IX/11]

SKV B/1: *Amarus*, ed. Leoš Faltus, Marie Kucerová and Miloš Štědroň; introduction by Jiří Vysloužil (Prague: Bärenreiter, 2000) [III/6]

SKV B/3: *Čarták on Soláň*, ed. Jan Hanuš and Miloš Štědroň; introduction by Theodora Straková (Prague: Supraphon, 1981) [III/7]

SKV B/4: *The Eternal Gospel*, ed. Leoš Faltus and Miloš Štědroň; introduction by Jan Trojan (Prague: Bärenreiter, 2002) [III/8]

SKV B/5–I: *Glagolitic Mass*, ed. Leoš Faltus and Jiří Zahrádka; introduction by Jiří Zahrádka (Prague: Bärenreiter, 2011) [III/9]

SKV B/5–II: *Glagolitic Mass*, September 1927 version, ed. Jiří Zahrádka (Prague: Bärenreiter, 2011) [III/9]

SKV C/1: Male Choruses I, ed. Leoš Faltus and Petr Oliva; introduction by Ivo Stolařík (Prague: Supraphon, 1983) [IV/1, IV/4–IV/11, IV/15, IV/17, IV/19, IV/22, IV/24–IV/26]

SKV C/2: Male Choruses II, ed. Leoš Faltus and Petr Oliva; introduction by Theodora Straková (Prague: Bärenreiter, 2011) [IV/16, IV/28, IV/31, IV/33–IV/36, IV/38, IV/42–IV/45]

SKVEJ C/3: Female Choruses, ed. Miloš Štědroň and Jiří Zahrádka; introduction by Jiří Zahrádka (Brno: Editio Janáček, 2002) [IV/39, IV/40, IV/41]

SKVEJ C/4: Mixed Choruses, ed. Leoš Faltus and Jiří Zahrádka; introduction by Alena Němcová (Brno: Editio Janáček, 2007) [IV/12, IV/14, IV/18, IV/21, IV/23, IV/27]

SKVEJ D/1–1: Suite for strings, ed. Leoš Faltus and Jiří Mottl; introduction by Svatava Přibáňová (Brno: Editio Janáček, 2002) [VI/2]

SKVEJ D/1–2: *Idyll* for strings, ed. Leoš Faltus and Jiří Mottl; introduction by Svatava Přibáňová (Brno: Editio Janáček, 2003) [VI/3]

SKVEJ D/2: Suite Op. 3, ed. Leoš Faltus and Jarmila Procházková; introduction by Jarmila Procházková (Brno: Editio Janáček, 2012) [VI/6]

SKV D/4: *Lachian Dances*, ed. Jarmil Burghauser and Radomil Eliška; introduction by Miroslav Barvík (Prague: Supraphon, 1982) [VI/17]

SKV D/6: *The Fiddler's Child*, ed. Jarmil Burghauser and Radomil Eliška; introduction by Jiří Vysloužil (Prague: Supraphon, 1984) [VI/14]

SKV D/7: *Taras Bulba*, ed. Jan Hanuš and Jarmil Burghauser; introduction by Svatava Přibáňová (Prague: Supraphon, 1980) [VI/15]

SKVEJ D/8: *The Ballad of Blaník*, ed. Karel Steinmetz and Miloš Štědroň; introduction by Jarmila Procházková (Brno: Editio Janáček, 2003) [VI/16]

SKV E/1: Compositions for Violin and Piano, ed. Jan Krejčí and Alena Němcová; introduction by Alena Němcová (Prague: Supraphon, 1988) [VII/3, VII/4, VII/7]

SKV E/2: Compositions for Violoncello and Piano, ed. Jiří Fukač and Bedřich Havlík; introduction by Jiří Fukač (Prague: Supraphon, 1988) [VII/5 and VII/6]

SKV E/3: String Quartet No. 1, ed. Leoš Faltus and Miloš Štědroň; introduction by Miloš Štědroň (Prague: Supraphon, 2000) [VII/8]

SKV E/4: String Quartet No. 2, ed. Leoš Faltus and Miloš Štědroň; introduction by Miloš Štědroň (Prague: Bärenreiter, 2009) [VII/13]

SKVEJ E/4 [!]: *The Diary of One Who Disappeared*, ed. Leoš Faltus and Alena Němcová; introduction by Alena Němcová (Brno: Editio Janáček, 2004) [V/12]

SKV E/5: *Capriccio*, ed. Leoš Faltus and Jarmila Procházková; introduction by Jarmila Procházková (Prague: Bärenreiter, 2002) [VII/12]

SKVEJ E/5 [!]: *Nursery Rhymes*, ed. Leoš Faltus and Alena Němcová; introduction by Alena Němcová (Brno: Editio Janáček, 2006) [V/17]

SKV E/6: *Youth*, ed. Jan Doležal and Leoš Faltus; introduction by Svatava Přibáňová (Prague: Supraphon, 1990) [VII/10]

SKVEJ E/7: *Concertino*, ed. Leoš Faltus and Eva Drlíková; introduction by Eva Drlíková (Brno: Editio Janáček, 2001) [VII/11]

SKV F/1: Compositions for Piano, ed. Ludvík Kundera and Jarmil Burghauser; introduction by Ludvík Kundera (Prague: Supraphon, 1978) [VIII/6, VIII/12, VIII/13, VIII/17, VIII/18, VIII/19]

SKV F/2: Compositions for Organ, ed. Miloslav Buček and Leoš Faltus; introduction by Theodora Straková (Prague: Supraphon, 1992) [VIII/2, VIII/3, VIII/4, VIII/7, III/9 No. 7 (organ solo)]

SKVEJ F/3: Fugues for piano 1879–80, ed. Leoš Faltus; introduction by Jakob Knaus (Brno: Editio Janáček, 2008) [incl. facsimiles, from X/6]

SKVEJ G/2: *Folk Dances in Moravia*, ed. Jarmila Procházková and Jitka Matuszková; introduction by Jarmila Procházková (Brno: Editio Janáček, 2005) [VIII/10, VIII/14, VIII/15, V/6, other transcriptions from the 1890s not in *JAWO*]

SKV H/2: *Singing Teaching Manual*, ed. Milena Duchoňová and Leoš Faltus; introduction by Milena Duchoňová (Prague: Supraphon, 1980) [V/5]

SKV H/3: *The Danube Symphony*, ed. Leoš Faltus and Miloš Štědroň; introduction by Jarmila Procházková (Prague: Bärenreiter, 2009) [IX/7]

SKV H/4: *The Wandering of a Little Soul*, ed. Leoš Faltus and Miloš Štědroň; introduction by Jarmila Procházková (Prague: Supraphon, 1997) [IX/10]

SKVEJ I/1–1: Literary Works I, ed. Theodora Straková and Eva Drlíková (Brno: Editio Janáček, 2003)

SKVEJ I/1–2: Literary Works II, ed. Theodora Straková and Eva Drlíková (Brno: Editio Janáček, 2003)

SKVEJ I/2–1: Theoretical Works I, ed. Eva Drlíková, Leoš Faltus, Svatava Přibáňová and Jiří Zahrádka (Brno: Editio Janáček, 2007)

SKVEJ I/2–2: Theoretical Works II, ed. Eva Drlíková, Leoš Faltus, Svatava Přibáňová and Jiří Zahrádka (Brno: Editio Janáček, 2008)

SKVEJ I/3–1: Folkloric Studies I, ed. Jarmila Procházková, Marta Toncrová, Jiří Vysloužil (Brno: Editio Janáček, 2009)

SKVEJ J/1: Liturgical Compositions, ed. Leoš Faltus and Kateřina Hnátová; introduction by Kateřina Hnátová and Alena Němcová (Brno: Editio Janáček, 2007) [II/1–II/9, II/12–13, IX/5]

Edition Peters in Leipzig issued new editions of *Youth* (1979), the *Sinfonietta* (1980), *Concertino* (1982), *The Cunning Little Vixen* (1985) and the solo piano works (1987), all edited by Miroslav Barvík and Reiner Zimmermann. Apart from *Vixen* (intended for hire only), these included useful prefaces and critical reports.

Several of Janáček's greatest works were published by UE. In 1969 the firm published a study score of the Kovařovic version of *Jenůfa* in a critical edition by Joannes Martin Dürr. Starting in the 1990s, UE began to publish study scores of the operas in editions based on the original sources that are both scholarly and practical. This series includes *Káťa Kabanová* (ed. Mackerras, 1992), *Jenůfa* (1908 version, ed. Mackerras and Tyrrell, 1996), *The Cunning Little Vixen* (ed. Zahrádka in consultation with Mackerras, 2009) and *The Makropulos Affair* (ed. Zahrádka in consultation with Mackerras, 2016). UE has also produced matching revised vocal scores. *From the House of the Dead* (ed. Tyrrell in consultation with Mackerras) is due for publication in 2019. A critical edition of *The Excursions of Mr Brouček* (ed. Zahrádka in consultation with Mackerras) is available for hire from UE. In a co-publication with Editio Moravia, Brno, UE issued a vocal score of *Šárka* (ed. Zahrádka; full score for hire), as well as the first version of the *Nursery Rhymes* (ed. Němcová) and the piano duet version of *Jealousy* (ed. Němcová). UE has also published Paul Wingfield's edition of the 'Erstfassung (1927)' of the *Glagolitic Mass*. In 2017 UE published a new critical edition of the *Sinfonietta* (ed. Zahrádka). Henle and UE have co-published new critical editions of *Youth* (2015), the *March of the Bluebirds* (2016) and *In the Mists* (2016), all edited by Jiří Zahrádka. More chamber and piano works are due to follow.

Elegy on the Death of my Daughter Olga [*Elegie na smrt dceri Olgy*] for solo tenor, mixed chorus and piano (IV/ 30).   Janáček's daughter Olga died at 6.30 a.m. on 26 February 1903 at the age of twenty. A few weeks later (on 15 March), two poems appeared in the newspaper *Moravská orlice* in Russian and Czech under the collective title 'A reminiscence of 27 and 28 February 1903'. The Russian version is dedicated to 'Lev Grigorievich Janáček' and the Czech version 'in memory of Olga Janáčková'. The Russian text is signed 'M. B.'. This was Maria Nikolayevna Veveritsa, Olga's Russian teacher, whose poetry also adorns Olga's tombstone. Veveritsa was a member of the Russian Circle in Brno, as were

Janáček and Olga, where she not only taught the Russian language but also folksong and dances. She was particularly admired for her readings from Russian literature. Janáček derived the text of the *Elegy* from part of Veveritsa's Russian poem in *Moravská orlice*, underlining the bond that father and daughter found in their love of Russian literature. According to Vladimír Helfert's introduction in the first edition, Janáček wrote the word 'Elegy' in Russian on the title page of the autograph manuscript (now lost). He completed it on 28 April 1903 and made some revisions on 28 March 1904. Janáček dedicated this tender and intimate tribute 'In memory of my Olga'. Helfert described the *Elegy* as being 'filled with the spirit of reconciled pain [and] resigned grief, under which beats the wounded heart of this loving father'. The first known performance took place after Janáček's death, on 20 December 1930, when it was broadcast on Brno Radio, conducted by Břetislav Bakala. Though publication was planned by HMUB in 1938 (for which Helfert wrote his preface), the *Elegy* was not published until 1958. *HelEle, JAWO, JYL1*.

Elgart, Jaroslav (b. Ivančice, 10 May 1872; d. Brno, 17 May 1955), Czech surgeon. Elgart went to school in Brno before studying medicine in Prague. In his early years he was an enthusiastic member of the Brno Sokol, as was Janáček. Elgart published an article for the Sokol on the benefits of gymnastics in 1895, the same year in which Janáček's *Music for Club-Swinging* (VIII/13) was published by the Brno Sokol. After completing his medical training in Prague, Elgart worked as a doctor at the Hospital of the Brothers of Mercy in Old Brno before being appointed director of the new Franz Josef Jubilee Hospital in Kroměříž, which opened on 23 October 1910 (it became Kroměříž Hospital after Czechoslovak independence). Elgart led the hospital with distinction until 1939. In his capacity as a member of the Brno Theatre Družstvo, Elgart had been a steadfast supporter of Janáček's cause. After moving to Kroměříž, he planned a concert of Janáček's chamber music, writing on 22 March 1912 to ask Janáček if he could lend the material for 'the *Fairy Tale* and perhaps the *Kreutzer Sonata* Trio'. It is not known if this concert took place, though Elgart put on three concerts of chamber music for the Moravan Choral Society that year – on 14 February, 17 March and 13 April – and it is possible that Janáček's music was performed in the April concert. Later in 1912, Janáček consulted Elgart for treatment of a severe attack of rheumatism, and it was probably at the start of 1913 that Janáček added a dedication on the manuscript of the *Fairy Tale**: 'To the Senior Consultant Dr Jaroslav Elgart'. This was in gratitude for the treatment he had received, and as a mark of Elgart's enthusiasm for Janáček's music. On 2 February 1913, Elgart wrote to thank Janáček for the dedication: 'You do me an honour with the dedication of the *Fairy Tale*, which I don't deserve, whatever my abilities, since we haven't yet treated your illness. But you've given me great joy, and I must work hard to merit it as far as I am able.' Elgart organised another concert for Moravan in Kroměříž on 9 February 1925, including *The Diary of One Who Disappeared* and the *Fairy Tale*. His younger brother was the writer Karel Elgart Sokol (1874–1929), who was a pupil of Janáček at the Teachers' Institute and a member of the KPU. *BalMor, JAWO, KLJ, KroNem*.

The Eternal Gospel [*Věčné Evangelium*], Legend for soloists, chorus and orchestra (III/8). The first mention of *The Eternal Gospel* in Janáček's correspondence is during 1913 and the work was certainly completed by early 1914 (there are no dates on the manuscript sources). The first performance was given at the Smetana Hall in Prague on 5 February 1917, conducted by Jaroslav Křička with Gabriela Horvátová* (soprano), Antonín Lebeda (tenor), the Hlahol Choral Society and the Czech Philharmonic. The concert was attended by Janáček, who was also present at rehearsals. The Brno premiere was on 18 February 1919, when it was conducted by Ferdinand Vach*, with Stanislav Tauber* as the tenor soloist. Janáček made revisions before the performances in 1924 given to celebrate his seventieth birthday, in Brno on 19 October and in Prague on 8 December. On both occasions, the tenor soloist was again Stanislav Tauber.

The title comes from the poem by Jaroslav Vrchlický* published in his collection *Frescoes and Tapestries* (Prague, 1891). It describes the mystic teaching of the twelfth-century Italian abbot Joachim of Fiore (c. 1135–1202) founded on his interpretation of the vision of an angel in the Apocalypse (Revelation 14:6). A medieval theologian may seem an unlikely subject for the agnostic Janáček, but the composer himself gave a clue to its appeal when he described the work's opening theme as representing 'open arms longing to embrace the whole world': in other words, what drew him to the text was its visionary humanity rather than Joachim's biblical exegesis. Janáček's setting of this unorthodox, pantheistic vision is an impressive example of his musical language as it developed after *Jenůfa*, full of surging lyricism and memorable ideas. Stylistically there are similarities with *Fate*, with the music of the 'Fifteenth Century' Excursion in *Brouček* and with *The Fiddler's Child*. Even the opening of the First String Quartet is hinted at in the solo violin writing. Reviewing the premiere in *Hudební revue* (February 1917), Ladislav Vycpálek provided a vibrant impression of the qualities of this underrated score: 'Janáček sees everything as drama. His *Eternal Gospel* is also a dramatic scene. I had the impression that the composition was taking place on the tops of high mountains in the glow of blood-red rays that pierced the darkness. Towering in the gloom, the ecstatic light of the prophet, who tells of the wings of his voice flying to the dark unknown, and of the coming of the Third Kingdom. Everything is, in a sense, unclear, indefinable by colour, but full of ardour, and of mighty gestures and apocalyptic ecstasy.' The vocal score was published by SNKLHU in 1959 and a critical edition of the work appeared as SKV B/4 (2002). *JAWO, JYL2, LHM, SimHyp, TroVěč, VogJan.*

The Excursions of Mr Brouček (I/6 and I/7)

1. *The Excursion of Mr Brouček to the Moon*, Burlesque opera in two acts (origi-nally three acts). Words after Svatopluk Čech* arranged by the composer with additions by Viktor Dyk* (I/6). Janáček's musical setting of Čech's satirical novel was originally conceived as a single opera: *The Excursion of Mr Brouček to the Moon*. He already knew the story well, having read it when it first came out in 1888, and even reprinted an extract from it in the magazine he edited (*Hudební listy*). It was twenty years later, in 1908, that he secured the rights from Čech's heirs, and he started composing on 27 March, before he had a libretto. Karel Mašek sent the first part of the text on 17 May, but by October there was trouble: Mašek had delivered one scene but refused to write any more. Meanwhile, the composer Karel Moor was surprised to hear that Janáček was at work on a Brouček opera since he, too, had just secured the rights from Čech's heirs to write one of his own. Janáček wrote to Moor explaining that he had already written an act of his opera. He hadn't (but no doubt hoped it might

stop Moor). Moor's operetta with spoken dialogue, *The Excursion of Mr Brouček to the Moon*, was staged in 1910. Meanwhile, Janáček had been left without a librettist after Mašek's withdrawal and he now turned to Zikmund Janke, a medical doctor with literary aspirations who was an acquaintance from summer visits to Luhačovice. Janke delivered his version of Act I, Scene 1 in December 1908, but any further collaboration with him was scuppered by Janáček's decision to introduce parallels between the characters in the earth and moon scenes – something that is not in Čech's novel. By September 1909, Janáček had finished this scene (originally Act I), mostly to his own libretto but using a little material from Mašek and a few words from Janke. Janáček began Act I, Scene 2 (originally Act II) on 10 February 1910 to his own libretto, finishing it by April 1911. He completed Act II (originally Act III) mostly to his own libretto, but he asked František Gellner to provide him with some additional verses. Work on this was completed by 12 February 1913, and Janáček then put *Brouček* to one side for more than two years.

It was probably the acceptance of *Jenůfa* at the Prague NT that encouraged Janáček to look at the opera again. He asked Jiří Mahen* to help him revise the text, but Mahen provided an entirely new libretto which Janáček discarded almost completely, and F. S. Procházka* assisted with the end of the opera. When he turned to Viktor Dyk*, he found much the most useful of his collaborators. Dyk did the bulk of the revisions between June and October 1916, and it was at this point that the structure was settled, changing what had originally been a four-act design into two acts and an Epilogue. Janáček started to compose the music for the Epilogue on 25 October 1916, finishing his revision on 29 March 1917, with some additional suggestions about the libretto from Max Brod. After almost ten years, *The Excursion of Mr Brouček to the Moon* was complete, and for the 'Moon' Excursion alone, Janáček had worked with seven other librettists.

After the success of the Prague *Jenůfa* in 1916, Janáček had no problem finding a publisher for his new opera. HMUB accepted it for publication, and proofs of Acts I and II were engraved between 17 November 1916 and 22 January 1917. Janáček withdrew the version of the Epilogue he had originally sent, and on 18 February 1917 he promised to send its replacement 'soon'. That never came and the first score of *Mr Brouček's Excursion to the Moon* as Janáček left it in March 1917 was only issued (for hire) in 2003, edited by Jiří Zahrádka. In fact, by the end of March 1917, Janáček already had new plans for his 'Moon' Excursion: to make it the first part of an operatic diptych.

As with everything else to do with the 'Moon' Excursion, the dedication was a tortured affair. Initially Janáček asked Karel Kovařovic* to accept it in June 1916, which he did 'with joy and thanks as a rare gesture from the composer himself, intended for all the members of the company for performing *Jenůfa*'. By the time the proofs of the planned HMUB edition were printed six months later, Janáček had changed his mind, dedicating the work to Gabriela Horvátová*, with whom he was still having a torrid affair. Nothing further happened with the publication of the opera at this stage, and by the time the 'Moon' Excursion had become the first part of a larger work, Janáček's affair with Horvátová was over and the Czech nation had become an independent republic. In the end, the opera was dedicated to neither Kovařovic nor Horvátová, but to President Masaryk* (see below).

The synopsis (below) includes a description of the Epilogue, which is only performed when the 'Moon' Excursion is given as a stand-alone opera. The first performance of *The Excursion of Mr Brouček to the Moon* in the form Janáček fixed by March 1917 was given, in the edition prepared by Jiří Zahrádka, on 17 November 2010 at the Brno NT, conducted by Jaroslav Kyzlink and directed and designed by Pamela Howard.

2. *The Excursions of Mr Brouček,* Opera. Part I: The Excursion of Mr Brouček to the Moon. Part II: The Excursion of Mr Brouček to the Fifteenth Century. Libretto after Svatopluk Čech, the first part written by Viktor Dyk, the second by Fr. S. Procházka (I/7). After nearly a decade of toil and trouble over the 'Moon' Excursion, it is astonishing to find Janáček eager to compose another Brouček opera as a companion piece, but this is exactly what he did, turning from lunar travel to time travel with Čech's second novel, set in the fifteenth century. Fortunately, it turned out to be a much more straightforward process. On 24 March 1917, Janáček wrote to F. S. Procházka proposing that he should write a libretto on Čech's second Brouček story. Procházka agreed and turned out to be a thoroughly efficient librettist, sending his work in regular instalments. Janáček started composing in early May 1917 and worked quickly: he had a fair copy of Act I by the end of August. Act II was finished on 18 September. By 3 December 1917, Janáček had completed the final scene, in which Brouček wakes up in the courtyard of the Vikárka to find Würfl peering at him in a barrel. During the composition process, Procházka had to endure Janáček making enormous cuts to his libretto, since the composer had failed to tell him that the 'Fifteenth Century' Excursion was only intended to fill half an evening, but Procházka was an amiable collaborator as well as a reliable one. From start to finish, the second Excursion took eight months. In January 1918, Janáček made a few final changes to what had now become an 'opera', no longer 'burlesque', in two parts, comprising both the 'Moon' and 'Fifteenth Century' Excursions. The complete work was performed for the first time at the Prague NT on 23 April 1920, conducted by Otakar Ostrčil*. The vocal score was already in print by then. Janáček had been signed up by UE after the Prague *Jenůfa* and they issued the first edition of the *Brouček*, using the plates engraved for the abandoned HMUB edition for much of the 'Moon' Excursion. It was published in September 1919, several months before the Prague premiere, and now carried a dedication 'To the Liberator of the Czech Nation, Dr T. G. Masaryk'. The front cover, printed in many colours with a pictorial design depicting Brouček and other characters, was designed by Láďa Novák*. The first Brno production was of *Mr Brouček's Excursion to the Moon* only, but in the version as it appears in the diptych rather than the original version (with Epilogue), which had to wait until 2010 for its premiere (see above). *Brouček* was given complete at the Brno NT on 27 November 1937, conducted by Milan Sachs, with the orchestration extensively revised by Sachs and Vilém Tauský*. The Prague NT brought its production to the Edinburgh Festival on 5 September 1970, conducted by Jaroslav Krombholc*. The first London production was given at English National Opera on 28 December 1978, conducted by Charles Mackerras*, and he conducted a new production there on 16 December 1992. On 20 December 2003, the new critical-practical edition by Jiří Zahrádka was given for the first time at the Prague NT, conducted by Mackerras.

Despite its long and troubled genesis, *Brouček* is one of Janáček's most vibrantly original works, by turns funny, strange, tender and inspiring. The novels of Svatopluk Čech and Janáček's operatic treatment of them certainly have their comic moments: the figure of Brouček is constantly ridiculed, as are the more ludicrous aesthetes in the 'Moon' Excursion. But there are serious sides to this opera, above all the profound sense of national pride that runs through the 'Fifteenth Century' Excursion. Janáček's score is full of variety, whether in the extraterrestrial sounds of the Moon music, or the radiant orchestral interlude which follows – a tone poem in miniature – bringing the action back from the Moon to Prague. At the end of the 'Moon' Excursion, Málinka and Mazal sing in soaring octaves that evoke the end of Act I of Puccini's *La Bohème*, while the Hussite Hymns and celebrations before and after the Battle of Prague in the 'Fifteenth Century' Excursion are as stirring as any patriotic chorus in opera. The instrumentation has some unusual features: nowhere else in his operas does Janáček call for bagpipes, but they add a distinctive reedy colour to the 'Fifteenth Century' Excursion, as does the organ, an instrument Janáček used in *Fate* but not in any other operas. Otherwise, the orchestration has many of the characteristics of Janáček's later operas, with a fondness for high timpani writing, fragments of brass fanfares that are used to generate the propulsive energy of the victory scene in the Old Town Square, and woodwind writing that can shift from impressionistic shimmering one moment to hymn-like richness the next (for instance, in the orchestral interlude of the 'Moon' Excursion). *Brouček* is scored with an opulence that underlines the celebration of Czech nationhood lying at its core. It was composed at a time when the quest for independence from the Habsburg Empire was evolving from being an aspiration to becoming a reality, and the heart-felt nobility of the music for the Liberation of Prague in the fifteenth century leaves no doubt about its contemporary resonance for Janáček. Finally, the sense of place is an essential component of *Brouček*. Two historic locations in the city of Prague – the narrow lanes around Prague Castle in Hradčany and the Old Town Square – are not only settings for the opera but (like Luhačovice in *Fate**) they give the work some of its unique character. *JAii, JAv, JAWO, JODA, ŠouBro, VogJan.*

SYNOPSIS

The Excursion of Mr Brouček to the Moon

Act I, Scene 1: Prague, 1888. Vikárka street in Hradčany on a moonlit night. The beer-soaked Matěj Brouček tries to find his way home after an evening's drinking at the Vikárka Inn. He comes across Málinka, distraught about the two-timing behaviour of her lover Mazal, who is Brouček's tenant. Málinka threatens to kill herself. In an attempt to calm her down, the inebriated Brouček promises to marry her. He quickly retracts the offer and instead dreams of escaping to a less stressful life on the moon.

Act I, Scene 2: A moonscape. The moon turns out to be the worst possible choice for the robustly philistine Brouček: it has become a colony for the artists and intellectuals he so despises, and he finds himself in the company of the avant-garde lunar artist Blankytný (the lunar parallel to Mazal). Blankytný describes his platonic passion for the moon-maiden Etherea (Málinka), who arrives with her radical sisterhood in tow to sing an ode to healthy living. Improbably, she falls for Brouček and flies away with him on Pegasus to the Temple of the Arts.

Act II, Scene 1: The Lunar Temple of All Arts. Etherea and Brouček arrive in the Temple of the Arts. At first Brouček's appearance causes alarm, but he is soon accepted as the newest artistic craze and shown the very latest in lunar art. A banquet of sniffing flowers does nothing to improve his mood, and when he is attacked for eating a sausage, he flees, leaving the aesthetes, complete with their latest Child Prodigy, singing hymns to art. An orchestral interlude leads to the next scene.

Act II, Scene 2: Prague. Mazal and Málinka return home as dawn is breaking. A waiter tells them that Brouček has been found in a drunken stupor, but their thoughts are elsewhere as they sing tenderly of their love for each other.

Epilogue [only when the 'Moon' Excursion is performed as a single opera]. Brouček awakes at noon at home. Before he has had time to recover from his lunar dream, Málinka and Mazal arrive and try to persuade him to allow Mazal to stay in the flat. Brouček is taken aback by the appearance of Málinka/Etherea, and agrees without protest. Finally he tries to placate his housekeeper, who is appalled at his dissipated ways. He promises, as only a Brouček would, to buy her a new apron for her next birthday.

The Excursion of Mr Brouček to the Fifteenth Century

Act I, Scene 1: The castle of Wenceslas IV. Brouček has been arguing with his drinking cronies about the subterranean tunnels beneath medieval Prague. He staggers home only to find himself in an underground cellar, where he encounters shadowy figures from the distant past. The poet Svatopluk Čech appears. He laments the moral decline of the Czech nation, where heroes have been replaced by self-indulgent nonentities (like Brouček). Čech sings of how he longs to write anthems for a nation reborn to its former greatness.

Act I, Scene 2: The Old Town Square, 1420. Brouček emerges near the Old Town Square, but everything looks unfamiliar to him. The city is under siege from the German armies of the Holy Roman Empire. Due to his dreadful Czech, Brouček is initially taken for a German spy by the Hussite rebels, but he manages to bluff his way out of trouble.

Act II, Scene 1: Domšík's house. Brouček has been taken to the home of the Sacristan, Domšík, and his daughter Kunka. The Hussite armed men sing a stirring hymn in preparation for the conflict that is to come. Brouček is horrified when his host explains that he is expected to join in the defence of the city, and in the heat of the battle he slips away at the first opportunity.

Act II, Scene 2: The Old Town Square. The people of Prague celebrate a famous victory, but it has come at a price: Domšík is among those killed and his servant Kedruta offers prayers while Kunka is distraught. Brouček is discovered in hiding and accused of treason. His sentence is death in a burning barrel.

Act II, Scene 3: The courtyard of the Vikárka Inn. Back at the Vikárka Inn – and back from the fifteenth century – the landlord Würfl finds Brouček in a barrel. Relieved to be home, Brouček boasts to Würfl how he bravely fought to liberate Prague – but begs him not to tell anyone.

Facsimiles Janáček's handwriting has a well-deserved reputation for being notoriously hard to decipher, especially in his later works. The supplements at the end of SKV and SKVEJ volumes often include extensive facsimiles of his autographs, as well as pages from authorised copies. Aside from those reproductions, a few of Janáček's autograph manuscripts have been published as facsimiles. They include the first movement of the *Sinfonietta** (as *Fanfáry ze Sinfonietty*, SHV, 1963), the *Moravian Folksongs** VIII/23 (as *Patnáct moravských lidových písní*, Panton, 1978), the *Album for Kamila Stösslová** (Moravian Museum, 1994; version with English commentary, 1996) and the fourth movement of *In the Mists** (as *V mlhách IV. Věta*, Moravian Museum, 1998). Facsimiles of nine works written during Janáček's studies at the Prague Organ School have been published as the *Sborník skladeb z pražských studií 1874–1875* (Editio Janáček, 2001), revealing that his early handwriting was a lot more meticulous than in his later manuscripts. A complete facsimile of Janáček's article 'Pro pár jablek?' (XV/296) has also been published (Brno City Museum, 1958). *JAWO.*

Fairy Tale [*Pohádka*] for cello and piano (VII/5). Inspired by Vasily Zhukovsky's poem *The Tale of Tsar Berendyey*, Janáček's *Fairy Tale* exists in three versions: the first (1910) and third (1923) in three movements, and the second (1912) in four movements. The earliest version, dated 10 February 1910 on the autograph, was performed at the Brno Organ School by Rudolf Pavlata (cello) and Ludmila Prokopová (piano). Janáček revised and expanded the work for a performance on 22 September 1912 given by Antonín Váňa and Jaroslav Krupka. The programme for this concert described the work as consisting of 'four evocative pictures' and the title was given as 'Fairy Tale about Tsar Berendyey'. Correspondence with Váňa from February 1913 indicates that Janáček produced another revision at the time, but this has been lost. Finally, Janáček established the definitive version of the *Fairy Tale* in 1923. It was performed at the Brno Beseda on 7 March 1923 by Julius Junek and Růžena Nebušková. Final revisions were made before the publication of the score by HMUB in 1924. The *Fairy Tale* has a dedication to Dr Jaroslav Elgart*.

Janáček's programme for the work was not printed in the first edition, but it was quoted by Bohumír Štědroň in his introduction to the 1949 HMUB edition. Headed 'From a Fairy Tale', it reads: 'Once upon a time there lived Tsar Berendyey, who had a beard down to his knees. He had been married for three years and lived with his wife in perfect harmony, but God had not yet given them any children, which grieved the Tsar terribly. One day the Tsar felt the need to inspect his kingdom. He bade farewell to his wife and for eight months he journeyed on his travels.' The *Fairy Tale* appeared in SKV E/1 (1988). The main text presents the 1923 version, but a supplement includes facsimiles of the 1910 version and the suppressed fourth movement (Adagio) of the 1912 version. Janáček's only other work for cello and piano, the *Presto* (VII/6) that was possibly intended as a movement of the *Fairy Tale*, was first published by Editio Supraphon in 1970 and this also appears in SKV E/1. *FukVio, JAWO.*

Fate [*Osud*], 'Three scenes from a novel' on a libretto by Fedora Bartošová after a scenario by Janáček (I/5). The first version of *Fate* was started by 8 December 1903 and finished by 12 June 1905. It was subsequently revised in 1906 and again in 1907. The final revision was finished by 19 November 1907, the date on which Janáček submitted the score to the Vinohrady Theatre in Prague. It was never performed in Janáček's lifetime. The work was first heard in 1934 on Brno Radio conducted by Břetislav Bakala*. These broadcasts introduced *Fate* piecemeal: Acts I and III were given on 13 March, Act II on 2 July and the complete opera on 18 September. It is rare for a living person to inspire two operas, but such was the case with Kamila Urválková (see Urválková, Kamila*). She was the title character of the 1897 opera *Kamilla* composed by Ludvík Vítězslav Čelanský* after their affair ended badly, and was portrayed as Míla Válková in Janáček's *Fate* after Janáček had become infatuated with her in 1903. Čelanský's portrayal of Kamila as disloyal and feckless smacks of revenge; her treatment in *Fate* is rather more sympathetic, though Urválková might have hoped for a stronger repudiation of Čelanský's depiction – and for her stage self to make it to the end of the opera alive. Both operas have librettos by the composers themselves, though Janáček sent his ideas to Fedora Bartošová*, a teacher and friend of Janáček's daughter Olga, who versified the text for him. Both have a creative artist as the central male role: the poet Viktor in *Kamilla* and the composer Živný in *Fate*. In the character of Živný, Janáček created a kind of fantasy alter ego of himself, with elements of Čelanský, reflecting both their turbulent relationships with the same woman.

Though *Fate* was not staged in Janáček's lifetime, it came tantalisingly close to a production at the Vinohrady Theatre in Prague. Negotiations were protracted and often bad-tempered. By a curious coincidence, the man most eager to put it on was the Vinohrady Theatre's music director – none other than Ludvík Čelanský. These plans foundered, but it would have been a piquant state of affairs if the two composers who had both fallen under Urválková's spell had collaborated on an opera inspired by her.

Fate also has important roots in a real place. Janáček's amorous adventures at Luhačovice* in 1903 provided the direct inspiration for *Fate*. He enjoyed being away from home (and from Zdenka), and the spa town became a favourite haunt, where he met two of the great loves of his life – Kamila Urválková in 1903 and Kamila Stösslová in 1917 – and spent time with another, Gabriela Horvátová, in 1916. Back in Brno after his visit in 1903, Janáček decided to use his encounter with Urválková as the basis for an opera, and that October he wrote to tell her about his plans for a 'modern' libretto, its first act 'completely realistic, drawn from life at a spa. There's plenty of material there!' He originally devised a plot based on their relationship (whether real or imagined), but the story took a more convoluted turn and the composer Živný emerged as the central character.

The plot of *Fate* may be confusing and outlandish – in that sense it could be seen as Janáček's *Il Trovatore* – but, like Verdi's opera, the music transcends the improbable story. *Fate* was composed straight after *Jenůfa* and it shows a composer moving forward with new confidence as he neared his fiftieth birthday. When Charles Mackerras conducted it for Welsh National Opera, he described *Fate* as 'an extraordinary departure after *Jenůfa*', and there's a coherence, terseness and power in the music that point towards the later operas, not least in the handling of short, obstinately memorable motifs. As Jan Smaczny put it (*Opera*, September 1989, p. 1142): 'None of the later operas would have been half so good without the miraculous control of episode and motif that Janáček exhibits in *Fate*.' One clue about the musical influences that prompted this 'extraordinary departure' can be found in the opera's subtitle: 'Three scenes from a novel'. In May 1903, on a visit to Prague, Janáček saw Charpentier's *Louise*, subtitled a 'musical novel'. With its cast of artistic types, contemporary setting and precise (Parisian) locations, the similarities are clear. John Tyrrell has pointed out further parallels: the 'speech melodies' of Charpentier's street cries, the use of elaborate and varied choral textures, and even the inclusion of a viola d'amore in the orchestra (a plan eventually abandoned by Janáček).

The 'modern' and 'realistic' setting Janáček outlined to Urválková is apparent from the start: in contrast to the rustic clacking of the millwheel at the beginning of *Jenůfa*, *Fate* opens in a busy contemporary town with a brilliant orchestral waltz teeming with rhythmic energy and played, according to the stage directions, from the bandstand in the main square. This exhilarating, ostinato-fuelled opening scene introduces a large cast of individuals and includes some exciting choral writing – an important feature of the whole opera. The sustained vigour is stilled only by Míla's bitter reflections provoked by a bouquet of red roses. Act I is divided into no fewer than sixteen linked 'scenes', an indication of the constantly shifting action, with vignettes that can change almost as quickly as camera shots in a film. The handling of the crowd and the chorus is spectacular in this act. One example begins with the rehearsal for the women teachers' choir (Janáček had run one in his earlier years), which grows into a multi-layered chorus culminating in an aptly cosmopolitan setting of a mock folksong in praise of the sun. The music teems with vitality, evoking a bustling resort, and these choral episodes provide a context for (and contrast with) the more intimate scenes between Živný and Míla. In those, Janáček captures the conversational nature of their exchanges, the vocal lines often hesitant. Perhaps the most remarkable feature of the first act of *Fate* is its almost symphonic trajectory, the action propelled with drive and élan.

At the start of Act II, the apparently idyllic mood as Míla and Doubek listen to Živný playing his opera at the piano is undermined by the orchestra: nervous rising scales (uneasy variants of the scales heard in Act I when Míla and Živný first met) suggest all is not well. The delicate instrumentation of this short act originally included Janáček's first use of the viola d'amore. Equally unusual in an operatic context is the piano part. In Act III, as the students in the hall of the Conservatory improvise thunder and lightning after a real storm has passed, the full organ makes a startling appearance. Živný's vision of Míla ('a white face, so pale and so sad. Now I see you clearly once more') is marked to be sung 'in the ecstasy of madness', and the music mirrors Živný in its hallucinatory intensity. The closing scene brings some of the finest music in the whole opera. Over a rumbling ostinato in the lower strings, Živný revives. At the close, the orchestra takes up the rhythm of Živný's final phrase, hammering it home as the broken composer is led away.

The first performance of *Fate* was given in 1934, six years after Janáček's death, when his pupil Břetislav Bakala conducted a broadcast for Brno Radio and he did so again in 1948; in 1954 Bakala gave a concert performance at the Brno Festival. *Fate* finally reached the stage in 1958 in a misguided 'flashback' version that sandwiched the first two acts between two halves of the third. This was given on 25 October 1958 under František Jílek, and the next day it was given in Stuttgart (where two of the smaller roles were taken by Fritz Wunderlich and Anja Silja). There have been several productions since, outstanding among them David Pountney's for English National Opera (1984, revived 1987), conducted by Mark Elder, that vindicated a return to Janáček's original structure. For many years this was the only one of Janáček's mature operas for which the vocal score was only available on hire. In 2013 Bärenreiter published a new edition, and a critical edition of the full score followed as SKV B/5 (2016), edited by Jiří Zahrádka.

The first commercial recording, released by Supraphon in 1976 (with the music in the order Janáček intended), was made with Brno NT forces conducted by František Jílek. In 1989 Charles Mackerras recorded the work with Welsh National Opera, using Rodney Blumer's English translation. Both these recordings do justice to a score that John Tyrrell has described as containing 'some of Janáček's most incandescent music'. *JAWO, JODA, JYL1, VogJan, ZahOsu.*

SYNOPSIS

Fate is an experiment in semi-autobiographical opera about a composer (Živný) writing an opera about another composer (Lenský) – who turns out to be one and the same composer. The other principals are his lover Míla and her crazed mother, with a very large supporting cast of smaller roles and a chorus of schoolgirls, schoolmistresses, students and guests at the spa. Dramatically it is often confusing. Some productions have attempted to clarify matters by using a 'flashback' version, but this is now regarded as wrong-headed, doing nothing to elucidate the plot and violating Janáček's intentions.

Act I: Fifteen years ago. The magnificent spa of Luhačovice. Upstage centre stands the resplendent Janův dům [Jan's House]. On the right, an imposing spa hotel ... On the left the Amantka spring and behind it an elaborate bandstand. Crowds promenade in the sunshine. Míla catches sight of the composer Živný, her former lover, and the two have an uncomfortable reunion: we learn it's not their first meeting when she asks if he's come for their baby. Intimate conversational scenes are intercut with large-scale choruses sung by various guests at the spa. Míla's mother, already on the brink of insanity, wanders around the town in search of her daughter and is appalled to learn that she's gone off with Živný.

Act II: A family setting. Four years later. Živný's study. A piano to the left. ... About 6 o'clock on a winter evening. Živný and Míla are at home with their young son Doubek. Živný plays through parts of his opera, while Míla listens and asks if he regrets having written 'these tunes that still accuse me' – a suggestion, perhaps, that Živný may have something of Čelanský about him as well as Janáček. Later in the act, Míla's mother enters, proclaiming 'Don't come near me, I'm not crazy!', though her behaviour suggests otherwise. Now thoroughly deranged, she hurls herself off a balcony. In trying to save her, Míla is also dragged to her death. When Doubek asks, 'Where's my mummy?', Živný enters with Míla's lifeless body.

Act III: The present. The Great Hall of the Conservatory. On the left a magnificent organ ... In the centre, a concert grand piano. The heat of a summer day. Živný muses on his opera, and on 'Lenský'. Pressed by his students for an explanation, Živný offers mystification instead: 'Lenský? You could say I know him intimately.' His student Verva isn't fooled ('Lenský must be Živný himself'). After seeing a vision of Míla during a storm, Živný faints, then makes a shaky recovery. Asked by Verva about the music for the final scene, Živný replies: 'Music for the final scene? That is still in God's hands, and there it will stay!' before being led away by his son Doubek, who is now a young man.

The Fiddler's Child [*Šumařovo dítě*], ballad for orchestra after the poem by Svatopluk Čech (VI/14). After the first Prague performance of *Amarus* on 6 October 1912, Janáček was asked to write a new orchestral work by Vilém Zemánek*, chief conductor of the Czech Philharmonic at the time. Janáček worked quickly and sent the piece to Zemánek on 28 April 1913. The premiere was scheduled for 15 March 1914, with the Czech Philharmonic conducted by Janáček. Since he already had decades of conducting experience, it is surprising that Janáček requested only two rehearsals for a difficult new work. The first rehearsal was a disaster and he asked Zemánek to postpone the performance. Plans for the following season fell through and in the end Otakar Ostrčil* gave the premiere with the Czech Philharmonic on 14 November 1917, a concert Janáček attended. In a letter to Ostrčil he thanked him for 'an excellent performance' of *The Fiddler's Child*, adding that 'you have been kind to me since our first meeting [in 1914] and now I like what you are doing. You have entered right into my soul – the work was deeply felt inside you even though it is not easy to understand.'

The critics were less kind to the work. Zdeněk Nejedlý* was particularly brutal, dismissing it as a 'theoretical experiment', complaining about the overt pictorialism of the music and regretting that Janáček was using such 'trivial means' to express his ideas. Despite Nejedlý's reaction, *The Fiddler's Child* was performed several more times during Janáček's lifetime. On 8 December 1924, it was the first orchestral work by Janáček to be played in London, when Henry Wood* conducted it with the Queen's Hall Orchestra. Talich* conducted it in the gala concert with the Czech Philharmonic for Janáček's seventieth birthday on 8 December 1924, and František Neumann* introduced the work to Brno on 1 November 1925.

In spite of the cancellation of the proposed premiere, *The Fiddler's Child* was published promptly: a pocket score was issued by the KPU in November 1914 in honour of Janáček's sixtieth birthday, and with a dedication to Zemánek. *The Fiddler's Child* was published as SKV D/6 (1984), including facsimiles of the autograph manuscript and authorised copy in a supplement.

The poem by Svatopluk Čech* (originally published in the magazine *Lumír* in 1873 under his pseudonym Václav Benda) was also called *The Fiddler's Child*. It tells a particularly gruesome tale, with a rural setting that would have appealed to Janáček as the son of a village schoolmaster. A destitute fiddler has died and his sickly child has been entrusted to the care of an old woman, as has his fiddle. At midnight the woman sees an apparition of the dead fiddler at the cradle of his child, luring the infant with his music to a better world. At precisely the moment when the dead fiddler kisses the child, the old woman scares the ghoul away by making the Sign of the Cross. In the morning the mayor of the village arrives to find the fiddle gone, and the old woman rocking the child's lifeless body. Given Janáček's literary imagination, it is no surprise to find him making alterations to Čech's plot. The original poem was printed in the first edition of the score, but it is misleading in view of Janáček's changes: in his version, the fiddler is still alive at the start of the work, the child falls mortally ill before the fiddler's death, the old woman does not appear at all, and the mayor has a sinister musical presence throughout (a steady four-note theme first heard on cellos and double basses). There is music of great beauty in this short work, not least the fiddler's promise of 'wonderful dreams' (Janáček's own phrase) that are shattered when his child dies. *JAWO, SimHyp, VysŠum.*

Firkušný, Leoš [Leopold] (b. Napajedla, 16 July 1905; d. Buenos Aires, Argentina, 9 July 1950). Czech musicologist, brother of Rudolf Firkušný*. Firkušný attended Vladimír Helfert's* classes on musicology and aesthetics at the Masaryk University. His doctoral thesis (1933) was on 'The Influence of Lachian and Valachian folk music on the Compositional Development of Leoš Janáček'. Firkušný wrote several books on Janáček, mostly on the operas, including a monograph on *From the House of the Dead* in 1937 that includes illustrations of the manuscript. In 1948 Firkušný was invited to lecture on Czech music in London, where he met Rosa Newmarch's daughter, who gave him Janáček's letters to her mother with a view to their eventual publication. In 1949 Firkušný and his wife, the singer Růžena Hořáková, settled in Buenos Aires. Here, Firkušný helped to arrange the first performance of *Jenůfa* at the Teatro Colón on 30 June 1950, when the opera was conducted by Karl Böhm with Tiana Lemnitz in the title role, Margarete Klose as the Kostelnička, Anton Dermota and Ludwig Suthaus as Laca and Števa, and Růžena Hořáková as Grandmother Buryja. Firkušný died suddenly ten days later. *ČHS, FisJan, PetFir.*

Firkušný, Rudolf (b. Napajedla, near Zlín, 11 November 1912; d. Staatsburg, New York, 19 July 1994), Czech pianist, brother of Leoš Firkušný*.   The young Ruda Firkušný started to take lessons in theory and composition with Janáček from 1917 (aged five), while he studied the piano with Ludmila Tučková (1917–20) and Růžena Kurzová (1920–7). As well as giving him regular lessons, Janáček took Firkušný to performances of his works, including *Káťa Kabanová* and *The Cunning Little Vixen*. Since Firkušný was not studying the piano with Janáček, it is hard to determine which works he may have played for the composer, but he saw him regularly over several years and Janáček asked him to play for Rosa Newmarch* when she visited Brno in April 1922. At the outbreak of World War II, Firkušný fled Czechoslovakia, settling in New York in 1940. He recorded Janáček's solo piano music for Columbia in 1952–3, for Deutsche Grammophon in 1971 and for RCA in 1989. He recorded the *Concertino** in 1947 (for Concert Hall) and 1954 (for Columbia). In 1970 he recorded the *Concertino* and *Capriccio* (for Deutsche Grammophon), and again in 1991 (for RCA).

   Firkušný recalled his lessons with Janáček in an interview with Elyse Mach: 'Nothing was ever planned: each meeting was a surprise for me because everything was so spontaneous. Sometimes we sat together at the piano and played music for four hands; at other times he demonstrated works for me, like Debussy's *La Mer*; and at other times he brought out his latest opera *Káťa Kabanová*, which was almost ready for publication, put it on the music rack and asked me to play.' Firkušný recalled that Janáček insisted on 'an original composition for each session ... and he showed me why he thought I had done certain sections in a particular way, or why he thought they could have been done differently. ... Janáček was the greatest influence on my musical life. He wasn't really the ogre that people made him out to be.' *CurDis, MacPia, PohRud.*

Foerster, Josef Bohuslav (b. Prague, 30 December 1859; d. Nový Vestec, 29 May 1951), Czech composer.   Like Janáček, Foerster studied at the Prague Organ School (1879–82) with František Skuherský*. Though they were to develop in very different ways (Foerster was sometimes criticised in his lifetime for a lack of national character in his music, including, privately, by Janáček), there are some interesting parallels in their careers. Both worked as teachers and both had literary talents, often fashioning their own librettos. In 1895–6 Foerster completed his opera *Eva*, based on Gabriela Preissová's play *The Farm Mistress*, at the same time as Janáček was working on *Jenůfa*, based on Preissová's *Její pastorkyňa*. In 1897 Janáček and Foerster both set Vrchlický's poem *Amarus*. Janáček's version is for soloists, chorus and orchestra, while Foerster's is a melodrama for reciter and piano (it was published in 1898 as his Op. 30a). In 1923 Foerster composed a *Glagolitic Mass* Op. 123 for mixed chorus and organ (published in 1929), his restrained setting pre-dating Janáček's by four years (both composers used the text edited by Josef Vajs published in *Cyril* in 1920). Contacts between the two composers were cordial, though Janáček expressed reservations about Foerster's *Eva* in a letter to Gabriela Horvátová: 'The *setting* of the work, that Moravian-Slovak spirit, freshness, colour, impetuousness – to take all that away and compose *in a universal way*! Only Foerster could do that!' Janáček was more interested in Foerster's *The Invincible Ones* (*Nepřemožení*) when UE sent him a copy in 1918: 'A story – I don't know how it happened – that is full of echoes of my libretto for *Fate*! Charming music, pale as the moon.' Foerster attended the Vienna premiere of *Jenůfa* in 1918, and on 27 October 1922 went to a rehearsal of *Káťa Kabanová* in Prague, writing to Janáček the same day: 'I heard part of the ensemble rehearsal (at the piano) for the chance meeting of Káťa and Boris and I was transported. I don't know your new work yet, but that scene caught my heart and I had to tell you and thank you.' *HilBri, JYL2.*

Folk Ballads (26 Folk Ballads) [*26 balad lidových*]   In 1921 Janáček planned a collection of twenty folksong arrangements with the collective title *Twenty Folk Ballads*. These were sent to HMUB on 1 May 1921 and comprised three works: the *Folk Nocturnes* (IV/32), the *Five Folksongs* (IV/37) and the *Songs of Detva* (V/1). Soon afterwards, Janáček added the *Six Folksongs sung by Eva Gabel* (V/9). The first two sets to be published (in 1922) were the *Six Folksongs sung by Eva Gabel* and the *Folk Nocturnes*, with title pages that give the collective title *26 Folk Ballads* as well as individual titles for each set. Though listed on the 1922 title page, the *Songs of Detva* and *Five Folksongs* were not published until HMUB issued a complete edition as a single volume in 1950. See *Folk Nocturnes** (IV/32) and *Six Folksongs sung by Eva Gabel** (V/9). *JAWO, LánJan.*

Folk Dances in Moravia [*Národní tance na Moravě*], folk dance arrangements for piano (two and four hands), compiled and arranged by Janáček with Lucie Bakešová*, Xavera Běhálková* and (for Vol. 3 only) Martin Zeman (VIII/10).   The tunes included in this collection were mostly collected in 1888–9. Ten of the dances were performed at the Brno Beseda on 7 January 1891 (played by Antonina Nikodemová and Anna Kumpoštová at an evening for the Vesna Society). The first volume of six dances was published by the end of January, printed in Brno for the authors (Janáček, Bakešová and Běhálková), and a second volume of a further six dances appeared at the end of the year. A third volume was published in 1893, with Zeman added as a collaborator. In the original edition, the dances are published with explanations of the steps illustrated with diagrams, and there are two different piano arrangements of each dance, for piano solo and for piano duet. For the 'Starodávný' (No. 6 in Vol. 1), Janáček also provides a version for cimbalom. In response to a letter from Bakešová asking him to make the arrangements, Janáček had set out what he hoped to achieve: 'The accompaniment for a song or dance, and the independent form adopted by the composer ... must be of the same style as the melody.' After the original publication of the dances in 1891 and 1893, they were not reprinted until 1953, with the piano duet versions printed as a supplement. A critical edition appeared in SKVEJ G/2 (2005). *JAWO, ProNar.*

Folk Nocturnes [*Lidová nokturna*] (*26 Folk Ballads* II), Evening songs of the Slovak people from Rovné. Arrangements of seven folksongs for 'folk duet' (two-part female voices) and piano (IV/32).   Probably completed before 22 May 1906. In 'An Evening with Leoš Janáček' (XV/182), an interview for the magazine *Dalibor* with Adolf Piskáček, Janáček described the folksongs he transcribed at Makov near Velké Rovné (now in the Žilina region of Slovakia) between 1901 and 1906: 'In the evening, after sunset, girls meet at the back of the cottages and one of them, the best singer, stands in front of the others leading the singing. She sings the first line and the others join in, holding hands, with an unusual melody which carries over the hilltops, falls into the valleys and dies away beyond the river in the dark forest.' Piskáček asked Janáček if he planned to publish the songs and Janáček replied that he had rehearsed 'about five of them' in Brno, adding that a proposed performance in Prague 'unfortunately did not happen'. The first performance was at the Brno Organ School on 5 December 1907 in a concert organised by the KPU. Ludvik Kundera* mentions that the *Folk Nocturnes* were sung by 'a small women's chorus' but gives no further details. A review by Karel Sázavský in *Dalibor* (14 December 1907) described the work as 'a series of folksongs for two voices that breathed an atmosphere of warm, beautiful summer nights. Janáček's arrangements, which adhere faithfully to the original in terms of both harmony and style, are masterpieces of folksong treatments. ... The songs themselves are of such a rare and interesting type that the universal wish was to hear them again.' The *Folk Nocturnes* were first published by HMUB as Vol. II of *26 Folk Ballads* (see Folk Ballads*) in 1922. In 1938 Břetislav Bakala made an arrangement for voices, two clarinets, two cimbaloms and string orchestra. *JAWO, KunJan, PisVeč.*

Folksong Editions   Janáček collaborated on five collections of folksongs, the first three with František Bartoš* and the other two with Pavel Váša*. These volumes represent Janáček's most important contributions to folksong collecting, editing and study in the strict sense: transcriptions rather than arrangements. Janáček's methods for folksong collection (and those of his closest collaborators such as Hynek Bím* and Františka Kyselková*) usually involved careful transcriptions, made on-site using traditional musical notation. For a few years (1909–12), Janáček and his collaborators also used a phonograph*. These are Janáček's major folksong editions:

A Bouquet of Moravian Folksongs [*Kytice z národních písní moravských*], 1890 (XIII/1), collected by František Bartoš and Janáček (his name is given on the title page as Lev Janáček). It was published by Emil Šolc* in Telč in 1890 and contains the words and tunes of 174 Moravian folksongs. An introduction partly written by Janáček describes musical features of the songs and how to perform them. The collection sold out within a few months and Šolc published a second edition in 1892. Šolc also asked Janáček to arrange some of the songs for voice and piano, and these were published in 1892 and 1901. See *Moravian Folk Poetry in Songs** (V/2).

A Bouquet of Moravian, Slovak and Czech Folksongs [*Kytice z národních písní moravských, slovenských a českých*], 1901 (XIII/2). For this third edition of the

Bouquet, published by Šolc in 1901, Bartoš and Janáček added Slovak and Czech songs.

Moravian Folksongs Newly Collected [*Národní písně moravské v nově nasbírané*], 1901 (XIII/3). After organising the 'Moravian Days' at the 1895 Ethnographic Exhibition in Prague, Janáček and Bartoš turned their attention to what would become their most important collection: *Moravian Folksongs Newly Collected*, published complete in 1901 by the Czech Academy. This contains 2,057 numbered songs and dances, and many more (unnumbered) are included in Janáček's long introduction, 'On the Musical Aspect of Moravian Folksongs'. The scope of this collection is reflected in its sheer size: the introduction and main body of the book amount to well over 1,300 pages. Most of the songs are given as single-stave tunes with words, but some (e.g. Nos. 1729–39 and Nos. 1789–1809) are given in score to illustrate traditional accompaniments by folk instruments. The collection is classified by song type: ballads, love songs, wedding songs, marriage songs, songs of daily life, laments, military songs, comic songs, drinking and festive songs, dances, religious songs, legends, and an appendix of street cries.

From the New Collection of Moravian Folksongs [*Z nově sbírky národních písní moravských*], 1911–12 (XIII/4). Published in *Večery*, the literary supplement to *Lidové noviny* on 23 December 1911 and 6 January 1912, this is a collection of twenty-five songs and dances compiled by Janáček and Pavel Váša. Some were later included in XIII/5.

Moravian Love Songs I [*Moravské písně milostné I*], 1930–6 (XIII/5). Edited by Janáček and Pavel Váša, this large collection has 150 numbered items, but counting the many variants it actually includes a total of 951 songs, 412 of them newly collected and 539 taken from earlier collections. It was published for the State Institute for Folksong by Orbis in six fascicles between 1930 and 1936, when the whole set was issued in a slipcase. The introduction, dated 14 June 1928, is largely by Janáček. Most of the songs in this collection were already prepared for publication at the end of 1913, but war intervened and the project was delayed. In 1927 Janáček spent time during a tea with President Masaryk to tell him about the forthcoming publication of the *Moravian Love Songs*, a project that he considered the culmination of his work in folksong studies. It includes indexes by textual incipits, melodic incipits, singers, places and collectors. *JAWO, LJFD1, ProVza.*

From the House of the Dead [*Z mrtvého domu*], Opera in three acts with libretto by Janáček after Dostoyevsky's *Notes from the House of the Dead* (I/11). Janáček's last opera was composed between 18 February 1927 and 7 May 1928, with revisions and corrections up to 20 June 1928 and possibly later. Dostoyevsky's *Notes from the House of the Dead*, first published in the magazine *Vremya* [*Time*] in 1860–2, was an unorthodox choice for an opera. There is little in the way of conventional narrative in this semi-autobiographical novel, but Janáček chose monologues drawn from Dostoyevsky that create scenes teeming with internal drama, erupting into climaxes that can be disturbingly violent. These tales of suffering, depravity, revenge and wrongdoing are described by prisoners who emerge from the chorus to tell their stories, holding back little in their descriptions of deceit and brutality. But Janáček's superscription at the top of his score, derived from Dostoyevsky, reads 'In every creature, a spark of God': for Janáček, as for Dostoyevsky, there were glimpses of compassion, dignity and hope to be found within the prison walls.

While Janáček was composing *The Cunning Little Vixen* and *The Makropulos Affair*, he was quite forthcoming in letters and interviews about progress on them, talking about his choice of sources (usually in *Lidové noviny*) giving an impression of what audiences might expect to see and hear, and even printing fragments of the scores. But he gave very few clues about *From the House of the Dead* and it is not even possible to establish when he first read Dostoyevsky's book. He owned two copies: a Russian edition published in Berlin in 1921 and an undated Czech translation. Janáček's first specific mention of the project came on 12 February 1927 in an open letter published the following day in *Lidové noviny* but addressed to Max Brod. Janáček wrote: 'Here I am close to Feodor M. Dostoyevsky. He found in *The House of the Dead* a good man's soul ...' A few weeks earlier, he had confided to Brod in a private letter that he was casting around for a project: 'All I want now is to come across a free libretto, so as not to be limited, bound, from a rather different world. In short I don't yet know myself whether it will be gouged in the earth – or in some sort of spiritual sphere.' With *From the House of the Dead* he seems to have found what he was looking for.

The evidence of the autograph manuscript suggests that Janáček wasted no time getting to work on *From the House of the Dead*: the earliest date on the manuscript is 18 February 1927, less than a week after his open letter. He quickly drafted a scenario and started the score, finishing the first draft of Act I by early April and making rapid progress over the next few months. On 29 July 1927, *Lidové noviny* reported that the opera was 'already finished in rough outline' but that Janáček had wanted to keep its composition 'secret'. The paper published a longer version of the same interview three days after Janáček's death, which revealed that his wish to keep the work secret was because he intended to enter it for an opera competition held by the Prague NT. This isn't a very convincing explanation, since Ostrčil in Prague would have been extremely happy to take any new opera by Janáček. John Tyrrell has speculated that 'another reason for Janáček's silence might also have been the foreboding that this would be his last opera.' A compelling detail in support of this idea is that not even Kamila Stösslová heard much about Janáček's work on the opera until the first version was finished in October 1927 (the statement in *Lidové noviny* that it was 'finished in rough outline' at the end of July was unduly optimistic). In the dozens of letters he wrote to Stösslová between February and October 1927, *From the House of the Dead* gets only a few brief mentions, but on 16–17 October he announced: 'My dear soul, yesterday and today I've finished that opera of mine: *From the House of the Dead*. A terrible title, isn't it?' Two major revisions followed over the next few months. A new version of the first two acts was finished just before Christmas 1927. On 18 December he wrote to Kamila that 'there now remains for me to tidy up just the last act. Then a heavy weight will fall from me!', and the revision of Act III was finished on 4 January 1928. The long monologue for Šiškov – a superb musical structure but an immensely harrowing narrative – cost him a great deal of effort, but on 4 January he was able to tell Kamila: 'Opera finished. The work finished. I just want to see you now and have joyful moments.'

Janáček undertook another complete revision of the opera in the first half of 1928, and between March and June the work was copied under Janáček's close supervision by his two most faithful and reliable copyists: Václav Sedláček* and Jaroslav Kulhánek*. Both were musicians in the orchestra of the Brno NT (Sedláček was a flautist and Kulhánek a trombonist) who had first-hand experience of playing Janáček's idiosyncratic and often extremely demanding orchestral writing in the opera house. By the time they worked on copying this opera they were also experienced at deciphering Janáček's handwriting, a task made all the more difficult in *From the House of the Dead* because the autograph manuscript was written not on conventional ruled music paper but on plain sheets, with the staves hand-drawn by Janáček. After the copied scores of each act had been made, Janáček began the painstaking process of checking and correcting them to establish a definitive musical text. He completed his checks for Acts I and II by 1 July 1928, and took Act III with him to his cottage in Hukvaldy. He died on 12 August before he was able to do the final checks on Act III.

These circumstances contributed to the subsequent history of the opera. Preparing the score was put in the hands of two pupils, Osvald Chlubna* and Břetislav Bakala*. They believed that Janáček's autograph was a sketch (not an unreasonable assumption given its unorthodox appearance) and that he had left the work unfinished, especially in terms of its orchestration. Certainly the sound of this opera is unlike any other and Chlubna made extensive changes to the instrumentation, and even invented a new ending to replace Janáček's original. It was with these far-reaching revisions (along with changes to the libretto by Ota Zítek*) that the opera was first performed at the Brno NT on 12 April 1930 (conducted by Bakala), and published the same year by UE. For the next three decades it was performed in this version, and in the 1950s Supraphon and Philips issued recordings including Chlubna's triumphalist ending. In 1958 Jaroslav Vogel* conducted Janáček's original ending at the Prague NT, the first time it had been heard. Rafael Kubelík* produced a new edition based largely on Janáček's autograph manuscript that went some way to restoring the composer's first thoughts, introducing his edition at a concert performance in Munich in 1961. In 1964 Bohumil Gregor* conducted a new production at the Prague NT which was taken to the 1964 Edinburgh Festival. Charles Mackerras* used Kubelík's edition for the first staging of the work in London, at Sadler's Wells Theatre in 1965. What these performances revealed was a score of astonishing boldness, with an austerity and economy that reflects the compactness and harshness of Dostoyevsky's novel.

Apart from the Tartar boy Aljeja – the Kamila character in this opera, written for a mezzo-soprano – the voices are all male (with the exception of the small role for a Prostitute in Act II). The chorus is an almost constant presence and Janáček writes music of searing intensity (and considerable difficulty) for it. The unusual instrumentation (chains, a saw, a pick and shovel, anvil blows and 'the clanging of work tools') are no mere sound effects but part of an extraordinary orchestral palette in which conventional instruments (often stretched to the limit) also add to the raw, visceral sonority of this opera, especially through Janáček's use of wide spacing and extremes of high and low registers. These were the passages that Chlubna felt needed filling out: this was music of an uncompromising sparseness and ruggedness of a kind Janáček had not written before. With the completion of John Tyrrell's new edition, the revelation of recent performances that have returned to Janáček's original orchestration is that the composer knew exactly what he was doing.

When Charles Mackerras recorded it for Decca in 1980, he asked Tyrrell to remove many of Chlubna's additions and to include as much as possible from the authorised copy of the score. In the years following that recording, Tyrrell delved much further into the sources of the opera and completed a new critical-practical edition for UE that presented Janáček's opera as he had left it. This was first performed at the Royal Opera House, Covent Garden in March 2018.

To hear the composer's own version of *From the House of the Dead* is particularly significant since Janáček considered it to be his greatest work for the theatre. The close of the opera finds Janáček at the peak of his creative powers: the prisoners sing a fervent hymn to freedom as the eagle they have nursed back to health soars into the skies, the chains are struck from Gorjančikov and he walks to liberty: in his words, to a new life and the resurrection of the dead. But Janáček saves a cruel twist to the last: as Gorjančikov leaves, the guards order the prisoners back to their never-ending grind. It's brutal and shocking – but that defiant spark in each of the prisoners continues to burn. Janáček himself reflected on what had inspired him to write this extraordinary work; after he died in August 1928, a note about the opera was found in his clothes:

> Why do I go into the dark frozen cells of criminals with the poet of *Crime and Punishment*? Into the minds of criminals and there I find a spark of God. You will not wipe away the crimes from their brow, but equally you will not extinguish the spark of God. ... See how the old man slides down from the oven, shuffles to the corpse, makes the sign of the cross over it, and with a rusty voice sobs the words 'A mother gave birth even to him!' These are the bright places in the house of the dead.

JAWO, JODA, JYL2, PalJev, TyrSim, VogJan.

SYNOPSIS
Act I: The yard of the prisoners' quarters of a Russian prison camp on the River Irtysh. Early morning. Winter, snow, frost. The prisoners get up. Two get into a fight and there's talk that the new arrival will be a nobleman. He is Alexandr Petrovič Gorjančikov, a political prisoner. The Prison Governor interrogates him and orders him to be beaten. The prisoners have found a wounded eagle and tease the bird until the guards order them to their work. Skuratov, one of the prisoners, recalls his previous life in Moscow, while another, Luka, tells how he started a riot and killed an officer in his first prison camp. As Luka describes his own beating, Gorjančikov is dragged in, half dead.
Act II: A year after Act I. Summer sunshine. The Bank of the River Irtysh. Gorjančikov has befriended the young tartar Aljeja and offers to teach him to read. The prisoners finish work and a holiday begins. The Priest blesses the food and the river. Skuratov tells his story: he loved a German girl, Luisa, but when she was to be married to an old relative, Skuratov shot the groom. To celebrate the holiday, the prisoners stage a play about Don Juan and Kedril and a pantomime about a beautiful but fickle miller's wife. After the plays, the Stubborn Prisoner, jealous of the friendship between Gorjančikov and Aljeja, wonders how wealthy Gorjančikov must be to drink tea in prison, then attacks Aljeja, who is left badly injured.
Act III, Scene 1: The prison hospital. Towards evening. Gorjančikov cares for Aljeja, who can now read and write. Luka lies dying of tuberculosis. Šapkin tells

the story of his arrest as a vagrant. During the night, Šiškov shares his story, constantly interrupted by Čerevin: a rich merchant had a daughter, Akulka, who was jilted by Filka Morozov. Derided by the whole village and her own family, she married Šiškov, who discovered on their wedding night that she was a virgin and had been a model daughter. After she confessed that she still loved Filka, Šiškov took her into the forest and slit her throat. At that moment Luka dies and in a shocking moment of recognition, Šiškov realises that Luka was Filka. *Act III, Scene 2: Setting as in Act I. The hospital wing at the back. Sunshine.* The drunken Prison Governor apologises to Gorjančikov for having him beaten and tells him that he has been pardoned. As Gorjančikov looks forward to freedom and a new life, the prisoners release the eagle before the guards order them back to work.

From the street 1 October 1905   See *1. X. 1905* (VIII/19)

Funeral, Janáček's   Janáček died shortly before 10.00 a.m. on the morning of Sunday, 12 August 1928 at Dr Klein's sanatorium in Ostrava. News travelled extremely quickly back to Brno. One of the first people to hear the news was František Neumann, about an hour after Janáček's death. He informed the mayor of Brno, who took charge of the funeral arrangements, and black flags were flown from the National Theatre. The scheduled performance that evening was Smetana's *The Bartered Bride*. There was insufficient time to change this, so Neumann conducted Smetana as planned and announced Janáček's death at the end of Act I. At the end of the performance, Neumann conducted the Funeral March from Beethoven's 'Eroica' Symphony. By the end of the day, Brno was a city in mourning. Janáček's body was brought from Ostrava on the Sunday night and placed in the chapel of the Augustinian Monastery in Old Brno.

When Zdenka Janáčková returned from Ostrava, she met Neumann on 13 August to discuss arrangements for the funeral, which was to take place in the National Theatre. The date was set for 15 August. On the Monday and Tuesday (13 and 14 August), Janáček's death dominated the newspapers: in *Lidové noviny* on 13 August, the whole front page (and part of page 2) was devoted to Gracian Černušák's long obituary, illustrated with the famous drawing by Eduard Milén. The following day there were further tributes and a formal half-page announcement printed within a thick black border:

> Josef Janáček announces on behalf of all his family the death of his beloved brother, Dr Leoš Janáček, composer and Professor of the Master School of the State Music Conservatory. He died unexpectedly in Moravská Ostrava on Sunday, 12 August 1928 at the age of 74. The funeral takes place on Wednesday, 15 August 1928, at 10.30 a.m. in the foyer of the National Theatre in Brno then at the Central Cemetery.

On the morning of the funeral, *Lidové noviny* printed the arrangements. These went ahead as announced, with one significant exception:

> The vestibule of the National Theatre will be accessible to the public. Access to the foyer will be reserved for representatives of cultural and public institutions. The memorial ceremony will begin at 10.30 a.m. with an extract from *The Cunning Little Vixen* (orchestra and soloist Mr Arnold Flögl). The memorial ceremony will close with Janáček's *Glagolitic Mass* performed by the chorus of the Brno Beseda with orchestra and soloists from the National Theatre.

3. Janáček's funeral procession at the Brno National Theatre (now the Mahen Theatre), 15 August 1928.

If the *Glagolitic Mass* had ever been contemplated, Jaroslav Kvapil* would surely have vetoed doing such a difficult work on little or no rehearsal (the choir had last sung it at the Prague premiere, several months earlier). The ceremony began in the National Theatre with the final scene from *The Cunning Little Vixen*, as Janáček had requested. Arnold Flögl sang the Forester and František Neumann conducted. This was followed by speeches, including from Ota Zítek on behalf of the theatre, and Boleslav Vomáčka on behalf of the Czech Academy. Other spoken tributes were given by Jan Kunc (Brno Conservatory), Max Brod (Janáček's German friends), Alois Hába (Prague SMH), Pavel Haas (KMS) and Stanislav Tauber (PSMU). Kvapil then conducted the Brno Beseda choir and the orchestra of the National Theatre in part of Dvořák's Requiem. Other prominent musicians who attended included Otakar Ostrčil, Oskar Nedbal, Jaroslav Vogel and Jaroslav Křička. Zdenka Janáčková, accompanied by Marie Stejskalová, recalled that she was in no state to take in either the speeches or the music.

Just before noon, the coffin was taken out of the theatre to the sound of four French horns. The report in the following morning's edition of *Lidové noviny* (16 August) described what happened next: 'Just then the sun broke through and deep emotion seized the large crowd in front of the theatre. The men bared their heads and all the electric lights in the city came on. Three vehicles filled with floral tributes drove at the head of the cortege ... through streets lined with thick crowds.' At the cemetery, the funeral rites were spoken by Father Albín Zelníček, and Janáček's body was lowered into the grave as French horns again played. František Neumann spoke briefly, his words reported in *Lidové noviny*: 'We Czech musicians stand here as poor orphans.' The paper noted: 'The funeral ceremony came to a close with the Czech national anthem, during which many of Janáček's friends wept.' That evening, Neumann conducted a memorial performance of *Jenůfa*. Two days later, Zdenka Janáčková recalled a second ceremony at the Central Cemetery, to move Janáček from the temporary location where he had been buried at the funeral to his final resting place: 'On Friday 17 August in the morning, we met at Leoš's present grave, the mayor and his wife, Director Neumann and some others. Mrs Tomešová [the mayor's wife] placed a bunch of flowers on the transferred coffin; I placed a bouquet of red roses. The coffin was lowered into the new grave, and covered with soil. And so, after six days of restless journeying, Leoš's body found peace after death.' MLWJ, ZahDiv.

Glagolitic Mass [*Mša glagolskaja*] for soloists, mixed chorus, organ and orchestra (III/9). Janáček first contemplated writing a Mass in about 1921, when he met Leopold Prečan* (appointed Archbishop of Olomouc in 1923) in Hukvaldy. They discussed the state of church music, and apparently Prečan suggested that Janáček should write a new setting of the Mass in Old Church Slavonic. There is a sketch from the early 1920s for two movements (which bear no relationship to the finished work), suggesting that Janáček may have considered writing a piece for liturgical use at the time (Prečan or another of Janáček's clerical friends no doubt told him that the Mass in Old Church Slavonic had been authorised for use in the Catholic liturgy in 1920). Janáček saw Prečan again in July 1926, when the Archbishop attended the rainy celebrations for the unveiling of a plaque on the composer's birthplace. Janáček started work on his new Mass in Luhačovice* on 2 August 1926. Much of it was composed on the harmonium in the chapel of the Augustinian House, and Janáček even gave a private play-through there for two friends (see Harmonium*). After making revisions in September 1926, he finished a draft in October and gave the manuscript to Václav Sedláček* for copying. Janáček made further changes and added the organ solo by December 1926. So extensive were the revisions Janáček made on Sedláček's copy in the first half of 1927 that a second copy was made by Jaroslav Kulhánek*, dated 1 September 1927. Before and after the first performance on 5 December 1927, Janáček revised the work again, making changes that can clearly be seen between the two versions published as SKV B/5-1 (1928 version) and B/5-2 (September 1927 version). The most important differences can be summarised as follows: in the September 1927 version, the 'Introduction' ('Úvod') includes passages written simultaneously in triple (3/4) time and quintuple (5/8) time. Janáček rationalised this into consistent triple time for the 1928 version. In the 1927 version, the 'Gospodi pomiluj' was in 5/4 and this was reworked by Janáček in 4/4 in the 1928 revision. The eruption for three timpanists in the 'Raspet' ('He was crucified') section of the 'Věruju' in the 1927 version was cut. In the 'Svet', fourteen bars were cut, probably during rehearsals. There are also extensive differences in the solo vocal parts of the two versions. Paul Wingfield's edition of the 1927 version (which presents a slightly later stage of the revision process than Jiří Zahrádka's) has nine movements, opening with the 'Intrada', the work's closing movement. This symmetrical structure reflects the movement listing in the programme for the premiere. Zahrádka's 'September 1927' version keeps the eight-movement order on the grounds that the evidence of the printed programme has no direct authority from the composer. Ludvík Kundera finished arranging the vocal score in early 1928, and noted in an article published on 22 February (*Tempo*, Vol. 7, No. 5) that some of the revisions were made after the Brno premiere, in particular the cuts in the 'Raspet' section of the 'Věruju'. Kundera's manuscript vocal score contains a number of further corrections in Janáček's hand. UE published the vocal score, with a pictorial cover by Eduard Milén*, on 6 April 1928, just before the Prague premiere (8 April 1928), which incorporated Janáček's revisions. This was described in Janáček's thank you note to the Brno Beseda (12 April 1928) as a 'beautiful performance ... perfect in every way'. While the vocal score was in proof, Janáček added the dedication 'To Dr Leopold Prečan, Archbishop of Olomouc', in acknowledgment of his role as the work's instigator. The full score was issued in March 1929.

The first performance was given at the recently opened concert hall of the Brno Stadion on 5 December 1927, with Alexandra Čvanová* (soprano), Marie Hloušková (contralto), Stanislav Tauber* (tenor), Ladislav Němeček (bass), Bohumil Holub (organ), the chorus of the Brno Beseda and the Brno NT orchestra conducted by Jaroslav Kvapil*. The Prague premiere in the Smetana Hall on 8 April 1928 had the same soloists, organist and chorus, but this time Kvapil conducted the Czech Philharmonic. The earliest performances outside Czech lands were conducted by Alexander Zemlinsky* in Berlin (28 February 1929) and by Kvapil with the Orchestre de la Suisse Romande and Brno Beseda chorus at the ISCM Festival in Geneva (7 April 1929). On 29 November 1929, an unusual programme of Purcell's *Dido and Aeneas* and the *Glagolitic Mass* was given by the Rotterdam Toonkunst choir, conducted by Evert Cornelis

(1884–1931). The British premiere was given by Henry Wood* at the Norwich Festival (23 October 1930) and the US premiere by Artur Bodanzky* at the Metropolitan Opera in New York (26 October 1930). Overseas critics were baffled by the work. When Zemlinsky conducted it in Berlin, Adolf Weissmann (*Die Musik*, May 1929) described the piece as 'mosaic-like', and Max Marschalk in the *Vossische Zeitung* (1 March 1929) criticised its 'extraordinary severity and complete lack of inner cohesion'. The Rotterdam performance was reviewed in *Voorwaarts* (2 December 1930), whose critic characterised the work as 'godly gypsy music'. After the New York premiere, Olin Downes (*New York Times*) wrote that the work was 'fantastically, impractically, and inarticulately original'. It was decades before the *Glagolitic Mass* was more widely recognised by non-Czechs as a work of major importance. Among the first was Alec Robertson, who described it as 'amazingly original, and of the most tremendous interest throughout' in his 1953 *Gramophone* review of the recording, conducted by Břetislav Bakala.

The attraction for Janáček of setting the Mass in Old Church Slavonic was twofold: it avoided the ecclesiastical trappings of Latin and served as an expression of his own Pan-Slavism – he saw Old Church Slavonic as the ancient wellspring of the Czech language. To Janáček's irritation, this was not how critics interpreted the Mass. Ludvík Kundera*, who had arranged the vocal score, declared in his article for *Tempo* (22 February 1928) that Janáček was 'now an old man, and a firm believer', provoking a memorably tetchy postcard from the composer on 28 February: 'No old man! No believer! You youngster!' In an interview a week later, Janáček added: 'not until I see for myself!' The fact that Janáček composed this piece at all prompts questions about whether there was a little more to it than that. In no sense was he conventionally religious, but several of his most important works are concerned with the central Christian tenets of redemption and resurrection. The *Glagolitic Mass* is something rather different: it represents the fullest and most dramatic expression of Janáček's pantheism, his belief (articulated in different ways in *The Cunning Little Vixen* and *From the House of the Dead*) that God is to be found in every living thing. His musical response to the Ordinary of the Mass was to explore its dramatic potential, and to present it as an explicitly Czech act of collective celebration: as he put it, the chorus represented 'our people', the tenor solo was the Celebrant, and the soprano solo in the 'Slava' was 'a girl – an angel'. The identity of the girl is easily inferred from his letters to Kamila Stösslová, but Janáček, with his monastery education, also knew that it was the angels who first sang 'Glory to God in the highest', the words set here. Janáček was 'no believer' in any traditional sense, but in the *Glagolitic Mass* his mystical notion of the universe as a manifestation of the divine finds a glorious musical manifestation.

On 27 November 1927, *Lidové noviny* published an article in which Janáček wrote about his inspiration for the work, combining pantheism and Slavdom:

> The balmy breeze of the Luhačovice woods was always like incense to me. The cathedral grew to the gigantic size of a mountain, reaching into the misty vaults of the sky. The bells that rang out were those of a flock of sheep. In the tenor solo I hear a high priest, in the soprano a girl – an angel, in the chorus, our people. The candles are the tall pines in the forest, lit by the stars, and somewhere in the ceremony I see the princely vision of St Wenceslas. I hear the language of the apostles, Cyril and Methodius.

4. Jaroslav Kvapil with the Beseda brněnská chorus and the orchestra of the Brno National Theatre on stage in the Stadion Hall where the *Glagolitic Mass* was given its premiere by the same forces in December 1927. This photograph was taken in March 1928 before a performance of Handel's *Judas Maccabeus*.

The same day he revealed a more private programme to Kamila Stösslová*. There was the same open-air cathedral, but now it was populated by animals and birds who were there to witness the wedding of Janáček and Kamila:

> I've set it in Luhačovice. Good, eh? Where else could it stand than there, where we were so happy! ... Two people enter the cathedral. They walk solemnly as if along a wide road, on a carpet that is a green lawn. And these two want to be married. It's strange that all the time it's just the two of them there. Priest, come at last! Nightingales, thrushes, ducks, geese, make music! Their general [i.e. Janáček] wants to marry that little black girl, small and tender – you, dear Kamila.

Though Janáček considered the revised 1928 version the definitive state of the work, Paul Wingfield's edition, presenting an earlier version, benefited from outstanding advocacy by Charles Mackerras*, who recorded it twice (for Chandos, and for Supraphon on DVD): it was the only version he performed from 1994 onwards, believing it to be the truest reflection of Janáček's bold conception. The 'September 1927' version edited by Zahrádka has also been recorded by Tomáš Netopil for Supraphon and Jiří Bělohlávek for Decca. Most other recordings follow the 1928 version. Mackerras's first Supraphon recording (1984) used the 1928 version but restored the fourteen bars cut from the 'Svet' during rehearsals. *JAWO, JYL2, WinGla, ZahGla, ZemEss.*

Gott erhalte den Kaiser!, music by Joseph Haydn, arranged for voice(s) and organ (XII/1). Janáček's version of the Austrian *Kaiserhymne* has an unusual place in his arrangements of music by other composers in that it is the only one he extensively reharmonised. The autograph manuscript is undated, but this arrangement must have been made for official use at one of the state institutions where Janáček taught (the Teachers' Institute and the Czech Gymnasium) between 1872 and 1903. Janáček's annotation 'Varhany' ['Organ'] on the top system looks much later than his handwriting in the 1870s, suggesting a date nearer 1900. The reproduction of Janáček's manuscript on p. 83 is the first publication of this arrangement. *JAWO.*

Gregor, Bohumil (b. Prague, 14 July 1926; d. Prague, 4 November 2005), Czech conductor. Gregor studied double bass at the Prague Conservatory and was a conducting pupil of Pavel Dědeček and Alois Klíma. Between 1949 and 1951, he worked at the Brno NT, where he first came to know Janáček's operas. At the Prague NT in the 1950s, he conducted revivals of *Jenůfa** and *The Cunning Little Vixen**, and a new production of *The Excursions of Mr Brouček** (17 December 1959). From 1958 to 1962, he was chief conductor in Ostrava, where he conducted new productions of *The Excursions of Mr Brouček* (28 June 1959) and *Káťa Kabanová** (1 October 1960). In the 1960s, Gregor conducted a series of new Janáček productions in Prague, including *From the House of the Dead* (24 April 1964, with Janáček's original ending), *The Cunning Little Vixen** (24 June 1965), *The Makropulos Affair** (15 October 1965) and *Jenůfa* (30 May 1969), most of which formed the basis for the Supraphon recordings of the operas made between 1964 and 1972. Over the next three decades he conducted many further Janáček productions in Prague and abroad. Gregor's recordings remain valuable: they are performed by singers who knew the works extremely well, and conducted with unfailing sensitivity. *NDPrOA, PřiLed.*

5. *Gott erhalte den Kaiser!* Autograph manuscript of Janáček's unpublished arrangement.

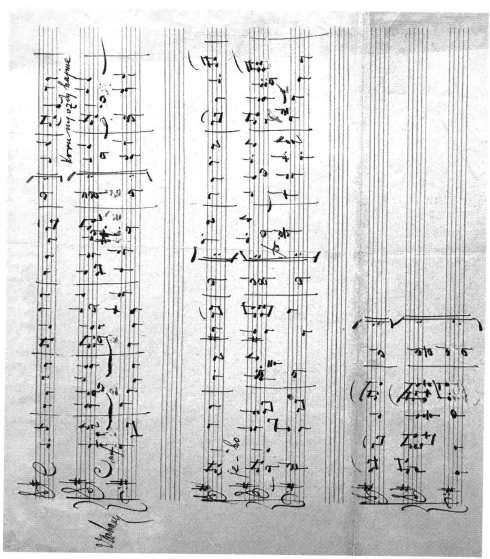

Haas, Pavel (b. Brno, 21 June 1899; d. Auschwitz-Birkenau extermination camp, 17 October 1944), Czech composer. In September 1920, Haas joined Janáček's Master School in Composition* and, under Janáček's supervision, completed his *Chinese Songs* Op. 4 and *Scherzo triste* for orchestra Op. 5. He graduated from the class on 28 June 1922, submitting a revised version of his First String Quartet. Haas's String Quartet No. 2 was subtitled 'From the Monkey Mountains' (a nickname for the mountains in the Vysočina region on the border of Moravia and Bohemia) and played at a KMS concert on 16 March 1926. A work full of surprises (including percussion in the final 'Wild Dance'), the influence of Janáček, particularly the First String Quartet, is occasionally apparent, especially in the first movement.

Haas and Břetislav Bakala* had been friends since student days. Bakala conducted an orchestral suite based on Haas's opera *The Charlatan* for Brno Radio on 13 June 1937, and the opera itself had its premiere at the Brno NT on 2 April 1938, conducted by Quido Arnoldi. Haas was arrested by the Nazis in 1941 and deported to Theresienstadt concentration camp. There he composed the *Study for Strings*, which was conducted by his fellow prisoner Karel Ančerl* in September 1944. A month later, Haas and Ančerl were transported to Auschwitz-Birkenau, and Haas was murdered in the gas chambers on the day he arrived. In 2002 the Pavel Haas Quartet took its name from the composer and in 2014 the Moravian Museum in Brno held the exhibition *Pavel Haas: Janáček's most talented pupil* to mark the seventieth anniversary of his death. *PedHaa, SpuHaa, VuhKMS.*

Hail Mary [*Zdrávas Maria*] for solo tenor, mixed chorus, violin and organ (II/14). Janáček composed this setting of the *Ave Maria* ('Hail Mary') in Czech by July 1904. It was written at the request of Countess Leopoldina Serényi, who remained involved with Luhačovice's cultural life after the spa was bought by František Veselý's consortium from her family in 1902. Serényi wrote to Janáček on 22 July 1904: 'I was delighted by the beautiful *Hail Mary* that you dedicated to me. I am very sorry that it was not possible to put this lovely composition into the programme this year because the concert had to be given earlier, but it will certainly be in our benefit concert next year.' Written soon after *Jenůfa*, Janáček's choice of a traditional Marian prayer is unsurprising: Jenůfa's prayer in Act II of the opera ('Zdrávas královno') is a Czech setting of another well-known prayer, the *Salve Regina* ('Hail Holy Queen'). The *Hail Mary* exists in two versions, the second of which enables performance without a choir. In the UE first edition (1978), both versions are printed. This work is not to be confused with Janáček's *Ave Maria* (IV/16, 1883), a chorus for male voices which sets a passage from Canto III of Byron's *Don Juan* in a Czech translation. *JAWO, KLJ, ProLuh.*

Halfar the Schoolmaster [*Kantor Halfar*], chorus for male voices (IV/33). The first of Janáček's choruses setting poems by Petr Bezruč*, *Halfar* was completed by 24 October 1906. The poem is based on real events: Bezruč's friend Ondřej Boleslav Petr (1853–93) was a teacher and Czech nationalist whose passion for teaching the Czech language led to his dismissal by the authorities. Having lost his job, Petr was then abandoned by his lover and ended his own life. This is similar to the tragic story of Bezruč's poem (originally called *Rektor Halfar* when it appeared in Bezruč's *Slezské číslo* in 1903, and the title Janáček gave his chorus until its publication in 1923). It was a text with an autobiographical resonance for Janáček too. As John Tyrrell put it, 'In some ways he was the schoolmaster Halfar, clinging on to the Czech language just as his father and grandfather, both schoolmasters, had done.' Janáček revised the chorus before it was published by HMUB in 1923, the title now changed to *Kantor Halfar*.

Janáček sent a copy in October 1906 to the Smetana choral society in Plzeň, which had sung Janáček's 'Ach vojna, vojna' (IV/17, No. 3) several times in 1905, including in Spa, Belgium (probably the first time Janáček's music had been performed in public outside Czech lands). A change in conductor may explain why it was another five years before *Halfar* was performed by the Smetana society, at Plzeň on 27 May 1911, under Antonín Arnet. In 1918 *Halfar* was taken up by Ferdinand Vach* and his PSMU. They sang it at Luhačovice on 3 August 1918, going on to give many more performances, and the first edition has a dedication to Vach. *Halfar* was also performed in Prague (24 October 1922) by the Prague Teachers' choral society under Metod Doležil. From a musical point of view, Janáček's Bezruč choruses are a remarkable group and *Halfar* resembles a miniature drama. As Tyrrell wrote: 'something came alive in these works, something that prefigures the urgency of the music of his last decade'. *JAWO, JYL1, ŠmoSbo, StrMuž, VogJan.*

Harmonium The harmonium (reed organ) was often found in private homes and small chapels in the late nineteenth and early twentieth centuries. Janáček had one at his cottage in Hukvaldy and used to compose on it, playing late into the night. In the summer of 1926, Janáček composed the *Glagolitic Mass** on the chapel harmonium of the Augustinian House in Luhačovice. František Kolář, an acquaintance from Brno, remembered Janáček's private play-through of the work, as Tyrrell relates: 'Kolář and his wife ... called on the composer at his rooms at the Augustinian House. Janáček greeted them in his dressing gown and in a state of elation: he had been composing the Mass that he had promised to the Archbishop. And despite the Kolářs' protests that there were sick people in the building, Janáček dragged them off to the chapel for the first "performance" of the work, which took place, very energetically, on the chapel harmonium with Janáček barking out the voice parts in a hoarse baritone.'

The first versions of five pieces from *On the Overgrown Path** were originally written for harmonium and published in 1901 and 1902. The first version (1901) of *Our Father** includes a part for harmonium; and the *Five Folksongs* (IV/37) composed in 1912 (part of the *26 Folk Ballads* – see Folk Ballads*) originally had harmonium accompaniment. *JAWO, JYL2.*

Helfert, Vladimír (b. Plánice, 24 March 1886; d. Prague, 18 May 1945), Czech musicologist. Helfert studied at the Charles University in Prague with Otakar Hostinský (1904–6) and subsequently worked with Zdeněk Nejedlý (who married Helfert's sister). Helfert came to Brno in 1919, establishing the music archive of the Moravian Museum and, in 1921, the Department of Musicology at the Masaryk University, leading him to be described by Jiří Vysloužil as 'the founder of musicology in Moravia'. When he arrived in Brno, Helfert, as a Nejedlý protégé, was sceptical about Janáček. Within a few years he had completely changed his opinion, becoming a committed champion of Janáček's music and a strong supporter of the composer's honorary doctorate (see Masaryk University*). In 1924 Helfert became the founding editor of the Brno journal *Hudební rozhledy**. His articles and reviews of Janáček (edited by Bohumír Štědroň) appeared in 1949 as *O Janáčkovi*. Substantial sections of Helfert's *Česká moderní hudba* (1936) are devoted to Janáček, and the book was attacked by Nejedlý and his acolytes. Helfert was also a lexicographer, and co-edited Part II of the *Pazdírkův Hudební slovník naučný* (1937–40).

Only the first volume of Helfert's biography of Janáček was finished (*Leoš Janáček: I. V poutech tradice*, 1939), covering his life and work up to *Šárka*. It is a magnificent torso, leading John Tyrrell to describe Helfert as Janáček's 'ideal biographer'. Helfert also wrote a monograph on František Neumann (1936). An outspoken opponent of the Nazis, Helfert was interrogated and arrested by the Gestapo in November 1939 and imprisoned in Brno's Špilberk Castle, then in Wrocław until 1942. After being released on health grounds, Helfert was arrested again in June 1944, imprisoned in Prague and finally at Theresienstadt concentration camp. By the time he was released on 24 April 1945, his health was ruined and he died three weeks later. His pupils included Leoš Firkušný, Jan Racek, Theodora Straková and Bohumír Štědroň. *ČHS, PečHel.*

Her Stepdaughter See *Jenůfa* (I/4)

Heřman, Jan (b. Neveklov, 31 August 1886; d. Prague, 30 September 1946), Czech pianist.   From 1914 until his death, Heřman taught at the Prague Conservatory while maintaining his career as a concert pianist. He played *On the Overgrown Path* in Prague on 3 November 1923, and *1. X. 1905* and *The Diary of One Who Disappeared* in a concert at the Vinohrady Theatre on 23 November 1924. The composer was present on both occasions. In a letter of 7 February 1926, Janáček recalled that the original ideas for the *Concertino**had occurred to him as he was walking back from the November 1924 performance of the *Diary*, in which Heřman had performed the piano part 'magnificently, like nobody else'. The *Concertino* was dedicated 'to Jan Heřman' on the first edition (1926) but, to Heřman's annoyance, Janáček did not entrust him with the premiere and Heřman seems not to have played it during Janáček's lifetime. *ČHS, JAWO.*

Hertzka, Emil (b. Budapest, 3 August 1869; d. Vienna, 9 May 1932), Austrian music publisher.   Hertzka studied chemistry, musicology and literature at the University of Vienna. In 1893 he joined the firm of Josef Weinberger, moving to UE when it was founded in 1901. He became its Director in 1907, changing the publishing policy to concentrate on living composers. It was a personal contact between Hertzka and Max Brod that led to him offering Janáček a contract for *Jenůfa** in November 1916. UE went on to publish all Janáček's later operas, the *Glagolitic Mass**, *Nursery Rhymes** and *Sinfonietta** (see Universal Edition*). Janáček's contact with UE was usually through Hertzka himself. Their relationship was generally cordial and survived some difficult moments (above all, when UE inadvertently gave the impression that they were rejecting *The Cunning Little Vixen* in 1924). Hertzka was a striking figure. Hans Heinsheimer, who worked in UE's opera department, wrote in *Menagerie in F sharp* that Hertzka 'was a man nobody who had ever laid eyes on would ever forget. He was very tall. ... His penetrating eyes flashed brilliantly out of a huge forest of grey hair that covered his head, face and chest. ... Hertzka was generally known as Wotan'. In terms of his achievements, his expansion of the UE catalogue and his promotion of new music led Paul Stefan to write that 'when the history of the music of our time is written, Hertzka's name will stand above all others as the great originator'. *FELJ, HeiErs, HeiMen, HilBri, JAWO, KLJ, ÖBL.*

Hipp Chronoscope, a scientific instrument designed to make precise measurements of very short periods of time. The German clockmaker Matthäus Hipp presented his chronoscope, an electromagnetic precision timer, in 1848. After Wilhelm Wundt (1832–1920) recommended the use of Hipp's chronoscope in his *Grundzüge der physiologischen Psychologie* (1874), it was adopted by experimental psychologists. Janáček read the expanded 1908–11 edition of Wundt's book, making copious notes on his copy. The earliest indication that he had access to a chronoscope came in 'Moravany! Morawaan', published in *Lidové noviny* on 6 April 1918 (XV/216), which includes precise measurements of short units of time. By February 1922, he had acquired his own machine, and on 12 March 1922 the *Prager Presse* published Janáček's 'Hipp's Chronoscope' (XV/236). As a discussion of the benefits of a scientific instrument, it is a curiously poetic piece of work: 'O sweet little window, a strange view into consciousness that is measured by the Hipp apparatus. No truth, no lie of music escapes you in this thousandth part of a minute.' Hipp chronoscope measurements appeared in his later writings about speech melody. 'He had an excellent ear' (*Lidové noviny*, 8 January 1924, XV/249) included a young woman saying 'You weren't there!' Janáček commented that these words 'wanted to be absorbed in tears. I measured them. They are squeezed into 0.00077m HCh.' Whether this calibration of speech was anything more than pseudo-science is open to question, but the chronoscope was a device which Janáček hoped would enable him to refine his studies of speech and yield psychological insights. His chronoscope is in the Janáček Archive in Brno. *SteJan.*

Hollander, Hans (b. Břeclav, 6 October 1899; d. Oxford, 3 October 1986). Hollander studied in Vienna with Guido Adler, then moved to Brno, where he met Janáček in 1928. He taught at the Brno Musikverein (1928–38) and worked for the German-language radio. Hollander escaped to Britain in 1938. In a letter to Janáček (7 June 1928), Hollander recalled their meeting a few months earlier, when Janáček had spoken about *From the House of the Dead*. With this letter, Hollander sent some recent articles he had written on Janáček and mentioned that a 'larger study' was due to be published in 1929 ('Leoš Janáček and His Operas', *Musical Quarterly*, Vol. 15, No. 1, January 1929). Written while Janáček was still alive, the *Musical Quarterly* article reported that he was 'working on a new opera founded on Dostoyevsky. What Janáček now seeks to express in music is the kinship of every human being to God, the divine spark that persists in every individual, however depraved and debased.' Hollander also asked Janáček to inscribe a photograph, reproduced as the frontispiece of his biography, *Leoš Janáček: His Life and Works* (1963). *FisCze, HolJan.*

Hollmann, Otakar (b. Vienna, 29 January 1894; d. Prague, 9 May 1967), Czech pianist. Hollmann initially trained in Vienna as a violinist but lost the use of his right hand as a result of a bullet wound during World War I. Unable to play the violin, he studied the piano with Adolf Mikeš at the Prague Conservatory (1919–24), and in 1925–6 studied composition with Vítězslav Novák. He wrote to Ludvík Kundera on 15 January 1926 asking him to approach Janáček to write a piece for him, and on 11 June 1926 he wrote to Janáček directly but received no reply at the time (see *Capriccio**). In May 1927, Hollmann secured Janáček's agreement to give the premiere of the *Capriccio*. He visited Janáček in Brno on 6 February 1928 to play him the work, impressing the composer with his performance. He gave the first performance on 2 March at a concert put on by the Organisation of Czechoslovak War-Invalid Officers in the Smetana Hall in Prague. Three decades later, in May 1956, Hollmann recorded the *Capriccio* for Supraphon, with an ensemble conducted by Jarmil Burghauser. Several other Czech composers wrote works for Hollmann, including Martinů, Schulhoff and Foerster. *JAWO, PřiHad, ProCap.*

Holst, Gustav (b. Cheltenham, 21 September 1874; d. London, 25 May 1934), British composer.   While visiting Eastern Europe in 1927–8, Holst wanted to meet Janáček and had been urged by Rosa Newmarch* to hear Janáček's operas. The two composers had dinner together on 7 January 1928 (Alois Hába was also present) and Janáček reported to Mrs Newmarch on 12 January 1928: 'I saw Mr Holst in Prague. We sat together at the Obecní dům. They will perform his orchestral suite *The Planets* in Prague. He wanted to hear one of my operas. He came to the wrong address! All the theatres except Olomouc ignore me here.' Holst's interest in Janáček seems to have run in the family: his daughter Imogen conducted a Janáček Centenary Concert at the Aldeburgh Festival in 1954, including the *Nursery Rhymes. JYL2, KLJ.*

Horvátová, Gabriela [Horvátová Noltschová, Gabriela] (b. Varaždin, Croatia, 25 December 1877; d. Prague, 29 November 1967), Croatian mezzo-soprano.   On 1 March 1903, Horvátová appeared at the Prague NT for the first time, was engaged as a member of the company one month later, and remained until her retirement in 1930. She sang two Janáček roles at the National Theatre: the Kostelnička in *Jenůfa** and, on just two occasions (29 May and 10 June 1924), Kabanicha in *Káťa Kabanová**. For her farewell performance on 18 May 1930, she sang the role she had made her own in 1916: the Kostelnička.
    By the time Horvátová sang the part in the Prague premiere of *Jenůfa* on 26 May 1916, Janáček had already fallen for her. Zdenka Janáčková's memoirs document his increasing infatuation with Horvátová: returning to Brno from rehearsals in Prague 'he spoke only of her', and by the end of the rehearsals 'he was completely besotted'. Over the next few months Janáček visited Horvátová in Prague at every opportunity, and in the summer of 1916 they spent time in Luhačovice. Zdenka confronted Janáček about his relationship with Horvátová and he admitted that he now thought of Horvátová as his wife. This admission brought the Janáčeks' marriage close to breaking point, and on 19 January 1917 they signed a pre-divorce settlement agreeing to run the household together and not to disturb domestic harmony. The friendship between Janáček and Horvátová cooled over the next year and by June 1918 their affair was over. Janáček was working on *The Excursions of Mr Brouček** during the years of his affair with Horvátová, and their letters include extensive discussion of the work. An edition of *The Excursion of Mr Brouček to the Moon* reached the proof stage in 1917, before being abandoned. Its title page had a dedication 'to Mrs Gabriela Horvátová Noltschová, the Kostelnička'. By the time the 'Moon' Excursion had become part of *The Excursions of Mr Brouček*, Janáček's affair with Horvátová had ended and the opera was dedicated to President Masaryk. In 1929 Horvátová appeared as the Kostelnička in a silent film of *Jenůfa*, and in 1935 she made a

recording of 'Co chvíla' (the Kostelnička's aria from Act II) for Radiojournal (see Recordings before 1960*). *JAvi, JAWO, MLWJ, NDPrOA.*

Hradčany Songs [*Hradčanské písničky*], choruses for solo soprano, female voices, flute and harp (IV/40).   Composed on 1–3 February 1916, these three choruses set poems from F. S. Procházka's *Hradčanské písničky*, first published in 1904. Procházka* was Janáček's favourite poet at the time, and the following year he was to prove an admirably efficient librettist for *The Excursion of Mr Brouček to the Fifteenth Century*. Each of the *Hradčany Songs* was composed in the space of one day. 'Golden Lane' is for unaccompanied chorus, SSAA; 'The Weeping Fountain' introduces a solo flute and a solo soprano; 'Belvedere' is the longest of the set, and is scored for solo soprano, SSAA chorus and harp. Janáček asked Procházka's permission to set the poems two days after finishing the songs: 'They have moved me deeply. I think they speak with the music of truth. Will you give me permission to use them for a composition?' Procházka readily agreed, asking only that they should not be mixed with other texts. 'Golden Lane' was first performed by the VSMU under Ferdinand Vach* in Prague on 26 December 1916. The whole set was given by the same performers in Brno on 24 November 1918, attended by Janáček. The songs were published by HMUB in 1922. The critical edition in SKVEJ C/3 (2002) includes Janáček's first version (before revisions) in a supplement.

All three poems evoke locations in Hradčany (Prague Castle). Golden Lane is the small street between the White Tower and Dalibor Tower. (In 1916–17, 22 Golden Lane was the home of Franz Kafka.) 'The Weeping Fountain' refers to the Singing Fountain in the Royal Gardens, in front of Queen Anne's summer palace. 'The Belvedere' refers to the summer palace itself. Janáček wrote a programme note for 'Golden Lane', possibly for the first performance: 'Heavy, like the drip of boiling oil, tone falls on tone, each laden with so much sadness – sadness without end! And where is consolation? In the splendour of Golden Lane? What started as an even rhythm settles into a meditation. The weeping whose end you never hear fades away: the golden chambers and the wide halls are still poor! The sounds of the whole chorus, with their weighty intoning, glitter like tears on a mourning veil. They seek their final understanding in the union of bitter pain. It is like the quiet howl of a black night.' *JAiii, JAWO, ZahŽen.*

Hrazdira, Cyril Metoděj (b. Rájec nad Svitavou, 16 January 1868; d. Brno, 3 December 1926), Czech composer and conductor.   Hrazdira studied with Janáček at the Brno Organ School (1885–8). Between 1888 and 1891, he played in the band of the 93rd Infantry Regiment in Olomouc, where he met the likes of Fibich, Foerster and Dvořák. Hrazdira was conductor of the Brno NT from August 1903 until January 1907, in the theatre that was located on the corner of Žerotín Square and Veveří Street. He conducted the premiere of *Jenůfa** on 21 January 1904, and the second production in 1906. His own opera *Ječmínek* was performed in March 1904, two months after *Jenůfa*. Hrazdira later took up posts in Ostrava, Split, Ljubljana and Zagreb. His operetta *Aviatik Meridon* (*Aviator Meridon*) was first performed at Ostrava in December 1910. Hrazdira's songs *Nálady a Rozmary* were dedicated to Janáček. *HraHud, PazHud, VěžZpí.*

Hudební besídka, musical magazine founded in 1924.   One of two short-lived journals published by Oldřich Pazdírek in Brno between 1924 and 1928 (the other was *Hudební rozhledy**), *Hudební besídka* (which translates as 'The Music Party') was subtitled a 'magazine for young people' and edited by Josef Gregor (1892–1957). Janáček contributed to *Hudební besídka* as both composer and writer, and he was the subject of numerous articles. His first contribution to the magazine was 'In the year 1874!' (XV/275), a reminiscence of the only time he saw Smetana. Vol. 3, No. 2 (October 1926) has Janáček's photograph on the front cover, and this is followed by a series of articles about him: Josef Beran writes about Janáček's house in the grounds of the Organ School (with photographs of the exterior and interior), Gregor reports on the ceremony in Hukvaldy at which Janáček unveiled a plaque on his birthplace (quoting extensively from Janáček's speech). The first part of Jan Mikota's account of Janáček's recent trip to England is followed by Gregor's commentary on the Suite for strings and his arrangement of the *Andante* for three violins (made with Janáček's consent). The second part of Mikota's article appeared in the Christmas number (December 1926), as did Janáček's article 'Christmas Lights' (a reprint of an article published in 1909), including Janáček's arrangement of the Christmas carol *Narodil se Kristus Pán* (VIII/20). The number for March–April 1928 included the first edition of Janáček's *March of the Bluebirds** (VII/9) and the second printing of his *Lullaby** (V/14). *HudBes.*

Hudební listy, musical magazine founded by Janáček in 1884. Between 1884 and 1888, Janáček not only edited *Hudební listy* but was also a major contributor. The magazine was supported financially by the Brno Beseda. Janáček first proposed the idea at a committee meeting of the Beseda on 24 November, and on 13 December 1884 the first issue appeared. The launch of the magazine coincided with the opening of the Brno Provisional Theatre (forerunner of the Brno NT), and Janáček wrote extensively about opera during the four years of the magazine's existence (when Janáček fell out with the Brno Beseda in 1888, *Hudební listy* ceased publication). In the first number, Janáček pledged to publish substantial and impartial reviews of opera and theatre (writing most of the opera reviews himself), while also promising essays on the history and theory of music, reviews of new publications and items of musical news. In the first year, Janáček wrote at length about Wagner's *Tristan und Isolde*, as well as reviews of performances at the Brno theatre, including Smetana's *The Bartered Bride* and *The Kiss*, Johann Strauss's *Die Fledermaus*, Suppé's *Boccaccio*, Verdi's *Il Trovatore* and *La Traviata*, Gounod's *Faust*, Weber's *Der Freischütz* and Blodek's *In the Well*. In the second year, Janáček reviewed Dvořák's *The Cunning Peasant*, and on 24 February 1886 he launched a tirade against the theatre's management: 'Complete stagnation at our opera house! No point in speaking about such a desert. Instead let me put forward a few brief thoughts about the Czech theatre in Brno.' He first attacked the obtrusive prompter (a 'barbarism') and then turned to the orchestra: 'The basis of an opera company is a good orchestra and a good chorus. ... To give a modern opera, in which every instrument takes part in the dramatic action, without a complete orchestra is not only ridiculous but is an invitation to ruin the audience's taste.' Janáček was also worried about unduly safe repertoire: 'Above all, it is necessary to pay attention to modern works, and especially those composed here at home ... the repertoire should include operas of all tendencies, styles and eras.' On 15 January 1887, Janáček wrote a sarcastic review of Karel Kovařovic's opera

The Bridegrooms: 'Which tune has stuck in your mind? Which motif at least?' (XV/70). Kovařovic* did not forget Janáček's comments, and this review might have been one of the reasons for Kovařovic's later reluctance to accept *Jenůfa* at the Prague NT. In the final number of *Hudební listy*, Janáček again called for a better orchestra, equipped with better instruments, and he encouraged the formation of a society to promote chamber music. *Hudební listy* provides an insight into Janáček's thinking about opera when he was composing *Šárka*. It includes early articles about his understanding of harmony and form, and reveals him as a plain-speaking critic. The complete journal is available free to download from Editio Janáček. *HudLis, JAWO, JYL1, ZemEss.*

Hudební matice and its successors The principal Czech publisher of Janáček's music, nationalised in 1950, later privatised and now Bärenreiter Prague. Founded in Prague in 1871, its first publication was Smetana's *The Bartered Bride* (1872). In 1907 Umělecká beseda established a foundation for its music-publishing activity under the name Hudební matice Umělecké besedy (HMUB). In May 1917, it issued the second edition of the vocal score of *Jenůfa** with a piano reduction by the firm's director, Otakar Nebuška*. Meanwhile, Nebuška had been pressing ahead with plans to publish *The Excursion of Mr Brouček to the Moon*, and proofs of the first two acts had been engraved in January 1917. At this point, Janáček withdrew the opera's Epilogue for revisions and promised a new version 'soon', which never materialised. In the end, plans foundered, and *Brouček*, now comprising two Excursions, was issued by UE in 1919. Despite Nebuška's efforts, by the time the Czechoslovak Republic was proclaimed on 28 October 1918 the firm had just one Janáček work in its catalogue: the vocal score of *Jenůfa*.

On 5 February 1921, Nebuška wrote to Janáček with a proposal to publish some choruses and other compositions. A few weeks later, on 22 March 1921, Nebuška asked about three specific works: *The Diary of One Who Disappeared*, the Violin Sonata and *Fairy Tale*. Janáček invited a representative of HMUB to come to the premiere of the *Diary* on 18 April 1921, but nobody came, so he gave the work to Pazdírek in Brno instead. He signed an agreement in April 1921 for the works that eventually became the *26 Folk Ballads* (see Folk Ballads*), and the following month he agreed to the publication of choruses including *Halfar the Schoolmaster**, *The Seventy Thousand**, *The Czech Legion**, *The Wolf's Trail**, *Kašpar Rucký** and the *Hradčany Songs**, and asked for a quick decision about the Violin Sonata. By 9 December 1921, he was becoming impatient: 'What's up with the Violin Sonata? They are asking me about it at the Prague Conservatory. Will it be printed by the end of February 1922?' HMUB finally began to issue its newly acquired Janáček pieces in March 1922, starting with the Sonata for Violin and Piano* and the first two parts of the *26 Folk Ballads* – the beginning of a steady stream of publications. For Janáček's seventieth birthday, the firm issued Max Brod's biography in March, followed by the *Fairy Tale** and *I. X. 1905** later in the year. Though Nebuška continued to work for the firm, the publishing programme was directed from 1924 onwards by Václav Mikota (the elder brother of Jan Mikota), who remained long after its nationalisation in 1950. Internal documents (published in Lána 2017) show that in 1924–5, Mikota sought further reforms in order to keep the firm solvent and active. Janáček editions continued to appear, including *Taras Bulba** (arranged

91

for piano duet by Bakala) in March 1925, the String Quartet No. 1* and *Youth**
in April, and *The Wandering Madman** in June. The *Concertino** followed in
January 1926. The full score of *Taras Bulba** appeared near the end of 1927
and the *Lachian Dances** were published in August 1928. Thanks to Oldřich
Lána's research (2017), it is possible to see how HMUB's Janáček editions sold,
based on the royalty statements Mikota compiled for Janáček up to 1927. The
Violin Sonata was much the most successful chamber work, with healthy sales
of 359 copies. The *Hradčany Songs* sold well (513 parts, 124 scores), as did *The
Seventy Thousand* (296 parts, 211 scores) and *Halfar the Schoolmaster* (396 parts,
149 scores). Others were disappointing: the piano duet arrangement of *Taras
Bulba* sold a mere 50 copies between 1925 and 1927, even though it was the
only available version, and two choruses (which, after all, sell in multiple copies)
had dismal sales: 58 copies of *Kašpar Rucký* and 57 copies of *The Wandering
Madman*. Some works that Janáček had signed over to HMUB did not appear
for many years. With *The Czech Legion* there was regular correspondence and
even a meeting (in November 1923) to discuss changes prior to publication, but
it was ninety years later when it finally appeared in print in SKV C/2 (2011).

HMUB operated not only as Janáček's publisher but also put on concerts,
secured state subsidies for international travel (including the London visit in
1926*), administered royalties and served as the principal promoter for his
music in Czechoslovakia and abroad. With the Czech Philharmonic, the firm
organised the grandest of the seventieth birthday concerts for Janáček on 8
December 1924 in the Smetana Hall (see Masaryk, Tomáš Garrigue*).

After Janáček's death, HMUB continued to issue works for the first time,
of which the most important were *Amarus** (vocal score by Nebuška) and the
String Quartet No. 2*, both in 1938. It also published new editions of several
works, including *Jenůfa* in 1934 (edited by Vladimír Helfert) and *Taras Bulba* in
1947 (edited by Otakar Šourek), which were among the first attempts at critical-
practical editions of works by Janáček (see Editions, Critical and Scholarly*). In
1950 HMUB was nationalised and merged with the state-owned Orbis. From
1953 to 1960, its activities were under the aegis of the SNKLHU, its music
department still headed by Václav Mikota. On 1 January 1961, it became the
Státní hudenbí vydavatelství (State music publishers) and in 1967 this was
renamed Editio Supraphon, the name under which it continued to operate until
1989. After the Velvet Revolution, the firm was returned to private ownership.
Following a protracted privatisation process, it was acquired by Bärenreiter,
Kassel and renamed Bärenreiter Prague. Links between Editio Supraphon and
Bärenreiter had already been close thanks to joint publication of the Janáček
Complete Edition (SKV), and the firm became part of the Bärenreiter group in
1999. *FELJ, JAWO, KLJ, LánJan, SkaSed, ŽeňHud.*

Hudební rozhledy, the title of two different Czech musical periodicals. The
first *Hudební* ('Musical perspectives' or 'Musical views') was one of the journals
published by Oldřich Pazdírek in Brno between 1924 and 1928 (the other was
*Hudební besídka**). It was edited by Vladimír Helfert*, who was joined by Ludvík
Kundera* from Vol. 2 (1925–6). *Hudební rozhledy* was an energetic advocate of
Janáček's music, and Vol. 1, Nos. 3–4 (15 November 1924) was a special number
to celebrate Janáček's seventieth birthday. It included personal reminiscences
by František Mareš, Ferdinand Vach* and Karel Sázavský. František Waic wrote

on the choruses for the PSMU, Jaroslav Kvapil* on Janáček's teaching at the Organ School, Václav Kaprál on Janáček's choral technique and his approach to opera, Ludvík Kundera on the piano works, Osvald Chlubna* on orchestration and theoretical writings, Otakar Nováček on speech melodies, and Josef Černík on Janáček's theory of composition. Helfert wrote on *Šárka* and reviewed Brod's biography. In Vol. 3 (1926–7), Kundera wrote about *The Makropulos Affair* (Nos. 2 and 3), and the leading article in Vol. 3, No. 7 (April 1927) was a review of 'Janáček's new works': Kundera on the *Nursery Rhymes* and Helfert on the *Sinfonietta*. *Hudební rozhledy* published Adolf Veselý's 'Last interview with Leoš Janáček' in November 1928 (Vol. 4, Nos. 4–8).

In October 1948, a completely different journal called *Hudební rozhledy* began publication in Prague (its first issue had Janáček on the front cover) and has continued to the present day. It also published books, including Bohumír Štědroň's *Dílo Leoše Janáčka* (1959), *Leoš Janáček: Sborník statí a studii* (1959, a collection of essays by Josef Stanislav, František Pala, Jan Šmolík and Josef Veselka) and *Leoš Janáček a soudoba hudba* (1963, the proceedings of the 1958 international Janáček conference in Brno).

Hukvaldy, village in Moravian-Silesian region, 30 km (18 miles) south of Ostrava in the Beskydy hills. Hukvaldy is where Janáček was born on 3 July 1854 and where he succumbed to his final illness in August 1928. It is dominated from above by the ruins of a thirteenth-century castle. The village itself includes the former palace of the Archbishops of Olomouc that now houses local government offices. Janáček's father Jiří was appointed schoolmaster at Hukvaldy in 1848, where he worked and raised his large family in near poverty (the salary of a Hukvaldy teacher was among the lowest in the region). He died in 1866 after several years of ill health. Janáček visited Hukvaldy in 1881 to introduce his fiancée Zdenka to his mother (who died in 1884), but he appears not to have visited again until 1888.

Janáček's sister Josefa taught needlework at the school from 1876 to 1892, but she was not able to put her brother up for a long stay when he visited in 1888. He rented a room in the house of Vincenc Sládek, and over the years the Sládeks and Janáčeks developed a close friendship. Vincenc Sládek (1865–1944) worked as a gamekeeper in the local forest, married to Antonie. Sládek's brother Jan was a shoemaker who also worked as a guide at Hukvaldy castle. Janáček and his daughter Olga were particularly fond of Vincenc and Antonie Sládek's children, Vincenc (Vincek) and Ludmila (Lidka), and Janáček noted down their speech melodies. When Janáček stayed with the Sládeks in the winter of 1904, he heard about the recent death of Alžběta Gygarová, a little girl who had lived across the road from them. Rumour had it that Alžběta had been beaten to death by her father, and Janáček's account of her short life (and her speech melodies notated on a previous visit) became one of his most remarkable articles, 'Alžběta' (1907, XV/189). As Procházková and Volný point out, the official record gives Alžběta's cause of death as a blocked intestine.

Thanks to the local brewing family of Joseph Jung, and his wife Marie Jungová (see Jungová, Marie*), Janáček was introduced to local folk musicians on visits to Hukvaldy from 1888 and throughout the 1890s, and Olga Janáčková became friends with Marie, Ema and Františka, the granddaughters of Joseph and Marie Jung. The family took a leading role in the cultural life of the

6. *Ukvalská lidová poezie v písních* [*Hukvaldy Folk Poetry in Songs*], first edition, published by A. Píša, Brno, 1899.

village and sang in 'The Circle Under the Acacia', the group to whom Janáček dedicated his *Hukvaldy Folk Poetry in Songs* (V/4) in 1898. The group met on the open ground near the church, where benches under the acacia trees made for an agreeable spot to sing.

The schoolhouse in which Janáček was born is located near the centre of the village (see Dwellings*). Nearby is the church of St Maximilian (built 1759–69),

7. Hukvaldy, 'Birthplace of the master Dr Leoš Janáček', including views of the castle, the church and the schoolhouse where Janáček was born. Postcard dated 1934.

where Janáček first played the organ. Janáček transcribed two folksongs about the 'little church in Hukvaldy', and arranged both tunes in *Hukvaldy Folk Poetry in Songs*. The cottage Janáček bought from his sister-in-law in 1921, and where he spent much of his time away from Brno in his later years, is now the Leoš Janáček Memorial (Památník Leoše Janáčka, see Dwellings*).

When *The Cunning Little Vixen* had its first performance on 6 November 1924, 'The Circle Under the Acacia' sent congratulations, and Janáček wrote to his old friend Marie Jungová on 9 November: 'I am sure you were close at hand when The Circle Under the Acacia remembered me on the occasion of *The Cunning Little Vixen*. Please extend my respectful thanks to all! There is so much for which I owe thanks to Hukvaldy.'

At the top of the village square, a stone gateway serves as the entrance to parkland below Hukvaldy Castle. A short walk through the park leads to the most endearing Janáček memorial: a bronze statue of Vixen Bystrouška by Karel Vávra (1914–82) installed on 20 June 1959. The statue was stolen two months later and replaced in 1962. In 2015 it was stolen again and the replacement (by Adam Krhánek) was unveiled at a ceremony in April 2016, at which folksongs were performed by a children's choir and fanfares were played on a pair of hunting horns. *ProVol, TyrInt.*

Idyll [*Idylla, Idyla*], for string instruments (VI/3). The autograph manuscript of Janáček's *Idyll* for strings is dated 31 July 1878–29 August 1878. It was started during a visit to the Steinmeyer organ factory at Oettingen in Bavaria. All seven movements except the Scherzo were completed by 24 August. The Scherzo was finished in Prague on 29 August, when it was inserted as the sixth movement, with the Moderato now placed seventh and last. On 15 December 1878, the *Idyll* was performed at a concert of the Brno Beseda conducted by Janáček. A review in *Moravská orlice* by Berthold Žalud* (20 December 1878) noted that Janáček's melodies were 'becoming more folkish, the harmonies more original and his composition in general more transparent'. Janáček conducted the *Idyll* again at the Beseda on 12 December 1880. The score and parts were kept in the archive of the Beseda, and in 1907 Cyril Metod Hrazdira borrowed them for a performance. It seems he didn't return the material, and the work was finally tracked down by Helfert in 1937. Orbis published it in 1951. A critical edition appeared as SKVEJ D/1–2 (2003). While still very much a work of Janáček's youth, with a clear debt to Dvořák, the *Idyll* shows, as Svatava Přibáňová put it, 'the first inklings of an emerging voice'. *JAWO, Přídy.*

Images of Janáček The Janáček iconography is particularly rich in photographs, paintings, sculptures and drawings. Published Janáček iconographies include Bohumír Štědroň's *Leoš Janáček v obrazech* (1958), Theodora Straková's *Iconographia janáčkiána* (1975) and Svatava Přibáňová and Jiří Zahrádka's *Leoš Janáček ve fotografiích* (2008). Caricatures and graphic works are reproduced in Libuše Janáčková's *Leoš Janáček a Lidové noviny* (2014). The first book to include extensive photographs and illustrations was Adolph Veselý's *Leoš Janáček: pohled do života i díla* (1924), and there are sixty pages of plates in Daniel Müller's *Janáček* (1930).

1. *Photographs.* The most extensive pictorial representations of Janáček are in photographs. There are 241 of them, taken between 1874 and 1928, in Přibáňová and Zahrádka, a comprehensive collection, superbly reproduced. They range from portraits to informal snapshots, showing Janáček alone, with family and friends, and even with his dogs, Čert (No. 53) and Čipera (No. 68). They document his visits abroad (to Venice, London, Frankfurt and Berlin), as well as to Luhačovice, Písek and Prague. These photographs are a precious source of information about Janáček's changing appearance, his friends and his travels.

2. *Paintings.* Three oil portraits of Janáček date from opposite ends of his career. The first was painted in 1881 by Josef Ladislav Šichan (1847–1918) with a companion portrait of Zdenka, both done at the time of their wedding (at which Šichan was the best man).

In 1926 Gustav Böhm (1885–1974) painted a large oil portrait of Janáček (now in the Leoš Janáček Memorial in Brno). Böhm had been in friendly contact with the composer for several years. His portrait was probably started in February 1926, but on 24 May Janáček wrote asking him to delay further work as he was about to go to London and suggested that Böhm might finish the portrait in June.

František Ondrúšek (1861–1932) made his first portrait of Janáček (a pastel study of him standing) at Hukvaldy in June 1926. In February 1927, Janáček sat for a second portrait (seated) at the artist's home in Bystřice pod Hostýnem. He wrote to Zdenka on 11 February: 'I'm doing well with Mr Ondrúšek. His work is good.' This portrait now belongs to the Brno Conservatory, and there is a preliminary sketch in the Janáček Archive.

A painting called *At Stopka's* [*U Stopků*] by A. Kalvoda (either Alois or Antonín Kalvoda) used to hang in Stopka's Pilsner pub at Česká No. 5. This group portrait depicted Janáček, Břetislav Bakala, Jiří Mahen, Bohumil Holub and Alois Mrštík gathered around a table, talking over beers. When Stopka's was restored, the painting disappeared and the only surviving evidence for it is an undated newspaper reproduction in the Janáček Archive.

3. *Sculptures*. Of the numerous Janáček sculptures, statues and reliefs in Brno, Prague, Olomouc, Hukvaldy and elsewhere, the outstanding example is the bronze bust by Jan Štursa (1880–1925), one of the leading Czech sculptors of the time. He was in touch with Janáček on 15 September 1924 to arrange a sitting four days later, writing that 'we could possibly start immediately if it's convenient for you'. Commissioned for the National Theatre in Brno, Štursa's sculpture was one of his last works, as in May 1925 he committed suicide. Janáček was present when it was unveiled in the foyer of the Mahen Theatre on 24 January 1926. Štursa's sculpture is now in the entrance hall of JAMU.

Emil Hlavica (1887–1952) was a member of the KPU. He designed at least two different plaques of Janáček: one (facing left) is illustrated in Janáček's autobiography so must date from 1924 or earlier; the other (facing right) is dated 1926. Hlavica also designed a bust that stands in the National Park in Štramberk, near Nový Jičín. It was unveiled on 3 July 1927 and is a handsome memorial, set on a plinth in a stone gazebo. In 1971 Hlavica's original was moved to the museum in Nový Jičín and replaced by a replica.

In terms of sheer size, no statue of Janáček can compete with the large bronze (4 m/13 ft high) on the piazza of the Janáček Theatre in Brno. Designed by Stanislav Hanzl and installed in 1975, this monumental work shows the composer standing in an overcoat. Inside the theatre, there is a bronze bust of Janáček by Miloš Axman (1962) installed in the theatre when it opened in 1965.

4. *Drawings, Caricatures and Graphic Art*. Janáček's striking physical features, including his mane of white hair, made him a good subject for caricaturists. *Lidové noviny* was a newspaper that included numerous illustrations, and several caricatures of Janáček appeared in its pages between 1919 and 1928, drawn by Eduard Milén*, Hugo Boettinger ('Dr Desiderius', 1880–1934) and Ondřej Sekora (1889–1967). The most famous of them is the pen-and-ink drawing by Milén used on the front page of *Lidové noviny* on 13 August 1928, which announced Janáček's death. Drawings of Janáček for other publications include Boettinger's cartoon of Janáček sitting on a cloud with a choir of angels for J. L. Budin's *Muzikantské dušičky* (Prague, 1922) and Sekora's caricature showing Janáček in a bowler hat and coat for *Hudební rozhledy* (15 December 1926). The Brno artist Helena Bochořáková-Dittrichová (1894–1980) was influenced by Frans Masereel, and her graphic novel *Z mého dětství* was published in 1929. The Moravian Gallery in Brno has two prints by her of Janáček, both undated: one of him in profile, and a linocut of him seated.

5. *Film*. Two very short films are known of Janáček. One shows him in Prague and is unpublished. The other shows him on a steamboat trip during the Prague ISCM Festival in May 1925. According to Přibáňová and Zahrádka, this film was shot at the request of Maria Calma-Veselá, who can be seen wearing a wide-brimmed hat being greeted by Janáček. It was published in *Leoš Janáček: dokument o životě a díle*, directed by Jaromil Jireš (Supraphon 140041-2, VHS tape). The best-known feature film about Janáček's life is also directed by Jireš: *Lev s bílou hřívou* (The Lion with a White Mane) was released in 1986 and published on DVD by Bontonfilm (D005568).

6. *Stamps, Coins and Medals*. Janáček has featured several times on Czech postage stamps. The first stamp was after a design by Karel Svolinský with a face value of 1.60 Kč, issued on 19 June 1953. A year later, on 22 May 1954, a new Janáček stamp using a different design by Svolinský (with a value of 40 h)

Když se L. Janáček vracel z pražského výletu na měsíc:

(vysl. v 0·99"
H. Ch.*

jedu spiclavou...

8. Ondřej Sekora: 'When Leoš Janáček returned from the Prague *Excursion to the Moon'*, cartoon in *Hudební rozhledy*, 15 December 1926.

was issued to celebrate the Year of Czech Music as one of a set of three that also included Dvořák and Smetana. On 26 November 1982, Janáček appeared on a stamp with a face value of 4.40 Kč, a depiction of the bust by Miloš Axman. Janáček was featured on a Czech Republic stamp in 2004, in a set showing Czech operas: Smetana's *Dalibor*, Dvořák's *Jacobin* and Janáček's *Jenůfa* (10 Kč).

In 2004 the Czech National Bank issued a 200 Kč silver coin to mark the 150th anniversary of Janáček's birth, designed by Jiří Věneček. Janáček also appeared on a bronze medal designed by Václav Adolf Kovanič in 1958 to mark the 30th anniversary of the composer's death. *IcoJan, JanLid, JYL2, MülJan, PřiZah, StěObr, VesJan.*

In the Mists [*V mlhách*], for piano (VIII/22). The inspiration for *In the Mists* may have been a recital organised by Janáček at the Brno Organ School on 28 January 1912, when Marie Dvořáková played Debussy's *Reflets dans l'eau* and *Doctor Gradus ad Parnassum*. *In the Mists* certainly shows the influence of Debussy, though it is also a nostalgic reflection of Janáček's childhood. On 21 April 1912, Janáček sent a manuscript of the work to Jan Branberger, asking if he would review it in the magazine *Čas* (an article by Jindřich Pihert duly appeared in the 5 December 1912 issue). Later the same year, Janáček sent a copy to Karel Hoffmeister, who had been asked by the KPU to judge a competition for a new work. Hoffmeister returned the manuscript on 25 November 1912, and Janáček made revisions before publication by the KPU a year later, presented to Club members as a gift for the year 1913. In correspondence with Branberger, Janáček gave the title as *Mhy* (*Mists*), but on an early authorised copy *Mhy* has been crossed out by Janáček and replaced with *V mlhách*.

The premiere was given by Marie Dvořáková* on 7 December 1913 at Kroměříž. She played it in Brno on 24 January 1914, at an Organ School concert in the Lužánky Hall attended by Janáček. The first known performance in Prague was not until 16 December 1922, when it was played by Václav Štěpán.

In February 1923, HMUB approached Janáček about publishing a new edition, and Štěpán prepared the revised text according to the composer's instructions. Janáček made final changes himself and was grateful to Štěpán for his careful addition of performance instructions and pedal markings. This revised edition, based on the original plates with alterations, was published in 1924 and includes an important revision in the last movement (bars 117–124). *In the Mists* was included in SKV F/1 (1978), and a critical edition by Jiří Zahrádka was published by Henle in 2016. A facsimile of the autograph manuscript of the fourth movement was published by the Moravian Museum in 1998. *JAWO, ŠtěMlh, ZahMlh, WinMlh.*

ISCM (International Society for Contemporary Music) Festivals The ISCM was founded in 1922 to promote contemporary music, with Edward J. Dent as its president and an international jury whose membership changed from year to year. The first ISCM Festival took place at Salzburg in 1923. On 5 August 1923, the Sonata for Violin and Piano* was played by Stanislav Novák and Václav Štěpán with Janáček present. He was the oldest composer on that year's programme, but it was the first time he had been to an international chamber music festival. The Violin Sonata was well received: as he wrote to Rosa Newmarch on 13 August, 'I think they liked it. I travelled to Salzburg and met many important people from the musical world' (those present included Berg, Schoenberg, Prokofiev, Szymanowski, Poulenc, Kodály and Hindemith). The 1925 Festival was in two parts: in Prague (May) and in Venice (September). Janáček was represented by the Prague premiere of *The Cunning Little Vixen* (18 May), and in Venice the Czechoslovak Quartet played the String Quartet No. 1* (4 September). He went to Venice with his wife Zdenka (a rare trip abroad together) and enjoyed the visit, writing about it in 'Basta!' (*Lidové noviny*, 8 November 1925, XV/281). The 1927 Festival was in Frankfurt, and the *Concertino** was played by Ilona Štěpánová-Kurzová on 30 June. In an interview with *Literární svět* (8 March 1928), Janáček declared that 'International festivals deserve more attention here at home. ... We had a victory at the Frankfurt festival [with the *Concertino*] – and how tough it was. And let me tell you ... we shall keep trying.' *JYL2, ZemEss.*

Janáček Dome   **See Demänovská Freedom Cave**

Janáček Family
1. Wife and Children
Janáčková, Zdenka, née Schulzová (b. Olomouc, 30 July 1865; d. Brno, 17 February 1938), wife. Zdenka Schulzová moved to Brno in 1872 when her father Emilian Schulz became Director of the Teachers' Institute. In 1877 Janáček started giving her piano lessons, and she witnessed his early triumph conducting Beethoven's *Missa solemnis* at the Brno Beseda on 2 April 1879. When Janáček left to study in Leipzig in September 1879, he maintained close contact with her through letters (written in German) which give a minutely detailed account of his studies. In January 1880, he told her that she had inspired him to write his 'Zdenčileoš Fugue' (X/6, No. 14), declaring that 'I thought of you during the whole work and thereby we created it together'. Between 29 January

and 22 February, Janáček composed his *Theme and Variations* for piano (VIII/6), telling Zdenka that 'you'll like them, and should they ever be published, they will carry your dear name'.

The engagement of Janáček and Schulzová was formally announced on 1 July 1880. They were married a year later on 13 July 1881 – two weeks before the bride's sixteenth birthday – at the Augustinian Monastery. During their honeymoon they visited Dvořák in Prague. Back in Brno, the marriage soon began to unravel: Zdenka was frightened by Janáček's violent outbursts, and relations with his in-laws deteriorated. If anything, the birth of Olga in 1882 made matters worse. For a time they lived apart and divorce papers were drawn up (not for the last time). Once they were back together again, it was an uneasy truce. Zdenka and Olga visited Janáček at Luhačovice in 1886, but he largely ignored them, and Zdenka's discovery of an amorous note signed 'Marie' led to a confrontation. The birth of Vladimír in 1888 served as a distraction, but when he died at the age of two and a half, Janáček appeared to react coldly. In 1894 Marie Stejskalová came to work as the Janáčeks' housekeeper and remained until Zdenka's death in 1938. She proved to be a devoted companion in whom Zdenka could confide. After Olga's death in 1903, there was a brief reconciliation between Zdenka and Janáček. When Kovařovic rejected *Jenůfa* at the end of April 1903, Zdenka wrote in her memoirs: 'I couldn't bear that. However he'd behaved to me … I'd always believed in his mission as an artist, and I also believed in the beauty and the greatness of *Jenůfa*.' That summer Janáček met Kamila Urválková* in Luhačovice, and when Zdenka discovered Urválková's letters the inevitable cycle of confrontation, contrition and awkward silences began again.

On 2 July 1910, the Janáčeks moved into the new house in the grounds of the Organ School that was to be their home for the rest of their lives. Zdenka recalled 'a peaceful time full of contentment'. With her unshakable belief in her husband's talent, the acceptance of *Jenůfa* in Prague should have been a moment of shared triumph for them, but Janáček's infatuation with Gabriela Horvátová* put paid to that, and Zdenka's years of 'contentment' were over. Of all the women Janáček fell for, Horvátová was the one for whom Zdenka reserved her deepest resentment, seeing her as a philandering opportunist. In January 1917, at the height of his infatuation with Horvátová, divorce documents were drawn up again. Even before matters had cooled between Janáček and Horvátová, he had met Kamila Stösslová* in Luhačovice during his summer visit in 1917. This soon developed into a life-changing passion, but in spite of Janáček's obsessive involvement with Kamila, the relationship between Zdenka and Janáček remained on a relatively even keel over the next few years. She basked in the celebrations of his seventieth birthday and the award of his Honorary Doctorate from the Masaryk University in January 1925. After the Prague premiere of *The Cunning Little Vixen** on 18 May 1925, Janáček showed a tenderness that Zdenka hadn't experienced for decades and they returned to Brno in high spirits. She wrote: 'Suddenly there was a different atmosphere in the house: cheerfulness, brightness, intimacy.' For Zdenka this felt like a reconciliation, even if what had motivated Janáček in the first place was his irritation with Kamila for not turning up to the *Vixen* in Prague. In September 1925, Zdenka travelled with her husband to the ISCM Festival in Venice (stopping off in Písek to spend a night with the Stössels en route, an uncomfortable experience for Zdenka). She also travelled with him to Berlin for *Káťa Kabanová* in 1926. When Zdenka wanted to decorate their home in April 1927, she took a decision that she later called a 'mistake which I'll always regret'. To get Janáček out of the house while the painting was done, she decided to send him off to the Stössels in Písek. After Janáček's return, Zdenka found a stash of letters from Kamila in his study. It was, she said, 'as if someone had thrust a knife into me'.

Still Zdenka didn't give up the fight. They had a blazing row on New Year's Day 1928, when Janáček announced that he was off to Prague and then spending a few days in Písek. In April she wrote in her memoirs that 'for me it was now certain that Leoš's relationship with Mrs Stösslová was fateful for us', and added that her greatest concern was the damage Stösslová might do to his reputation. In July 1928, Janáček announced to Zdenka that he would be going to Hukvaldy with Kamila, and with reckless insensitivity the date he chose to leave was 30 July, Zdenka's birthday. As Kamila waited for him at the station, Janáček's last conversation with his wife was recorded in her memoirs: 'I turned my head away: "Must it be so?" "It can be and it must be." He kissed me vigorously and left.' When Zdenka heard the news of Janáček's death at a sanatorium in Ostrava, she rushed there only to find that he'd already been moved to the mortuary. She blamed his death on the 'frivolous and thoughtless' Kamila 'who had every quality other than what was needed to nurse a sick man'.

It's hard not to feel a great deal of sympathy for Zdenka. In 1935 she embarked on her memoirs, with Marie Trkanová as her amanuensis. Though written from her own viewpoint, they are largely accurate, apart from playing down the importance of Kamila Stösslová in Janáček's final decade. Zdenka's treatment of her husband's legacy was, as John Tyrrell put it, 'largely benevolent', and she was never in any doubt about his value as a composer. For almost half a century she provided Janáček with unwavering loyalty, a well-run home and the stability he needed to compose. *JYL1, JYL2, MLWJ, PřiThe, ZemJan.*

Janáčková, Olga (b. Brno, 15 August 1882; d. Brno, 26 February 1903), daughter. During the last stages of her pregnancy, Zdenka had to oversee the move into a new flat in 2 Monastery Square (Klášterní náměstí), but when she went into labour she stayed with her parents. Janáček celebrated the news of Olga's birth at a banquet in the Augustinian Monastery, but it was only after one of the priests took him to task that he went to visit his wife and daughter. The marriage between Janáček and Zdenka was at a low point when Olga was born, and she spent much of her infancy in the home of Zdenka's parents. As Janáček and Zdenka's relationship began to improve, he started to visit, but Zdenka recalled that he 'did not know what to say' to his young daughter. As Olga started to grow up, Janáček's feelings changed markedly, and her cheerful presence around the house helped to keep the peace between her parents. She particularly loved visits to Hukvaldy, and confided to Josefa Jungová on 2 December 1897: 'Whenever I remember Hukvaldy here in Brno, I always feel so depressed that I can't live there forever. Only there, amid sincere people, am I always happy. Here there is nothing but hypocrisy.'

Olga aged eighteen was described by her mother as 'slender, quite tall, with exquisite small hands and feet … kind, natural and cheerful'. She was also successful at managing her squabbling parents (see Vítězslav Novák* for details of his witnessing this in 1900). Olga did very well at school, but left at sixteen, partly because of her precarious health. She had already demonstrated a gift for languages, and after leaving school she continued to study Russian (with Janáček's approval). Like her father, Olga was an enthusiastic member of the Brno Russian Circle. She began an intense relationship with Otakar Vorel, a medical student training in Vienna. Zdenka and Janáček both disapproved, but Olga and Vorel decided they would marry as soon as he qualified. Olga's parents insisted that all contact should cease, but Marie Stejskalová helped to arrange clandestine meetings, and in September 1900 Olga even managed to smuggle Vorel off to Hukvaldy. By the time she went to Russia in 1902, the relationship was over. Accompanied by Janáček (who returned a few days later), Olga went to St Petersburg in March 1902. In mid-April Janáček told her that he was working on Act II of *Jenůfa*. At the end of April, she fell ill with typhoid fever and made a slow recovery, followed by a relapse in June. Both parents rushed to St Petersburg, and Zdenka remained. Several weeks later, Olga was allowed to travel and Janáček met them in Warsaw. The plan was to take her to Hukvaldy, but her condition deteriorated on the journey and the family went straight to Brno. Olga was suffering from chronic rheumatic heart disease. Her bed was moved into Janáček's study. Beautiful, clever and headstrong, Olga knew she was dying. In heartbreaking scenes described by Zdenka, Olga asked to hear her father's new opera: 'Daddy, play *Jenůfa* for me. I won't live to hear it.' On 22 January 1903, Olga asked for the Last Rites. Janáček wrote down the words of his dying daughter during the last two days of her life, a document of unbearable poignancy. Olga died early in the morning (6.30 a.m.) on 26 February with the family kneeling at her bedside. Čert, the family dog, kept his own vigil, refusing to leave her room. The funeral took place on 28 February at the Augustinian Monastery, and Olga's coffin was taken to the Central Cemetery. The next day, a Sunday, Janáček and Zdenka visited her grave together for the first and only time: after that visit Janáček always insisted on going by himself. He dedicated three works to her: the song 'Uncertainty' ['Nejistota'] (No. 28 from *Moravian Folk Poetry in Songs** V/2) on the autograph manuscript in 1896, the *Elegy on the Death of my Daughter Olga** and *Jenůfa**, her most enduring memorial. *JYL1, MLWJ, PřiThe, ZemJan.*

Janáček, Vladimír (b. Brno, 16 May 1888; d. Brno, 9 November 1890), son. Vladimír was, according to Zdenka, 'the pride of his father'. She described him as having 'dark eyes after Leoš, golden-haired, dark eyebrows, lovely white skin – an exquisite child. He was always high-spirited, he laughed and sang the whole day long.' He was talking fluently at the age of two and a half, and his devoted father was quick to spot signs of musical promise, delighted that he sang in tune and showed an interest in the piano. Zdenka quoted Janáček saying to him: 'My boy, you'll be a musician.' Vladimír succumbed to scarlet fever in October 1890 and meningitis followed. His sister Olga was inconsolable and Zdenka grieved for a long time afterwards. Janáček's reaction was more complex: he wouldn't talk about his son, and refused to visit Vladimír's grave with Zdenka. Years later, in his autobiography, he wrote that '*Jenůfa* will be bound with a black ribbon to commemorate the long illness, pain and cries of my daughter Olga and my little boy Vladimír.' *JYL1, MLWJ, ZemJan.*

2. Parents

Janáček, Jiří (b. Albrechtičky, near Nový Jičín, 4 October 1815; d. Hukvaldy, 8 March 1866), father. Jiří completed his preparatory training as a teacher in

Příbor and took up his first post in August 1831 at Neplachovice, near Opava. Though he only stayed in this post for a year, one of his pupils was Pavel Křížkovský*, who never forgot the fatherly support his teacher gave him (in 1865 he was able to reciprocate by taking Jiří's eleven-year-old son into the choir of the Augustinian Monastery). Jiří married Amalie Grulichová on 24 July 1838 in Příbor. He was appointed to the school at Hukvaldy in June 1848 and remained there for the rest of his life. In 1858 Jiří's health deteriorated and he was unable to continue full-time teaching (one of his assistants was his son Karel). Despite living in humble circumstances, Jiří was a fine musician who made sure his children had a good musical education. Janáček was taught at the village school and his father also gave him piano lessons. In 1926, at a ceremony to unveil a plaque on his birthplace, Janáček recalled his earliest musical education: 'Just what did he [Jiří] want to make of me back then? ... I, a boy of eight, took on many Beethoven sonatas at the old piano.' Jiří's lessons were strict, but as Janáček said in his speech: 'I forgive him everything, and I've never had bad memories of Beethoven either.' His father died a few months after Janáček started school in Brno. *JYL1, ProVol.*

Janáčková, Amalie, née Grulichová (b. Příbor, 13 April 1819; d. Hukvaldy, 16 November 1884), mother. Amalie Grulichová was the daughter of Karel Grulich, a tailor in Příbor. She married Jiří Janáček on 24 July 1838. Like her husband, she was a musician who sang and played the guitar and organ. According to Procházková and Volný, Amalie was 'remembered as a small woman, strict and demanding, but good-natured'. After her husband's death, Amalie moved back to her family in Příbor and suffered a tragedy in April 1868 when her daughter Rosalie died. Janáček visited her in 1869, and a decade later she seems to have been living in Brno, receiving financial support from Janáček and his brothers. Janáček apparently promised his mother that she could come to live with him and Zdenka, but in December 1881 Amalie wrote: 'You mustn't worry that you'll ever see me in Brno, for with a bleeding heart I have left Brno for ever.' Many years later, Janáček blamed Zdenka for refusing to give his mother a home. By December 1882, Amalie was living with her daughter Eleonora in Švábenice. In 1884 she developed stomach cancer and in October that year she moved to Hukvaldy to be with her daughter Josefa. Shortly before Amalie died, Josefa wrote to Janáček: 'Please, when I let you know of her death, come to the funeral. It's mother's only wish as you're still her special favourite.' Janáček did not attend her funeral. She was buried in Rychaltice. *JYL1, ProVol.*

3. Siblings

Janáček's siblings who survived were Viktorie (1838–94), Eleonora (1840–1919), Josefa (1842–1931), Karel (1844–1919), Bedřich (1846–1918), Rosalie (1850–68), František (1856–1908) and Josef (1858–1941).

Eleonora was greatly liked by Zdenka, who found her sister-in-law to be 'gentle, kind and attentive ... always a welcome guest'. Known as 'Lorka', she was also Olga's favourite aunt. According to Zdenka, Eleonora often complained that [Janáček] 'didn't like her and it was clear they didn't get on'.

Josefa married Jindřich Dohnal (1868–1939) in 1892 (becoming Josefa Janáčková-Dohnalová) and moved with him to the Ostrava area before returning to Hukvaldy in 1901, when Dohnal became headteacher of the school. The marriage foundered and they were already separated (living on separate floors of the schoolhouse) when Janáček and Zdenka visited in 1915. In 1919 Josefa divorced Dohnal (who married one of his former pupils). In her memoirs, Zdenka recalled Josefa's fiery temperament, but later she saw in her a fellow sufferer: Josefa 'knew what marital infidelity felt like'. After Janáček purchased the Hukvaldy cottage in 1921, Josefa worked as his custodian and housekeeper.

František was the sibling to whom Janáček was closest. He trained as an engineer and moved to Gleiwitz in Silesia (now Gliwice, Poland), where he married Marie [Máša] Koziczińska in 1883. In 1895 they moved to St Petersburg, where Janáček visited in 1896 and Olga went in 1902. Owing to František's poor health, they moved back to Hukvaldy in 1905. Marie remained in the house after František's death. In 1921 she accepted Janáček's offer to buy the Hukvaldy house (see Dwellings*) and moved back to Poland. *JYL1, ProVol.*

Jealousy **(Prelude to *Jenůfa*)** [*Žárlivost* (Úvod k *Její pastorkyni*)] for orchestra (VI/10).   Originally conceived as a prelude to *Jenůfa*, *Jealousy* was composed by 31 December 1894 in a version for piano four-hands. After making some revisions, Janáček completed the orchestration by 16 February 1895. The first performance took place at the Rudolfinum in Prague on 14 November 1906, with the Czech Philharmonic conducted by František Neumann*. In his note on the work for *Dalibor* in 1906, Janáček gave the title as 'Úvod k *Její pastorkyni*' (Introduction to *Jenůfa*). In a later note for a concert in Brno on 13 October 1917, Janáček called the work 'Úvod k *Její pastorkyni – Žárlivost*'. It was played on that occasion by the visiting Prague NT orchestra, conducted by Karel Kovařovic*. The note Janáček wrote for this concert is misleading, as he quoted from the earlier version for duet which differs significantly from the orchestral version (presumably Kovařovic was using the only copy of the score). Janáček ended his note: 'The Prologue is tightly compact and is only an epigraph to *Jenůfa*. As to motifs, it is in no way linked with the opera.' The orchestration was retouched by Kovařovic, presumably for the Brno performance in 1917. His pencil alterations on Janáček's authorised copy were identified by Jiří Zahrádka*, who prepared a new edition of *Jealousy* for UE. The work was given without retouchings by the Brno Philharmonic under Jakub Hrůša on 18 September 2016. *Jealousy* was published by the Czech Music Fund in 1957 for hire only. A new edition, revised by Osvald Chlubna with an introduction by Theodora Straková, was issued in 1964. Straková drew attention to the quotation of 'Žárlivec' ['The Jealous Man'] from Sušil's 1860 collection of Moravian folksongs. Janáček had used it as the basis for his earlier chorus of the same name (IV/19, No. 3). Straková also argued that 'The connection between *Jealousy* and *Jenůfa* was much deeper than Janáček admitted', basing this on 'several identical motifs in *Jealousy*' and 'thematic sketches written in the libretto of *Jenůfa*'. Further evidence that Janáček considered it to be part of the opera – at least up to the point when *Jenůfa* was completed in 1903 – is that *Jealousy* was copied into the score of the whole work. *Jealousy* was never performed as the overture to the opera in Janáček's lifetime, but it was used for a 1959 production in Greiz (then in East Germany). On 9 June 1941, Břetislav Bakala* conducted extracts from the original version of *Jenůfa* for Brno Radio, beginning the broadcast with *Jealousy*. *JAWO, StěZur, StrŽár.*

Její pastorkyňa   See *Jenůfa* (I/4)

Jenůfa [*Její pastorkyňa*, literally 'Her Stepdaughter'], opera in three acts after the play of Moravian rural life by Gabriela Preissová (I/4). Composing *Jenůfa* was a long process, including a gap of four years between Acts I and II. The first contact between Janáček and Preissová about setting her play *Her Stepdaughter* [*Její pastorkyňa*] was in November 1893, renewing their contact from two years earlier, when Janáček had composed *The Beginning of a Romance**. Initially Preissová told Janáček (6 November 1893) that the play was 'not suitable for musical setting'. He seems to have talked her round, as there are extensive annotations on his copy of the play made between 18 March 1894 and 11 February 1895. Janáček first started work on *Jealousy**, originally planned as the overture, finishing its early version for piano four-hands on 31 December 1894. Progress was slow on Act I, which was probably finished in 1897, though there are no dates in the manuscript to confirm this. Marie Stejskalová, who had started to work for the Janáčeks in 1894, recalled Janáček beginning the opera, composing whenever time allowed: 'He seldom had time for it during the day, but devoted all his free evenings to it ... and while others went to sleep when they got home, he sat down to work. ... I brought a lamp into his study filled to the brim with paraffin and the next day I took it away empty. The mistress would look at it: "He's been writing through the whole night again." Sometimes it seemed to me that the master was battling with *Jenůfa*, as if he went into his study not to compose it but to have a fight with it.'

After completing Act I, Janáček put the opera to one side, turning his attention to other projects including *Amarus* (III/6) and the huge folksong collection with Bartoš, *Moravian Folksongs Newly Collected* (XIII/3). He took up *Jenůfa* again before the end of 1901 and finished Act II by summer 1902 (the copy of the vocal score is dated 8 July 1902). Stejskalová particularly remembered the composition of Jenůfa's Prayer in Act II and makes an intriguing comment on the role of the Kostelnička: 'That tough love of the Kostelnička – that's him. There is much of his own character in that part. When Oluška [Olga] got typhoid fever for the second time in Russia [April 1902], the master once came to me in the kitchen. "Máŕa, do you know the *Salve Regina*? I know the *Ave Maria* but I've forgotten this one.' I went to get my prayer book, and looked up the *Salve Regina* ['Zdrávas královno' in Czech]. The master took the book into the study and after a while I heard the beginning of the song (Jenůfa's Prayer) that has now gone around the world. People weep during it. I think this is because the master's heart so wept and bled when he wrote it.'

Composition of Act III coincided with Olga's final illness and death, a time of unbearable sadness in the household. On 26 February, a few days before Olga died, she asked her father to play through *Jenůfa*, because she would never hear it in the theatre. According to Stejskalová, after Janáček played it through to the end, he got up from the piano and Olga said to him: 'It's beautiful. What a pity I won't see it.' Given the circumstances in which the last two acts were composed, it was inevitable that Janáček would dedicate the work to his daughter's memory. On the first edition of the vocal score, one page has the inscription 'To the memory of Olga Janáčková'.

The first performance was given in the Veveří Theatre on 21 January 1904, conducted by Cyril Metoděj Hrazdira*. Despite being played by an orchestra that was far smaller than Janáček envisaged (and missing several instruments, including the harp and cor anglais), the opera was a great success in Brno.

Reviews by Brno critics were predictably positive (several were written by former pupils of the composer), but the most interesting reaction came from a Prague critic who attended the premiere. Emanuel Chvála (1851–1924) reviewed the opera for *Národní politika*, and this was reprinted in the Brno paper *Moravská orlice* on 28 January 1904. Noting that there was little in the way of conventional lyricism, Chvála felt that Janáček's approach was suited to the 'plasticity of the declamation' in Preissová's play. The use of a prose libretto has Chvála comparing *Jenůfa* to Charpentier's *Louise* – a parallel that must have delighted Janáček – and Chvála went on to say the opera's success 'was pervasive and increased from one act to the next'. He particularly admired the intensification of the drama during Act II, remarking that this 'visibly excited the audience'. Chvála's reaction is perceptive and fair-minded. Unlike some of the Brno reviews, it's not an unqualified rave (he has some qualms about Janáček's lack of conventional musical development), but this was a critic from Prague expending a good deal of space on a new opera that he clearly felt was worthwhile. Other Prague critics opted for the easier gambit of dismissing the work as being of merely local importance in Brno. Janáček's pupil Václav Kaprál recalled the euphoria of the occasion, and the lively discussion about *Jenůfa* among Janáček's students: 'We students occupied almost the entire gallery of the Old Theatre at Veveří and breathlessly watched the progress of the performance. Janáček was wildly applauded and after the performance he was carried on the shoulders of the soloists (as far as I remember they were still in costume) from the theatre to the Beseda House. The dramatic significance of the work was immense. From the musical point of view it made an impression of complete newness and divided us students into fervent upholders or fierce antagonists of its unusual style. At that time opera was judged according to the standards of Wagner, which made it impossible for staunch Wagnerites to be able to take music that was so completely opposed to Wagner in character. Janáček was able to suggest life and truth with great spontaneity. ... We held our ground, and proved to the Wagnerites that Janáček was an utterly different case, and therefore entirely right.'

As soon as *Jenůfa* was finished, in the spring of 1903, Janáček tried to interest the Prague NT in producing it. Its swift rejection was the first of many such rebuffs (see Kovařovic, Karel*). Janáček tried to interest other conductors in *Jenůfa* too: on 9 December 1904, Gustav Mahler, the conductor of the Vienna Hofoper, wrote to Janáček: 'Unfortunately it is impossible for me to leave here at the moment. But I would certainly be interested in getting to know the work, so I would ask if you could send me a vocal score with a German translation.' Sadly, Janáček couldn't, as there was no German libretto at the time. Before the opera was revived on 6 October 1906 (with Hrazdira again conducting), Janáček started a thorough revision and made cuts. After the 1906 performances, Janáček continued his revisions, completing the changes to Act II on 10 January 1907 (oddly enough, the only date to be found on the earliest copy of the full score that had been made several years earlier by Josef Stross). At a committee meeting of the KPU on 2 December 1907, it was decided that the Club would start to publish music. Janáček suggested that they might like to start with *Jenůfa* and by March 1908 finished copies were ready (see Brno: Club of the Friends of Art in Brno*).

Janáček became disheartened over the seemingly fruitless battle to have *Jenůfa* produced in Prague, but after the Brno revival in 1911 others, including influential figures in the KPU such as František Veselý*, took up the cause, with his wife Maria Calma-Veselá* and Josef Peška*. Eventually Kovařovic relented (see Kovařovic, Karel* for discussion of the acceptance of *Jenůfa* in Prague, and Kovařovic's changes). The Prague premiere on 26 May 1916 launched Janáček's international career, and even though it used Kovařovic's substantially reorchestrated version, this did nothing to dim Janáček's enthusiasm. The consequences of the Prague performance were far-reaching: Janáček found an energetic new supporter in Max Brod*, and through Brod he was taken up by UE in Vienna. UE issued a new vocal score in December 1917 that included Brod's German translation, following this in September 1918 with the full score.

On 1 February 1918, *Jenůfa* was given in German at the Vienna Hofoper, conducted by Hugo Reichenberger, with Maria Jeritza* in the title role. Between 1918 and Janáček's death in 1928, there were around seventy productions of *Jenůfa*, and it took its place in the repertoire of German and other European opera houses. It took longer to reach London: the British premiere was at the Royal Opera House on 10 December 1956, conducted by Rafael Kubelík*. Since then, it has been performed regularly all over the world. The new edition by Charles Mackerras* and John Tyrrell* of the 1908 version (the last revision Janáček made himself before publication of the Brno vocal score in 1908) introduced audiences to the sound of the opera as Janáček had intended, discarding Kovařovic's reorchestrations in favour of Janáček's own. This edition was not only true to Janáček's intentions, but it also revealed a work with greater sinew and rugged strength, closer to his later operas. Since the publication of the Mackerras and Tyrrell edition in 1996, it has become the version that is usually performed. On 15 May 2004, Warsaw Chamber Opera gave the first performance of the reconstructed 1904 version by Mark Audus (published by UE for hire only). This remarkable piece of reconstructive surgery marked another important step in the history of *Jenůfa*, enabling the work to be heard as it had been at the historic Brno premiere, before Janáček himself revised it.

Janáček said that including folksongs in *The Beginning of a Romance** had been a lapse of taste, and the search for authentic folk material in his next opera, *Jenůfa*, has long proved to be a red herring, despite the folkish elements such as the Recruits' Chorus in Act I. Other musical features are of far greater significance. In *Jenůfa* Janáček found his original operatic voice, evolving a style of vocal writing in which characters are sharply differentiated by the music they are given to sing, while much of the larger-scale musical argument is articulated by the orchestra. The orchestral colours are often arresting, not least the xylophone, and Janáček's harmony is far richer than in any earlier work (with sudden modulations used to heighten dramatic tension). Above all, *Jenůfa* is an opera of radiant lyricism, the expressiveness of Jenůfa's music set in even sharper relief by the belligerent writing for the Kostelnička. Janáček's other great achievement in *Jenůfa* is his perfecting of dramatic timing: the pacing of Act II, in particular, has a variety, sweep and intensity that make an overwhelming impact in the theatre. *AudJen, FELJ, GryKPU, JAWO, JODA, JYL1, ŠtěZur VogJan, ZahDiv.*

SYNOPSIS

Act I: The Buryja Mill, late afternoon. The opera opens with the clacking of the mill wheel, represented by a xylophone. Jenůfa is waiting anxiously to hear if her beloved Števa has been conscripted: she is carrying his child and her secret will soon be known. She is relieved to learn that he has not been called up, and so he will be able to marry her before the pregnancy becomes too obvious. Meanwhile, Laca – Števa's jealous half-brother – secretly loves Jenůfa. Števa staggers in drunk with the other recruits and they break into a rowdy dance. Jenůfa's stepmother, the Kostelnička (literally the 'village sacristan'), gives Števa an ultimatum: he can only marry Jenůfa if he abstains from drinking for a year. Jenůfa begs Števa to marry her as soon as possible. His drunken response is to tell her that she is prettiest of all the girls and that he loves her 'rosy-apple cheeks'. Grandmother Buryja sends him away to sleep off his drink. After Števa has gone, Laca seizes the chance to turn Jenůfa against Števa, taunting her with flowers that Števa had been given by one of his other female admirers. Jenůfa remains steadfast. Laca then tries to kiss her but she pushes him away. In a jealous rage, he slashes her cheek with a knife.

Act II: The Kostelnička's house, five months later. Winter. Everyone thinks Jenůfa has been sent away, but the Kostelnička has hidden her in her home, where she has given birth to a boy. Jenůfa loves the child, but the Kostelnička cannot bear the shame. She sends for Števa secretly and gives Jenůfa a sleeping potion. When Števa arrives, the Kostelnička tells him about the baby and begs him to marry Jenůfa. Števa refuses, as he has become engaged to Karolka, the Mayor's daughter. The Kostelnička then turns to Laca, who is only too happy to marry Jenůfa, but he is so distressed to hear about the baby that the Kostelnička sees lying as her only option: she tells Laca that the child has died. Worse still, she next turns this lie into a shocking reality: with the baby under her arm, she sets out for the millstream to drown him in the freezing water. Jenůfa wakes up as the Kostelnička returns. The Kostelnička tells her she has been in a fever for two days, during which the baby has died. She also tells her of Števa's forth-coming marriage, but Laca returns and offers to marry Jenůfa, insisting that he loves her. She agrees to become his wife. The Kostelnička is gripped by guilt at what she has done, and sees 'the icy hand of death, forcing its way in' as the wind blows the door open at the height of a storm.

Act III: Two months later. Spring. The marriage between Jenůfa and Laca is about to take place. The Mayor and his wife come to pay their respects. Laca tells Jenůfa that he has overcome his resentment for Števa and invited him to the wedding with his bride-to-be, Karolka. The village girls sing a song to Jenůfa, and Grandmother Buryja gives the couple her blessing. Just as the Kostelnička is about to bless them, there is a commotion outside: the body of a baby has been found in the thawing river. From the clothes the baby was wearing, Jenůfa realises that this must be her own child. The villagers turn on Jenůfa, assuming that she must have killed the baby. The Kostelnička confesses to her crime, begging the crowd not to blame Jenůfa. As the Kostelnička is led away to face her punishment, Jenůfa calls upon the villagers to forgive the Kostelnička just as she has. Jenůfa tells Laca that he is free to go, but he promises to stay with her forever. Moved by his devotion, Jenůfa realises that God has blessed their union.

Jeritza, Maria [Marie Jedličková] (b. Brno, 6 October 1887; d. Orange, New Jersey, 10 July 1982), Czech soprano. Jeritza made her debut at Olomouc in 1910, and sang at the Vienna Hofoper (later Staatsoper) from 1912 to 1935.

On 16 February 1918, she sang Jenůfa in the Viennese premiere of *Jenůfa**, giving ten performances in 1918 and returning for two more in 1926. Janáček described Jeritza's Jenůfa as 'ideal' in a letter to Gabriela Horvátová. Recalling the premiere in her memoirs, Zdenka Janáčková wrote that 'Jeritza shone, with her silvery voice, deeply felt acting and beautiful fair-haired appearance. She was the best Jenůfa I ever saw and heard.' Jeritza first appeared at the Metropolitan Opera in New York in 1921, and there on 6 December 1924 she sang the title role in the American premiere of *Jenůfa*. Lawrence Gilman in the *Herald Tribune* wrote: 'It is not easy to imagine a more perfect embodiment of the role of the ill-used peasant girl than Jeritza's. Her handling of the scene in which she learns of the death of her child is as beautiful and affecting a thing as she has done here; it is on a par with her Tosca for veracity and skill and power.' *JYL2, MetArc, WieArc.*

Jílek, František (b. Brno, 22 May 1913; d. Brno, 16 September 1993), Czech conductor. Jílek attended the Brno Conservatory, studying the piano and composition with Jaroslav Kvapil* and conducting with Antonín Balatka and Zdeněk Chalabala. In the 1930s, Jílek worked as a repetiteur at the Brno NT, and in 1939 he was appointed second conductor at the Ostrava National Theatre under Jaroslav Vogel*, remaining there until 1948. Jílek became principal conductor of the Brno NT in 1952, holding the post until 1978. As well as conducting a very wide repertoire, he oversaw the move into the Janáček Theatre in 1965, inaugurating the new opera house with *The Cunning Little Vixen* on 2 October. He worked closely with Václav Nosek*, a conductor and the company's dramaturg, from 1952 to 1982. Together they planned the 1958 Brno Janáček Festival, during which Jílek conducted *Jenůfa*, *The Cunning Little Vixen*, *From the House of the Dead*, *The Excursions of Mr Brouček* and the stage premiere of *Fate*. Jílek left the opera in 1978 to become principal conductor of the Brno State Philharmonic, retiring in 1991. He made a number of Janáček recordings for Supraphon, including *Fate** (its first commercial recording), *The Excursions of Mr Brouček**, *Jenůfa** (with Gabriela Beňáčková in the title role) and the *Glagolitic Mass**. Between 1986 and 1993, he recorded a complete series of Janáček's orchestral works with the Brno State Philharmonic, issued on three CDs. Jílek's 1976 Brno Radio performance of *The Beginning of a Romance** was published on CD by Multisonic. *BarJíl.*

Journalism, Janáček's   See separate entries for: *Hudební besídka*; *Hudební listy*; *Lidové noviny*

Jungová, Marie, née Adamková (b. Velký Petřvald, 1839; d. Hukvaldy, 29 January 1926). Jungová was the daughter of a landowner in Velký Petřvald. In 1861 she married Josef Jung, a brewer in Hukvaldy. She was a prominent member of Hukvaldy society and established the singing group 'Pod akátem' ('The Circle Under the Acacia'), in which most of her family sang (see Hukvaldy*). From 1888 onwards, she introduced Janáček to several local folk musicians, notably the cimbalom player Jan Myška. In gratitude for introducing him to Myška, Janáček dedicated the edition of two *Valachian Dances* (VI/4), published by Bursík and Kohout in April 1890, 'to the esteemed Mrs Marie Jungová'. Her husband Josef subsidised the publication by purchasing a number of copies of the score. When Janáček published the definitive form of the work as the six

Lachian Dances* (VI/17) in 1928, he added a preface dated 22 May 1928 (first printed in *Lidové noviny* on 27 May, XV/310). It's a touching and nostalgic recollection of an evening at the long-closed tavern 'U Harabiša', where he heard some of the music that inspired the dances: 'I am sitting here bent over the proofs of the *Lachian Dances*. I see the room of the tavern in the notes of every bar. It is overcrowded with sweating, red-cheeked folk. All of them are moving, swinging and turning. All those who took part in that frenzied summer night's dance are no more. Gone is the poet Šťastný, gone is Professor Batěk, gone is Mrs Marie Jungová ... In memory of all of you who were witnesses of that warm night and who are now sleeping the eternal sleep – a song of praise to my homeland, my Lachian country.' *BarLaš, LJFD1, LJLD1, ProVol.*

Jurjevskaja, Zinaida [born Zinaida Lenkina] (b. Tartu, Estonia, 10 June 1892; d. near Andermatt, Switzerland, 3 December 1925), Estonian soprano.   She went to study at the St Petersburg Conservatory in 1912, and made her debut at the Mariinsky Theatre in 1919. In December 1922, she gave a concert in Berlin and was immediately signed by the Berlin State Opera. In March 1924, she sang the title role in the Berlin premiere of *Jenůfa**, conducted by Erich Kleiber*. Six months later, on 10 October, Jurjevskaja recorded Jenůfa's Prayer (Act II, Scene 6) with the Orchestra of the Berlin State Opera and an unnamed conductor (probably Max Saal). Not only does Jurjevskaja give an impressive performance but this record is also the earliest recording of any music by Janáček (it has been reissued on CD by Preiser). Janáček probably never heard it, as he did not own a gramophone. Jurjevskaja's end was tragic. After a performance of *Götterdämmerung* on 29 November 1925, she left Berlin for Switzerland. On 3 December, near Andermatt, she set out in bad weather for the Devil's Bridge (Teufelsbrücke) in the Schöllenen Gorge and never returned. She is presumed to have taken her own life. Police later found a razor blade and bottles of poison near where she had fallen.

Jurkovič, Dušan (b. Turá Lúka, near Myjava, Slovakia, 23 August 1868; d. Bratislava, 21 December 1947), Slovak architect.   After formal studies in Vienna, Jurkovič travelled throughout Moravia, Valachia and Western Slovakia to study local architecture and woodworking. He designed the traditional buildings for the Valachian Village at the 1895 Prague Czecho-Slavonic Ethnographic Exhibition*, where some of Janáček's folk musicians performed. It is probable that Jurkovič and Janáček met at the exhibition. Jurkovič moved to Brno in 1899, after which he saw Janáček frequently.

Jurkovič's architectural style, blending elements of Viennese Jugendstil and vernacular folk art, is apparent in his remodelling of Luhačovice (mostly in 1902–3). His new or restored buildings included the Hotel Jestřabi, the Music Pavilion, the Valašska, Vlastimila and Chaloupka Villas, the Hydrotherapy Institute and swimming pool, and the Janův dům [Jan's House], renamed the Jurkovič House in 1948. His most important building in Brno is the Jurkovič Villa in Brno-Žabovřesky (Jana Nečase No. 2), now administered by the Moravian Gallery in Brno. It was completed in 1906. From 26 August to 20 September that year, the KPU organised an exhibition there. Jurkovič and his family lived in the house until moving to Bratislava in 1918.

Janáček and Jurkovič both served on the committee of the KPU and shared an interest in folk music. On 24–27 July 1914, they went to Valašská Bystřice to photograph the locations in which songs were performed. In an undated letter from 1913, Jurkovič wrote to tell Janáček about a manuscript collection of folksongs he had found twenty-five years earlier in the estate of his uncle Jozef Miloslav Hurban (1817–88). He told Janáček that the songs were 'all collected at the Moravian border where the dialect of Czech is probably closest to Slovak'. At some stage he lent this collection to Janáček and wrote on 19 June 1927 asking him to return 'the three notebooks of songs collected in western Slovakia about a hundred years ago'.

It's possible to see parallels between the work of Janáček and Jurkovič in the first decade of the twentieth century: both of them studied and then subsumed folk art into their own wholly original language, whether in Jurkovič's villa in Žabovřesky or in Janáček's *Jenůfa* and *Fate*. After World War I, Jurkovič returned to Slovakia and designed a number of houses in Bratislava (including his own villa) which demonstrate a more geometric and abstracted style. *DušJur, HorPet, JurDům, ProLuh.*

Kafka, Franz (b. Prague, 3 July 1883; d. Kierling, near Vienna, Austria, 3 June 1924), Czech writer.   Kafka and Janáček met through their mutual friend Max Brod* on at least two occasions: for the first time in Brod's Prague apartment and for the second time when Janáček was in Berlin for the premiere of *Jenůfa* at the Staatsoper under Erich Kleiber on 17 March 1924, a few weeks before Kafka's death. Brod sent Kafka his German translation of *Jenůfa* in October 1917, and Kafka replied: 'I have received *Jenůfa*. Reading is music. The text and music have indeed important lessons for us. Your German translation is the work of a giant. How well you make the repetitions breathe with such life! May I mention a few small things?' Kafka then listed a number of suggested alterations, some of which were taken into subsequent printings of the German-language libretto of *Jenůfa* published by UE (described in detail by Procházka 1982). Brod wrote a touching letter to Janáček on 13 June 1924: 'You probably know already that I have lost my best friend – the poet Franz Kafka whom you met at my home and most recently in Berlin at Anhalter Station. He was buried here on Wednesday.' After Kafka's death, Brod became his literary executor. *ProKaf.*

Kalda, Ozef [Josef] (b. Nové Město na Moravě, 4 August 1871; d. Prague, 1 January 1921). Czech writer.   The poems set by Janáček in *The Diary of One Who Disappeared** were first published in *Lidové noviny* on the front pages of the issues for 14 and 21 May 1916. They were headed 'From the writings of a self-taught man' and the author of the poems remained a mystery until the 1990s, when Jan Mikeska and Jiří Demel demonstrated that Kalda had written them. The discovery of a letter from Kalda to his friend Antonín Matula, found in Matula's family papers, sent three weeks after the poems were published, confirmed the authorship. Kalda was brought up in Zlín, and became an employee of the Buštěhrad Railway in 1891. His poetry drew on regional dialects, and Janáček may well have believed that the texts were folk poems. Kalda died on 1 January 1921 and never knew of Janáček's settings. His other works included *Ogaři [The Lads]*, first published in 1905 and subtitled 'Scenes from Moravian Valachia for children'. In 1919 Kalda turned this into an opera libretto, which was set to music by Jaroslav Křička. Though nothing came of it, the writer Josef Peška wrote to Janáček on 19 December 1915 recommending Kalda as someone who could help with the troublesome libretto of *The*

Excursion of Mr Brouček to the Moon, describing him as 'brilliant, and as original as the Russians'. *JYL2, KLJ, MikTaj, NěmZap, ZahZap, ZemJan.*

Kantor Halfar **See *Halfar the Schoolmaster* (IV/33)**

Kašpar Rucký, chorus for soprano solo, solo quartet and female voices (IV/41). Completed on 12 February 1916, this was the third of the works for female chorus that Janáček composed in January and February that year, preceded by *The Wolf's Trail** (IV/39) and *Hradčany Songs** (IV/40). *Kašpar Rucký* sets a poem from F. S. Procházka's *Hradčanské písničky*, first published in 1904. The poem and Janáček's autograph both give the title as 'O Kašparoví Ruckém' ('About Kašpar Rucký'). The first edition was published by HMUB in 1925 and included a German translation by Max Brod. A critical edition was published in SKVEJ C/3 (2002).

Kašpar Rucký (d. 1612) was a historical figure. He worked at the court of Rudolf II, where he had a rather shadowy role as an adviser and valet to the Emperor. Like Rudolf himself, he seems to have had an interest in alchemy. Rudolf died on 20 January 1612 and Rucký was arrested soon afterwards, accused of stealing one of Rudolf's magical tinctures. He killed himself in prison and his body was cut up and burned. While the real Rucký had more in common with Karel Čapek's (and Janáček's) Hieronymus Makropulos (Emilia Marty's father in *The Makropulos Affair*), Procházka depicts Rucký as a kind of quack, hawking potions around Prague and using them to seduce girls. He is brought to justice and condemned to die a slow and painful death, but is found hanging in his cell. He comes back to haunt Prague as an agent of the devil, with attendant witches and ghouls, terrorising its inhabitants as the King looks on aghast.

While Ferdinand Vach and his VSMU took up the other works for female chorus in 1916, *Kašpar Rucký* had to wait another five years, until Metod Doležil* performed it with his Prague Women Teachers' Choral Society. An exceptionally demanding work, Janáček was anxious about how well it would go at the premiere in Prague on 6 April 1921. After the concert, he wrote to Max Brod: 'You have no idea how scared I was to come to Prague to hear *Kašpar Rucký*. I was afraid they wouldn't be able to manage it and would make an utter shambles of it! But it turned out well.' Brod himself was so impressed with it that he volunteered to make the translation that appeared in the first edition. *JAWO, JYL2, SusJan, ZahŽen.*

Káťa Kabanová, opera in three acts with libretto by Janáček after Alexander Nikolayevich Ostrovsky's play *The Thunderstorm* [*Groza*] in the Czech translation by Vincenc Červinka (I/8). Composed between January 1920 and April 1921, with minor revisions in December 1921; interludes added in November 1927. Janáček tried to contact Vincenc Červinka* to ask about his translation of *The Thunderstorm* in October 1919 (it had been published in 1918 as *Bouře*), but Červinka was away in the United States. He returned to Prague just before Christmas to find a note from Janáček requesting permission to use the translation as the basis for an opera libretto. Červinka wrote to Janáček (on 31 December): 'I give my permission most willingly for the use of my translation of *The Thunderstorm* and in the case of a stage production I would ask for a 2% royalty. If, with my modest knowledge of Russian conditions and background, I can be of any assistance to you it goes without saying that I am always at your disposal.' By the time Janáček replied to thank Červinka on 10 January 1920, he had already started work on the opera. According to Marie Stejskalová, composition began on 5 January, and on 9 January Janáček wrote to Kamila Stösslová: 'I have begun writing a new opera. The chief character in it is a woman, gentle by nature. She shrinks at the mere thought [of hurting, of evil]; a breeze would carry her away, let alone the storm that hangs over her.' During the summer of 1920, he met Červinka at Luhačovice. Červinka recalled that Janáček 'told me enthusiastically with what relish he was working, and how it flowed from his hand. He was looking forward to the thought that this time he would make a breakthrough in Prague more quickly than with *Jenůfa*.' After the holidays, Janáček resumed work, completing Act II on 15 October 1920 and Act III on 24 December. By 17 April 1921, he had made a complete revision. The only difficulty that remained was choosing a title. On 31 March 1921, Janáček wrote to Červinka for advice: 'I have finished the opera. The trouble is what to call it. There are already several *Thunderstorms* in music and opera [notably the opera by Zdeněk Fibich and the cantata by Vítězslav Novák]. So that name is not a good idea. Furthermore this natural phenomenon is not the mainspring of the action. It is *Kateřina* who holds the psychological interest of the story. Director [Gustav] Schmoranz mentioned to me that *Kateřina* might be taken as Catherine the Great. He suggested the name *Káťa*. Boris and Tichon call her that. I'd therefore be in favour of this title. What do you think about it?' Červinka liked the idea, but added a suggestion of his own: 'I completely agree with you that the name of your new opera ... will have to be differentiated from all the earlier *Thunderstorms*. ... Your calling it *Káťa* would perhaps be the happiest solution. *Káťa Kabanová* would possibly be a little broader.' Janáček quickly adopted Červinka's suggested title, using it on 14 April 1921 in a letter to Otakar Nebuška.

František Neumann* was eager to secure the premiere of Janáček's new opera for the Brno NT. *Káťa Kabanová* was finished on 17 April 1921, and on 26 April Neumann wrote to the composer: 'May I ask that you entrust your opera *Káťa Kabanová* to us for its first performance? It is very important to me that the new work of our foremost Moravian composer should also be given its first performance in Moravia.' Prague was also eager to perform the work and Janáček was in correspondence with Otakar Ostrčil* in May 1921, but as he told Stösslová (23 May), 'I don't have much stomach for the Prague theatre.' The vocal score was prepared by Janáček's pupil Břetislav Bakala*, who also coached the singers for the Brno premiere.

Káťa Kabanová was first performed at the Brno NT on 23 November 1921, with Marie Veselá* in the title role, conducted by František Neumann. Max Brod reported on an 'unprecedented success'. He noted: 'After only the first act, the audience was not content just to recall the performers to the stage more than ten times. "Author! Author!" thundered again and again ... until Janáček himself appeared with that touchingly courteous smile on his great kind face. ... It was uncommonly moving to see this youthfully vigorous old man on the stage which still reverberated with the magical sounds of his passionate score.' On 24 December 1921, Ostrčil wrote that the Prague NT 'will put it on as soon as Universal Edition delivers the material'. By September 1922, Ostrčil had a printed orchestral score and rehearsals were in progress the next month.

Janáček attended these and made a few adjustments to the orchestration. He wrote to Ostrčil (2 November 1922) that 'the work is safe in your hands. I'm looking forward to it and have no fears!' The Prague premiere took place on 30 November 1922.

Meanwhile, the first performance abroad was given at Cologne Opera on 8 December 1922, conducted by Otto Klemperer*. The pianist and writer Julius[z] Wolfsohn (1880–1944), working in Cologne at the time, wrote to Janáček requesting information about the opera. The composer replied from Hukvaldy on 2 September 1922 with a five-page letter, written in German. Janáček wrote that 'The work flowed from my pen just like the beautiful river Volga. Should I now catch the waves? Impossible. The motifs are transformed as if "by themselves". It seems to me that even when a motif rises up threateningly, it has its germ in the still, dreaming waters. For instance, [the timpani motif at the start of the prelude (four Fs, four B flats)] threads its way through the whole work. The whole weight of the drama lies in it.' He contrasts this with its subsequent transformation on oboes and sleigh bells, commenting that 'when a motif becomes so fundamentally different I feel that it must be so – I don't think any more about it'. In a subsequent letter, Wolfsohn encouraged Janáček to say more about other motifs in the opera, and most unusually the composer did so. Janáček's reply, dated Brno, 2 November 1922, is written on the sheet of manuscript music examples that Wolfsohn had sent. Janáček labels some of these as follows: 'Lightning' (Act I, Fig. 5, bars 1–2, muted trumpets), 'Accusation' (Act I, Fig. 6, bars 1–2, strings), 'The pure, unstained Káťa' (Act I, Fig. 31, bars 7–14), 'Suffocating atmosphere', at the start of Act II (bars 1–3) and 'The heart falters', at the start of Act II, Scene 2 (bars 1–2). For Janáček, these descriptions of the extra-musical associations for his operatic motifs are very rare. What is more, on the verso of the same sheet of manuscript paper, he expanded some of his remarks, adding: 'The motifs should not vanish but must continuously *live* and radiate life.' (Facsimiles of both letters are reproduced by Plamenac.)

The Cologne performance under Klemperer was poorly received, but there were successful productions in Bratislava (24 March 1923), Ostrava (18 January 1924), a new Brno production (16 October 1924) and Berlin (31 May 1926). Janáček went to the Berlin *Káťa*, conducted by Fritz Zweig, with his wife Zdenka, who later recalled a glittering occasion, 'an entirely distinguished audience, splendid instruments in the orchestra, the very best cast, magnificent sets, in the intervals huge applause and calls for the composer ... both of us were thoroughly delighted. After the performance there was a reception with dazzling guests: Schoenberg, Schreker, Kleiber, almost every outstanding Berlin artist.' Janáček himself praised the performance in *Lidové noviny* (13 June 1926): 'The performance yielded humbly to the commands in the score. All the notes became animated: they had their space and their time. ... And how the storm in the third act raged in the orchestra of 95 players! Such productions dazzle. They open wide the gates of the world for the work.' For the production at the German Theatre in Prague (21 January 1928), Janáček composed two interludes in November 1927 to cover the scene changes in Acts I and II. If anything, the 1928 Prague production, conducted by Steinberg, pleased him even more than Berlin (see Steinberg, Hans Wilhelm*).

Václav Talich* conducted a new production of *Káťa* at the Prague NT on 16 September 1938 using his own (extensive) reorchestrations, while a few months

later Jaroslav Vogel* conducted the work in Ostrava (7 December 1938) using
the original orchestration (as did most other productions). A new production
at the Prague NT conducted by Talich opened on 25 April 1947, and a later
performance was seen that autumn (on 15 October) by Talich's pupil Charles
Mackerras*: his first experience of a Janáček opera and a decisive moment in
his career. In 1951 Mackerras conducted the work at Sadler's Wells in London,
the first Janáček opera to be staged in the United Kingdom. Supraphon made
the first complete recording in March 1959 with Prague NT forces conducted
by Jaroslav Krombholc, using Talich's reorchestration. Charles Mackerras's
Decca recording in 1976 not only used Janáček's original orchestration but also
included the interludes composed in 1927. A second Mackerras recording was
made in Prague in 1997. A Brno Radio broadcast from January 1953 (published
by CRQ editions) is of particular interest as it is conducted by Břetislav Bakala,
who was involved with rehearsals for the world premiere and who arranged the
vocal score at Janáček's request. Bakala also uses the original orchestration and
includes the interludes.

The vocal score was first issued by UE in February 1922 and the full score
followed in August–September 1922. In 1971 Charles Mackerras prepared a
new edition based on the authorised copy corrected by Janáček and František
Neumann. This was used for his 1976 Decca recording and published by UE
in 1992.

There is no dedication on any edition or on the manuscript sources, but
Janáček's correspondence with Kamila Stösslová indicates that it was dedicated
unofficially to her (see Stösslová, Kamila*).

Káťa Kabanová includes some of the most tender and lyrical music to
be found in any of Janáček's operas, but it also has moments of formidable
dramatic power (often featuring the eight-note 'fate' motif). The evocations of
nature (the wordless chorus embodying the Volga, the sounds of the thunderstorm) point the way forward to *The Cunning Little Vixen*. Reviewing the work in
Rovnost, Janáček's pupil Václav Kaprál wrote that '*Káťa Kabanová* is much more
concisely written than *Jenůfa*. The first act, in particular, gives the impression
of a unified gradation, varied by an episode of unrivalled beauty when Káťa
remembers the church services of her childhood [Act I, Scene 2, Fig. 7]. ... The
music in this opera is not as simply expressed as in *Jenůfa* and its richness is
polyphonic, especially in the first act. However, it is polyphony in the Janáček
sense, somehow creating emotion from fragments. ... The work overflows with
inventive ideas. The orchestral writing shows that Janáček's technique is in the
front rank of contemporary music.' The double love duet at the end of Act II,
with its rapturous music for Káťa and Boris and its folk-like material for Varvara
and Kudrjáš, is intensely expressive, and the final scene is a monologue for Káťa
that leads to her suicide and its brutally concise aftermath. The opera as a whole
shows Janáček at his most inspired both in terms of the music and his dramatic
pacing. *JAWO, JODA, PlaKat, PřiKat, TyrKat, VrbStá.*

SYNOPSIS

*Act I, Scene 1: The Russian town of Kalinov on the Volga in the 1860s. Outdoors,
after church.* After an orchestral prelude, Váňa Kudrjáš, a scientist and teacher,
admires the beauty of the river, but the servant Glaša is unimpressed. Dikoj
arrives with his nephew, Boris Grigorjevič, and berates him. Dikoj leaves after

learning that Kabanicha, the matriarch of the Kabanov family, is not at home. Boris explains to Kudrjáš that he tolerates Dikoj's bullying in order to collect his inheritance, which Dikoj controls. Boris also tells Kudrjáš that he is in love with Káťa, the wife of Tichon Kabanov. Káťa appears and Kabanicha reproaches Tichon for his inattentiveness and for spoiling Káťa. Tichon grumbles to Varvara, the Kabanovs' foster child, who says he should spend more time defending Káťa rather than resorting to drinking.

Act I, Scene 2: Inside the Kabanov house later the same day. Káťa reminisces about her childhood to Varvara and says she dreams of having a man who loves her. Tichon enters to say his farewells; he is going to Kazan on Kabanicha's behalf. Káťa wants to go with him, but when he refuses to take her she asks him to make her swear not to speak to strangers while he is away. Kabanicha tells Káťa how to behave while Tichon is away, and he echoes his mother's instructions to Káťa: that she must treat Kabanicha like her own mother and not look at other men.

Act II, Scene 1: Inside the Kabanov house, late afternoon. Kabanicha complains that Káťa is not demonstrating enough sorrow during Tichon's absence. After Kabanicha leaves, Varvara shows Káťa the key to the garden where Varvara intends to meet Kudrjáš later. She hints that Káťa might want to do something similar and gives her the key. Káťa takes it nervously, after deciding that she will meet Boris. As evening falls, Kabanicha reappears with a drunk Dikoj.

Act II, Scene 2: Outside the Kabanovs' garden gate at night. Kudrjáš is waiting for Varvara when Boris appears, hoping to meet Káťa. Kudrjáš warns him of the risk he is taking. Varvara arrives, and leaves for a stroll along the river with Kudrjáš. Káťa enters and Boris declares his love. Though knowing it will ruin her, she admits her own feelings for him. They embrace and leave. Kudrjáš and Varvara return and Káťa and Boris are heard in the distance singing an ecstatic duet, before Kudrjáš announces that it is time for them all to go home.

Act III, Scene 1: Two weeks later, a ruined building by the river. Kudrjáš and his friend Kuligin take shelter as a storm approaches. Others join them, including Dikoj. Kudrjáš tries to calm Dikoj by telling him that the storm is just electricity, but this enrages Dikoj, who insists that lightning is a punishment from God. Varvara tells Boris that Tichon has returned. Kabanicha arrives with Tichon and Káťa. The storm returns and Káťa confesses to Tichon that she has met Boris during his absence. She rushes out into the storm.

Act III, Scene 2: On the banks of the river. Tichon and Glaša are searching for Káťa. Varvara and Kudrjáš decide to leave for Moscow to start a new life. Káťa appears, regretting her confession and longing to see Boris one last time. He enters and they embrace, but he tells her that his uncle is sending him away. At first she begs him to let her go with him, then realises that this is impossible and bids him farewell. Káťa imagines how nature will flourish over her grave, then throws herself into the river. Kuligin sees this and raises the alarm. Though Tichon wants to help Káťa, Kabanicha stops him. He blames his mother for Káťa's suicide. Dikoj brings in Káťa's corpse. As Tichon weeps over the body, Kabanicha gives chilling thanks to friends and neighbours for their kindness.

Keys, Janáček's choice of In his mature works, Janáček showed a marked preference for flat keys, often with modal inflections such as flattened sevenths. Examples include E flat major (the end of *Jenůfa**), A flat major (the end of the

Glagolitic Mass* and much of *The Eternal Gospel**) and, especially, D flat major (the key in which the *Sinfonietta**, *Taras Bulba**, *The Excursions of Mr Brouček**, *The Cunning Little Vixen**, *From the House of the Dead** and the String Quartet No. 2* all end). Other flat keys that appear in his music include G flat major (the orchestral interlude before the final scene of *The Excursion of Mr Brouček to the Moon*), B flat minor (the start and finish of *Káťa Kabanová**), A flat minor (the end of the String Quartet No. 1*) and more extreme keys such as C flat major (Káťa's first entrance in Act I of *Káťa Kabanová**) and G flat minor (the third movement of the String Quartet No. 1*). Occasionally Janáček combines two tonal areas simultaneously, as in the start of *Fate*, where a bass line on D flat is combined with leaping violin figurations in A major. Janáček also used sharp keys, of course, though less often at climactic moments or at the close of works. However, the end of Act II of *Káťa Kabanová* is in E major, the end of *Fate** is in C sharp minor and the end of *The Excursion of Mr Brouček to the Moon* is in A major. Janáček's choice of keys, and his sudden shifts from extreme flat to extreme sharp keys, can create difficulties in performance, particularly for string players, but they are an essential component of his musical style.

Janáček abandoned the use of key signatures in his operas from *Brouček* onwards and in most of his mature instrumental music, though one of the more controversial policies of SKV has been to add key signatures where editors see fit to do so. Janáček's own practice of leaving them out seems more appropriate since his music shifts so freely (and often rapidly) through a series of keys. His works often begin and end in different keys, and the preference for A flat major, A flat minor and D flat major seems to be determined by their particular resonance and sonority.

Kleiber, Erich (b. Vienna, 5 August 1890; d. Zurich, 27 January 1956), Austrian conductor. Kleiber spent his childhood in Vienna and Prague. He studied art history and aesthetics at the Charles University and music at the Prague Conservatory, where he studied composition and conducting, learning Czech in the process. He obtained his first post at Darmstadt in 1913, followed by positions in Wuppertal, Düsseldorf and Mannheim. In August 1923, he made his debut at the Berlin State Opera conducting *Fidelio*, and a few days later was appointed Generalmusikdirektor. One of his first triumphs was the Berlin premiere of *Jenůfa* on 17 March 1924. The dress rehearsal on 15 March was a great success, as Janáček wrote to Zdenka: 'In twenty-seven years nobody can remember a dress rehearsal like today's for *Jenůfa*. A huge theatre, full of all the Berlin critics. Endless curtain calls for the singers and conductor and me! The effect is like nowhere else. All original folk costumes, a gift of our Embassy to the State Opera. The conductor Kleiber has no equal.' He wrote to Kleiber from Brno on 22 March, explaining which aspects had most impressed him: 'You felt the climactic moments in my work and presented them bathed in sunshine. They used to make the Recruiting Song into a blatant military march, and you instilled into Jenůfa's aria the glow of young hearts. ... You made the endings of all the acts work magnificently. It is you who have at last made *Jenůfa* appear great, not Prague or Vienna. If I may ask you for something, it is to play the introduction to the first act just a little quicker to give it a sense of restlessness, and put the xylophone on stage near the mill, where its icy tone will be damped.'

In December 1927, Kleiber began rehearsals for the German premiere of *The Makropulos Affair*. The production was scheduled for May 1928 but it was cancelled (see *The Makropulos Affair**). Kleiber remained enthusiastic about Janáček, recording the first of the *Lachian Dances* with the Berlin Philharmonic on 13 September 1930 for Ultraphon (issued on CD by Preiser). In 1955 he recorded *Taras Bulba* with the Czech Philharmonic, but this is unpublished. *JAWO, JYL2, SimZam.*

Klemperer, Otto (b. Breslau, 14 May 1885; d. Zurich, 6 July 1973), German conductor. Starting with his years at Cologne Opera (1917–24), Klemperer became an enthusiastic advocate of Janáček's music. On 16 November 1918, he conducted the German premiere of *Jenůfa* in Cologne. It was given in the face of considerable opposition: members of the chorus refused to sing, and the local press objected to performing a work by a Czech at a time when, according to the *Rheinische Musik- und Theaterzeitung,* 'our Austrian brothers have to suffer so much under the effrontery of uncultured Slavs'. A year after the Brno premiere of *Káťa Kabanová*, Klemperer conducted the first production to be given outside Czechoslovakia, at Cologne Opera on 8 December 1922. Again, local critics dismissed the work, though there was some grudging praise for Rose Pauly's *Káťa* and Klemperer's conducting. Klemperer later attempted to secure *The Makropulos Affair* and *From the House of the Dead* for the Kroll Opera in Berlin (there are letters to Janáček asking about both works). He did not conduct either work, but *From the House of the Dead* was done at the Kroll in 1931, conducted by Fritz Zweig. Klemperer made a speciality of the *Sinfonietta**. He first conducted it in Wiesbaden on 9 December 1926, and gave the US premiere in Carnegie Hall on 4 March 1927 with the New York Symphony Society. Olin Downes reviewed the concert in the *New York Times*, praising the performance and the work itself for the 'joyous play of short and rhythmical fragments, a freedom from the shackles of traditional form, and a genuine freshness of feeling'. The performance of the *Sinfonietta* that Klemperer conducted at the Kroll Opera in Berlin on 29 September 1927 was attended by Janáček and described by him as 'unrivalled by anyone anywhere'. Klemperer continued to conduct the work in later life, including performances with the Concertgebouw Orchestra (1951) and Cologne Radio SO (1956) that have been released on CD. *HeyKle, JAWO, KLJ.*

Klub moravských skladatelů   See Brno: Moravian Composers' Club

Klub přátel umění v Brně   See Brno: Club of the Friends of Art in Brno (KPU)

Kolář, Emil (b. Rosice, 4 August 1866; d. Brno-Židenice, 9 August 1938), Czech teacher. Kolář held teaching posts in Rosice and then Ivančice, where he worked from 1892 to 1905. From 1906 to 1918, he taught in Brno-Židenice. Between 1897 and 1902, Kolář edited six volumes of *Slovanské melodie*, anthologies of pieces for harmonium. The first five volumes were published by Josef Vávra and the sixth by Kolář himself. Vol. 5 included the first publication of Nos. 1, 2 and 10 of *On the Overgrown Path**, Series I, and Vol. 6 included Nos. 4 and 7. Though the individual pieces are untitled, the collective title of the work appears on the contents pages of the *Slovanské melodie*. Kolář also composed choruses on texts by Petr Bezruč. *ČSHS, JAWO.*

Komenský, Jan Amos   See *Lullaby* (V/14)

Kovařovic, Karel (b. Prague, 9 December 1862; d. Prague, 6 December 1920), Czech composer and conductor.   After completing his training at the Prague Conservatory, Kovařovic joined the orchestra of the Provisional Theatre (later the National Theatre) in Prague as a harpist and clarinettist. He conducted at the Brno NT in 1885–6, and in January 1887 his opera *The Bridegrooms* was given a scathing review by Janáček in *Hudební listy*, which may have started the hostility between them. In 1900 Kovařovic became the music director of the Prague NT, serving until his death (his final performance was of Smetana's *Dalibor* on 28 October 1920), raising the standard in all aspects of the company's work, especially the orchestra. Kovařovic was a composer whose operas were successfully produced at the Prague NT, mostly before he became music director there. One of his more familiar orchestral pieces, the *Miner's Polka* recorded by Talich, was taken from his incidental music for František Ferdinand Šamberk's play *The Excursion of Mr Brouček to the Exhibition … with a Prologue: The Dream on the Moon*, which opened at the Prague NT on 18 June 1894.

Kovařovic's name is best remembered for his attitude to *Jenůfa**. Janáček took the score to Prague just days after the death of his daughter Olga in 1903, but it was rejected on 28 April 1903. After the Brno premiere in January 1904, Janáček wrote on 9 February with a 'renewed request that the Prague National Theatre should grant a hearing to *Jenůfa*', adding that 'my only complaint is that it was unjust to turn down *Jenůfa*' and wondering if it was because of the 'Moravian character of the work'. Kovařovic replied on 4 March, saying that Janáček was wrong to describe the rejection of the opera as unjust: 'I became convinced that we could not accept your opera for performance. My fears continue that your work, at least on *our* stage and before *our* audience, would not meet with the complete success that we would wish both for you and for us. This is not however because of the Moravian character of the work (where did you get that impression?).' *Jenůfa* was published by the KPU in 1908 and revived in Brno in 1911. At this point František Veselý, chairman of the KPU, proposed a new appeal to the Prague NT. He wrote to the chairman of the National Theatre committee, Jaroslav Hlava, who replied that since Janáček had already felt it necessary to revise *Jenůfa*, this was 'proof that it is not such a masterpiece as you imagine' and that he would be better off writing something completely new for the theatre. It was the sustained campaign in 1915 by Josef Peška, František Veselý and his wife Marie Calma-Veselá that finally persuaded Kovařovic to take *Jenůfa* seriously, and on 20 November 1915 Janáček was finally able to write to Kovařovic: 'Dr František Veselý is the reason why yesterday I sent you the full score of *Jenůfa*. I have two requests for you should you want to perform this work at the National Theatre: don't delay it, and take on the conducting yourself.'

Kovařovic did a lot more than the conducting. He made it a condition of performing the work that it should be done with his revisions to the orchestration and his suggested cuts. Initially, at least, Janáček didn't seem to mind. After the first orchestral rehearsal he wrote to his wife on 13 May 1916 that it was 'wonderful' and that at the end of Act II 'they played it in such a way that one trembles. After the rehearsal Kovařovic and I embraced; we were both overcome.' Five days later, on 18 May, Janáček wrote to Zdenka: 'Kovařovic said yesterday, "I think of it as if it were *my* work". And also, with what love and dedication he is working on it! The other day he sat over the score until 5 in the morning! ... There have been as many as twenty-three orchestral rehearsals ... and on top of those there will be another five!' In his letter to Zdenka on 22 May, Janáček mentioned the final scene of the opera, in which Kovařovic's addition of canonic imitative phrases is one of his most blatant retouchings. Janáček didn't seem to have a problem with this, writing: 'The ending sounds like a hymn, the victory of pure love!' A week after the premiere, Janáček wrote to Kovařovic offering him the dedication of his next opera, *The Excursion of Mr Brouček to the Moon* (as it then was). Kovařovic replied on 8 June, accepting the dedication 'with joy and thanks' (though in the end *Brouček* was dedicated to President Masaryk) and asking Janáček about a gala performance of *Jenůfa* planned for the Emperor's birthday on 18 August: 'Would you not like to *conduct* this performance? It would increase not a little the glamour of the whole evening!' Janáček declined, saying that *Jenůfa* was in the best possible hands with Kovařovic. It was in this version that *Jenůfa* started to be become widely known: during Janáček's lifetime there were more than seventy productions, and from 1919 onwards the Kovařovic version was even used in Brno. If Janáček had serious objections to Kovařovic's reorchestrations, would he have permitted them to be used in his home town?

Janáček's resentment dates from 1923, when he discovered that Kovařovic's widow was receiving a 1% royalty on performances of the opera. In a series of letters to Otakar Ostrčil (Kovařovic's successor), he denounced Kovařovic's work as unnecessary and damaging to his reputation. On 21 September, he wrote: 'gossip is now circulating in Prague that Kovařovic did all the orchestration of *Jenůfa*, just as in Brno stories are being spread that *Káťa Kabanová* was orchestrated by God knows who!' Kovařovic's widow started legal proceedings to secure a share of the royalties in perpetuity, but in February 1924, UE settled the matter: the case had no merit as Kovařovic had agreed to do the work for a flat fee that was paid to the widows and orphans fund of the Prague NT. Though Břetislav Bakala had made a compelling case in 1941 for reverting to Janáček's original, it wasn't until John Tyrrell and Charles Mackerras prepared an edition based on Janáček's own 1908 Brno version (UE, 1996) that the opera was heard as the composer intended.

Viewed from the perspective of a century later, it is clear that Janáček's own *Jenůfa* should be heard, and that Kovařovic's interventions seem superfluous and often gratuitous. But Janáček's own view was more nuanced. He bitterly resented Kovařovic's failure to take the work in the first place, but once the opera was put on in Prague he was delighted with the results. Janáček made no objection to UE using Kovařovic's revisions when it published the orchestral score in August 1918. A year later, *Jenůfa* was the first Janáček opera to be staged in Brno under František Neumann's direction (23 August 1919) – the start of an extraordinarily productive relationship – and it was Kovařovic's version that was used. For better or worse, Kovařovic's version of *Jenůfa* secured Janáček's reputation as an opera composer, and its success in 1916 undoubtedly gave Janáček the new-found confidence that enabled him to compose his later operatic masterpieces. *ČSHS, JODA, PetKov, TyrCze.*

Král, Alois (b. Senetářov, 30 July 1877; d. Tišnov, 27 February 1972), Czech teacher and speleologist. Král was taught by Janáček at the Teachers' Institute in Brno, and under his influence became interested in folksong. His first teaching post was in Březová in south-eastern Moravia, and from here he sent Janáček a number of folksongs. In 1902 he moved to a new teaching post in Uherský Brod. Janáček and Král remained in friendly contact and on 16 September 1913, Janáček wrote: 'Are you still in [Uherský] Brod? Well? Do you still visit caves?' In a letter dated 30 December 1913, Král reported to Janáček that he had 'started to explore upper Slovakia; I climbed Kriváň [a mountain in the High Tatras] this year and looked at the area around St Mikuláš – the Liptovský mountains with the Demänovská ice cave'. He was subsequently appointed to a school in Liptovský Mikuláš (then known as Liptovský Svätý Mikuláš) and continued his exploration of the area. On 3 August 1921, Král made his great discovery of the Demänovská Freedom Cave*. He wrote to Janáček on 14 June 1922, inviting his old teacher to visit the cave, which Janáček did on 7 August 1922. It was thanks to Král that the 'gigantic dome' inside the cave was named after Janáček. *JYL2, KLJ, TěsDem.*

Křížkovský, Pavel (b. Holasovice [then Kreuzendorf], near Opava, 9 January 1820; d. Brno, 8 May 1885), Czech composer and conductor. Křížkovský came from a poor background and attended school in Opava as a choral scholar, where he was encouraged by Jiří Janáček, then at the start of his teaching career. He arrived in Brno in 1843, became a novice at the Augustinian Monastery in 1845, and was ordained priest in 1848. All the while, he continued with musical activities, as a viola player and as a founder member of the Brno Männergesangverein. He wasn't the only member of the monastery to have outside interests. When the Bishop of Brno made a visitation in 1854 he noted with alarm that the philosophy teaching was full of 'pantheistic fantasies', that Gregor Mendel was spending too much time studying science at a secular institution, and that Křížkovský was an outstanding musician 'whose conducting wins him applause'. The bishop concluded that the Monastery was not functioning as it should, that too much emphasis was placed on science and education, and that the best thing would be for it to be dissolved. Abbot Napp used his considerable influence to stave off this potential disaster, and continued to allow the careers of gifted members of the community like Mendel and Křížkovský to flourish. In 1860 Křížkovský became the first conductor of the Brno Beseda, staying in the post until 1863, when the Bishop finally insisted that he should devote more time to music at the Monastery. He conducted the choir of the Augustinian Monastery from 1848 until he moved to Olomouc in 1872, when Janáček succeeded him. Janáček learned a lot from Křížkovský, but regarded him with admiration rather than warmth. Of Křížkovský's conducting, he said: 'No musician could reach so boldly, so surely, as he could into the depths of a soul, into the expression of another soul, another composer.' Janáček aimed to emulate this when he succeeded Křížkovský at the Monastery in 1872, and at the Brno Beseda in 1876. Janáček only started to compose after Křížkovský had moved to Olomouc, but he was influenced by some of his teacher's compositions, especially the secular choruses based on folksongs using texts from Sušil's collection. Křížkovský's Czech sympathies, reflected in his compositions, influenced Janáček's own musical formation, and his earliest choruses written for Svatopluk are indebted to Křížkovský.

In 1883, after a decade in Olomouc, Křížkovský had a stroke and moved back to the Monastery in Brno. Janáček conducted the music at his funeral, including a setting of the chorus *Take your rest* on a poem by Sušil that Křížkovský had originally composed for Sušil's funeral in 1869. Janáček later produced his own setting of the same poem (IV/24). In 1875 he had written a more direct homage: the *Chorale fantasia* for organ (VIII/4) contains references to the closing chorale from Křížkovský's cantata *SS Cyril and Methodius*. *JYL1, OreMen.*

Krombholc, Jaroslav (b. Prague, 30 January 1918; d. Prague, 16 July 1983), Czech conductor. As a student at the Prague Conservatory in 1937–40, Krombholc studied conducting with Pavel Dědeček* and later with Václav Talich* (1940–2). Between 1941 and 1982, he conducted at the Prague NT, including three operas by Janáček which he performed regularly: *Jenůfa* (from 1942 onwards), *Káťa Kabanová* (from 1957 onwards) and *The Excursions of Mr Brouček* (from 1968 onwards). He also conducted the Prague NT at the Edinburgh Festival in *Káťa Kabanová* (1964) and *Brouček* (1970). In his Prague Janáček performances, he worked with many of the outstanding Czech singers of the day, including Marie Veselá, Štěpánka Jelínková, Libuše Domanínská, Marta Krásová, Beno Blachut and Karel Berman. Krombholc was married to the soprano Maria Tauberová (1911–2003), who sang the Vixen in the 1937 Prague production of *The Cunning Little Vixen* under Talich. In March 1959, Krombholc made the first recording of *Káťa Kabanová** for Supraphon, a passionate and dramatic performance that preserved Talich's retouchings of the score. Myto issued a live performance of *Jenůfa* conducted by Krombholc at the Vienna State Opera in 1964, with a cast including Sena Jurinac and Martha Mödl. *NDPrOA, PřiLed.*

Kubelík, Rafael (b. Býchory, 29 June 1914; d. Kastanienbaum, Switzerland, 11 August 1996), Czech conductor, son of the violin virtuoso Jan Kubelík (1880–1940). Kubelík studied conducting with Pavel Dědeček* at the Prague Conservatory. After two years as Talich's assistant at the Czech Philharmonic, he became music director of the Brno NT (1939–41), where he conducted a production of *Jenůfa** (7 January 1941). Between 1942 and 1948, Kubelík was chief conductor of the Czech Philharmonic. On 6 June 1946, he conducted Janáček's *Sinfonietta** in the closing concert of the first Prague Spring Festival, and a few months later made the work's first recording (for HMV on 4–5 October). At the end of October 1946, he took the Czech Philharmonic to Paris for three concerts sponsored by UNESCO, where he conducted the *Sinfonietta* and *Taras Bulba*. In May 1948, Kubelík conducted the *Glagolitic Mass*, *Jenůfa* and *Amarus*, all with the Czech Philharmonic, but two months later he left Czechoslovakia to escape the Communist regime, only returning in 1990. Between 1949 and 1953, he was chief conductor of the Chicago SO, where he performed the *Sinfonietta* (2 November 1950). Kubelík conducted the *Glagolitic Mass* with the Concertgebouw Orchestra in Amsterdam (2 May 1950), and in June 1954 he led a revival of *Káťa Kabanová** at Sadler's Wells in London. The following year he became music director of the Royal Opera House, Covent Garden, where he gave the British premiere of *Jenůfa** (10 December 1956). In 1961 Kubelík was nominated music director of the Bavarian Radio SO in Munich, and Janáček's music appeared frequently in his programmes. On 17 November 1961, Kubelík gave the premiere of his new edition of *From the House of the Dead**, the first attempt to present Janáček's authentic score of the work. Other works performed with Bavarian Radio included *Jenůfa* (1961), *Amarus* (1969), the *Glagolitic Mass* (1964, 1976), *Sinfonietta* (1962, 1968, 1970, 1976, 1981), *Taras Bulba* (1963, 1970) and the *Capriccio* and *Concertino* (both with Rudolf Firkušný, 1970 and 1971). Apart from *Amarus* and the two operas, Kubelík recorded all these works with Bavarian Radio forces for Deutsche Grammophon. In 1970 he conducted *Jenůfa* at the Bavarian State Opera (a live audio recording was released by Myto and another performance was televised). Kubelík included Janáček in many of his programmes as a guest conductor, and in 1977 he conducted *Káťa Kabanová* at San Francisco Opera. Kubelík played the piano for a recording of *The Diary of One Who Disappeared** with Ernst Haefliger made in Zurich in 1963. Kubelík's advocacy of Janáček in Western Europe and the USA from the 1950s onwards did much to bring the music to international audiences. Kubelík's Bavarian Radio recordings of the *Sinfonietta* and *Taras Bulba* remain among the finest ever made, and his *Jenůfa* from the Bavarian State Opera is electrifying.

Kudláček, František (b. Milevsko, 11 May 1894; d. Brno, 26 August 1972), Czech violinist. Kudláček studied at the Prague Conservatory, graduating in 1914. After war service, he was engaged by František Neumann to be leader of the Brno NT orchestra. He began teaching at the Brno Conservatory in 1921 and founded the Moravian String Quartet*, which he led until 1958. Kudláček worked closely with Janáček. He gave the first performance of the Sonata for Violin and Piano* at the KMS (24 April 1922), and played first violin in the premiere of the *Concertino** (16 February 1926) and at the ISCM Festival in Frankfurt (30 June 1927). On 18, 25 and 27 June 1928, Kudláček led the Moravian Quartet in private performances at Janáček's home of the 'Intimate Letters' Quartet, and he led the work's premiere in the Brno Beseda on 7 September 1928, less than a month after the composer's death. With the Moravian Quartet he broadcast Janáček's First String Quartet for RAVAG (Vienna Radio) on 15 April 1928. As leader (concert master) of the Brno NT orchestra, Kudláček played in the world premieres – all attended by Janáček – of *Káťa Kabanová**, *The Cunning Little Vixen** and *The Makropulos Affair**, the *Glagolitic Mass**, *Taras Bulba** and the *Lachian Dances**. Kudláček was married to the singer Ludmila Kvapilová (1894–1948), the sister of Jaroslav Kvapil, who was the solo contralto in the first performance of *The Diary of One Who Disappeared** (18 April 1921) and created the role of Fekluša in *Káťa Kabanová* (23 November 1921). *ČSHS, JAWO.*

Kulhánek, Jaroslav (1881–1938), Czech trombonist. Like most of Janáček's copyists, Kulhánek was an experienced orchestral player. He was principal trombone of the Brno NT orchestra from 1919 to 1938. He first worked as Janáček's copyist on *The Cunning Little Vixen**, making the authorised copy that was commissioned by the Brno NT and used by František Neumann for the world premiere. Kulhánek's authorised copy of *The Makropulos Affair** was also made for the Brno NT and was the score used by Neumann. Kulhánek shared copying duties for *From the House of the Dead** with Václav Sedláček, his colleague in the opera orchestra. Sedláček made the authorised copy of Act I and part of Act II, while Kulhánek did the rest of the opera. Kulhánek's other assignments for Janáček included an authorised copy (and the orchestral parts) for the *Glagolitic Mass**, the first version of the *Nursery Rhymes** (V/16) and the authorised copy of the *Capriccio**. *JAWO, ZahGla, ZahMak, ZahVix.*

Kunc, Jan (b. Doubravice nad Svitavou, 27 March 1883; d. Brno, 11 September 1976), Czech composer. Kunc attended the Teachers' Institute, where he was taught by Janáček, and then moved to the Brno Organ School for further study with Janáček, graduating in 1903. Between 1906 and 1910, he studied composition privately with Vítězslav Novák*. He taught at the Brno Organ School (1910–13). From 1919 until 1945, he worked at the Brno Conservatory, succeeding Janáček as its director in 1920, when Janáček started the Master School in Composition (in the same building, but administered by the Prague Conservatory). Kunc wrote for *Lidové noviny* from 1909 to 1918, and for *Hudební revue* where, in March and April 1911, he published the first detailed account of Janáček's life and work. This examined Janáček's activities as a conductor, theorist, folksong collector, teacher and composer, with a final section on Janáček's personality. Though Kunc and Janáček had argued over the word setting in *Jenůfa*, it is clear from this substantial article that Kunc was eager to promote the work of his former teacher. Kunc's compositions include choruses on poems by Petr Bezruč* and Rudolf Těsnohlídek*, and an early setting of a text by Fedora Bartošová* (the librettist of *Fate*). In 1907 he made a setting for chorus and orchestra of Bezruč's *The Seventy Thousand*, performed in Brno on 5 April 1908. Kunc stated in his 1911 article that it was Janáček's dissatisfaction with Kunc's setting that led Janáček to make one of his own. *ČHS, JODA, KuncHR.*

Kundera, Ludvík (b. Brno, 17 August 1891; d. Brno, 12 May 1971), Czech pianist and writer. After attending school in Brno, Kundera continued his studies at the Philosophical Faculty of Charles University in Prague. During World War I, he served in the Czech Legion in Russia. He started to teach at the Brno Conservatory in 1921, and remained there until the Nazis removed him in 1941. In 1925 he attended Alfred Cortot's masterclasses in Paris, and the same year he completed his doctorate in musicology at the Masaryk University. As a piano teacher at the Conservatory, Kundera worked closely with Janáček, and he was asked by the composer to make the vocal scores of two major works, *The Makropulos Affair** (1926) and the *Glagolitic Mass** (1927–8), both under Janáček's supervision and published by UE.

In June 1922, Kundera was one of the founding officers of the KMS (along with Jaroslav Kvapil and Vilém Petrželka). He appeared in many of the Club's concerts, and on 3 March 1925, he played Schoenberg's Op. 11 piano pieces and extracts from *Gurrelieder* with Hana Pírková in the presence of their composer. He was the named pianist for several pieces in a concert on 25 April 1927, including the premiere of Pavel Haas's song-cycle *Vyvolená*. No pianist was listed for the last item on the programme, the first performance of Janáček's *Nursery Rhymes** (V/17), but it is likely that he played this too (when the work was given again on 14 April 1929, Kundera was named as the pianist). During the 1920s, Kundera gave regular two-piano concerts with his friend Václav Kaprál. He was the soloist in the first performance of the Piano Concerto by Vítězslava Kaprálová (1915–40) – Kaprál's daughter – given with the Brno Radio Orchestra conducted by Kaprálová on 15 October 1936.

Kundera was active as a critic in the Brno press, particularly in *Hudební rozhledy*, becoming co-editor in its second year (1925–6). His contributions included articles about several important Janáček premieres: the *Concertino** (15

February 1926), *The Makropulos Affair** (15 November 1926 and 15 December 1926) and the *Nursery Rhymes** (15 April 1927). For the Janáček seventieth birthday number (15 November 1924), Kundera wrote a survey of Janáček's piano works. He also wrote for *Listy Hudební matice* (*Tempo: Listy Hudební* *matice* from October 1927), including an article on the *Glagolitic Mass** in February 1928.

Kundera was involved in the early years of the Complete Critical Edition, and was co-editor of the first volume to be published (SKV F/1), which appeared after his death. In 1948 Kundera published two scrupulously researched books on aspects of Janáček's activities in Brno: at the Organ School (*Janáčkova varhanická škola*, Olomouc: Velehrad, 1948) and at the KPU (*Janáček a Klub přátel umění*, Olomouc: Velehrad, 1948). Kundera made two recordings of Janáček's works: the *Concertino** in 1948 and the first-ever recording of the *Capriccio** in 1950, both with Břetislav Bakala*. His son is the author Milan Kundera. *ČSHS, HudRoz, VohKMS.*

Kundera, Milan (b. Brno, 1 April 1929), Czech-born writer, son of Ludvík Kundera. In 2004 Kundera published *My Janáček* (*Můj Janáček*), from which the chapter about *The Cunning Little Vixen** subsequently appeared in *Encounter* (English edition 2010). Kundera writes about his love for Janáček's music and demonstrates a deep understanding of it. The insights in his little book, beautifully expressed, give it a special place in the Janáček literature. *KunEnc, KunMůj.*

Kvapil, Jaroslav (b. Fryšták, near Zlín, 21 April 1892; d. Brno, 18 February 1958), Czech composer, conductor and pianist. Kvapil was born in the same small town as Břetislav Bakala*. From 1902 to 1906, he was a chorister in Olomouc Cathedral under its choirmaster Josef Nešvera (1842–1914). He then studied with Janáček at the Brno Organ School, graduating in 1909. Kvapil completed his musical studies with Max Reger at the Leipzig Conservatory. He worked as organist in Olomouc in 1914–15, and served as a soldier in World War I. Kvapil taught at the Brno Conservatory (1919–47), and in 1920 he became conductor of the Brno Beseda. On 19 October 1924, he conducted a programme of Janáček's works for chorus and orchestra: *Our Father**, *Amarus**, *Čarták on Soláň** and *The Eternal Gospel**. Kvapil conducted the world premiere of Janáček's *Glagolitic Mass** in Brno on 5 December 1927, and gave the Prague premiere on 8 April 1928, both with the choir of the Brno Beseda. Janáček was delighted by the Prague performance (the first time his definitive revision of the work had been heard). He described it in a letter to the Brno Beseda (12 April 1928) as 'a beautiful performance ... perfect in every way', and praised 'especially the work of Prof. Kvapil'. Kvapil was also a brilliant pianist. With Ludvík Kundera and Vilém Petrželka, he was one of the founding officers of the KMS in 1922 and appeared as a pianist and composer in many of their concerts. At these concerts he gave with František Kudláček the premiere of Janáček's Sonata for Violin and Piano* (24 April 1922), and he played *1. X. 1905** on 19 January 1925 to mark the twentieth anniversary of the demonstrations that inspired it. At the Brno Beseda on 26 October 1925, he performed *The Diary of One Who Disappeared** (with Stanislav Tauber and Marie Hloušková as the soloists), and gave the premiere of the original version of the *Nursery Rhymes** (V/16).

In 1912 a committee of Prague musicians (Josef Bohuslav Foerster, Karel Hoffmeister and Jan Branberger) recommended two manuscripts that had been submitted anonymously for a competition organised by the KPU. These were a group of songs by Kvapil, and Janáček's *In the Mists*. Janáček urged the Club to print Kvapil's songs rather than *In the Mists*. In the end both works appeared in 1913. A review of Kvapil's songs appeared in *Lidové noviny* on 27 November 1913 signed '–c', the mark used by Jan Kunc. Though he was well aware they were by a very young composer, this didn't stop him from criticising the songs for being too reminiscent of Janáček ('Janáček appears in the declamatory style as well as in the repetition of words and in the piano with the repetition of small rhythmic and melodic motifs') and finding 'a contradiction between the words and the music' and 'inconsistent form'. At a committee meeting of the KPU the day after this appeared, Janáček is reported to have said that Kunc 'not only excoriated the songs of Mr Kvapil ... but also complained that the publisher should have issued piano music rather than songs, though he himself submitted songs that were rejected [by the jury]'. Kvapil's Second Symphony was given its premiere under František Neumann on 9 October 1922, and his Violin Concerto was first performed by František Kudláček and Neumann on 6 March 1928. Kvapil's *100 Slováckých písní* (Kroměříž: Pithart, c. 1917) were dedicated to Janáček.

Kvapil is not to be confused with the dramatist and librettist Jaroslav Kvapil (1868–1950), a director of the Prague NT and the librettist of Dvořák's *Rusalka*. *ČSHS, JYL2, KunKva, ZahGla.*

Kyselková, Františka, née Klimešová (b. Kamenice, near Jihlava, 27 March 1865; d. Brno, 23 July 1951), Czech folksong collector. Kyselková was the most productive of Janáček's folksong collectors: the Ethnographic Institute in Brno holds more than 4,200 tunes that Kyselková collected in Moravia and Slovakia. She graduated from the Teachers' Institute in Brno in 1884 and took up a post in Ivančice. In 1888, after marrying František Kyselka, she moved to Ořechov near Brno and was encouraged by Lucie Bakešová* to collect folksongs. She had collected over a hundred songs from the Brno region before the 1895 Czecho-Slavonic Ethnographic Exhibition, and these were subsequently included in the Bartoš-Janáček *Moravian Folksongs Newly Collected* (XIII/3), published in 1901. Janáček invited her to become an external member of the Working Committee on Czech Folksong in Moravia and Silesia in 1906, and a permanent member in 1909. That year, Janáček gave Kyselková and Hynek Bím* the task of making field recordings using a phonograph*. Janáček later asked her to catalogue the collections of the State Institute for Folksong. Kyselková's collecting activity concentrated on the Brno region between 1890 and about 1906, but after that she began collecting in her native region of Horácko in Western Moravia, where she collected more than a thousand folksongs. Her later collecting activity concentrated on the area near Uherský Brod in south-east Moravia, near the border with Slovakia. Kyselková was particularly interested in Slovak folksongs, and between 1906 and 1912 she discovered and recorded the songs of seasonal Slovak workers in the area; among them was Eva Gabel (see *Six Folksongs sung by Eva Gabel**).

In her memoir, *How I Collected Folksongs* [*Jak jsem sbírala národní písně*] (Brno, 1936), Kyselková recalled some of the difficulties she encountered as a folksong collector around 1900: 'At first the work was very hard. It would have been easier for a man. A male collector can meet for a friendly chat in the pub, inspiring high spirits, which always helps. This, of course, was not possible for me. ... It was often the case that a willing singer began to sing songs that he or she liked but that were not genuine folksongs. I was happy to go on overcoming these obstacles, especially as I could see how the results accumulated and that my work was good, as Mr Janáček told me several times.' *JYL1, ProVza.*

Kytice z národních písní moravských See *Moravian folk poetry in songs* (V/2)

Kytice z národních písní moravských (with Bartoš)   See **Folksong Editions**

Kytice z národních písní moravských, slovenských a českých (with Bartoš)   See **Folksong Editions**

Lachian Dances [*Lašské tance*], folk dances arranged for orchestra (VI/17).   By 1889 Janáček had completed at least eight folk dance arrangements for orchestra, two of which were published as *Valachian Dances* by Bursík and Kohout in 1890 (VI/4), and further arrangements were finished by 1893. Janáček returned to his early dances three decades later, and by October 1924 he had established a definitive suite of six dances with the title *Lachian Dances*, which were first performed on 2 December 1924 by the Brno NT orchestra conducted by František Neumann*. Janáček discussed publication of the *Lachian Dances* with HMUB in 1925 and again in 1927, when an agreement was reached in June, though publication was postponed until the following year. Janáček corrected the proofs in May 1928 and wrote the preface, 'My Lachia' (first printed in *Lidové noviny* on 27 May, XV/310). Janáček died on 12 August 1928, and the three-volume score of the *Lachian Dances* was published about two weeks later, by the end of the month.

For Janáček, the *Lachian Dances* were a nostalgic evocation of the time he first heard the tunes in the late 1880s with friends such as the poet Vladimír Šťastný (1849–1910), the philologist František Batěk (both from Brno) and Mrs Marie Jungová, a friend from Hukvaldy. All three were fondly remembered in Janáček's preface: 'Gone is the poet P [i.e. V.] Šťastný, gone is Professor Batěk, gone is Mrs Marie Jungová ... In memory of you who were witnesses of that warm night and who are now sleeping the eternal sleep – a song of praise to my homeland, my Lachian country.'

The first performance in Germany was given in Mainz on 3 October 1928, conducted by Paul Breisach, and the British premiere was given in the Queen's Hall, London on 19 August 1930, conducted by Henry Wood*. In October 1929, Otakar Pařík recorded Nos. 2 and 6 with the Radiojournal orchestra of Prague Radio, and on 13 September 1930, Erich Kleiber recorded No. 1 with the Berlin Philharmonic (see Recordings before 1960*). The first miniature score (Orbis, 1951) is based on the 1928 HMUB edition and includes a preface by Bohumír Štědroň. A critical edition by Jarmil Burghauser and Radomil Eliška appeared as SKV D/4 (1982). *BarLaš, JAWO, JYL2, ProVol.*

Lada, Josef (b. Hrusice, 17 December 1887; d. Prague, 14 December 1957), Czech artist.   Lada began contributing to *Lidové noviny* in 1919. His illustrations to a series of nursery rhymes printed in *Lidové noviny* in 1925–6 delighted Janáček, and on 9 March 1927 he wrote to the artist about his own musical settings: 'I even added a musical twist to the eighteenth song, I think. The joke in the music is very much in keeping with your illustrations. They want these little songs to be finished by 4 April. I asked them if your illustrations might be shown [at the concert]. It would be wonderful if they were in colour. Could you add colour to them? I will send you a score with your pictures stuck in so that you can see which ones I have chosen.' Lada tried to add colour to the plates of his illustrations, but couldn't get the paints to adhere. The performance of the *Nursery Rhymes* (V/17) took place on 23 April without Lada's illustrations, but Janáček also wanted to include them in the vocal score. On 10 July 1927, he wrote to Lada asking him to contact UE with his terms for using eight illustrations. These duly appeared, along with illustrations by Ondřej Sekora and Jan Hála, in the vocal score published on 28 September 1928, six weeks after Janáček's death. Lada made new colour versions of his illustrations for a film of Janáček's *Nursery Rhymes* directed by Eduard Hofman in 1949. In 1941 Lada produced a large print called *The Forester's Dream* (*Hajného sen*) depicting a forester falling asleep by a tree in a clearing, surrounded by animals including a fox, a badger and an owl: an image that is almost certainly based on the final moments of Janáček's *The Cunning Little Vixen*. JanLid, JAWO, JosLad, KLJ.

Lašské tance See *Lachian Dances* (VI/17)

Lehner, Ferdinand Josef (b. Rokycany, 6 June 1837; d. Prague, 1 March 1914). Following his ordination in 1862, Lehner served as a chaplain in the Karlín district of Prague from 1865 until 1892, when he became parish priest of St Ludmila at Vinohrady. At Karlín he established a choir school that gained a reputation for singing Renaissance polyphony, including Masses by Palestrina. In 1874 Lehner founded *Cecilie*, a 'journal for Catholic music' (continued as *Cyrill* from 1879). Lehner advocated reform and high standards in church music, views he shared with Janáček's teacher Pavel Křížkovský*. During Janáček's stay in Prague in 1874–5, not only did Lehner provide him with regular meals, but also arranged for a piano to be installed in his flat. According to Janáček: 'One fine day, all of a sudden, there was a piano standing in my little room in Štěpanská ulice. I related the inexplicable incident to Father Lehner ... A knowing smile stole over his good-natured face. At the end of the school year the piano vanished from my flat again just as quietly.' In 1877 Lehner was the first person to publish any music by Janáček, when the motet *Exaudi Deus* (II/4) appeared in a musical supplement to *Cecilie*. Lehner's hymnbook *Mešní kancionál* was first published in Prague by Mikuláš and Knapp in 1875. It was probably when Janáček and his new wife Zdenka visited Lehner on their honeymoon trip to Prague in 1881 that the idea of writing some harmonisations for tunes in Lehner's hymnbook came up. As one of the very few people with any knowledge of Janáček's music at the time, Lehner was enthusiastic and offered to publish them in *Cyrill*. This never happened, and Janáček's *Ten Czech Hymns from the Lehner Hymnbook for the Mass* (II/10) were instead published in 1882 by Winkler in Brno. In 1889 Winkler published an expanded edition, including three additional hymns and revised harmonisations of the others. HelJan, JYL1, KLJ.

Leipzig To further his musical studies, Janáček applied for leave from the Teachers' Institute in 1879–80 and set out for Leipzig, then the musical centre of Germany. His principal teachers at the Leipzig Conservatory were Oscar Paul (1836–98) for harmony and counterpoint, and Leo Grill (1846–1919) for musical form. Janáček arrived in Leipzig on 1 October 1879, found lodgings on the second floor of No. 1 Plauensche Strasse and made arrangements to hire a piano. The next day he went to the Conservatory for the first time, auditioning successfully with a prelude by Bach and a study by Anton Rubinstein. The Conservatory at that time was housed in a building Janáček described in his autobiography as 'A shed with a wooden partition. Very dark. At one end an old piano fitted with a pedal board – this is where organ practice is done. All desire to go there soon vanishes.'

Despite the dismal accommodation of the Conservatory, Janáček wasted no time getting down to composing. He was an argumentative student who complained that if he did what Leo Grill asked, 'I should need to forget what imagination is.' He went to rehearsals in the Gewandhaus (across the courtyard from the Conservatory), where Carl Reinecke's conducting failed to impress (Janáček grumbled about sluggish speeds and complacency). In spite of complaining about the rule-bound teaching and slapdash music-making that he found in Leipzig, his letters to Zdenka Schulzová give a comprehensive account of his composing activity. Only a few of these Leipzig works survived. The *Romance* for violin and piano (VII/3), composed on 16 November 1879 (published by HMUB in 1938), was originally one of six. It is also possible that the *Dumka* for violin and piano (VII/4) was one of the Leipzig romances. Janáček composed the *Thema con variazioni* for piano (VIII/6) between 29 January and 22 February 1880, describing them as 'Zdenka's variations' (HMUB, 1944). While working on the violin romances, Janáček also composed fugues for piano (X/6). There were fourteen of them in all, written as exercises for Oscar Paul and Leo Grill. On 14 February 1880, Janáček performed three fugues in a concert at the Leipzig Conservatory, including the one he called the 'Zdenčileoš' fugue. These three fugues, long thought lost, were rediscovered in 1998 in a manuscript made by Josef Chmelíček (a Brno theologian who collected fugues). An edition by Lehel Donáth with an introduction by Jakob Knaus was published in 2008 as SKVEJ F/3.

Several other works were composed during Janáček's Leipzig stay, including a piano sonata, a violin sonata, the scherzo of a symphony and a song cycle, all of them now lost (see X/5 to X/14). Janáček left Leipzig on 24 February 1880; his time had not been wasted. As John Tyrrell put it, 'the most positive outcome was the secure technical grounding that he built up with Grill, which enabled him to work quickly and extract the maximum out of any musical material'. *HelJan, JAWO, KnaFug, KnaInt, VesJan, VogJan.*

Lidová nokturna See *Folk Nocturnes* (IV/32)

Lidové noviny, Brno daily newspaper. *Lidové noviny*, literally the 'People's newspaper', was founded by Adolf Stránský in 1893 and its first editor-in-chief was Emil Čermák. The first issue appeared on 16 December 1893, and Janáček's feuilleton 'The Music of Truth' (XV/143) – an account of the folk music he heard and the musicians he met in Valachia and Moravian Slovakia – was printed on its front page. He was a contributor for the next thirty-five years, particularly from 1919 onwards, when Arnošt Heinrich became the editor-in-chief. Heinrich maintained its political orientation of Moravian national liberalism, and encouraged leading Czech writers and artists to contribute. Janáček's articles for *Lidové noviny* were intermittent at first (there were none at all between 1896 and 1905), but in the 1920s he became a regular contributor. The subjects range far and wide. Examples include accounts of new works ('Glagolitic Mass', 27 November 1927, XV/297), recollections of childhood ('Without drums', 16 April 1911, XV/199), descriptions of speech melodies ('Smetana's daughter', 3 December 1924, XV/255), reflections on the creative process ('Silence', 15 August 1919, XV/219), birdsong ('These lovers! A spring study', 16 April 1922, XV/238), folk music ('Mayor Smolík', 18 March 1923, XV/245), landscapes ('Springs', 8 September 1922, XV/242), reports on trips abroad ('Berlin', 15 May 1924, XV/253) and the plight of gypsy children ('Pepík and Jeník', 2 April 1928, XV/307). Janáček's literary style is distinctive: energetic and loosely structured, the prose often peppered with terse outbursts or imaginary conversations. He is sometimes whimsical and nearly always sharply observant. Janáček is never a predictable writer: there are unexpected associations of ideas, and his prose has a kind of spiky succinctness.

As well as writings, Janáček also contributed original pieces of music to *Lidové noviny*. A piece from *On the Overgrown Path** (Series II, No. 1) was printed in the paper's literary supplement *Večery* (30 September 1911), as was the *Krajcpolka* (V/6, No. 5, 17 February 1912). The article 'Early morning lights' (24 December 1909, XV/194) included Janáček's arrangement of the carol *Narodil se Kristus Pán* (VIII/20), and a number of shorter works were included in other articles. An extract from the fanfares of the *Sinfonietta** (bar 76 to the end) were published in a facsimile of Janáček's manuscript ('Festival fanfares', 4 July 1926). *Lidové noviny* was the first Czech daily to publish political cartoons, and it developed a strong visual and graphic identity thanks to its art editor, Eduard Milén*, with illustrations by Josef Lada*, Ondřej Sekora, Josef Čapek*, Hugo Boettinger, Stanislav Lolek* and Milén himself (see Images of Janáček*). *Lidové noviny* also provided Janáček with material. Two examples stand out: the drawings by Stanislav Lolek and accompanying story by Těsnohlídek that inspired *The Cunning Little Vixen*, and the series of children's nursery rhymes published in the paper in 1925–6 (illustrated by Lada, Sekora and Jan Hála) that gave Janáček the idea for his *Nursery Rhymes* (V/16 and V/17). The drawings from the paper were subsequently used to illustrate the music in the first edition of the vocal score (1928, see *Nursery Rhymes**). *Lidové noviny* offered Janáček both a platform for his writings and a source of inspiration for some of his music. *JanLid, JAWO, LJLD1, TauJan, ZemLid.*

Lolek, Stanislav (b. Palonín, near Šumberk, 13 November 1873; d. Uherské Hradiště, 9 May 1936), Czech artist. Lolek is best known for his drawings that inspired Těsnohlídek's story *Liška Bystrouška* (*Vixen Bystrouška*). He had studied at the Písek School of Forestry before training as an artist. He enrolled at the Academy of Fine Arts in Prague in 1895, and the landscapes for which he was best known were influenced by Impressionism.

Jaromír John (1887–1952) was responsible for acquiring the cartoons about Vixen Bystrouška for *Lidové noviny*. He visited Lolek (then living in Prague) to ask if he could provide some illustrations for the paper. Lolek explained that he would not be able to help as he was a landscape painter, but John spotted a pile of cartoons half-hidden on the floor, depicting 'a furious hunter with a bristly beard and a kind of sly vixen'. Despite Lolek's protests, he took these back to Brno. Words needed to be put to them and Těsnohlídek was asked to provide them. He recalled that at first this was a chore:

Vixen Bystrouška exasperated me. Dr Markalous [Jaromír John] brought Lolek's pictures and the editors wanted some humorous verses to go with the drawings. Nobody wanted to do this, so it was shoved onto my desk and one lunchtime I took the drawings with me to Bílovice nad Svitavou. A railway official was travelling back by train ... He took the drawings from me, started laughing, and didn't stop until I promised to write something to go with it. Some time in February I set to work on it. I threw away the first chapter and went to listen to how woodcutters speak. And then it wrote itself. It was the magnificent spring of 1920 ... I scribbled so wildly that the printer couldn't read it and threatened to strike and I was instructed to dictate it into a machine. When it came out in the paper, it was like a hallucination. People went crazy. ... When Veselý first told me that Janáček was planning to turn it into an opera, I thought he was pulling my leg.

Lolek's drawings and Těsnohlídek's text were published in instalments in *Lidové noviny* between 7 April and 23 June 1920. The following year, Těsnohlídek's story was republished in book form with Lolek's illustrations (Brno: Polygrafia, 1921). *JanLid, KLJ.*

London visit in 1926   In January 1926, Rosa Newmarch* wrote to Janáček proposing a visit to London: 'I have suggested to the Legation here that you should pay us a visit to London. I should like to have you and dear Mrs Janáčková as my guests, and while you are here we will organize a concert of your work. An operatic performance is impossible, I fear.' On 15 February, Janáček accepted the invitation and arranged for a copy of the newly published *Concertino* to be sent to Newmarch. Over the next few weeks she discussed various possibilities for the programme of the London concert, as well as making all the other arrangements.

Janáček and Jan Mikota* (who acted as Janáček's interpreter) arrived at Folkestone on 29 April, where Mrs Newmarch's daughter Elsie met them. In London that evening, they were received by Jan Masaryk (the Czech Ambassador in London and son of the President) and by Newmarch herself. Janáček and Mikota stayed at the Langham Hotel in Langham Place, a short walk from the Wigmore Hall and opposite where Broadcasting House now stands. A reception at Claridge's followed the next day.

On the morning of Sunday, 1 May, Janáček attended a rehearsal for the Violin Sonata at the home of Adila Fachiri (10 Netherton Grove, Chelsea), followed by a rehearsal for the *Fairy Tale* at the home of the critic H. C. Colles in the afternoon. Dinner that evening was at Les Gobelins Restaurant in Heddon Street (just off Regent Street) with Sir Henry and Lady Wood, Newmarch and her daughter Elsie.

On 2 May, Janáček spent the morning attending rehearsals for the String Quartet No. 1, *Youth* and the *Concertino* before a trip to Chorleywood in Hertfordshire to visit Henry Wood at Apple Tree Farmhouse. He then travelled back to London to give a speech at the Czechoslovak Club, paying warm tribute to his host, Mrs Newmarch, and contrasting the works in the Wigmore Hall concert (which he claimed, quite wrongly, that he could 'accomplish in two or three days') with his most important pieces: 'There are some compositions on which one works for years. Perhaps, one day, you will hear them in London too. I mean, my operas. In them a nation is celebrated in its true form: firm, resolute and unyielding!'

The next morning, 3 May, Janáček visited London Zoo, where he noted down the cries of monkeys and a walrus, and he then did some sightseeing by the Thames, including Westminster Abbey, the Houses of Parliament and the Cenotaph. On 4 May, he went to a rehearsal by Henry Wood (Queen's Hall was next door to the Langham Hotel), then to a reception at the School of Slavonic Studies at London University. At this event a choir from Mansfield Road School, Gospel Oak, sang a selection of English folksongs and madrigals conducted by their headmaster Mr Miles, and Herbert Hayner sang two of Janáček's *Silesian Songs* (V/13) in English translations by Rosa Newmarch. Robert Seton Watson gave a speech about cultural relations between Britain and Czechoslovakia, to which Janáček responded, his words noted down by Jan Mikota: 'The moment I saw these young singers who sing so beautifully, I felt as if I were at home. Why at home? Because of the folksongs. I, too, have lived with folk music since I was little. In a folksong the whole man is present, body and soul, his milieu, everything. ... If I grow as a composer, I grow only from folksong and from human speech, and I am confident that I will keep on growing. I laugh at those who offer only acoustic sound.'

On 5 May, Janáček and Mikota dined with Seton Watson. The concert took place at the Wigmore Hall the following day (6 May), despite the considerable problems caused by the General Strike (3–12 May). Janáček wrote to his wife on the morning of the concert: 'A terrible situation has developed with this General Strike. Cars do not run in London and it is impossible to walk the distances. Trains are at a standstill. ... Naturally the concert today is in the air too. ... Today they even shouted at our driver. Be glad that you are at home.' Several of the musicians had to walk long distances to get to the hall (Leon Goossens recalled that it took him three hours) and there were no printed programmes, only a flyer circulated in advance. No reviews appeared in the daily papers, as they were not printed during the strike. The works performed were the String Quartet No. 1*, Sonata for Violin and Piano*, *Fairy Tale** and *Youth**. The *Concertino* was dropped from the programme after Janáček decided it needed more rehearsal – and after an unsuccessful attempt to bring Ilona Štěpánová-Kurzová to London as a replacement for Fanny Davies (described by Janáček to his wife as 'an old scarecrow'). Though Janáček was impressed by the wind players at the rehearsal of *Youth* (on 3 May he told Zdenka that it was 'interpreted excellently'), at the concert only Fachiri's playing stood out for him. On 7 May he wrote to Zdenka: 'Except for the Violin Sonata, they did not play in a way that satisfied me. The ground is prepared, but I doubt that what I have sown will grow.' Following the concert, Janáček stayed with Jan Masaryk for two days before returning home via Vlissingen in the Netherlands, where Mikota took the well-known photographs of Janáček notating the sounds of the sea. *FisJan, JYL2, MikJan.*

Lost works   Most of Janáček's lost works date from the early part of his career, whether in Brno in the 1870s or during his years of study in Leipzig and Vienna. A few later works have also disappeared, most tantalisingly the Piano Trio, which was performed several times and which appears in the worklist of Brod's 1924 biography. Works in this category are those for which there is documentary evidence that they once existed, for instance mention in concert programmes, Janáček's correspondence, reports of pupils and reviews. Full

WIGMORE HALL

WIGMORE STREET, W.1

THURSDAY
AFTERNOON **MAY 6 at 3**

Under the Patronage of:

HIS EXCELLENCY THE CZECHOSLOVAK MINISTER

and Mme. MASARYK

LEOŠ JANÁČEK

During the visit to England of The Czechoslovak Composer,

A Concert of his Chamber Music will be given

ARTISTS :

ADILA FACHIRI   **MANNUCCI**   **FANNY DAVIES**
VIOLIN   'CELLO   PIANO

THE WOODHOUSE STRING QUARTET   **THE LONDON WIND QUINTETTE**

STEINWAY GRAND PIANOFORTE

TICKETS (including Tax) : **Reserved 12/-, 8/6 & 5/9   Front Row Balcony 5/9   Unreserved Area & Balcony 3/-**

Tickets may be obtained at the BOX OFFICE, Wigmore Hall, Libraries, usual agents and of
FRED WILLIAMS CONCERT & OPERATIC DIRECTION, 73, Mortimer Street, London, W 1   Tel. Museum 3220

VAIL AND CO., PRINTERS, LONDON, W.1   P.T.O.

9. Announcement for the concert of Janáček's music at the Wigmore Hall, London, on 6 May 1926.

details of these works are given in section X of *JAWO*. See Leipzig*, Vienna* and Piano Trio* (X/22). *BroJan, JAWO, JYL1, JYL2, KnaFug, KnaInt, VesJan, VogJan.*

Löwenbach, Jan (b. Rychnov nad Kněžnou, 29 April 1880; d. New York, 13 August 1972), Czech lawyer and writer.   An expert on copyright, Löwenbach worked for HMUB from 1908 until his resignation in 1925, and from 1916 he

LEOŠ JANÁČEK

Zde Janáček svou bílou hřívu složil,
jenž roků sta se na Moravě dožil.
Byl přes to mlád! Neb v šedesátce let
svou operu zřel prvně provádět.

Na věky potřel starou melodii
svou slavnou nápěvkovou theorií.
Znal nápěvky všemožných živých tvorů
a řeči spád i náměsíčních sborů.

Teď duše jeho vzlétla k nebi vzhůru
nápěvky sbírat andělského kůru.

8

10. J. L. Budin (pseud. Jan Löwenbach) and Dr Desiderius (pseud. Hugo Boettinger): 'Leoš Janáček' from *Muzikantské dušičky* [*Musical Souls*], published by A. Srdce, Prague, 1922.

advised Janáček on negotiations with foreign publishers, including UE, and with the Prague NT. The correspondence between Janáček and Löwenbach was published in 1958, edited by Ivo Stolařík. Under the pseudonym J. L. Budin, Löwenbach published *Muzikantské dušičky*, a collection of humorous poems about musicians (Prague: Srdce, 1922) with illustrations by 'Dr Desiderius' (Hugo Boettinger). Janáček is the subject of one of the poems. Its first line includes the phrase 'Janáček with his white mane' ('Janáček svou bílou hřívou'), which may have inspired the title of Jaromil Jireš's 1986 film *The Lion with the White Mane*. Löwenbach's poem ends with the couplet 'His soul now flies into the skies / Collecting angels' speech melodies', illustrated by a Boettinger cartoon showing Janáček notating the speech melodies of angels above the Brno skyline. Other poems are about Janáček's associates, including František Neumann*, František Ondříček*, Otakar Ostrčil*, František Spilka*, Václav Štěpán*, Václav Talich* and Ota Zítek*. *BudMuz, JODA, LánJan, StoLöw.*

Luhačovice, spa town 110 km (70 miles) east of Brno in the Zlín region. Along with Hukvaldy and Brno, Luhačovice has a central place in Janáček's creative and personal life. Janáček stayed there regularly from 1903 onwards, and it's likely he had visited at least twice before, in 1886 and 1892. With the spa transformed by the improvements instigated by its director František Veselý* and the new buildings designed by Dušan Jurkovič*, it became the holiday destination of choice for Janáček: between 1903 and 1928 he went there almost every year, usually for two or three weeks in July or August. In earlier years he stayed in the Vlastimila, the Janův dům and the Hotel Jestřabí, and from 1918 to 1928 he stayed at the Augustinian House (Augustiniánský dům), which still

Luhačovice.
Hudební pavilon.

11. The Music Pavilion at Luhačovice designed by Dušan Jurkovič. Postcard from 1910.

operates as the Hotel Augustiniánský dům (its Leoš Janáček Suite commemorates Janáček's visits there). Though his 1903 article 'My Luhačovice' evokes the busy Promenade, in general Janáček avoided the crowds and preferred to take long walks along country paths. His reason for choosing Luhačovice was partly to take various cures for his health, partly to have a rest, and partly as a place to meet friends, especially female friends: in his autobiography he described Luhačovice as 'an annual gathering of beautiful women'. He was clearly impressed by the alterations he found in 1903, sending a postcard to Zdenka on 17 August: 'The spa has been changed, expanded, made more beautiful.' The 'annual gathering of beautiful women' involved some specific individuals: it was in Luhačovice that he spent time with three of the most important women in his life. He met Kamila Urválková* there in 1903, took Gabriela Horvátová* in 1916, and first encountered Kamila Stösslová* in 1917. Luhačovice also had very close connections with two major works: *Fate** and the *Glagolitic Mass**. No wonder Janáček attached such importance to the place.

Janáček's longest article about Luhačovice appeared in *Hlídka* in 1903. 'My Luhačovice' (XV/173) described his impressions of the town, interspersing these with a huge array of speech melodies recording the people he met on the Promenade. The highlight is Janáček's encounter with Kamila Urválková, unnamed but unmistakable, the 'magic' of her beautiful voice described in dream-like terms: 'The *violetta d'amour* of these speech melodies cast their spell. They were brought alive with almost theatrical power. They fell like evening shadows suddenly turning into unhappy memories ... "What is love?", they ask the five-year-old boy. I hear the well-mimicked reply: "When Nana and Johan love each other!"' The references to Urválková's mood reflect how Míla appears in Act I of *Fate*, while the words of the little boy went into Act II almost unchanged. With its description of a large cast of characters (even including the spa orchestra), bristling with activity and energy and with sudden shifts of mood and perspective, 'My Luhačovice' reads like a prose blueprint for the opening scenes of *Fate*.

Until 1901, Luhačovice was owned by the aristocratic Serényi family, and guests were predominantly wealthy and usually German. However, Janáček's teacher Pavel Křížkovský stayed there in 1884, and Janáček's autobiography mentions a 'Czech Society' led by the lawyer and organiser of the Sokol movement in Brno, Ctibor Helcelet (1844–1904). Janáček's connection with the Serényi family can be seen in his *Hail Mary** (II/14), which is dedicated to Countess Leopoldina Serényi (1872–1917). In 1902 Count Serényi sold Luhačovice to a consortium of Moravian doctors, led by František Veselý.

Act I of *Fate* was set in Luhačovice, and the other work closely linked to the town is the *Glagolitic Mass*, which Janáček started composing there during his stay in August 1926, with a sustained effort over a two-week period to produce a first draft of the work. Janáček wrote in *Lidové noviny* in 1927 that 'the Luhačovice rain' and 'the balmy breeze of the Luhačovice woods' were an important influence on the work. To Kamila Stösslová he was more explicit, telling her: 'I've set it in Luhačovice. Good, eh? Where else could it stand than there, where we were so happy!' For ten blissful days in August 1927, Janáček was together with Kamila in Luhačovice, happy to be seen in public with her and for them to be photographed together. His last visit was in July 1928. *HorPet, JYL1, JYL2, KLJ, LázLuh, ProLuh, VokLuh.*

Lullaby [*Ukolébavka*], arranged by Janáček for voice and piano (V/14). This arrangement was made in 1920. The words and melody were printed in the *Informatorium školy mateřské* [*Nursery School Handbook*] (1632) by the Czech educational reformer Jan Amos Komenský (1592–1670), also known as Comenius. Komenský advocated the use of music to calm young children and to help develop musical memory. He included an example of a lullaby suitable for infants, beginning with the words 'Spi, mé milé poupě' ['Sleep, my dear bud']. Janáček made his arrangement for voice and piano as a contribution to the *Kniha Komenského*, edited by František Pražák and published in Brno in 1920 to commemorate the 250th anniversary of Komenský's death. In 1928 the *Lullaby* was reprinted in *Hudební besídka* and had acquired further significance for Janáček: one of his recurring fantasies was that Kamila Stösslová* was pregnant with his child, and on 16 April 1928 he wrote to her: 'I take some old magazine into my hands and I see the title *Lullaby* to the words of Jan Amos Komenský by Leoš Janáček. It will be a magnificent little piece. At that time, years ago, I'd already composed a lullaby.' *JAWO, TyrInt.*

Mackerras, Charles (b. Schenectady, New York, 17 November 1925; d. London, 14 July 2010), Australian conductor. Brought up in Australia, Mackerras's first encounter with Janáček was playing *Youth* as an oboe student at the Sydney Conservatorium. After moving to London and starting work as an oboist and assistant conductor at Sadler's Wells Opera, he went to Czechoslovakia in 1947–8, on a British Council scholarship to study conducting with Václav Talich*. It was during this visit that he first heard Janáček's operas. His wife Judy (a clarinettist, who went with him to Prague) noted in her diary on 15 October 1947: 'Saw *Káťa Kabanová* at Národní Theatre. Superb performance. Talich.' Both Mackerras and his wife learned Czech at the time, and for the rest of his life he delighted in using the language when working with musicians in

Prague and Brno. He later recalled that during his stay in 1947–8 he saw nearly all the operas. In May 1948, he wrote to his mother: 'It is a terrible pity that these works are quite unknown outside this country. ... When I get back I shall do my utmost to persuade Sadler's Wells to perform one of them, though I don't suppose they will.' Fortunately, his prediction was wrong and on 10 April 1951, Mackerras conducted the British premiere of *Káťa Kabanová**, the first opera by Janáček to be staged in Britain. Though *Jenůfa* was produced at Covent Garden in 1956, and Mackerras conducted a warmly received revival of *Káťa* at Sadler's Wells in 1959, Janáček's music was still rarely heard in London when Mackerras first recorded it for Pye in 1959: the *Sinfonietta, Jealousy* and the preludes to *Káťa Kabanová, The Makropulos Affair* and *From the House of the Dead* with the Pro Arte Orchestra. Andrew Porter wrote in *Gramophone* (January 1960): 'At Sadler's Wells, where he introduced *Katya Kabanova* in 1951, and where he has just been in charge of a triumphant revival of the opera, Charles Mackerras has shown himself to be one of the finest Janáček conductors ... His readings convey a sense of burning belief in and love of Janáček's music; they are well prepared; yet on each occasion it is as if the strangeness and beauty of the music were being revealed for the first time.' In 1964 Mackerras conducted the London premiere of *The Makropulos Affair**, with Marie Collier an outstanding Emilia Marty, and a year later he conducted the first London performances of *From the House of the Dead** at Sadler's Wells, using Kubelík's edition. Ever since conducting *Káťa* in 1951, Mackerras had been aware of problems with the hastily prepared full score of the opera, and by 1971 he had completed a thoroughly corrected edition. He also prepared a new edition of *The Makropulos Affair* after introducing the work to London audiences. By the time he began recording the operas for Decca in 1976, Mackerras had an unrivalled knowledge of these works as both conductor and editor. The series began with *Káťa Kabanová* in 1976, followed by *The Makropulos Affair* (1978), *From the House of the Dead* (1980), *The Cunning Little Vixen** (1981) and *Jenůfa** (1982). He was invited to conduct Janáček's operas abroad (notably at the Metropolitan Opera), and late in his career he conducted *Káťa Kabanová* (2007) and *The Cunning Little Vixen* (2010) at Covent Garden. *Vixen* was the last opera he conducted there, a few months before his death.

At English National Opera, he conducted *The Excursions of Mr Brouček** in 1978 and 1992, and at the Prague NT he gave the first performance of the new edition by Jiří Zahrádka in 2003. Though both ENO productions were broadcast and a private recording was made of the Prague production, *Brouček* is the only Janáček opera (apart from *The Beginning of a Romance*) that Mackerras did not record commercially. He recorded *Fate* for EMI (1989, in English; reissued by Chandos). For Supraphon he recorded *Káťa Kabanová* (1997) for the second time, and *Šárka* (2000), both with the Czech Philharmonic. *The Cunning Little Vixen* was filmed at the Châtelet in Paris in 1995 and released on DVD. Later recordings of *Jenůfa* (2003) and *Makropulos* (2006) were released by Chandos, sung in English.

Mackerras recorded most of Janáček's major choral and orchestral works, including *Amarus** (Supraphon, 1984), the *Glagolitic Mass** in its final version with the Czech Philharmonic (Supraphon, 1984) and in Paul Wingfield's edition of the earlier version with Danish Radio forces (Chandos, 1994) and the Czech Philharmonic (Supraphon 1996, on DVD). The *Sinfonietta** and *Taras*

*Bulba** were recorded with the Vienna Philharmonic (Decca, 1980) and later with the Czech Philharmonic (Supraphon, 2002 and 2003), along with other works including *Schluck und Jau**. He recorded the *Concertino* and *Capriccio* with Mikhail Rudy (EMI, 1995). Mackerras was the recipient of many honours and awards. In 1978 he was presented with the Janáček Medal, and he was knighted in the 1979 New Year Honours.

Mackerras first recorded *The Cunning Little Vixen* for Decca before performing it in the theatre. His first stage production was with Welsh National Opera in 1987, and it became one of the operas he loved above all others. Like Janáček before him, Mackerras asked for the closing scene of *Vixen* to be played at his funeral at St Paul's, Covent Garden on 23 July 2010. *MacTyr, SimTyr.*

Mahen, Jiří [pseud. for Antonín Vančura] (b. Čáslav, 12 December 1882; d. Brno, 22 May 1939), Czech writer and librarian. Mahen worked for *Lidové noviny* (1910–19) and on the staff of the Brno NT (1918–20). In 1921 he became a librarian for Brno City Library, and its director from 1937. His suicide in 1939 was motivated by despair at the Nazi occupation. Two major institutions in Brno bear Mahen's name: the theatre where five of Janáček's operas had their world premieres has been known as the Mahen Theatre since 1965; and Brno Public Library (Schrattenbach Palace, Kobližná No. 4) has been known as the Jiří Mahen Library since 1959. On 28 May 1916, Mahen wrote to Janáček: 'Please accept my congratulations for the success of *Jenůfa* in Prague. Believe me, I was very pleased to hear about it.' The next month, Janáček asked Mahen if he could help to rewrite the troublesome libretto of *The Excursion of Mr Brouček to the Moon.* Mahen did not mince his words. In 1929 he recalled, 'I went to Janáček and told him directly that this was an incoherent ragbag and that the whole thing ought to be done again.' Mahen duly delivered his revision, only to read a newspaper report (in September 1916) that Janáček had asked Viktor Dyk* to take on the rewriting. Some acrimonious correspondence ensued, but Dyk brought matters to an amicable conclusion. Between 1920 and 1924, Mahen taught drama at the Brno Conservatory and is likely to have seen Janáček on a regular basis there. Mahen and Janáček were among those depicted conversing over beers in Kalvoda's group portrait *At Stopka's* that used to hang in Stopka's Pilsner pub (see Images of Janáček*).

Mahen was one of the most significant literary figures in Brno, the author of several successful plays, poetry and a volume of stories for children, originally entitled *Tales* (Brno, 1914) and reprinted in 1922 as *What the Fox told Me*, with illustrations by František Hlavica (who illustrated Janáček's feuilleton 'Mayor Smolík' for *Lidové noviny* in 1923, and designed the sets for the premiere of *From the House of the Dead* in 1930). After Mahen's suicide, *Lidové noviny* (24 May 1939) summarised his importance as follows: 'What musical life in Brno lost with the death of Janáček, drama and theatre has now lost with the passing of Mahen.' *EDMB, JODA, KLJ.*

Maixner, Vincenc (b. Prague, 17 March 1888; d. Prague, 24 May 1946), Czech conductor. Maixner worked at the Prague NT as a repetiteur from 1915, and as a conductor from 1918 to 1938. He conducted *Káťa Kabanová* in 1923, *The Cunning Little Vixen* in 1925, and on 21 February 1931, the Prague premiere of *From the House of the Dead**. Maixner's personal relationship with Janáček hit a low point in 1918, when he failed to deliver the promised vocal score of *The*

Excursions of Mr Brouček and when Janáček discovered that Maixner was having an affair with Gabriela Horvátová* (Zdenka Janáčková related in her memoirs that 'there was apparently a scene ... and Maixner told him that Mrs Horvátová was and would continue to be his mistress'). Once the Horvátová infatuation had blown over, Janáček, Maixner and his wife Sylvia Maixnerová (née Šebková) had a cordial correspondence. In a letter dated 2 December 1924, Maixnerová wrote about the 'great impression' *Taras Bulba* had made on her, hoped they would soon see Janáček in Prague, and asked Marie Stejskalová to send some of Mrs Janáčková's 'excellent recipes'. Stejskalová obliged and on 22 December 1924, Maixner wrote to Janáček: 'Thank you very much for the recipes: my wife was very happy with them, mainly because you had a part in sending them! ... The Janáček celebrations have nearly finished now and we were especially captivated by *Taras Bulba*, the String Quartet [No. 1] and the choruses.' *ČSHS, KLJ, NDprOA.*

The Makropulos Affair [*Věc Makropulos*], opera after Karel Čapek's comedy (I/10). Janáček saw Karel Čapek's *Makropulos Affair* in Prague on 10 December 1922, and approached Čapek informally through his sister, Helena Čapková in February 1923 (see Čapek, Karel*). Despite the author's initial scepticism about the play's suitability for operatic treatment (and his concerns that there might be legal or contractual problems), by October 1923, Janáček had a formal agreement. He got to work without delay and the opera was composed between November 1923 and December 1925: a first version was finished in February 1925 and Janáček then went through the whole opera making substantial changes (some of them during a summer break in the peace and quiet of Hukvaldy) before arriving at a definitive score.

Why was Janáček drawn to this thoroughly metropolitan comedy, its plot dominated by a long-running legal dispute? His previous opera had been the bucolic *The Cunning Little Vixen* and now he was turning his hand to something that could hardly be more different, apart from the strong female character at the centre of both stories. Janáček wrote to Kamila Stösslová on 28 December 1922, a couple of weeks after seeing Čapek's play: 'They have been giving *Makropulos* in Prague. A woman 337 years old, but at the same time still young and beautiful. Would you like to be like that too? And you know that she was unhappy? We are happy because we know that our life isn't long. So we need to make the most of every moment, to use it properly. It's all hurry in our life – and longing. The latter is my lot. That woman – the 337 year-old beauty – didn't have a heart any more.' In October 1925, Janáček told Adolf Veselý that the play had 'captivated me immediately', describing it as a 'modern historical opera'. In letters to Stösslová, his focus remained single-mindedly on the heroine: on 4 December 1923, three weeks after starting the opera, he wrote to her: 'I'm now doing that Brrr! But I will warm her up so that people sympathise with her. I might yet fall in love with her.' Two years later, the opera complete, he wrote to Stösslová on 5 December: 'I'm now finished with *The Makropulos Affair*. That poor 300 year-old beauty! People thought she was a thief, a liar, an unfeeling animal ... and her fault? That she had to live so long. I was sorry for her.'

Václav Sedláček completed a copy by 24 February 1926, to which Janáček added corrections. A second copy was made by Jaroslav Kulhánek for the Brno NT, which was used by František Neumann* for the world premiere. The first performance took place on 18 December 1926, conducted by Neumann and produced by Ota Zítek*, with a cast led by Alexandra Čvanová* as Emilia Marty. The day before the premiere, Janáček was worrying over details, writing to UE about some changes he'd made to the orchestration and the need for care over dynamics: 'A larger theatre, a larger orchestra needs different markings. The main thing is *not to drown the singers!* For the theatre here, the conductor Neumann took trouble and put in dynamic markings into his full score.' Neumann wrote a warm tribute to Janáček, published on the day of the premiere (see Neumann, František*). The performance itself was a great success, recalled by Ludvík Kundera: 'I remember the joyful premiere of *The Makropulos Affair*. We all felt at the time that a great work had been born here ... and among us was a highly delighted Janáček! He praised Neumann and his orchestra, and he praised the main characters, especially the unforgettable Alexandra Čvanová for her poetic and *mondaine* qualities.'

Janáček was very happy with the success of *Makropulos*, writing to Stösslová on 21 December 1926 that 'the Icy One has unexpected success! To the extent that everyone had cold shivers down their spines. They say it's my greatest work. But it's still possible to go higher!' The same day, he sent a note of thanks to the orchestra: 'I flushed hot at the thought that you would not bring it off, and that I had not brought it off. We walked past one another without speaking. And yet you brought it off superbly under Neumann's baton – and I brought it off too, I thank you for your performance.' When Čapek came to see the opera, his sister recalled that he was 'charmed and pleased ... Karel simply glowed. He also remarked that Janáček "did it a hundred times better than I could ever have imagined"'. Čapek must have been surprised (and evidently impressed) by Janáček's ending. In the play, Marty remains flippant to the end, and her last line is sardonic: 'Ha ha! The end of immortality!' In the opera, the final scene is a catharsis, with Marty finally able to die.

If anything, the success that awaited Janáček in Prague was even greater than it had been in Brno. When *Makropulos* was given its Prague premiere, conducted by Otakar Ostrčil, on 1 March 1928, it was given a rapturous reception and was acclaimed by almost all the critics. It was the most successful Prague premiere for Janáček since *Jenůfa*.

As with all Janáček's late operas, the score of *Makropulos* has a sonority that is completely individual. With the three acts set in a lawyer's office, an empty theatre and a hotel suite, the action takes place entirely indoors (it is the only Janáček opera with no outdoor scenes). Janáček matches this with music that is sometimes brittle and claustrophobic, and such nostalgia as there is in the opera – Marty recalling episodes in her impossibly long life – is very different from that in *The Cunning Little Vixen*. On the one hand, *Makropulos* is an uncompromisingly modern opera, even down to having one of the first operatic phone calls, the humming of the telephone wires imitated by a prickly violin motif marked to be repeated *ad libitum* (Act I, Fig. 30). On the other hand, Marty's origins as Elina Makropulos, daughter of the alchemist at the Prague court of Emperor Rudolf II (1552–1612), means historic times are evoked with a brutal lack of sentimentality, with hard-edged fanfare motifs. From the start of the prelude, the music has a nervous, restless energy. Janáček's use of short motifs is even more succinct than in his previous operas, and many of them are based on intervals of perfect fourths and fifths.

The orchestration is gleaming and intense, coloured by some unusual instruments, including children's (toy) drums and castanets, with the viola d'amore adding an aura of strangeness. The use of offstage trumpets and timpani is spectacularly effective, combining with the main orchestra in ways that serve to bind ancient and modern inextricably, from the prelude, to the final bars of the whole opera. The vocal writing is predominantly conversational, at times brittle (Dr Kolenatý, Albert Gregor), at others threatening (Baron Prus), and in just one case, tender (Krista). The score is driven by an orchestra teeming with rhythmic and motivic energy. As for Marty herself, in the first two acts her music, like her character, often has a quality of knowing indifference. This makes her great monologue in the last scene of the opera all the more overwhelming: in her final moments, Marty's music acquires breadth, opulence and soaring nobility. As he hinted to Stösslová, perhaps Janáček did fall in love with his chilly heroine.

The vocal score, arranged by Ludvík Kundera, was published by UE in December 1926. It included Brod's German translation as well as the Czech text. For many years, the full score was for hire only, but in 2016 UE put it on sale, edited by Jiří Zahrádka with performance suggestions by Charles Mackerras. A new edition of the vocal score appeared at the same time.

After the original productions in Brno and Prague, there were plans for the opera to be staged in Berlin in 1928, to be conducted by Erich Kleiber. Rehearsals started in December 1927 and the opening was scheduled for May 1928, but it was cancelled, apparently because of the refusal of the soprano Barbara Kemp to sing Emilia Marty. There were only two productions outside Czechoslovakia before World War II (Frankfurt in 1929 and the Theater an der Wien in Vienna in 1938). Deutsche Oper am Rhein (Düsseldorf) produced the opera in 1957, and it was a great success when Sadler's Wells gave the London premiere in 1964, conducted by Mackerras with Marie Collier in the title role. Emilia Marty became closely associated not only with Marie Collier, but also with Elisabeth Söderström, Anja Silja and Josephine Barstow, ensuring that *Makropulos* began to take its rightful place in the international repertoire. *JAWO, JODA, NosOpe, PřiLed, TyrInt, VogJan, ZahMak.*

SYNOPSIS

Act I: The clerk's room at Dr Kolenatý's office in Prague. The clerk Vítek is filing papers connected to the long-standing case of Gregor vs. Prus. Gregor, the plaintiff, enters to ask about the case's progress, followed by Vítek's daughter Krista (Kristina). An aspiring singer, she enthuses about the great prima donna, Emilia Marty. Dr Kolenatý enters his office with Marty herself. She, too, has come to find out about the progress of Gregor vs. Prus, and reveals an unusually thorough knowledge of it. Marty claims that Baron 'Pepi' Prus, who was thought to have died childless in 1827, was actually the father of Ferdinand Gregor, son of the famous opera singer Ellian MacGregor. Marty claims that the present Baron Prus has documents in his family archives that will settle the matter. Kolenatý is sceptical but Gregor urges him to look into the matter. After Kolenatý has left, Gregor offers Marty a reward if he wins the case, and she wonders if he could get hold of a sealed envelope in Prus's family papers. Kolenatý returns with Baron Prus, along with a bundle of documents, including love letters from Ellian MacGregor and the sealed envelope Marty was looking for. Prus points out that before Gregor can make his claim, written proof is needed to show that Ferdinand MacGregor was the son of Pepi and Ellian McGregor. Marty tells Dr Kolenatý that he will have it in the morning.

Act II: The stage of a large theatre, empty after the night's performance. A stagehand and a cleaning woman discuss Marty's performance. Prus comes looking for Marty, as does his son Janek (with his sweetheart, Krista). Gregor and Vítek come to congratulate Marty, but she merely insults them. The aged eccentric Hauk-Šendorf enters and says how much Marty reminds him of an old flame from fifty years ago, the Spanish dancer Eugenia Montez. Marty greets him in Spanish and tells him Eugenia is still alive. The others leave, but Prus questions her about other documents and love letters he has found in his papers. The love letters to Pepi Prus were only signed 'E. M.', so it cannot be proved that Ellian MacGregor was Ferdinand Gregor's mother. Furthermore, at Ferdinand's baptism, his mother had given the name Elina Makropulos and that only a descendent of hers can claim the estate. Desperate for the sealed envelope, Marty asks Prus to name his price, but he leaves. Gregor tells Marty how much he loves her, but she falls asleep, bored and exhausted. She wakes up to find Janek staring at her and seizes the chance to ask him to steal the sealed envelope. Prus overhears, orders Janek to leave, and agrees to give Marty the document if she will spend the night with him.

Act III: Emilia Marty's hotel room. Marty and Prus are in her hotel room. She demands the sealed envelope and he reluctantly hands it over. A maid enters to say that Prus's servant is downstairs with a message. Prus goes to find out what it is, and returns with the news that Janek has killed himself because of his unrequited love for Marty. Her response is to say that plenty of people kill themselves. Prus storms out. Hauk-Šendorf arrives, ready to whisk Marty off to Spain. She begins to pack her bags, but they are interrupted by the arrival of a group comprising Dr Kolenatý, Gregor, Krista, Prus and Vítek. Kolenatý suspects Marty is a fraud, as the letter purporting to be from Ellian MacGregor is in Marty's handwriting. Marty leaves. During her absence the others search her belongings. They find letters addressed to Emilia Marty, Ellian MacGregor, Eugenia Montez, Elsa Mueller, Ekaterina Myshkin and Elina Makropulos.

Marty returns drunk. She confesses her real identity: Elina Makropulos, born in Crete in 1575. She reveals the story of how her father, Rudolf II's alchemist, was made to experiment on his own daughter with a potion for eternal life. She has lived ever since, under different names and in different countries, but is feeling her strength ebbing away, needing the formula (in the sealed envelope) to rejuvenate herself. She collapses and the others realise she has been telling the truth. Marty revives, looking 'like a ghost or shadow', and the stage directions emphasise the strangeness of the situation: 'A pale green light floods the stage and the auditorium'. Marty now understands that she doesn't want the elixir after all: there is nothing more to be had from life, and she is dreadfully lonely. She forces the formula on to Krista, who holds it over a flame until it is completely burnt. Marty utters the start of the Lord's Prayer in Greek and willingly embraces death.

March of the Bluebirds [*Pochod Modráčků*] for piccolo and piano (VII/9). The autograph manuscript of this piece is dated 19 May 1924, but fragments of it had appeared in Janáček's feuilleton 'Berlin' (XV/253) published four days earlier. On the autograph and the first edition, the accompaniment is given as for 'bells [i.e. glockenspiel] and small drum', but is notated for piano (with the drum part indicated as trills). Janáček clearly intended the piano to imitate the sound of bells and drums. The title is a reference to the blue uniforms that used to be worn by choristers at the Augustinian Monastery in Old Brno, earning them the nickname 'Bluebirds'. The stimulus, however, was Janáček's memory of a Prussian marching band in 1866, in which 'tin drums whirled, and over them high piccolos squealed: ferocious music'. Janáček dedicated the piece to Václav Sedláček*. The first performance was given on 24 April 1926 by one of Sedláček's pupils, V. Pinkava (with Vilém Konopka, piano). It was first published in the March–April 1928 issue of the Brno music magazine *Hudební besídka* (straight after an article on the flute by Sedláček). In the summer of 1924, Janáček reworked *March of the Bluebirds* as the third movement of *Youth**. Henle published a critical edition by Jiří Zahrádka in 2016. *HudBes, JAWO, ZahPoc.*

Martinů, Bohuslav (b. Polička, 8 December 1890; d. Liestal, Switzerland, 28 August 1959), Czech composer. In spite of mutual acquaintance with the likes of Bakala* and Talich*, it seems that Janáček and Martinů never met. In a letter to Miloš Šafránek on 16 February 1935, Martinů ended with some thoughts on contemporary Czech composers: 'I have great respect for Vycpálek even if I have questions about his technique. I like Křička. Novák is not my thing and never was. Janáček I adore.' Martinů was also interested in Janáček's relationship to Moravian folksong. In the 1950s, he studied the Bartoš–Janáček *Moravian Folksongs Newly Collected* (1901) and made extensive notes on it. In 1955 he wrote: 'I know of nothing healthier than Moravian song. In this case we have the example of Janáček, who employed it and opened up a distinctive path, where music grows not from imitation, but straight from national song and language, and speaks straight to the heart.' *BMI, ZouMar.*

Maryčka Magdónova, two choruses for male voices (IV/34 and IV/35). Janáček made two completely different settings of Petr Bezruč's poem *Maryčka Magdónova* in quick succession. The first version (IV/34) was finished by 11 November 1906, only a few weeks after having secured Bezruč's permission to set it. The score and parts were copied and corrected by Janáček, but he seems to have had doubts about this setting and it was never performed in his lifetime. Josef Veselka and the Prague Philharmonic Choir made the first recording in 1977, and the score was published in SKV C/2 (2011).

Janáček's first setting of *Maryčka Magdónova* (IV/34) is in A flat major and is a virtuoso demonstration of his male-chorus writing in the wake of hearing Vach's PSMU. The setting is much freer and more rhapsodic than the familiar second setting, and perhaps this is why Janáček had doubts about it: in his first *Maryčka*, the folk-like rhythms of Bezruč's ballad are sometimes contradicted by the music.

The second setting (IV/35), in C sharp minor (ending in C sharp major), was finished by 21 March 1907 and is entirely different, with no relation to the earlier setting. Janáček played it to Ferdinand Vach*, who took it up with enthusiasm. He gave the first performance with the PSMU at Prostějov on 12 April 1908, and on 27 April 1908 the choir performed it at the Châtelet in Paris. The first Brno performance was given on 15 November 1908, at a concert attended by both Janáček and Bezruč. It became one of the great showpieces of the

PSMU, and they sang it in Moscow and Kiev (1913) and at the Queen's Hall in London (26 May 1919). By 1963 the PSMU had sung the work 485 times. It also recorded *Maryčka Magdónova*, under Jan Šoupal in 1948 and 1953, and under Antonín Tučapský in 1969. The first recording is one of the earliest of any work by Janáček, made by the Prague Teachers' Choir under Antonín Bednář for Radiojournal Prague in 1936. Fr. A. Urbánek in Prague first published the score in September 1909. A critical edition appeared in SKV C/2 (2011), where it can be compared with the first setting. Janáček's second setting shows the composer entirely rethinking his approach to Bezruč's poem. The music is simpler, its rhythms stronger, and the whole chorus is more tightly constructed, generating a dramatic intensity that makes it one of Janáček's most compelling choruses.

Bezruč's poem is brutal and tragic: Maryčka is a miner's daughter whose father is beaten to death and whose mother is crushed under the wheels of a coal-wagon. Hungry and starving, Maryčka goes to gather firewood on the estate of the 'Marquis Gero' (the Duke of Těšín), but she is caught. Unable to face the derision of the villagers in Frýdek, she throws herself into the River Ostravice. *CurDis, JAWO, VogJan.*

Masaryk, Tomáš Garrigue (b. Hodonín, 7 March 1850; d. Lány, 14 September 1937), first President of the Czechoslovak Republic. Masaryk and Janáček were both brought up in isolated parts of Moravia, both went to school in Brno, and both spent periods of study abroad. Patrick Lambert (1989) has explored parallels between them and found similarities in their political and philosophical outlook in later life. Masaryk was a passionate believer in the cause of Czech autonomy who taught philosophy at the Charles University in Prague. He escaped to London in 1914, where he co-founded the School of Slavonic Studies at London University and lobbied the allies in the cause of Czech self-determination. In 1918 he was elected the first President of the new Czechoslovak Republic. In conversation with Karel Čapek, Masaryk declared, 'When I chose realism and scientific method it meant that I had to control my own romanticism and to practice mental discipline. ... The method must be absolutely practical, reasonable, realistic – but the aim ... is an eternal poem. Goethe has a nice phrase: *Exacte Phantasie.*' In his speech on receiving his honorary doctorate from the Masaryk University in 1925, Janáček spoke in similar terms: 'Musical composition has the same thought processes as everyday life and in purely scientific work. There are no miracles in art. ... And the scientist cannot get by without *fantasie.*'

Janáček met Masaryk at Prague Castle on 24 April 1919 in a delegation from the Brno NT Družstvo (its management committee) to discuss the transfer of the German Theatre building to the National Theatre. This was almost certainly the occasion when Janáček asked permission to dedicate *The Excursions of Mr Brouček** to Masaryk. The President accepted, and a few months later Janáček also dedicated *The Ballad of Blaník** to him.

Masaryk was present at the gala concert in the Smetana Hall, Prague, for Janáček's seventieth birthday on 8 December 1924, with the Czech Philharmonic under Talich (*Fiddler's Child** and *Taras Bulba**), the Prague Teachers' Choir under Metod Doležil (*Maryčka Magdónova**, *The Seventy Thousand** and *The Wandering Madman**) and *Eternal Gospel** under Jaroslav Křička. Janáček was received in the President's box at the interval. He described the meeting as a 'good conversation of a quarter of an hour' and, among other topics, Masaryk asked him to speak frankly about Zdeněk Nejedlý and to talk about speech melodies. Janáček and Masaryk met again on 3 June 1927 in Prague Castle, at a gathering of the Republic's great and good: composers such as Suk and Foerster, and others from Janáček's circle, including the Archbishop of Olomouc, Leopold Prečan, and Gabriela Preissová. When Janáček spoke to Masaryk, their conversation was not about his latest compositions but about a project dear to his heart: the *Moravian Love Songs* (XIII/5).

On 8 January 1925, Masaryk wrote to Janáček about his retirement from teaching: 'When I talked to you at the concert held in honour of your seventieth birthday less than a month ago – and saw you full of creative power and radiant with joy over the successful performance of your compositions – I had no idea that your request for permanent retirement would be handed to me ... As a teacher you have brought up a generation of composers and enhanced the standing of the State Conservatory in Prague [through the Master School in Composition]. Your work over many years has enriched our musical life and brought to Czechoslovak music artistic works that we have valued at home and that have been recognised abroad.' *ČapMas, JYL2, LamMas.*

Masaryk University, Brno Tomáš Garrigue Masaryk called for the establishment of a Czech university in Moravia when he was a member of the Austrian Parliament (Reichsrat) in 1891–3, and others soon followed his lead. The movement for a Czech university became a matter of public dispute in Brno between German and Czech speakers, reaching a tragic climax with the manifestations on 1–2 October 1905 that led to the death of František Pavlík* and inspired Janáček's *1. X. 1905**. After the collapse of the Habsburg Empire, a Czech university was formally established in Brno on 28 January 1919 and named after Masaryk. Janáček was the recipient of its first honorary doctorate, awarded on 28 January 1925. The citation mentioned that he 'invented a new type of opera, contributed to the rebirth of choral singing ... and brought new and original elements to contemporary musical art. In the footsteps of his predecessors, he pursued a tireless study exploring and collecting Moravian folksongs.' Josef Suk prepared an eloquent speech for the occasion but was unable to deliver it at the ceremony because of time constraints (see Suk, Josef*).

Janáček was extremely proud of his honorary doctorate, and from 1925 onwards signed his name 'DrPh. Leoš Janáček'. On 2 April 1928, he finished the *Chorus for Laying the Foundation Stone of the Masaryk University in Brno* (IV/45), performed under Jaroslav Kvapil on 9 June 1928 at a ceremony attended by Janáček and President Masaryk*. The Masaryk University was a substantial beneficiary of Janáček's will, and Zdenka Janáčková also made a bequest. Thanks to Vladimír Helfert*, the Department of Musicology became a centre of Janáček research. His pupils included Leoš Firkušný*, Jan Racek, Bohumír Štědroň* and Theodora Straková*. The Communist authorities renamed the University after Jan Evangelista Purkyně in 1960, and it reverted to its original name in 1990 after the Velvet Revolution. A new generation of scholars began working on the *Complete Critical Edition* (SKV) in the 1970s, and since then the department has continued to play an important role in Janáček scholarship. Foreign musicians awarded honorary doctorates by the Masaryk University have included Charles Mackerras* (1994) and John Tyrrell* (2002). *JanMas, LHM.*

Mass in E flat, unfinished setting for soloists, mixed chorus and organ (IX/5). The Mass in E flat was a model for Janáček's class at the Organ School in the spring of 1908, as an example of a Mass setting for chorus and organ. One of his pupils at the time was Vilém Petrželka (1889–1967), who in 1942 came across his copy of the work dictated by Janáček while students were preparing to compose their own settings. In 1943 Petrželka made an edition which included a completion of the unfinished Credo, first performed on 7 March 1943 and conducted by Karel Hradil. Chorus parts were printed by HMUB in 1946, the year Rafael Kubelík conducted Czech Philharmonic forces in a performance of Petrželka's orchestrated version. The organ and vocal score was only published in 1972. A critical edition was published in SKVEJ J/1 and the introduction quotes Petrželka's comments:

> The unfinished Mass was not a student work but Janáček's demonstration of how to compose music based on church texts. I found the following parts ... completely finished: Kyrie and Agnus Dei, and an unfinished Credo of which almost two thirds was already finished in my notes and the notes of my fellow students. ... In the Kyrie there was no indication of tempo but instead the marking 'Very anxious mood'. The text is sung to what Janáček called the 'motif of anxiety'. I noted an interesting comment [by Janáček] on the Agnus Dei: 'the inspiration for the final motif was my memory of bells'. In the Credo there was another interesting note: 'the Credo came from the motif of the words Credo in unum Deum. The motif keeps the same expression all the time because it is like faith, which always remains sure and stable. Therefore the motif stays the same – only its harmony changes.'

A later completion made by Paul Wingfield drew on early sketches for the *Glagolitic Mass** to produce a new movement (a Sanctus) as well as a different completion of the Credo. *SKVEJ J/1.*

Master School in Composition On 1 September 1920, Janáček was named professor of the Master School in Composition by the Prague Conservatory. His classes were given in Brno, in the Chleborád Villa, the building that housed the Brno Organ School* and, since 1919, the Brno Conservatory*. According to his pupil Osvald Chlubna, Janáček's teaching in the Master School was less prescriptive than his class at the Organ School, as more advanced students came to develop and deepen their knowledge. Janáček's doctrine of composition in the Master School was, Chlubna wrote, that 'the essence of freedom in composition is the creation of new ideas in sound, to produce a more complex aural impression through what you see, what you touch and what you feel'. Janáček's pupils at the Master School included Břetislav Bakala*, Zdeněk Chalabala, Osvald Chlubna*, Pavel Haas* and Gustav Homola. *ChlJan.*

Mikota, Jan (b. Stádlec, near Tábor, 4 February 1903; d. Prague, 8 December 1978), Czech music publisher and publicist. Mikota worked for HMUB (succeeding his brother Václav as secretary) and for the Czechoslovak section of the ISCM. He got to know Janáček and his wife when he accompanied them to the ISCM Festival in Venice, a visit he recorded in several photographs. In 1926 Mikota accompanied Janáček to London, acting as his interpreter and assistant, transcribing his speeches and again taking photographs that provide a visual record of the visit, showing Janáček with Rosa Newmarch, Henry Wood, and several of the musicians who performed at the concert of his works on 6 May (see London visit in 1926*). Mikota also photographed Janáček on the return journey, including the memorable images of Janáček notating the sound of the sea at Vlissingen. His account of Janáček's London visit, 'Leoš Janáček v Anglii' ('Leoš Janáček in England') was published in *Listy hudební matice* (25 May 1926). The following year, 1927, Mikota accompanied Janáček to the ISCM Festival at Frankfurt. Mikota served as the publicist and tour organiser for the Liberated Theatre of Prague (Osvobozené divadlo) and was also a member of the experimental vocal ensemble Voiceband, founded at the theatre by Emil František Burian (1904–59). He was the younger brother of Václav Mikota. *MikJan, PřiZah.*

Mikota, Václav (b. Stádlec, near Tábor, 24 March 1896; d. Prague, 19 January 1982), Czech music publisher. Václav Mikota was secretary of HMUB from 1920 until 1924, then its managing director from 1924 until 1950 (when it ceased operations). He worked for its successors until 1960 (see Hudební matice and its successors*). Mikota's correspondence with Janáček between 1922 and 1928 provides valuable documentation of Janáček's relationship with HMUB. Mikota wrote an article, 'Leoš Janáček a Hudební matice', published in *Sedmdesát let Umělecké besedy 1863–1933*, ed. František Skacelík (Prague: Umělecká beseda, 1933). *KLJ, SkaSed.*

Milén, Eduard [born Eduard Müller] (b. Frýdštejn, near Liberec, 18 March 1891; d. Brno, 19 May 1976), Czech artist. Milén studied at the Academy of Applied Arts (1908–12) and Academy of Fine Arts (1912–14) in Prague. He came to Brno in 1917. His first contribution to *Lidové noviny* was in September 1919. He was appointed to the permanent staff of the newspaper in 1921, serving as graphic designer and art editor until 1948. He also worked for the Brno NT as a set designer, and was very active as a book illustrator. Milén later recalled, 'I came to know Janáček at the offices of *Lidové noviny*, where he would bring his original contributions from time to time. He did not come very often, which made him stand out all the more, and I remember vividly the exciting impression that Janáček made on me with his unusual appearance.' His first drawing of Janáček, a half-length portrait with his hand behind his ear, appeared in *Lidové noviny* on 21 September 1919 (reused, with a different caption, in 1924). A second portrait (printed on 29 August 1920) showed Janáček seated in a theatre box. In 1924 Milén designed a bookplate for Janáček on which the composer is depicted huddled against the cold in his coat. Milén was probably referring to his most famous portrait of Janáček when he recalled 'how Janáček's face changed when he was giving an enthusiastic speech about contemporary culture'. This celebrated image, drawn for the newspaper's editorial archives, was used on 13 August 1928 above the announcement of Janáček's death. The original drawing (in the Moravian Gallery, Brno) is undated.

In the spring of 1924, Milén designed the front cover of the vocal score for *The Cunning Little Vixen** (Janáček sent it to UE on 6 May). It's a wonderful illustration, capturing the human–animal femininity of the Vixen by portraying her as a young woman wearing a fox mask with a fox fur draped over her shoulder. Later in the year, Janáček chose Milén to do the set designs for the stage premiere of *The Cunning Little Vixen* (despite initial resistance from František Neumann and Ota Zítek). While Milén was drawing the sets and costumes, Janáček was a regular visitor to Milén, inspecting the work-in-progress, and he warmly praised the results which cleverly united the human and animal worlds.

Milén was asked by Janáček to design the cover of the vocal score for the *Glagolitic Mass**, and the composer requested an image that evoked the era of St Cyril and St Methodius rather than the present day. Milén had some misgivings about this and wrote to Janáček on 15 May 1928: 'Regarding the cover on your *Glagolitic Mass*, I note the following. As you requested, I did a design with St Wenceslas on the cover. ... It's a matter of personal opinion whether this image is suitable for the cover or not ... because your Mass is a modern one, having nothing to do with earlier compositions of that time, and therefore shouldn't have an image from that time on the cover. That would really be anachronistic. If I hadn't been following your wishes, I would have designed a completely modern image.' This letter was sent after the score had been published. The cover depicts a head surrounded by the words 'Mša Glagol'skaya' and 'Gospodi pomiluj' in the Glagolitic alphabet, and it has been used on editions of the vocal score ever since the first printing on 6 April 1928.

Milén also designed Janáček's tombstone in Brno's Central Cemetery (see Brno Central Cemetery*). *EDMB, JanLid, KLJ.*

Military music   Janáček's first recollection of a military band was in 1866, when as a boy chorister he watched Prussian soldiers in Brno, a memory that came back to him in 1924 when he visited Berlin for the premiere there of *Jenůfa*. In his feuilleton 'Berlin' (*Lidové noviny*, 15 May 1924, XV/253), he wrote: 'The Monastery Square in Old Brno was filled with the grey and red uniforms of the Prussian army during the summer holidays in 1866. The tin drums whirled and above them the high piccolos squealed. Ferocious music. ... As a boy of twelve, with my eyes popping out, I followed the wild tumult of the Prussian army on Pekařská Street and of Vídeňská here in Brno!' The 'ferocious music' of tin drums and piccolos was transformed into the *March of the Bluebirds** and subsequently reworked as part of *Youth**.

In Janáček's time, military bands in the Habsburg Empire usually included a string section, so they resembled conventional orchestras. At the Brno Beseda, Janáček collaborated with bandmasters such as Eduard Horný (1838–1907) and Josef Opelt (1841–?). In 1909, when Janáček conducted Gounod's *Mors et vita*, the orchestra was the Band of the Imperial Infantry Regiment No. 8. A review in *Lidové noviny* (11 March 1909) reported that 'Janáček's persuasive powers over his performers are legendary. The band of the Imperial Regiment No. 8 was elevated under his direction to a level that would have been unbelievable for anyone who did not hear it in person.' After World War I, Janáček remained on friendly terms with the regional leader of the army in Moravia and Silesia, General Alois Podhajský (whose daughter, Zdenka Podhajská, was the model for the pictorial cover of *Káťa Kabanová*). The band of the Imperial Regiment No. 8 became the Czech Infantry Regiment No. 43 and its conductor was František Zita (1880–1946). Podhajský and Zita arranged an event in honour of Janáček's seventieth birthday year on 23 January 1925 at the garrison headquarters. A few weeks later, Zita and the band played the *Lachian Dances* for a celebration of President Masaryk's birthday at the Beseda House (2 March 1925), and the following year, Zita and the band broadcast the dances on Brno Radio (10 November 1926).

Janáček's most famous piece influenced by military music is the *Sinfonietta**. In his letters to Kamila Stösslová, Janáček recalled listening with her to fanfares played by the band of the Regiment No. 11 'František Palacký' in Písek in June 1924. This was the direct inspiration of the Fanfares that begin and end the *Sinfonietta*. One of its original titles was 'Military Sinfonietta' and in a letter to his wife the day before the premiere, Janáček wrote: 'It's not just a Sinfonietta – it's a Military Sinfonietta! It sounds magnificent!' This performance was given on 26 June 1926, the first day of the Sokol rally, and the fanfares were performed again on 6 July in the Old Town Square at the climax of the Sokol procession through Prague. In both performances, it was military musicians who played the trumpet parts in the fanfares.

The *Capriccio* was first performed by Otakar Hollmann, a military veteran who lost his right arm in World War I. He visited Janáček on 8 February 1928 to play the work to him and asked about the unusual instrumentation: 'I asked him, Master, how did you get the idea to choose piano with only wind instruments, and these particular instruments. Janáček answered: A long time ago I was asked to write something for a military ensemble, and when I was pondering the composition for you, I suddenly remembered this request and so it occurred to me that I would combine the wind instruments with the piano and the military band with you.' *ProCap, ProMil, ZahSin.*

Mládí See *Youth* (VII/10)

Moor, Karel (b. Lázně Bělohrad, 26 December 1873; d. Prague, 30 March 1945), Czech composer.   Moor made musical settings of two poems by Petr Bezruč* that Janáček also set. In 1905 he composed a melodrama with orchestra on Bezruč's *Maryčka Magdónova* that was performed in Brno on 22 November 1906. It is likely that Janáček had already seen the score, as he wrote to Olga Vašková (Bezruč's sister) on 1 October 1906 asking for permission to compose a piece on *Maryčka Magdónova* in which he claimed that 'Moor didn't get it right. Perhaps I'll do better.' (Janáček's first setting of the poem was finished by 11 November 1906; he made a completely different setting by 21 March 1907.) In 1919 Moor wrote another melodrama based on Bezruč's *Kantor Halfar*, a poem which had been set by Janáček in 1906. In the 1908–9 season, Moor worked as assistant conductor to Rudolf Pavlata at the Brno NT. Moor composed an operetta on *The Excursion of Mr Brouček to the Moon*, which was completed by October 1908, first performed at Jaroměřice in 1910 and published privately the same year. *KLJ, MooVzp, TyrCze.*

Moravian Composers' Club   See **Brno: Moravian Composers' Club**

Moravian Folk Poetry in Songs [*Moravská lidová poezie v písních*; originally published as *Bouquet of Moravian Folksongs*], 53 folksong arrangements for voice and piano (V/2).   Following the success of the Bartoš and Janáček collection of 174 folksongs issued as the *Bouquet of Moravian Folksongs* by the publisher Emil Šolc in Telč (1890, reprinted in 1892; see Folksong Editions*), Janáček was asked to make arrangements of some of the same songs for voice and piano. These arrangements were made between about 1892 and 1901, but only one can be firmly dated: an early version of No. 28 ('Uncertainty' [Nejistota]) was written by Janáček in his daughter Olga's commonplace book on 5 October 1895. These arrangements mostly date from the time when Janáček was working on *Jenůfa* and they served as a kind of laboratory, balancing harmonic experimentation with preserving the authenticity of the songs, and resisting the temptation to produce accompaniments that were too ingenious. Vogel wrote that 'Janáček's work as an arranger of folksongs played an important part in awakening his Moravian awareness', and Janáček himself said that it was 'the way I purify my musical thoughts'. Emil Šolc* published two volumes of Janáček's arrangements in about 1892 and 1901. In 1908 Šolc reissued both volumes, giving the collection the title that has been used ever since: *Moravian Folk Poetry in Songs*. *JAWO, VogJan*.

Moravian Folksongs [*Moravské lidové písně*], folksong arrangements for piano (VIII/23). In the course of their extensive correspondence during 1921, Otakar Nebuška* at Hudební matice suggested that Janáček should make some new folksong arrangements for piano. They were completed by 1 January 1922. The autograph manuscript has been published in facsimile (as *Patnáct moravských lidových písní*, Panton, 1978) and shows how Janáček laid out the songs, with the text of one verse written over the piano music, and further verses added either at the foot of the same page or on an additional page. Once Nebuška received the manuscript of the songs, he seems to have had second thoughts about them, and on 21 February 1922, Janáček asked for them to be returned. HMUB finally published these arrangements in 1950, with an introduction by Bohumír Štědroň. Jaroslav Vogel regarded these arrangements highly: 'Despite being limited to the piano, this group of 15 songs is one of the most interesting of its kind. In them Janáček is relatively free from the "authentic" folk example. He accompanies the tunes, placed in only eight of the songs in the top part and in the rest in the middle parts or in the bass, with ostinato motifs, contrary motion, imitation and shifting rhythms ... Yet in spite of these technical tricks and considerable freedom of harmony, the spirit of the folksong is perfectly preserved.' The arrangements were made a few weeks before Janáček embarked on composing *The Cunning Little Vixen* (started on 22 January 1922) and just after the premiere of *Káťa Kabanová* (23 November 1921). In a letter to Max Brod on 10 January 1922, he confessed that 'my head is an empty shell, like after a fire. ... I dabble in folksongs and read Einstein. But the relativity of time and space is rather unsuitable for tones. We live by air and not by ether.' The 'dabbling' Janáček mentions here is a reference to these arrangements, which he seems to have done as a kind of recreation between operas. *JAWO, VogJan*.

Moravian Quartet Founded by František Kudláček* at the Brno Conservatory in 1921 as the Kudláček Quartet, it became the Moravian Quartet in 1923. Kudláček led the quartet until 1958. The other members in the 1920s were Josef Jedlička (violin II), Josef Trkan (viola) and Josef Křenek (cello). An important ensemble in Moravia, they gave the first performances of many contemporary works (as did the individual members of the quartet). The Moravian Quartet was closely associated with Janáček, and was one of the first ensembles to take up the String Quartet No. 1 after the Czech Quartet. All four members of the Moravian Quartet signed a postcard to Janáček on 25 November 1925, sending 'a souvenir from Znojmo where we played your quartet successfully', and the quartet broadcast the work for Austrian Radio on 15 April 1928. In May–June 1928, they made three visits to Janáček's home (18 and 25 May, 27 June) to play the String Quartet No. 2 for the composer. At the first rehearsal, Josef

Trkan played the viola d'amore (as Janáček originally planned) but this was found to be impracticable: on the two subsequent visits the work was played in Janáček's revision for a conventional string quartet. The first performance was given by the Moravian Quartet for an invited audience on 7 September 1928, and repeated on 11 September 1928 as part of the Exhibition of Contemporary Culture in Brno. When the work was published by HMUB in 1938, the score and parts were edited by Kudláček and Otakar Nebuška. *ČHS, VohKMS.*

Moravian Teachers' Choral Society (PSMU) [Pěvecké sdružení moravských učitelů] Ferdinand Vach recalled in 1924: 'When I founded PSMU in 1903, Janáček was not interested in the new choir until he heard us by chance in 1904 in Veselí nad Moravou. He was very surprised and immediately sent me two compositions.' This was the start of a productive relationship between Janáček and the PSMU that had a decisive effect on his creative output. Vach founded the choir with students and graduates of the Teachers' Institute in Kroměříž, but its personnel soon came from a wider group of singers and Vach moved rehearsals to Přerov.

Janáček heard the two choruses he had sent to Vach, 'If only you knew' and 'The Evening Witch' from the *Four Moravian male-voice choruses* (IV/28), on 26 November 1905. These were included in the PSMU tour in April 1906, including performances in Vienna, Munich, Nuremberg, Leipzig, Berlin and Dresden. The first edition, published by Mojmír Urbánek in 1906, has a dedication to the choir. By March 1907, Janáček had composed his second setting of *Maryčka Magdónova* (IV/35) and gave it to Vach, who conducted the first performance with the PSMU on 12 April 1908, after which it became one of the choir's showpieces (see *Maryčka Magdónova**). *The Seventy Thousand** (IV/36), the next of Janáček's Bezruč choruses, was composed by 8 December 1909 and rehearsed in Janáček's presence by Vach and the PSMU in 1910, after which Janáček withdrew the work to make some revisions. He sent the new version on 16 July 1912, but Vach was alarmed by the difficulty of the choral writing and considered it 'unperformable'. After *The Seventy Thousand* was published in 1923, Vach changed his mind about the work and the PSMU performed it on tour in Montpellier (6 and 10 December 1925), earning the dedication of *Our Flag** (IV/44): 'To the PSMU for *The Seventy Thousand* in France.'

Between January 1915 and February 1917, the PSMU's activities were suspended due to World War I. The re-formed choir performed *Halfar the Schoolmaster** at Luhačovice on 3 August 1918. This was the first of Janáček's Bezruč choruses, but he had originally given it to the Smetana Choral Society in Plzeň. From 1918 it became a staple of the PSMU repertoire. The choir gave the first performance of *The Czech Legion** (IV/42) on 26 September 1920 (in Kroměříž). Thanks to its strongly patriotic sentiments, this chorus became extremely popular in the early years of the Czechoslovak Republic and was performed thirty-seven times by the PSMU during Janáček's lifetime. *The Wandering Madman** (IV/43) was completed at the end of 1922. One of Janáček's most original (and difficult) choruses, scored for male voices with a solo soprano, it was first performed by Vach and the PSMU on 21 September 1924. *Our Flag** (IV/44) was finished in December 1925 and once again the PSMU gave the premiere, at Přerov on 18 October 1926.

12. Membership card for the Moravian Teachers' Choir (PSMU) using the design made specially for the choir by Alfons Mucha in 1911.

During Janáček's lifetime – between 1905 and 1928 – the PSMU not only performed Janáček's choruses in concerts all over Czech lands and in the cultural capitals of Europe, but the quality of the PSMU's singing inspired Janáček to write his most innovative choral works, culminating in *The Wandering Madman*.

Janáček was made an honorary member of the PSMU in 1911, the same year as Alfons Mucha, who had designed a magnificent poster for the choir.

After Janáček's death, the PSMU continued to perform his choruses. Vach stepped down for health reasons in 1935. In 1936 Jan Šoupal (1892–1964) was elected as his successor. Šoupal had sung tenor in the choir since 1917 and had studied with Jaroslav Kvapil, Ludvík Kundera and Bohumil Holub. Šoupal and the PSMU made recordings of Janáček for Ultraphon in the 1940s, including the three Bezruč choruses and *The Wandering Madman*; they recorded them again for Supraphon in the 1950s (see Recordings before 1960*). Given Šoupal's long experience as a member of the choir and his close association with Vach, his recordings with the PSMU are of particular interest. After Šoupal's death in November 1964, his successor was Antonín Tučapský (1928–2014), who remained until 1972, when the Communist Party local committee in Ostrava dismissed him from his university post and forced him to relinquish the choir (he emigrated to Great Britain). In 1975 Lubomír Mátl (b. 1941) became choirmaster, leading the choir for forty years, and in 2015 he was followed by his pupil Jiří Najvar (b. 1990). *ČHS, DesLet, JAWO, StoPSM*.

Moravská lidová poezie v písních See ***Moravian Folk Poetry in Songs*** (V/2)

Moravské lidové písně See ***Moravian Folksongs*** (VIII/23)

Mša glagolskaja See ***Glagolitic Mass*** (III/9)

Mucha, Alfons Maria (b. Ivančice, 24 July 1860; d. Prague, 14 July 1939), Czech artist. Mucha studied the violin and singing as a child in Ivančice. He first met Janáček in 1872, when he arrived in Brno to audition for a place in the choir at the Augustinian Monastery. Mucha's son Jiří wrote that 'Křížkovský ... took the candidate [Mucha] to the piano and gave him a long test in intonation and harmony. He was clearly happy with the result, but when he wanted to offer the boy the only remaining place, an 18-year-old youth came in. "I have just taken on a new *fundatista* [chorister]," he announced to Křížkovský, who stopped in his tracks: "and I have just found such a good alto."' The 'youth' in question was Janáček, soon to take over from Křížkovský. Mucha had more success auditioning for the choir of Brno Cathedral, and as a choral scholar he was educated at the Czech Gymnasium (1872–5). In 1885 he began studies in Munich before completing his training in Paris. His breakthrough came in December 1894, when he designed a poster for Sarah Bernhardt's production of *Gismonda*. The success of this poster helped to establish Mucha as one of the leading artists of Parisian art nouveau.

In 1910 Mucha returned to Bohemia, where one of his first major projects was the decor for the Obecní dům in Prague. The following year, he designed a poster for the PSMU depicting a woman in a South Moravian folk costume. From 1918 onwards, Mucha's work became a feature of everyday life in the new Czechoslovak Republic: he designed a set of postage stamps in 1918 and a series of banknotes issued between 1919 and 1931. On 14 April 1919, Janáček asked Mucha to design the front cover for the vocal score of *The Excursions of Mr Brouček**: 'The publishers, Universal Edition, would like very much to have the frontispiece in two or three colours and I must tell you frankly that I would very much like your work on the front cover. But can I ask you such a thing? Universal Edition is looking for a young artist and is offering 100 crowns. ... But do at least advise me

13. Janáček and Alfons Mucha in Luhačovice, 1922.

as to whom I could approach.' Mucha replied on 20 April 1919 in friendly terms: 'Your nice letter gave me great pleasure because I learn from it that your work *The Excursions of Mr Brouček* will soon see the light of day. I would very much like to talk to the publisher about the cover ... I have a lot of work on this week and on Saturday and Sunday there is an exhibition of some of my 'Epic' paintings [Mucha's *Slav Epic*, his magnum opus, produced between 1910 and 1926] – but then, immediately!' Janáček went to Mucha's exhibition and they met to discuss the *Brouček* cover. Mucha was unable to do it himself but recommended his friend Láďa Novák*. In 1922 Janáček and Mucha met again at Luhačovice, and Mucha wrote on 25 July to thank Janáček for a signed photograph of the two of them: 'Heartfelt thanks for your kind and affectionate memento. I too remember Luhačovice with great pleasure' (the photograph was taken by Janáček's pupil, František Rybka). One of Mucha's last great works was the mural *Czech Song*, for the Great Hall of the Hlahol Choral Society (Masarykovo nábřeží No. 16, Prague). After Hitler's occupation of Czechoslovakia in March 1939, Mucha was arrested by the Gestapo for his activities as a Freemason. Though he was released after a few days of questioning, his health never recovered. *KLJ, MucMuc, PřiZah.*

Na Soláni Čarták   See ***Čarták on Soláň*** (III/7)

Národní tance na Moravě   See **Folk Dances in Moravia** (VIII/10)

Naše vlajka   See **Our Flag** (IV/44)

Návod pro vyučování zpěvu   See *Singing Teaching Manual* (V/5)

Nebuška, Otakar (b. Mlada Boleslav, 28 May 1875; d. Prague, 28 October 1952), Czech music publisher.   During his years as a law student at the Charles University, Nebuška immersed himself in Prague's musical life and studied the piano with Adolf Mikeš. He became a member of the Umělecká beseda (Society of Artists) in 1900, where he established lasting friendships with Josef Suk and Vítězslav Novák. In 1907 Nebuška set up Hudební matice as the music publishing division of the Umělecká beseda. Between 1907 and 1924, he personally prepared most of its output for publication. He also contributed regularly to *Hudební revue*, the journal published by HMUB. Nebuška's earliest known contact with Janáček was in 1908, when he wrote to ask about the publication of *Jenůfa* by the KPU as he wanted to announce it in *Hudební revue*. By 1916 he was in contact about potential publications. The first was a vocal score of *Jenůfa** with the piano reduction revised by Nebuška (issued in 1917), a task he tackled with great attention to detail. He wrote to Janáček on 11 February 1917: 'Today I have been finishing the end of *Jenůfa* and by comparing your version and Kovařovic's I see a difference between them not just in the sound but also the composition itself. I ask for your decision by return of post which version you would like for the vocal score.' Nebuška wanted HMUB to publish a completely new opera by Janáček, and the firm had *The Excursion of Mr Brouček to the Moon* in proof by January 1917, but Janáček withdrew it a month later for revisions, and eventually it became part of *The Excursions of Mr Brouček**, published by UE in 1919. Following the postwar reorganisation of Hubdení matice, Nebuška wrote to Janáček on 5 February 1921 with an ambitious proposal to publish his works (see Hudební matice and its successors*). *ČSHS, JODA, KLJ, LánJan.*

Nejedlý, Zdeněk (b. Litomyšl, 10 February 1878; d. Prague, 9 March 1962), Czech musicologist and politician.   Nejedlý studied composition with Zdeněk Fibich in Prague and was a devoted advocate of Smetana (born, like Nejedlý, in Litomyšl). He was hostile to the music of Dvořák and his pupils, especially Josef Suk and Vítězslav Novák, who failed – as he saw it – to follow in Smetana's footsteps, and he also disliked most music from France and Russia. His attitude to Janáček became apparent in his book *České moderní zpěvohra po Smetanovi* [Czech modern opera since Smetana], published in 1911. Comparing Janáček's *Jenůfa** with Josef Bohuslav Foerster's *Eva* (also based on a play by Preissová), he argued that while Foerster composed with true feeling, Janáček was intent on pursuing a separatist Moravian agenda. Objecting to Janáček's 'naturalism', Nejedlý detected the influence of Balakirev and other Russian composers ('with their inadequacies') in what he dismissed as Janáček's 'experiment in Moravian opera'. He particularly objected to Janáček's theories of speech-melody, finding the results unconvincing, and he considered Janáček's view of Smetana to be suspect, declaring that he had been an 'opponent of Smetana', and 'still cannot be counted today as one of his adherents'. After the Prague premiere of *Jenůfa* in 1916, Nejedlý wrote a long review in *Smetana* (also published separately as a pamphlet), which further entrenched his critical view of the work and its composer. For Nejedlý the main problem remained the use of speech-melodies, and his 'sober assessment' of the opera was that it remained an 'outdated naturalistic experiment'. A year later, the 6 December 1917 issue of *Smetana* included Nejedlý's scathing review of *The Fiddler's Child** (VI/14), which he dismissed as a 'theoretical experiment' that relied on 'trivial means'. Even so, Nejedlý made the trip to Brno for the premiere of *Káťa Kabanová* (23 November 1921). On matters of folksong, Janáček and Nejedlý found common ground, and both served on the Folksong Committee in Prague. As John Tyrrell points out, 'one of the great ironies of Janáček's relationship with Nejedlý is that their surviving correspondence, which is exclusively on folksong matters, could not be more pleasant, friendly and constructive'. Nejedlý had joined the Czechoslovak Communist Party in 1921 and criticised what he considered to be the bourgeois policies of President Masaryk's government. He spent the war years in the Soviet Union. After returning to Czechoslovakia, he served as Minister of Culture and Education in 1945–6, and again from 1948 to 1953. *JYL1, JYL2, NejČes, NejJej, TyrNej.*

Neumann, František (b. Přerov, 16 June 1874; d. Brno, 25 February 1929), Czech conductor.   Neumann was born in Přerov, Moravia, and was originally apprenticed as a sausage-maker in his father's firm. He studied composition at the Leipzig Conservatory with Carl Reinecke and Salomon Jadassohn in 1896–7. On completion of his studies, he became chorus master at opera houses in Karlsruhe (under Felix Mottl) and Hamburg, became first Kapellmeister in Regensburg in 1899 and in Linz the following year. In 1904 he was appointed Second Kapellmeister at Frankfurt Opera, where he remained until 1919.

On 14 November 1906, Neumann conducted the first performance of Janáček's *Jealousy** with the Czech Philharmonic. It was with Janáček's enthusiastic recommendation that Neumann was appointed Head of Opera at the Brno NT in 1919 (see Brno National Theatre*). Neumann's enthusiasm for Janáček was clear from the start of his tenure: his inaugural production was a new staging of *Jenůfa** (23 August 1919), and this was followed by the world premieres of *Káťa Kabanová** (23 November 1921), *The Cunning Little Vixen** (6 November 1924), *Šárka** (11 November 1925) and *The Makropulos Affair** (18 December 1926), along with the Brno premiere of *The Excursion of Mr Brouček to the Moon* (15 May 1926). Neumann also conducted Janáček's major orchestral works, including the world premieres of *Taras Bulba** (9 October 1921), *Ballad of Blaník** (21 March 1920) and the *Lachian Dances** (2 December 1924), as well as Brno premieres of *The Fiddler's Child** and the *Sinfonietta**. All these performances were given in the presence of the composer. Neumann conducted the final scene from *The Cunning Little Vixen* at Janáček's funeral on 15 August 1928 (see Funeral, Janáček's*).

Neumann taught at the Brno Conservatory from 1919 onwards, and his pupils included Břetislav Bakala and Zdeněk Chalabala. He was also the composer of several operas, including *Beatrice Caracci*, given its premiere at the National Theatre on 29 April 1922, with principals including Marie Veselá and Karel Zavřel (the creators of Káťa and Boris in *Káťa Kabanová* a few months earlier). As well as Janáček, Neumann's large repertoire at the Brno Opera included Debussy (*Pelléas et Mélisande*), Falla, Fibich, Křenek (*Jonny spielt auf*), Martinů (the first performance of *The Soldier and the Dancer*), Novák, Ravel, Richard Strauss (*Elektra, Der Rosenkavalier* and *Josephslegende*) and Stravinsky (*Petrushka*, with sets by Josef Čapek), as well as Mozart, Wagner, Verdi, and cycles of operas by Smetana and Dvořák.

Neumann's early death meant that he left no commercial recordings, but he was unquestionably the conductor who advocated Janáček's works with the greatest authority and dedication during the composer's lifetime. He wrote little about the composer he did so much to champion, though an entry in his diary from 1925 reads simply: 'The aim of our theatre is completely different from Prague – Janáček.' On the day of the premiere of *The Makropulos Affair* (18 December 1926), *Divadelní list* published Neumann's eloquent appreciation of Janáček's operas:

14. Eduard Milén: portrait of František Neumann, pastel, undated but almost certainly 1924, the year in which Milén, Neumann and Janáček collaborated on the first production of *The Cunning Little Vixen*.

Just as Smetana was once a great innovator who had to suffer and fight, Janáček has had a similar fate. He has only recently been understood and appreciated in the wider world, and so far only *Jenůfa* has established itself with audiences. The time will come for his other operas. ... It sounds paradoxical, but it is a fact that today the 72-year-old Janáček is our youngest composer. Just as beneath his white hair his eyes have a youthful sparkle, so his music uses precise and well-established forms, but with fertile modern ideas full of fire and passion. With one brilliant idea after another, the music of his latest work, *The Makropulos Affair*, is no exception, and the end of the opera scales heights that only the greatest composers can achieve: Emilia Marty's farewell to the world invites comparison with the final scenes of *Otello*, Wagner's *Tristan* or Strauss's *Elektra*. Each sounds very different, but each gives us a glimpse, at least for a moment, of something that our eyes cannot see and that otherwise cannot reach our consciousness. Here we feel the breeze beyond the grave, but we do not feel horror or fear. Death is the longed-for saviour.

The National Theatre has prepared this production of Janáček's work with respect, diligence, reverence and love, lavishing the greatest care on it, as this work of genius truly deserves. It will be sufficient reward if this earns for the opera the understanding and admiration of the progressive members our audience. However, we firmly believe that after several hearings all our audience can respond to *The Makropulos Affair* with love.

HelNeu, JAWO, ZahDiv.

Neumann, Václav (b. Prague, 29 September 1920; d. Vienna, Austria, 2 September 1995), Czech conductor.   Václav Neumann studied the violin and conducting at the Prague Conservatory. His conducting teachers were Pavel Dědeček and Metod Doležil, both of whom had worked with Janáček. After graduating, he played in the Czech Philharmonic, and co-founded the Smetana Quartet in 1943, remaining with it until 1947, when he turned to conducting. In 1956 he began working at the Komische Oper in Berlin, where he conducted Walter Felsenstein's famous production of *The Cunning Little Vixen**. The original plan had been to produce *Káťa Kabanová*, but Felsenstein decided to stage *Vixen* instead. He wrote to Neumann telling him about the change, and the conductor replied on 21 February 1956: 'My relationship to both works is of the same intensity. But *Káťa* is about passion, pain and the innermost lyricism of the human soul. To perform *The Cunning Little Vixen* means sunshine, joy and happiness, and a positive affirmation of life. ... With *The Cunning Little Vixen* ... you become happy and enriched at the same time. You feel good about the world.' The production opened in May 1956 and it was one of the major landmarks in the international discovery of Janáček's operas. Sung in German, with a cast led by Rudolf Asmus as the Forester, it was extremely successful and Neumann conducted 213 performances out of 218, including visits to Wiesbaden, Paris and Prague. The last night was on 22 December 1964, and the following year Neumann conducted the version filmed for German TV. He made the first commercial recording of *Vixen* for Supraphon on 4–15 November and 12 December 1957, with Prague NT forces and the Forester again sung by Asmus (in Czech). A later Neumann recording of *Vixen* was made in 1979–80. His other Janáček for Supraphon included the The *Excursions of Mr Brouček* (recorded 9 April–30 May 1962) and *From the House of the Dead* (recorded 5–22 June 1979). He recorded *Taras Bulba*, the *Sinfonietta*, *Schluck und Jau*, the Violin Concerto (with Josef Suk) and the *Glagolitic Mass*, all with the Czech Philharmonic, of which he was principal conductor from 1968 until 1990. *KobExp.*

Newmarch, Rosa (b. Leamington Spa, 18 December 1857; d. Worthing, 9 April 1940), British writer. Newmarch had a particular interest in Russian and Czech music, and played an extremely important role in the promotion of Janáček in England. She arranged his visit to London in 1926 and was the dedicatee of the *Sinfonietta**. Newmarch first visited Prague in 1919, when she saw *Jenůfa* at the National Theatre. In 1922 she went to Brno, as noted in her diary: 'April 20: Went to Brno. *Katia Kabanova* – Supped with Janáček – wonderful man. Many meetings during next few days, before travelling to Bratislava.' Janáček inscribed a copy of the Violin Sonata to Newmarch on 20 April, and she attended its first performance (24 April) as well as seeing *Káťa*. After returning to England, Newmarch informed Janáček that she was arranging the London premiere of *The Diary of One Who Disappeared**, to be sung by the Danish tenor Mischa-Léon (pseud. for Harry Haurowitz), who went to Brno to sing the work for Janáček before the concert. In December 1922, Newmarch's pioneering article 'Leoš Janáček and Moravian Music Drama' appeared in *Slavonic Review*, including detailed discussion of *Jenůfa*, *The Excursions of Mr Brouček* and *Káťa Kabanová*, about which she wrote: '[Janáček] moulds the melodic curves of aspiration and spiritual exaltation, of fatal foreboding, of cruelty, dignity and madness into a work the truthfulness of which is burnt into us as we listen. *Káťa Kabanová* is as strong, as irreversible, as absolute in effect as an antique tragedy.'

In May 1925, Newmarch was in Prague to review *The Cunning Little Vixen* for *The Times*. She wrote: 'Janáček never repeats himself in his operatic works, but the power and freshness of *The Cunning Little Vixen* has an added quality for which one was hardly prepared – the quality of a new style. The myriad short themes, the outcome of a close observation of melodic speech and of nature's voices, are welded into a completely cohesive expressive language. The orchestration is brilliant and sure, and the colour effects infinitely varied. ... *The Cunning Little Vixen* will add lustre to Janáček's growing reputation.'

Newmarch's enthusiasm was backed by action, inviting Janáček to visit London in a letter of 29 January 1926 and making all the arrangements (see London visit in 1926*). A few months after his trip to England, Janáček wrote to Newmarch on 8 September, sorry that she hadn't been able to come to the premiere of the *Sinfonietta*, but adding: 'I am dedicating it to you and the Committee that invited me to London'. Janáček did not have all the names of the committee, so the eventual dedication was 'To Mrs R. Newmarch'. On 28 February 1927, Newmarch wrote to Janáček: 'How can I thank you enough for the dedication of the *Sinfonietta*? I am too proud of this honour, because you know, dear Mistr, that I have the conviction of your great and unique power. It is not a question of opinion. I feel it in my bones that your music is great music. Therefore, to be associated with it is a joy.' On 12 January 1928, Janáček wrote to Newmarch that he had 'finished the opera on Dostoyevsky's *From the House of the Dead*' and had met Gustav Holst* in Prague. Henry Wood conducted the *Sinfonietta* in London on 10 February 1928 (a concert broadcast by the BBC) and Janáček wrote to Newmarch on 18 February: 'I am happy about the performance of *Sinfonietta*. Be so good as to give my warm thanks to Sir Henry Wood. I am very grateful to him.' Janáček's last letter to Newmarch was written on 2 June

very grateful to him.' Janáček's last letter to Newmarch was written on 2 June 1928, reporting that *From the House of the Dead* 'is being copied at full speed' and that his Second String Quartet was about to be performed.

In Britain, Newmarch was way ahead of her time in her assessment of Janáček's music. From her first experience of his work, she considered him a figure of international importance and – particularly in the operas – a composer of the greatest emotional power and inventiveness. Few outside Brno – let alone in England – shared her view until many years later. Her last book, *The Music of Czechoslovakia* (published posthumously in 1942), made a compelling case for Janáček a decade before any of his operas had been heard in London. *FisJan, MikJan, NewCze, SteNew.*

Nosek, Václav (b. Starý Plzenec, 5 April 1921; d. Brno, 22 January 2000), Czech conductor and dramaturg. Nosek studied at the Prague Conservatory, where his teachers included Pavel Dědeček (conducting) and Jaroslav Řídký (composition). In 1952 he became dramaturg at the Brno NT, working closely with František Jílek, who was appointed principal conductor the same year. Together they planned the 1958 Brno Janáček Festival, a landmark in the renewal of Janáček's operas. Nosek conducted *The Makropulos Affair** in the Festival, prepared the edition of *Fate** conducted by Jílek at the work's stage premiere, and edited the Festival book, *Opery Leoše Janáčka na Brněnské scéne* (Brno, 1958). At Brno in 1974, Nosek conducted *From the House of the Dead** using his own edition based on the autograph and authorised copy, which attempted to restore Janáček's original version (a live recording was published by Supraphon). *ČHS, JAWO, NDBrOA, NosOpe.*

Novák, Láďa [Ladislav] (b. Prague, 7 October 1865; d. Prague, 16 January 1944), Czech artist. Novák studied architecture and civil engineering. He is best known as a graphic artist and for decorative facades on buildings. In 1919, on the recommendation of his friend Alfons Mucha*, he was asked by Janáček to design the front cover for the vocal score of *The Excursions of Mr Brouček**. Janáček wrote to Novák on 9 May to say that he had met Mucha and asking him to do the design. The efficient Novák sent his cover to Janáček ten days later and it subsequently adorned the UE vocal score. Janáček was delighted with the results, writing to Novák on 23 May: 'You have given me such a wonderful surprise that I do not know how to thank you. It's as though Brouček has come alive in front of my very eyes. His landlady – I just have her like Kedruta in the fifteenth century – so fitting! Etherea with the flower hat – and Málinka – with a money box! It's a masterly piece of work that you've done. And not just as a cover: I think it would make a wonderful theatre poster! In the meantime I thank you with all my heart. In one page you have captured the tone that I searched for in three or four hundred pages of piano score.' It was also in 1919 that Novák painted the striking art nouveau frescoes on the facade of Stopka's Pilsner Pub at Česká No. 5 in Brno, which became one of Janáček's favourite haunts. *KLJ, ZahFoo.*

Novák, Vítězslav (b. Kamenice nad Lipou, 5 December 1870; d. Skuteč, 18 July 1949), Czech composer. Novák studied composition with Dvořák at the Prague Conservatory. He played his Piano Quintet in A minor Op. 12 at a concert in Brno on 21 March 1897, and was introduced to Janáček by the violinist Rudolf

15. Vitězslav Novák, his wife Marie Nováková and Břetislav Bakala.

Reissig. Novák recalled in his memoirs that they discussed Moravian folk music and César Franck, and disagreed about both. Novák resolved in future to avoid talking about music with Janáček, but over the next few years they saw each other quite frequently. Novák visited the Janáčeks in Hukvaldy in the summer of 1897, and the two composers climbed Mount Radhošť with Reissig on 15 August. On this expedition they encountered a young woman from Fremštát who 'sang us a beautiful melancholy song' which Janáček notated, telling Novák he would include it in his forthcoming collection with Bartoš of *Moravian Folksongs Newly Collected* (XIII/3). In his memoirs, Novák grumbled that he 'looked in vain for this beautiful, typically Lachian song', and concluded waspishly that Janáček was 'not such an infallible authority on Moravian folksong'. On 18 August 1897, Janáček organised a concert in Hukvaldy at which Novák's *Three Czech Dances* Op. 15 were played by Novák and Janáček in their original version for piano four-hands. Soon afterwards, Novák dedicated Set II of his arrangements of Moravian folksongs (Op. 17) to Janáček. While Novák often found himself disagreeing with Janáček on musical matters, he was greatly impressed by Janáček's daughter Olga. On a visit to the family in Hukvaldy in 1900, he noted the disharmony between Janáček and Zdenka, but recalled that 'Janáček's young daughter Olenka dazzled us. This pale, blonde girl was the only link between her quarrelling parents, but for us it was an experience to look upon her gentle beauty.' After 1900, Janáček and Novák met less often.

As composers and teachers, Janáček and Novák could be considered rivals – Janáček certainly saw it that way, and he did not have a high opinion of Novák's music. When *The Storm* was given its triumphant world premiere in Brno on 17 April 1910, Janáček was one of the few to be lukewarm about what was certainly one of Novák's most successful works. Janáček's lack of enthusiasm may have been partly through irritation that the commission for a work to celebrate the fiftieth anniversary of the Brno Beseda had gone to Novák rather than to him. *ČHS, JYL1, JYL2, NovSob.*

Nursery Rhymes [*Říkadla*]: first version, for three voices, clarinet and piano (V/16); second version, for nine voices and ten instruments (V/17). The first version was started by 30 July 1925, when Janáček wrote from Hukvaldy to Kamila Stösslová* that he was 'setting nursery rhymes to music – they will be fun'. They also provided Janáček with a welcome distraction from his more arduous task that summer of revising *The Makropulos Affair*. The eight songs were finished before Janáček left for the ISCM Festival in Venice at the end of August, and the first performance took place on 26 October 1925 in the Brno Beseda as part of an evening given by the Czech Readers' Club. The performers included Stanislav Krtička (clarinet) and Jaroslav Kvapil (piano). Janáček was present, and according to Ludvík Kundera he was unhappy with the limited scope and sound of the *Nursery Rhymes* as they stood, though it was another year before Janáček expanded the work.

The second version (V/17) comprises an introduction and eighteen songs, scored for two sopranos, two altos, three tenors and two basses, and an ensemble that is endearingly odd even by Janáček's standards: two flutes (the second doubling piccolo), two clarinets (both doubling E flat clarinets), two bassoons (the second doubling contra-bassoon), an ocarina capable of playing C flat and A flat, a double bass, a child's drum and piano. The revisions and additions were made between 14 November and 27 December 1926, involving the composition of an instrumental introduction and ten completely new songs, as well as revisions of the eight earlier songs. Václav Sedláček's authorised copy is dated 21 January 1927, and the first performance took place in the Brno Beseda on 25 April in a concert given by the KMS. Janáček was away in Prague so could not be present, but the concert was broadcast and he heard it at the home of his friend Otto Kretschmer (see Radio Broadcasts during Janáček's Lifetime*). The performers were mostly from the Brno NT orchestra, including Václav Sedláček playing piccolo and ocarina, and Stanislav Krtička as the first clarinet. No conductor is named, but the evidence points to Břetislav Bakala. Not only did the singers in the first performance include Bakala's younger sister Antonie, and his wife Marie, but when the work was repeated at the KMS in 1929, 1935 and 1938, Bakala was identified as the conductor on each occasion.

Like *The Cunning Little Vixen*, the inspiration for *Nursery Rhymes* came from *Lidové noviny*. A number of traditional children's rhymes were published, with new illustrations, in the newspaper's 'Children's Corner' ('Dětský koutek'), a feature of the Sunday edition. The first of them, 'Frantíku, Frantíku', appeared on 4 January 1925, and 'Mole is crawling' ('Leze krtek'), the eighth and last of those chosen by Janáček for the first version, was published on 15 August, the earliest date on which Janáček could have composed his setting (which became the opening song of the first version). Each nursery rhyme ('Řikadlo') in *Lidové noviny* was accompanied by an illustration. Of the first eight, six were illustrated by Josef Lada and two by Ondřej Sekora. The rhymes chosen by Janáček for the new songs in the expanded *Nursery Rhymes* appeared between 23 August 1925 and 21 November 1926. Once again, the last rhyme to be printed in the newspaper ('The Turnip's Wedding' [Řípa se vdávala]) became the first song of the new version, coming straight after the instrumental introduction. Of this second group of rhymes, seven were illustrated by Lada, one by Sekora and one by Jan Hála; one is anonymous. For the premiere of the complete *Nursery Rhymes*, Janáček wanted to project the illustrations on to a screen and asked Lada if it would be possible to create versions of them in colour. Lada tried to do this but could not get paints to adhere to the plates (see Josef Lada*). In the end, the illustrations were not used at the concert, but reproductions were included in the first edition of the vocal score.

Inspired by these amusing texts and illustrations, Janáček produced one of his most delightful works, a brilliant demonstration of his late composing technique in miniature. The start of the introduction sets a mood that is at once folk-like, beguiling and strikingly modern, with the clarinet and ocarina answering each other over spiky bassoons. Throughout the *Nursery Rhymes*, the use of ostinato is ingenious, and the different levels of rhythmical activity within a single song are clearly audible: the clarinet semiquavers and slower piano chords in No. 14 ('The white goat's picking pears' [Koza bílá hrušky sbírá]), or the three layers, of clarinets, voices and the gently bucolic piano, in No. 16 ('Goat lies in the hay' [Koza leží na seně]). There is some extraordinary instrumentation of a sort that can be found in the late operas, but that is here presented in microcosm: the E flat clarinets at the end of No. 2 ('The Turnips' Wedding' [Řípa se vdávala]) or at their most stratospheric after Fig. 2 in No. 19 ('Bear was sitting on a tree-trunk' [Seděl medvěd' na kolodi]), the dialogue between piccolo and piano in No. 3 ('Nothing's nicer than the start of spring' [Není lepší jako z jara], or the whole ensemble (minus ocarina) in the joyous instrumental epilogue. In terms of its word setting, the howling dog in No. 8 ('Our dog' [Náš pes]) is a close relative of Lapák in Act I of *The Cunning Little Vixen*.

In March 1928, Janáček started to receive proofs of the vocal score arranged by Erwin Stein (a reduction for voices, viola and piano) and he sent corrections back to UE. The publication appeared in September 1928, a month after Janáček's death. Printed in oblong format (and with some copies bound in boards covered in bright red paper), it included the illustrations by Lada, Sekora and Hála that had originally appeared with the rhymes in *Lidové noviny* now printed side by side with the songs. The full score, which doesn't include the illustrations, was published by UE in April 1929. Following the Brno premiere, early performances included a broadcast on 3 December 1928 by the BBC (2LO): a live relay from the Arts Theatre Club in London conducted by Hermann Scherchen. Two of the songs from the first version were published as a musical supplement in *La Revue musicale* (August 1926), but the whole of the first version was only rediscovered in 1988 (in the archives of the Brno Beseda) and published in 1993 by UE and Editio Moravia, edited by Alena Němcová. A critical edition of the definitive second version was published in SKVEJ E/5 (2006), also edited by Němcová. *JanLid, JAWO, JYL2, NěmŘík.*

On the Overgrown Path [*Po zarostlém chodníčku*], miniatures ('drobné skladby', literally 'small pieces') for piano (VIII/17). These piano miniatures were composed between 1900 and 1911. In 1897 Josef Vávra*, a teacher in Ivančice, wrote to Janáček asking for a contribution to an anthology of music for harmonium containing 'the most beautiful Slavonic melodies'. Janáček was asked to provide folksong arrangements, and to include the words. Vávra's *Slavonic Melodies* started to appear in 1897. Three years later, Janáček wrote to Vávra offering him some harmonium pieces. Three pieces (Nos. 1, 2 and 10 of *On the Overgrown Path*) were published in Vol. 5 of Vávra's collection in 1901, and two more (Nos. 4 and 7) were included in Vol. 6 (1902), published by Vávra's collaborator Emil Kolář*. The collective title, *On the Overgrown Path*, was used for the first time in these collections but the pieces had no individual titles.

There things remained until 1908, when Jan Branberger and Janáček exchanged several letters about the possibility of publishing some or all of the *Overgrown Path* pieces in a series to be published by Bedřich Kočí in Prague. Nothing came of this and Janáček instead offered the pieces to Mojmír Urbánek, who turned them down in February 1909. The Brno firm of Arnošt Píša was more enthusiastic and agreed to publish the pieces. Janáček sent Series I to Píša in September 1911 and all ten pieces appeared in a single volume in December 1911, with their individual titles included.

Before Series I appeared, Janáček published another piece, described as the first in a 'new series' of *On the Overgrown Path*. It appeared in *Večery*, the literary supplement to *Lidové noviny*, on 30 September 1911. The authorised copy from which this was printed also contains Nos. 12 and 14, but these were not published during Janáček's lifetime. Nos. 11, 12 and 14, along with two earlier pieces that had been discarded from Series I, were published by HMUB in 1942 as Series II of *On the Overgrown Path*. The whole work was published in SKV F/1 (1978), which also included the harmonium version of No. 4.

An early performance of unspecified pieces from Series I was given on 6 January 1905 by an unnamed pianist at a concert organised by the Association of Women Teachers. On 20 September 1912, Vladimír Ambros played Series I at a concert in Frankfurt, Germany. The first performance Janáček is known to have attended took place more than a decade later, on 3 November 1923, when Jan Heřman played Series I at a concert of the SMH in Prague. The first recording of Series I was made for Ultraphon by Josef Páleníček in 1943.

Janáček's miniatures, like Schumann's, range from tender reminiscences to dark mood pieces. According to Ludvík Kundera, the cycle was based on memories of Janáček's childhood, but what the deeper programme for the set as a whole might be, or even the individual pieces, is hard to fathom: these are enigmatic and mysterious miniatures that seem to be confiding intimate secrets. 'Our evenings' [Naše večery], the first piece, begins benignly enough but has surprisingly discordant conflict at its centre. 'A blown-away leaf' [Lístek odvanutý], a piece of great tenderness, was described by Janáček in a letter to Jan Branberger of 6 June 1908 (before the individual titles had been settled) as 'a love song'. 'Come with us!' [Pojd'te s nami!] has the feeling of a folk dance, but there's sadness too, made explicit by Janáček's remarks on the closing bars that they depict 'a letter put away for ever'. 'The Frýdek Madonna' [Frýdecká Panna Maria] evokes a place that Janáček knew from childhood. 'They chattered like swallows' [Štěbetaly jak laštovičky] is another piece with a clear folk music influence, though it has hints of unease too, perhaps because of its predominantly minor key or its harmonic ambiguity. 'Words fail!' [Nelze domluvit!] was described in Janáček's 1908 letter as 'The bitterness of disappointment', made all the more acute by the moment of apparent reconciliation near the end. 'Good night!' [Dobrou noc] can be taken at face value, but Janáček's comment to Branberger that 'perhaps you'll hear parting in it' suggests a more permanent farewell, something underlined by the quietly obsessive rhythmic figure that runs throughout. 'Unutterable anguish' [Tak neskonale úzko] is a powerful lament. In his description of 'In tears' [V pláči], Janáček gives a clue to its very personal meaning: 'Perhaps you'll sense weeping in the penultimate number? The premonition of certain death. During the hot summer nights that angelic being lay in such mortal anguish.' In other words, 'In tears' is the most tender of elegies for Olga Janáčková. Janáček wrote that in the final piece, 'The screech-owl has not flown away!' [Sýček neodletěl!], 'the ominous motif of the screech-owl is heard in the intimate song of life'. He says nothing about whose 'intimate song' this might be, but the owl's presence is persistent and sinister, and at the end the whole piece seems to become enveloped in uneasy darkness.

The five pieces in Series II (Nos. 11–15) of *On the Overgrown Path* have no titles. The first piece, originally printed in *Lidové noviny* in 1911, maintains a mood of intimacy, uncertainty and emotional ambivalence similar to that of Series I. The other pieces in Series II are quite experimental: they begin to hint at a kind of pianistic expressionism, the music often unusually dissonant, and the ideas intense and disturbing. *JAWO, JYL1, VogJan.*

Operas seen by Janáček   Janáček only became interested in opera during his thirties, attending numerous performances at the newly established Provisional Theatre in Brno (forerunner of the Brno NT) from 1884 to 1888, when he was reviewing them for *Hudební listy*. After 1888, Janáček's attendance at operas became more patchy: for example, there's no evidence of him attending a single performance of *Le Nozze di Figaro*, *Die Zauberflöte*, *Die Meistersinger*, *Otello*, *Falstaff* or *La Bohème*. Dvořák's *Rusalka* and Mussorgsky's *Boris Godunov* he is known to have seen just once. He saw relatively little German repertoire (especially Wagner) because he refused on principle to go to the German Theatre in Brno, which opened in 1882. He came to know the building well later on: from 1919 it was the home of the Brno NT, where so many of his premieres took place. There are also operas Janáček wrote about without having seen them: he published a detailed analysis of Wagner's *Tristan und Isolde* in 1885, but did not see the opera in the theatre until 1922. The other Wagner operas he saw (all after 1906) were *Lohengrin*, *Tannhäuser*, *Der Fliegende Holländer*, *Die Walküre* and *Parsifal*. He saw only two operas by Richard Strauss: *Salome* and *Elektra*, and he saw Debussy's *Pelléas et Mélisande* once, in 1921. Though he was enthusiastic about Berg's *Wozzeck*, he never saw it. The operas he saw most often were Smetana's *The Bartered Bride* (more than a dozen times) and *Dalibor* (six times), and Verdi's *Il Trovatore* (seven times). Of those operas that are known to have made a particularly deep impression on him, he saw Charpentier's *Louise* once in 1903; Mascagni's *Cavalleria rusticana* twice in 1892, Tchaikovsky's *Eugene Onegin* twice in 1891 and 1903, and *The Queen of Spades* once in 1896; and Puccini's *Madama Butterfly* twice, in 1908 and 1919. Complete lists of all the operas Janáček saw are in Tyrrell *JYL1* and *JYL2*.

Opus numbers   Janáček gave opus numbers to three works. The *Theme and Variations* (VIII/6) was described in a letter to Zdenka on 20 February 1880: 'It is very nice and I see it as my first completely personal work, as my Opus 1.'

There is, however, no opus number on Janáček's autograph manuscript. The designation 'Op. 2' appears on the title page of the 1890 Bursík and Kohout edition of the *Valachian Dances* (VI/4). A manuscript volume of four pieces for orchestra (without a collective title) was designated 'Op. 3' by Janáček, and this was eventually published as the Suite Op. 3* (VI/6) in 1958. Occasionally 'Op. 60' has been given to the *Sinfonietta** (VI/18), but this is entirely spurious.

There have been several attempts to number Janáček's works. The numbering established for *JAWO* (1997) has started to gain general acceptance (see Catalogues of Janáček's Works*). *JAWO, JYL1.*

Ostrčil, Otakar (b. Prague, 25 February 1879; d. Prague, 20 August 1935), Czech composer and conductor. Ostrčil studied philosophy at Charles University, and took private lessons in composition from Zdeněk Fibich. His own operas enjoyed some success, but it was his advocacy of new music by other composers that was arguably his greatest achievement as chief conductor at the Prague NT. Ostrčil met Janáček at a concert by the Prague Teachers' Choir on 4 April 1914, and congratulated him after *The Seventy Thousand** (its first performance in Prague). This was the start of a musical friendship that soon bore fruit. Ostrčil attended the first night of *Jenůfa** at the Prague NT (26 May 1916) and wrote to the composer on 28 May, expressing his great admiration, and alluding to the coolness of relations between Janáček and the National Theatre over the years (specifically with its conductor Kovařovic): 'Your *Jenůfa* made a huge impression on me. Seldom have I left the theatre so taken by a work as on Friday's premiere. You know how to keep the listener as if in a vice for the whole evening. ... Accept from me, Maestro, my sincere congratulations on this well-deserved success and my wishes that the ice now already dispersed will open the way for all your works into the hearts of people.'

The following year, on 14 November, Ostrčil conducted the premiere of *The Fiddler's Child** with the Czech Philharmonic. In November 1919, an ailing Kovařovic told Janáček that Ostrčil would conduct the forthcoming premiere of *The Excursions of Mr Brouček**. On 29 January 1920, Janáček wrote to Ostrčil to say he would like to attend the orchestral rehearsals, in order 'to fill in things if I feel the need. Should you consider some colouristic retouching a good idea, don't hesitate to carry it out.' It was immediately clear from Ostrčil's reply that a much more welcoming regime was taking charge in Prague: 'I am overjoyed that I was allowed to rehearse your masterly work. It is a real treat for me, though the work – I admit – isn't easy. In the orchestra ... no need has been felt for any retouching. Besides, I think that the orchestral part will sound colourful without any retouching just as in that respect your *Fiddler's Child* sounded very rich, although not a single note was revised.' Following the premiere on 23 April 1920, Janáček sent Ostrčil several letters about details and small cuts and changes, but he was pleased with the result. Not always quick to praise conductors, he wrote to Ostrčil on 16 May 1920: 'I heard the last performance and its orchestral clarity – I thank you once again for your great work.'

Janáček kept Ostrčil informed about progress on his next opera, *Káťa Kabanová**, writing on 6 December 1920 that he was at the 'final chords'. Ostrčil was to be a consistent champion of Janáček operas despite being a close friend of Zdeněk Nejedlý*, Janáček's critical nemesis. He conducted the Prague premiere of *Káťa Kabanová* on 30 November 1922, having worked closely with

Janáček during rehearsals, filling the composer with confidence: on 2 November he wrote, 'I now know for sure that in your hands the work is safe. I'm looking forward to it and have no fears!' Janáček was full of praise for the conducting: 'Be true to yourself in everything. I would be pleased if *Káťa* were to be given everywhere as magnificently as you did it.' Preparations for *The Cunning Little Vixen** didn't go quite as smoothly – Ostrčil rejected Janáček's suggestion that Prague should take over Eduard Milén's sets for the Brno production – but the Prague premiere on 18 May 1925 was a success, and also had the distinction of being the first radio broadcast of an opera by Janáček. While generally pleased (he told Stösslová, 'They perform it excellently'), Janáček objected to Ostrčil's decision to use adults as the Hens and Fox Cubs, writing to Brod on 16 June that 'they must be a children's chorus. It was Mr Ostrčil's arbitrary decision to let monsters on to the stage.' Ostrčil conducted a new production of *Jenůfa** on 12 January 1926, for which the theatre paid a royalty to Kovařovic's widow for his part in the orchestration, much to Janáček's annoyance. He was also very hurt by what he imagined to be Ostrčil's rejection of *Šárka**, revealed in a tense exchange of letters in January 1926 (though Janáček ended his angriest letter with an olive branch: 'You were the only one whom I respected, and continue to respect'). This correspondence culminated in a remarkable letter from Ostrčil on 30 January: 'You know my attitude towards you. During my time at the National Theatre I have performed your *Excursions of Mr Brouček* which had not yet been played in Brno, *Káťa Kabanová*, *The Cunning Little Vixen* and now I have prepared a new production of *Jenůfa*. I have directed all the premieres myself and I have put all that I know into the preparation. The facts speak for themselves. ... As for *Šárka*, I had not anticipated that you were interested in its being performed at the Prague National Theatre ... I assumed that you yourself regarded the performance of this work [in Brno] as an interesting retrospective, shedding light on the beginnings of your work ... For [these] reasons, I did not apply to produce *Šárka* but it is also intolerable for news to be spread about that I turned it down when it was not even submitted. I look forward, however, to your new opera, *The Makropulos Affair*, and would regard it as an honour if you were to entrust it to the National Theatre in Prague for its first performance.' The world premiere took place in Brno, but the Prague production of *The Makropulos Affair** opened on 1 March 1928. Janáček was delighted by Ostrčil's preparation of an exceptionally difficult score, writing to Zdenka on 24 February: 'It has been rehearsed marvellously. Elina Makropulos [Naďa Kejřová] is outstanding both in voice and acting. The Brno orchestra is of course rather poor in comparison with the one here. Everybody was pleased that I praised it. Ostrčil valued that praise at half a million.' His optimism was well placed: along with *Jenůfa*, the first night of *Makropulos* was the most successful of all Janáček's Prague premieres. *EckJan, JAii, JAWO, JODA, PalPos.*

Osud See *Fate* (I/5)

Otče náš See *Our Father* (IV/29)

Our Father [*Otče náš*] for tenor solo, mixed chorus, harp and organ (IV/29). The original version of this setting of the Lord's Prayer in Czech was composed for a performance at the Brno NT on 15 May 1901. Given in aid of the Brno Women's Shelter, it included the Tyl theatre group (an amateur theatre club) enacting

a. Christus

b. Our Father, who art in heaven, hallowed be thy name

c. Thy kingdom come

d. Thy will be done on earth as it is in heaven

16. Józef Męcina-Krzesz: eight illustrations for 'Our Father', *Tygodnik ilustrowany*, 1898.

e. Give us this day our daily bread

f. And forgive us our trespasses, as we forgive those who trespass against us

g. And lead us not into temptation

h. But deliver us from evil. Amen.

tableaux vivants based on a series of paintings illustrating the Lord's Prayer by the Polish artist Józef Męcina-Krzesz (1860–1934). A member of the Women's Shelter committee was given a copy of the magazine *Tygodnik Ilustrowany* (28 October 1899) that included black-and-white reproductions of the paintings (the originals are lost). Janáček's setting was for solo tenor, mixed chorus, piano and harmonium, and divided into five numbered sections. At the premiere, the conductor was Max Koblížek, the tenor solo was sung by Miroslav Lazar (also known as Zdeněk Lev), with Ludmila Tučková (piano) and Rudolf Zahrádníček (harmonium). In 1906 Janáček revised the work. The division into five sections was removed and the instrumental accompaniment revised for harp and organ. It was first performed in this version by the Hlahol Choral Society in Prague, conducted by Adolf Piskáček. František Pácal was the tenor soloist and the organist was Josef Klička, with unnamed harpists (Janáček merely described them as 'two bad harpists'). Janáček was present at the performance. Pácal took over the tenor solos at the last moment and Janáček considered the whole performance to be under-prepared. On 19 October 1924, Jaroslav Kvapil conducted the *Our Father* with the Brno Beseda in a programme of Janáček's choral works to honour the composer's seventieth birthday.

Our Father is a transitional work that has some hints of how Janáček's choral style would develop in parts of *The Excursions of Mr Brouček** and in *The Eternal Gospel**. A review of the Prague performance in 1906 in *Smetana* claimed that it 'suffered from the lack of a coherent whole and did not leave the deeper and more lasting impression that a work of this serious musical theoretician would otherwise deserve'. Janáček sent off a furious note to the editor of *Smetana*, Jan Branberger, underlining that it was meant to be illustrative music: 'My *Our Father* refers only to Krzesz's pictures. Why was this relationship not taken into account? On the concert platform it was completely lost. Perhaps having the pictures in the programme would have helped. ... In Brno the work was sung to *tableaux vivants* and is remembered to this day.' Since the *tableaux vivants* were themselves developed from the reproductions of the paintings in *Tygodnik Ilustrowany* and Janáček lays such importance on the work only referring to the pictures in his letter to Branberger, perhaps the illustrations (murky as they are) should accompany performances as the composer suggested. *JAWO, JYL1, ŠtěOtč, Tygllu.*

Our Flag [*Naše vlajka*], chorus for male voices with two solo sopranos (IV/44). *Our Flag* was composed between December 1925 and March 1926 (just before Janáček started the *Sinfonietta*) on the poem 'Vlajka' [Flag] from F. S. Procházka's *Nové Hradčanské písničky* (Prague, 1924). Janáček wrote to Procházka* on 10 December 1925, asking him for some additional lines for the fifth stanza of the poem (and sending a tune which is different from the one he eventually used). Procházka sent the new lines by return of post. In another letter of 20 December 1925, Janáček argued that Procházka's title only made sense in the context of the other poems and suggested 'Naše vlajka'. Procházka agreed to his suggestion on 21 December. This friendly exchange of letters was Janáček's last communication with Procházka. *Our Flag* was dedicated 'To the PSMU for *The Seventy Thousand* in France', a reference to the successful performances of *The Seventy Thousand** (IV/36) given in Montpellier in December 1925. The first performance of *Our Flag* was given by the PSMU in

Přerov on 16 October 1926, conducted by Ferdinand Vach*, and they gave the Prague premiere on 28 December 1926. The first publication was in SKV C/2 (2011). *JAiii, JAWO, JYL2, StrMuž.*

Páleníček, Josef (b. Travnik, Bosnia, 19 July 1914; d. Prague, 7 March 1991), Czech pianist. Páleníček recalled that 'when I was a little boy ... I heard Janáček's *Jenůfa* in Olomouc. The next day I told my piano teacher, composer Jaroslav [*recte* Josef] Svoboda, about the experience, how the music kept me awake all night. Professor Svoboda excitedly proceeded to draw me a picture of Janáček. ... Later in Prague and later still in Paris I heard Ruda Firkušný play *On the Overgrown Path*; in Prague I also heard Janáček's symphonic and operatic works in monumental interpretations by Václav Talich. That's more or less how it started for me, and it was soon plain to me that I had fallen in love with the music in a way that would change my life.' Páleníček's first experience of *Jenůfa* must have been the Olomouc production that opened in October 1924. He gave his first recital in Olomouc in 1926, and in 1927 he began studies at the Prague Conservatory with Karel Hoffmeister (piano) and Otakar Šín (composition). After graduating, he continued advanced studies with Hoffmeister and Vítězslav Novák. In 1936–8 he studied in Paris with Albert Roussel (composition), Alfred Cortot (piano) and Pierre Fournier (chamber music). He returned to Prague in 1939, becoming a teacher at the Conservatory, and his large repertoire developed with Janáček's music at its core. During the 1940s, he made the first recordings of Janáček's major piano and chamber compositions, including *1. X. 1905** (*On the Overgrown Path** (Series I), *In the Mists**, *Fairy Tale** (with Miloš Sádlo), the Sonata for Violin and Piano* (with Alexander Plocek) and *The Diary of One Who Disappeared** (with Josef Válka and Růžena Hořáková). (See Recordings before 1960* for further details.) Páleníček recorded most of these works again later in his career, including *The Diary of One Who Disappeared* with Beno Blachut, Vilém Přibyl and Nicolai Gedda, as well as new recordings of piano works. He recorded the *Concertino** three times and the *Capriccio** twice. In 1975 Supraphon issued a selection from *Moravian Folk Poetry in Songs** (V/2) with Čeněk Mlčák and Páleníček. *ČHS, PalJan.*

Památník pro Kamilu Stösslovou   See *Album for Kamila Stösslová*

Pan-Slavism   Janáček's Pan-Slavism – the political and cultural union of Slav peoples – first manifested itself in 1869 when, as a teenager, he attended a celebration in Velehrad of Cyril and Methodius, the two saints linking Moravia to a wider Slavic world. By 1874 he had started to learn Russian and became an enthusiastic reader of Russian literature. Janáček's children, Olga and Vladimír, had the same names as the lovers in Pushkin's *Eugene Onegin* (Olga Larin and Vladimir Lensky), and it's difficult to imagine that this was a pure coincidence. In 1886, reviewing Ludvík Kuba's collection of Slav songs, Janáček made the extraordinary assertion that in future music would have no separate national styles: it would become 'only Slavonic, and not individually Czech, Russian etc.'. Coming from the composer who went on to forge his own uniquely Moravian modernism, particularly in works like *Jenůfa**, *The Cunning Little Vixen** and the Bezruč choruses, this is a decidedly odd remark. Perhaps in the 1880s he believed that it was the way forward for some kind of musical Pan-Slavism. By the time *Jenůfa* was performed in

Brno, he had produced a work that was essentially and inextricably Moravian rather than Pan-Slavic. Probably composed while he was at work on the first act of *Jenůfa*, the choral work *Lord Have Mercy* [*Hospodine!*] (III/5) is an interesting case. Scored for soloists, mixed chorus, brass, harp and organ, it sets the words 'Hospodine, pomiluj ny!' ('Lord have mercy on us'). A translation of 'Kyrie eleison', it is the oldest known song in Czech. The musical elements of Janáček's work give it a distinctly Pan-Slavic flavour: though the text is in Czech, the style of the setting closely resembles that of Russian Orthodox chant rather than Czech hymnody.

Though Janáček had a profound interest in Russia and Russian Literature*, his Pan-Slavism extended to other Slav nations and, on a specifically Czech level, to the distinctive regions of Moravia and Bohemia. His involvement with the Czecho-Slavonic Ethnographic Exhibition in 1895 is evidence of a growing interest in the different kinds of Slavonic culture within Czech lands. *Our Father** (IV/29) was based on paintings by a Polish artist, and it can be argued (as Tyrrell does) that *Fate** – set in the Moravian spa of Luhačovice but with a cast that is cosmopolitan – is a work that begins to explore a broader Slavism, reaching beyond Moravia. Janáček's next opera, *The Excursions of Mr Brouček**, amounts to a kind of ode to the Bohemian capital, Prague. Janáček's orchestral rhapsody *Taras Bulba** takes its inspiration from a novel that was written in Russian by an author who was Ukrainian (Gogol was descended from Ukrainian Cossacks), and that Janáček decided to dedicate retrospectively to the Czech armed forces. Janáček's last opera, *From the House of the Dead**, is one of his supreme achievements, and also one of his most overtly Pan-Slavic. In Janáček's version of Dostoyevsky's Siberian prison camp, he freely mixes Czech with snatches of Russian, Ukrainian and Moravian dialect to produce a polyglot libretto that encompasses much of the Slavic world as he saw it. *JYL1, JYL2.*

Pavlík, František (b. Ořechov, near Brno, 16 August 1885; d. Brno, 2 October 1905).   Pavlík was a joiner's apprentice who came to be regarded as a martyr for the cause of Czech education. His death inspired Janáček to compose *1. X. 1905**. Pavlík was fatally wounded by a bayonet on the steps of the Beseda House after the Austrian army was sent in to restore order during demonstrations in support of a Czech university in Brno on 1 and 2 October 1905. On Thursday, 5 October, *Lidové noviny* printed a memorial notice under the caption: 'František Pavlík from Ořechov, murdered in front of the Besední dům on 2 October at about 9 in the evening by a soldier of the 49th Imperial Infantry Regiment.' Below this is a harrowing account of the circumstances of Pavlík's death: 'An innocent 20-year-old boy František Pavlík was stabbed on the steps of Beseda House and terribly mutilated by piercing bayonets, rifle butts and swords. He fell to the ground, blood pouring from his wounds, and he died shortly afterwards.' Janáček was present at this protest and, after attempting to engage the Austrian soldiers with his walking stick (conjuring up an image worthy of Mr Brouček), he was dragged to safety inside the Beseda House. Janáček was among the thousands of mourners who attended Pavlík's funeral on 5 October. The inscription on Pavlík's grave in Brno's Central Cemetery reads: 'A simple Czech worker who had a royal funeral ... He fell in the struggle for a beautiful and noble idea.' A bronze plaque in

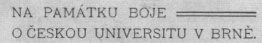

NA PAMÁTKU BOJE ━━━━
O ČESKOU UNIVERSITU V BRNĚ.

„Vidíme-li nespravedlivost a mlčíme-li k ní, pášeme ji sami". (Rousseau.)

„Život je založen na obětování se jednotlivců pro celek". (H. P. Blavacká.)

ČESKÝ DĚLNÍK
FR. PAVLÍK Z VEL. OŘECHOVA,
zavražděný německým vojákem od 49. pěš. pluku 2. října 1905.
oo oo
„Žádná smrt nemůže býti zlá, které předchází život dobrý".
Kramerius.

17. Memorial postcard commemorating František Pavlík whose death while protesting on behalf of a Czech university in Brno inspired Janáček's *1. X. 1905*.

Pavlík's memory, designed by Josef Axmann, was unveiled on the wall of the Beseda House on 4 October 1925. It was stolen during the war but Axmann cast a replacement which was installed on 17 November 1946. The protests in which Pavlík died led to the establishment of Brno's Masaryk University in 1919. *EDMB, JYL1, LN.*

Pazdírek, Oldřich (b. Horní Moštěnice, near Přerov, 18 December 1887; d. Brno, 3 August 1944), Czech music publisher. Oldřich Pazdírek came from a family of publishers and musicians. His uncles Bohumil (1839–1919) and František (1848–1915). Pazdírek compiled the *Universal-Handbuch der Musikliteratur* (Vienna, 1904–10), while his father, Ludevít Raimund Pazdírek (1850–1914), founded the first music publishing house in Moravia, initially in Horní Moštěnice, then Olomouc (1897) and finally Brno (from 1911). Oldřich Pazdírek took over his father's firm in 1919. He had a stroke of luck when nobody from Hudební matice turned up to the premiere of *The Diary of One Who Disappeared** on 21 April 1921, so Janáček gave the work to Pazdírek, who had the first edition on sale in September 1921. In 1924 Pazdírek launched two magazines, *Hudební besídka** (edited by Josef Gregor and aimed at younger readers) and *Hudební rozhledy** (edited by Vladimír Helfert and Ludvík Kundera). Both were enthusiastic advocates of Janáček's music. In 1926 Pazdírek published the score of the early Suite for strings (VI/2). The first part of Pazdírek's music dictionary (*Pazdírkův hudební slovník naučný*), edited by Gracian Černušák, appeared in 1929 (covering musical terms). The biographical part (co-edited by Helfert) reached the letter M before publication had to be abandoned due to the war. In 1939 Pazdírek issued the first volume of Helfert's Janáček biography, the only volume to be published. Later publications included *Spring Song* (V/3) in 1944, and a separate edition of the piano intermezzo (No. 13) from *The Diary of One Who Disappeared* with the title 'Intermezzo erotico' and an illustrated title page by František Drlík depicting a naked woman, printed in lurid shades of red, yellow and green. *FELJ, JAWO, KLJ.*

Peška, Josef [Karel Šípek] (b. Bohdaneč, 17 March 1857; d. Bohdaneč, 12 February 1923), Czech writer. Peška, who used the pseudonym Karel Šípek, was the author of four opera librettos for Karel Kovařovic*, including *The Dogheads*. He was on friendly terms with both Kovařovic and Gustav Schmoranz at the Prague NT. With František Veselý* and Marie Calma-Veselá*, Peška was instrumental in persuading Kovařovic to put on *Jenůfa** in 1916: as Calma-Veselá wrote in 1924, Peška 'acted in his decisive, energetic way. He let rip at Kovařovic and it's a wonder that this didn't put an end to his friendship with him.' František Veselý wrote to Janáček on 12 December 1915 that 'were it not for [Peška's] great influence on Schmoranz and Kovařovic as well as his continual daily contacts with the National Theatre, I don't know if our plan would have come off'. *JODA.*

Pěvecké sdružení moravských učitelů (PSMU) See Moravian Teachers' Choral Society

Phonograph Janáček was President of the Working Committee for Czech Folksong in Moravia and Silesia, formed at the end of 1905. In October 1909, an Edison Phonograph was delivered to the Working Committee to make wax cylinder recordings of folksongs in the field. The machine was in use between 1909 and 1912. Most of the cylinders were recorded by two of Janáček's most assiduous folksong collectors, Františka Kyselková* and Hynek Bím*, but occasionally Janáček himself used the machine. After 1912, Janáček and his folksong collectors returned to making handwritten transcriptions (which they had continued to make during the years when the phonograph was in use). The collection of wax cylinders was transferred to the State Institute for

Folksong Study in 1919, and this became the Institute for Ethnography and Folklore Studies in 1953. The collection of surviving cylinders remains there to this day. The phonograph recordings document several collecting trips. In November 1909, Kyselková (with Janáček present) recorded a group of Slovak seasonal workers at a farm in Modřice, near Brno. Most of the songs were sung by groups, but Janáček was particularly attracted by the singing of Eva Gabel, one of the few solo singers to be recorded by the phonograph. These recordings are of particular interest, as the songs Eva Gabel recorded were subsequently arranged by Janáček for voice and piano and published as *Six Folksongs sung by Eva Gabel** (V/9). Bím and Kyselková recorded singers in the Terchová Valley region in northern Slovakia on two trips during 1910. Kyselková and Bím recorded Moravian folksongs at Vnorovy in September 1911, and in May 1912, Janáček himself returned to Terchová to record the women singers there. The manuscript survives of his handwritten transcriptions made on this trip, noting that he transcribed the songs between 12 and 15 May, and that they were also recorded 'by phonograph'.

The surviving cylinders recorded by Janáček, Kyselková and Bím on the phonograph between 1909 and 1912 have been published on three CDs, together with a volume of scholarly studies, transcriptions of the texts, and a DVD including facsimiles of the handwritten transcriptions made at the same time. While these represent only part of what was recorded (wax cylinders can degrade quickly), they constitute a fascinating body of material, giving an insight into the types of singing Janáček and his collectors encountered in the field on folksong collecting trips. In the case of the Eva Gabel songs, they also present the raw material that Janáček subsequently fashioned into published arrangements. *ProVza.*

'**Piano Sonata**' See *1. X. 1905* (VIII/19)

Piano Trio for violin, cello and piano after Tolstoy's novella *The Kreutzer Sonata*, lost (X/22). This work was probably composed by December 1908, and first performed on 2 April 1909 at the Brno Beseda in a concert organised by the KPU. The performers were Pavel Dědeček (violin), Rudolf Pavlata (cello) and Růžena Fialová. According to the review of the premiere in *Lidové noviny* (8 April), the trio was in three movements. It had been written for a concert in honour, rather belatedly, of Tolstoy's eightieth birthday (7 September 1908). It was performed subsequently in Boskovice (14 August 1910), and Janáček received requests for the loan of the parts for performances in Prague (1910, 1917 and 1922), Kroměříž (1912) and Příbram (1914); it is likely that some of these took place. The Piano Trio appears in the lists of Janáček's compositions in Max Brod's 1924 biography and in Janáček's autobiography (Veselý 1924). Brod's list adds a note quoting Janáček: 'The Quartet was based on a few ideas from this.' This provides an important clue as to how a work that had several performances and appeared in two lists of Janáček's compositions overseen by the composer simply disappeared in about 1924.

In 1947 the violinist in the premiere, Pavel Dědeček, sent Jan Racek a description of the Trio:

I remember well the beginning of the first movement with sextuplets in the violin and violoncello and as far as I can still recall, it was written in 2/1 time (two semibreves per bar). Pavlata and I asked Janáček at that time what the opening depicted and he told us that it was the rumbling of a train in motion. ... The start of the work corresponded to Tolstoy's description [the novel begins in a railway carriage]. Otherwise, there was in the first movement, as far as I dimly remember, a fair amount of thematic brevity. The second movement, in A flat minor, was melodious and I seem to remember that it was in triple time. The movement was very beautiful and melodious and I remember that from the first bar of the violin part the melody, which started on the G string, climbed gradually to the E string. As for the end of the Trio, my memory fails me, and I can no longer remember how the closing bars went.

Almost forty years on, after an extremely busy musical career (latterly as a distinguished teacher of conducting at the Prague Conservatory), Dědeček's recollections are an impressive feat of memory, made all the more credible by his admission that there are some passages he simply cannot remember. He also appears to confirm that the work was in three movements. In 'Janáček's "Lost" Kreutzer Sonata' (1987), Paul Wingfield argued that the 'few ideas' mentioned by Janáček formed the substance of the first two movements of the String Quartet No. 1* (VII/8), and also proposed that reworking the music of the Trio is what enabled Janáček to appear to complete the Quartet in the space of little more than a week, between 30 October and 7 November 1923. This is a plausible suggestion, but against this is another comment by Dědeček's to Jarmil Burghauser (quoted in Vogel 1981, p. 297), in which he said that 'little of the material is used in the quartet'. A further complication is the existence of a fragment of music for violin, cello and piano among the sketches for *Čarták on Soláň* (thus placing it at about 1910 or earlier). This clearly uses the same musical material as the third movement of the String Quartet No. 1 (a transcription of the sketch is printed in Wingfield 1987, p. 240). At the very least, this means that one of the ideas was reworked for the Quartet, and it certainly suggests that there may well have been others. Any more than that remains speculation. The strong likelihood is that Janáček destroyed the Piano Trio once he had refashioned some of its music into the Quartet, a work with which he was completely satisfied.

A 'reconstruction' of the Piano Trio by Michal Hájků (pseud. for Jarmil Burghauser) was released on CD in 1995 (Tacet 083), played by the Abegg Trio. It is in four movements and is essentially a transcription of the String Quartet No. 1. A different reconstruction based on the surviving materials was made by Paul Wingfield but this is unpublished. *BroJan, JAWO, VesJan, WinJan.*

Píša, Arnošt (b. Dřiteč, near Pardubice, 14 April 1865; d. Brno, 25 June 1950), Czech publisher. Píša had premises in Brno at Česká No. 28. The firm opened in March 1898 and Píša's first publications of Janáček's music were issued in 1899: the *Singing Teaching Manual* (V/5) and *Hukvaldy Folk Poetry in Songs* (V/4). In early 1905, Píša published Janáček's *Moravian Dances* (VIII/18), inserting small printed slips to explain the dance steps. Píša issued the first edition of *On the Overgrown Path**, Series I (VIII/17) in November 1911. The firm's other major Janáček publication was the *Complete Harmony Manual*, first issued in 1911–12, with a revised edition in 1920. *EDMB, FELJ, SimMor.*

Písek Town in South Bohemia, about 100 km (60 miles) south of Prague. Janáček visited the town with Dvořák in 1883, and one of the earliest performances of his *Valachian Dances* (VI/4) took place there on 16 January 1891, at a ball including other Moravian dances. In later life, Písek acquired a central significance for Janáček as the home from April 1919 onwards of Kamila Stösslová* and her husband David Stössel, at Premyslová Street, No. 228. In his letters to Kamila he described Písek as 'heaven', and he visited it to see Kamila every year from 1924 until 1928. The visit in August 1925, en route to the ISCM Festival in Venice, was particularly awkward as Janáček was travelling with Zdenka and they both spent the night at the Stössels. They sat for a group photograph the next day at the Písek studio of František Zeman. Even by the standards of the time, three of the subjects look extremely uncomfortable, and only Janáček appears pleased to be there. In general, Janáček went to Písek to escape from Zdenka and to be with his muse. Before Easter 1927, he was particularly pleased when Zdenka made a decision she would 'always regret': to pack her husband off to the Stössels in Písek while the house was being redecorated. Through Stösslová, he made other musical acquaintances in Písek, including the headmaster Alois Kodl, and Cyril Vymetal, conductor of the local amateur orchestra. The most significant musical outcome of Janáček's visits to Písek (aside, of course, from those works inspired by Kamila's presence there) came in June 1924, when he heard some fanfares at a band concert which he went to with Kamila. He wrote to her on 29 March 1926 while at work on 'a beautiful little *Sinfonietta* with fanfares! I remember those fanfares in Písek.' (See Military Music* and *Sinfonietta**.) *JYL1, JYL2, MLWJ, TyrInt.*

Po zarostlém chodníčku   See *On the Overgrown Path* (VIII/17)

Počátek románu   See *The Beginning of a Romance* (I/3)

Pochod Modráčků   See *March of the Bluebirds* (VII/9)

Pohádka   See *Fairy Tale* (VII/5)

Potulný silenec   See *The Wandering Madman* (IV/43)

Prague Czecho-Slavonic Ethnographic Exhibition [Národopisná výstava českoslovanská v Praze], 1895.   This exhibition ran from 15 May to 28 October 1895, on the Exhibition Grounds at Stromovka that had been built for the 1891 Jubilee Exhibition. The information at the foot of the colourful poster for the Exhibition gave an idea of its scope: 'Ethnography: people and countries, languages, songs and dances, customs and costumes, folk architecture and folk art, literature, theatre, music, industry, agriculture.' It was an ambitious programme and one that took several years of planning. Janáček's involvement was with the 'Moravian Days' at the Exhibition. These provided an opportunity to promote Moravian folk music to a large number of visitors (over the whole period of the Exhibition, an estimated two million people attended), and for Janáček it came at a time when his folksong collecting activity was at its height. Janáček's role was to organise the musicians who would travel to Prague for the 'Moravian Days' on 15–18 August. The plan was to present entire ensembles from particular regions of Moravia, but this was something of a logistical nightmare: many of the musicians were working people – farm labourers, factory workers and the like. They all needed time off, and this was complicated by the fact that the 'Moravian Days' coincided with the harvest. Janáček had to find ways for all these performers to be transported to Prague from some of the remotest parts of rural Moravia, and somehow they all got there. On 15 August, the large Moravian contingent processed through Prague, resplendent in their folk costumes, with Janáček at the head of the procession. The complete programme of events for the 'Moravian Days' has been summarised by John Tyrrell:

> Each day in the afternoon, 15–18 August, there were demonstrations of the songs, dances and ceremonies that had been assembled and practised for the exhibition. On the opening day and the final day, a cross-section of all the groups performed in the exhibition amphitheatre. On 16 August there was a procession of Slovácko carnivalists through the exhibition site. The next day, 17 August, was devoted to Haná, with the 'Haná rights' group travelling on a cart through the exhibition and at 5 p.m. the other Haná groups performing in the exhibition amphitheatre; a Valachian evening was held in the Valachian village which had been assembled on the exhibition site.

During the course of the exhibition and its preparations, Janáček met two artists who were to become leading members of the KPU: the architect Dušan Jurkovič* and the artist Joža Uprka. *JYL1, VysJan.*

Prague German Theatre [Neues deutsches Theater, Deutsches Landestheater], German opera house in Prague. On 23 October 1926, the Prague German Theatre staged *Jenůfa**. The conductor was Alexander Zemlinsky*, then in his final season as music director, having taken up the post in 1911. Zemlinsky's repertoire in 1926–7 included recent novelties such as Křenek's *Jonny spielt auf* and Hindemith's *Cardillac*, as well as *Jenůfa*. Janáček did not attend the opening night. The *Prager Tagblatt* (31 October 1926) announced a second performance on 'Friday' (i.e. 5 November), noting that its 'premiere showed every sign of great success'. Janáček and his wife were present at the 5 November performance. The opera continued in repertoire until March 1927. William [Hans Wilhelm] Steinberg was hired by Zemlinsky in 1925 and promoted to music director at the start of the 1927–8 season. He was in charge of the new production of *Káťa Kabanová** that opened on 21 January 1928, and for which Janáček composed two new interludes (see Steinberg, Hans Wilhelm*). On 24 January, the *Prager Tagblatt* noted that the performance had been 'greeted with enthusiastic applause', and on 15 February, announcing a performance two days later, the *Tagblatt* hailed 'Janáček's extraordinarily successful opera'. On 27 January 1935, Steinberg's successor, George Szell, conducted a new production of *Jenůfa* at the German Theatre and this was broadcast (see listings in *Radio Wien*, 25 January 1935, p. 23). *VrbStá.*

Prague National Theatre [Národní divadlo]. Set on the banks of the Vltava, across the river from Prague Castle, the building was designed by Josef Zítek. It opened on 1 June 1881 with the world premiere of Smetana's *Libuše*. After further performances of *Libuše* and Meyerbeer's *Les Huguenots*, the theatre was closed for interior work to be completed. While this was being undertaken, fire broke out and destroyed much of the theatre. Zítek's pupil Josef Schulz oversaw the renovation, and the restored National Theatre opened on 18 November 1883, once again with *Libuše* and with newly installed electric lighting to replace the original gas lighting.

Given the battle it took for *Jenůfa** to reach the Prague stage in 1916 (see Kovařovic, Karel*), it is surprising that the ballet *Rákoš Rákoczy** had its world premiere at the Prague NT in 1891, when Janáček's name was barely known outside Brno. However, for the next twenty-five years, the Prague NT ignored his music. From the time Karel Kovařovic rejected *Jenůfa* in April 1903 until the Prague premiere in 1916, this was a source of enormous frustration to Janáček, not least because the Prague company was far better equipped to cope with the demands of the opera (when *Jenůfa* was given in Brno between 1904 and 1916, it was played by a small orchestra in cramped conditions, with instruments missing). With the appointment of Otakar Ostrčil as Kovařovic's successor in 1920, Janáček found a conductor eager to perform his later operas. Despite some personal differences, Ostrčil was a loyal advocate of Janáček from the 1920 world premiere of *The Excursions of Mr Brouček** onwards. The Prague premiere of *The Makropulos Affair** on 1 March 1928 was one of the greatest triumphs of Janáček's career. After Janáček's death, new Prague productions included *The Cunning Little Vixen*, *Káťa Kabanová* and *Jenůfa* conducted by Václav Talich, all in reorchestrated versions (see Talich, Václav*). In the 1950s, three operas were conducted by Jaroslav Vogel*, and between 1959 and 2002, Bohumil Gregor* conducted a distinguished series of performances. In 2003 *The Excursions of Mr Brouček* was conducted by Charles Mackerras* in the new edition by Jiří Zahrádka that restored Janáček's original orchestration. The following productions of Janáček operas were given at the Prague NT during his lifetime. Abbreviations: c.: conductor; d. director; des.: designer.

26 May 1916: *Jenůfa* (Prague prem.), c. Karel Kovařovic, d. Robert Polák

23 April 1920: *The Excursions of Mr Brouček* (world prem.), c. Otakar Ostrčil, d. Gustav Schmoranz, des. Karel Štapfer

30 November 1922: *Káťa Kabanová* (Prague prem.), c. Otakar Ostrčil, d. Robert Polák, des. Josef Matěj Gottlieb

18 May 1925: *The Cunning Little Vixen* (Prague prem.), c. Otakar Ostrčil, d. Ferdinand Pujman, des. Josef Čapek

12 January 1926: *Jenůfa*, c. Otakar Ostrčil, d. Josef Munclinger, des. Vladimír Hrska

1 March 1928: *The Makropulos Affair* (Prague prem.), c. Otakar Ostrčil, d. Josef Munclinger, des. Josef Čapek

JAWO, KonČte, NDPrOA, PřiLed.

Prague Organ School   In January 1874, Pavel Křížkovský* wrote a testimonial for Janáček, who was starting to think about applying for further musical studies. It provides a useful summary of Janáček's strengths as he approached his twentieth birthday: 'In the light of his unusual musical gifts, especially for playing the organ, should Mr Janáček be given the opportunity of getting an all-round knowledge of music and devoting himself to this art for a longer period under excellent teachers, a splendid result could be expected since his truly exceptional talent justifies such a hope.'

While the Prague Organ School was funded by the church and existed to train church musicians, it also taught composition, something that could not be studied at the Prague Conservatory at the time. As John Tyrrell put it: 'In 1874, the Organ School was by far the best place in Prague for a thorough theoretical and compositional training.' This is where Janáček arrived to study in early October 1874. He was virtually penniless but he was supported by a scholarship from the Moravian Regional School Board. When he arrived in Prague, Janáček was befriended by Ferdinand Lehner*, who gave him regular meals and arranged for a piano to be put in Janáček's lodgings. Lack of money meant that Janáček was unable to experience the cultural riches of Prague, though he did go to the concert in April 1875 that included the world premiere of Smetana's *Vltava*, where he saw the composer (see Smetana, Bedřich*).

At the Organ School, Janáček took courses in harmony, counterpoint, fugue, chorales, figured bass and improvisation. His most important teacher was František Skuherský*, the director of the Organ School, who taught composition and whose treatise on musical form had been published in 1873, the year before Janáček's arrival. During his academic year in Prague, Janáček not only filled thirteen manuscript books with prescribed exercises (VIII/1), but he was also an industrious composer. The pieces, composed between December 1874 and July 1875, were written by Janáček, in extremely neat handwriting, almost all of them carefully dated. Six of the compositions were Latin motets (II/1–6) and there were three works for organ: *Prelude* (VIII/2), *Varyto* (VIII/3) and the most substantial of them, the *Chorale Fantasia* (VIII/4). Covering nineteen pages of Janáček's Prague notebook (published in facsimile as *Sborník skladeb z pražských studií 1874–1875* in 2001), this work is in eight sections (later cut to six) and was performed by Janáček on 23 July 1875 as part of his final examinations at the Organ School. Janáček published a review (XV/2) in Lehner's journal *Cecilie* on 5 March 1875 which was critical of Skuherský's performance of Gregorian chant at the Piarist Church in Prague. While Janáček's plain speaking was an admirable quality in many ways, it was unusually bold of him to attack his teacher's approach to singing plainchant. He was briefly suspended from the Organ School, but Skuherský was not a man to hold grudges, and he readmitted Janáček after Easter.

Though Janáček had written some choruses for the Svatopluk Society the year before coming to Prague, the crucial importance of his time in the city was the development of his composing technique, ending with the *Chorale Fantasia* that was his most ambitious work to date. He graduated as the top student in the year. Once back in Brno, he was equipped to take the state exams that would allow him to teach music in schools. These he took and passed in October 1875, with a jury that included Skuherský. In June–July 1877, Janáček was back at the Organ School for a few weeks, and Helfert surmised that this was to study musical form with Skuherský privately. Janáček's Prague studies laid the groundwork for his future composing activity with a thoroughness – and a degree of personal success – that was not to be repeated when he studied in Leipzig and Vienna in 1879–80. Much of the credit must go to Skuherský, whose pupils not only included Janáček but also Josef Bohuslav Foerster. *HelJan, JAWO, JYL1, StrSbo.*

Prague: Society for Modern Music (SMH) [Spolek pro moderní hudbu].   The SMH was founded in Prague on 7 October 1920 on the initiative of Vítězslav Novák*, Josef Suk* and Otakar Ostrčil*. The first committee included Otakar Ostrčil (chairman), Václav Štěpán* (vice-chairman), Ota Zítek* (managing director) and Ladislav Vycpálek (archivist); Karel Hoffmann, Vincenc Maixner*, Václav Talich* and Boleslav Vomáčka also signed the report on the establishment of the society in *Hudební revue*. Emil Axman* was secretary from

1920 until 1927. The aim of the Society was to give public performances of contemporary piano, chamber and vocal works by Czech composers and leading composers from abroad. Concerts were held in the Mozarteum and later at the Prague Conservatory and the Umělecká beseda. The adventurous programmes may have been one reason for the precarious financial status of the SMH. It ceased to put on concerts in 1932 and was officially wound up in 1939. Janáček's music featured regularly on its programmes. It put on a performance of *The Diary of One Who Disappeared** at the Mozarteum on 10 December 1921. On 16 December 1922, the SMH gave the Prague premieres of the Sonata for Violin and Piano* and *In the Mists** (played by Václav Štěpán). A year later, on 3 November 1923, *On the Overgrown Path** (Series I) was given for the first time in Prague, played by Jan Heřman*. At the SMH concert on 17 October 1924 to celebrate Janáček's seventieth birthday year, the programme included the world premiere of the String Quartet No. 1* played by the Czech Quartet, along with the Violin Sonata, *Fairy Tale** and *Folk Nocturnes**. On 16 December 1924, Janáček was elected an Honorary Member of the SMH and was informed about this in a letter jointly signed by Emil Axman, Otakar Ostrčil and Václav Štěpán. *ČHS, JAWO.*

Prečan, Leopold (b. Velký Týnec, 7 May 1866; d. Svatý Kopeček, Olomouc, 2 March 1947), Czech clergyman.   Ordained in 1891, Prečan taught theology from 1902 at the University of Olomouc, and in 1923 he was appointed Archbishop of Olomouc. According to Janáček's pupil Father Josef Martínek, Prečan and Monsignor Jan Šrámek (later the Prime Minister of the Czech Government in exile) met Janáček in Hukvaldy in about 1921. Janáček told Martínek that they discussed the decline of church music and Prečan suggested that Janáček should write something himself. Five years later, Prečan and Janáček met again when the Archbishop attended a rain-soaked ceremony on 11 July 1926 to unveil the plaque on Janáček's birthplace. A few weeks later, Janáček was at work on the *Glagolitic Mass**. He wrote to Archbishop Prečan on 26 November 1927, inviting him to the premiere on 5 December: 'The *Glagolitic Mass* is deeply connected with your person. The impetus for the work came from those rainy Hukvaldy celebrations of mine which you took the trouble to participate in ... it would be a great honour for me to welcome your Lordship in Brno on this occasion.' Prečan replied on 28 November regretting that he couldn't attend. On 16 March 1928, while the vocal score was in proof, Janáček wrote to UE adding a dedication: 'To Dr Leopold Prečan, Archbishop of Olomouc.' This was published on 6 April 1928, and on 16 April, Prečan wrote to Janáček: 'Esteemed master! Please receive my most sincere thanks for the gracious dedication of the *Glagolitic Mass*. As soon as I get to see you in Hukvaldy I will not forget to thank you in person.' *JYL2, JAWO, KLJ.*

Preissová, Gabriela, née Sekerová (b. Kutná Hora, 23 March 1862; d. Prague, 27 March 1946), Czech writer.   Though born in Bohemia, Preissová moved with her husband to Hodonín in the Slovácko region of Moravia in 1880 and soon became a perceptive observer of the conventions and traditions of Moravian village life. She later wrote, 'I began to write about the things which surrounded me, my *Tales from Slovácko*. One of the first of these was called *The Beginning of a Romance**. The young Leoš Janáček liked this novella so much that he wrote a one-act opera based on it.' Preissová always remembered this work with affection, and as late as 1916 she asked Janáček to submit his 'finely honed comic opera *The Beginning of a Romance*' to the Prague NT. On 9 November 1890, Preissová's play *Her Stepdaughter* (*Její pastorkyňa*) opened at the Prague NT. Though enthusiastically received by the public, critics condemned it as gratuitous realism and the National Theatre closed the play after five performances. The furore shocked Preissová and she defended herself in a letter to the editor of *Pražské noviny*, explaining that her play was based on 'two real-life incidents, though much idealised! In the first, a lad wounded a girl in the face ... because he loved her himself. In the second, a woman helped her stepdaughter get rid of a love-child (the girl threw the baby into the sewer), but I did not want two murderesses. Jenůfa falls through love, but she has enough goodwill and strength to live a better life.' A production opened in Brno on 10 January 1891, and it is likely that Janáček saw the play then. Initially, Preissová was reluctant to give Janáček permission to set *Her Stepdaughter*, claiming it was 'not suitable for musical setting', but at the Brno premiere of *Jenůfa** (always known in Czech lands as *Její pastorkyňa*), any doubts she might have had were swept aside. Janáček considered setting Preissová's play *The Farm Mistress* in 1904, but made no progress with it. *JODA, JYL1, ZavPre.*

Přibáňová, Svatava, née Nováková (b. Neplachovice, near Opava, 7 March 1934; d. Brno, 27 September 2014), Czech musicologist. After graduating from Masaryk University, Přibáňová spent her entire career working at the Department of Music History of the Moravian Museum as a curator of the Janáček Archive. One of the leading Janáček scholars of her generation, she published several books, including *Leoš Janáček* (1984), *Hádanka života*, the complete edition of the correspondence with Kamila Stösslová (1990), *Svět Janáčkových oper*, including a chronology of Janáček opera performances (1998), *Káťa Kabanová na brněnském jevišti* (2003), *Thema con variazioni*, the correspondence with Zdenka and Olga Janáčková (2007), and *Leoš Janáček ve fotografích* (2008, with Jiří Zahrádka). Přibáňová wrote the introductions to three volumes of SKV as well as co-editing the theoretical works (see Editions, Critical and Scholarly*). *ČHS.*

Příhody lišky Bystroušky See *The Cunning Little Vixen* (I/9)

Procházka, František Serafínský (b. Náměšť na Hané, near Olomouc, 15 January 1861; d. Prague, 28 January 1939), Czech poet. Josef Peška* first recommended Procházka to Janáček in a letter of 19 December 1915: 'Turn to F. S. Procházka, editor of *Zvon*. A Moravian, a bright spirit and a brilliant versifier.' Janáček wrote to Procházka on 31 December 1915, enclosing the existing libretto of *The Excursion of Mr Brouček to the Moon* and asking the poet if he would be willing 'to take on the completion of the whole work'. Procházka replied a week later, on 6 January, having read the libretto carefully, making some suggestions about the ending. Before Procházka could give Janáček any of the *Brouček* text, the composer wrote to him (5 February 1916) with a quite different request, asking to set some of Procházka's *Hradčany Songs* to music. Procházka's only condition was that the songs be kept together. Janáček composed the *Hradčany Songs** (IV/40) quickly, and a few days later, by 12 February 1916, he had set another poem in the same collection, *Kašpar Rucký** (IV/41). Procházka sent his revision for the *Brouček* libretto on 3 April, admitting that it had been a laborious task to 'patch up and knit together' the work of earlier librettists, but Janáček was happy with the result, particularly the love duet for Mazal and Málinka. All this was going on as final preparations were being made for the Prague premiere of *Jenůfa* on 26 May 1916, and Procházka was quick to congratulate Janáček on 'the success of Moravia on the Prague stage'. In March 1917, Janáček asked Procházka to write the libretto for *The Excursion of Mr Brouček to the Fifteenth Century*. Procházka started work on 30 April 1917, and sent the last instalment on 5 November, with revisions a month later, accepting Janáček's cuts with good grace (see *The Excursions of Mr Brouček**). Janáček made contact again in December 1925, asking to set Procházka's poem 'Vlajka' ('The Flag') from the *New Hradčany Songs* as a chorus for male voices with two sopranos, and requesting some more lines. Ever helpful, Procházka sent the new lines by return of post and Janáček completed *Our Flag** (IV/44) on 29 March 1926. *JAiii, JAWO, JYL2.*

Procházková, Jarmila (b. Třebíč, 27 February 1961), Czech musicologist. Procházková worked at the Janáček Archive in Brno from 1987, and became its director in 1996. In 2004 she joined the staff of the Ethnographic Institute of the Czech Academy of Sciences in Brno, and from 2005 worked in Prague at the Institute's Department of Music History, serving as its head from 2014 to 2016. Procházková's extensive work on Janáček has included biographical and ethnographical studies. She has edited volumes of SKV and SKVEJ, and contributed introductions to others (see Editions, Critical and Scholarly*). Procházková edited the *Album for Kamila Stösslová** (1994). Her other books include studies of Janáček's associations with Hukvaldy (with Bohumír Volný, 1995) and with Luhačovice (2009). Procházková's innovative research on all aspects of Janáček and folk music has been of particular significance, including the encyclopedic *Janáčkovy záznamy* (2006). She has published and documented the phonograph* recordings made by Janáček and his fellow collectors from 1909 to 1912 in *Vzaty do fonografu* (2012). *ČHS, ProLuh, ProPam, ProVol, ProVza, ProZaz.*

Puccini, Giacomo (b. Lucca, 22 December 1858; d. Brussels, Belgium, 29 November 1924), Italian composer. John Tyrrell has suggested that 'a chance visit to a performance of *Madama Butterfly* seems to have set *Káťa Kabanová** in motion'. There is plenty of evidence to support this, notably a letter from Janáček to Kamila Stösslová written on 5 December 1919: 'I have just come from the theatre. They gave *Batrflay* [*Butterfly*], one of the most beautiful and saddest of operas. I had you constantly before my eyes. Butterfly is also small with black hair. You could never be as unhappy as her. ... I'm so unsettled by this opera. When it was new I saw it in Prague and many places still move me deeply.' Jaroslav Vogel claimed that 'the careful study [Janáček] made of Puccini was mainly dictated by his wish to master the weapons of the opposite camp.' This is debatable: like Janáček's later operas, several of Puccini's are very compact (notably *La Bohème* and *Tosca*), most of them have central characters who are women (Mimì, Tosca, Butterfly, Minnie, Turandot and Liù), and Puccini's vocal writing in duets often has climactic (or tender) moments with the voices in octaves. These traits don't necessarily suggest 'the opposite camp' in Janáček, but a similar one, with a preference for concise, fast-moving drama, an enhanced and colourful role for the orchestra, and a female character at the heart of the work. While there is little direct musical influence, the end of *The Excursion of Mr Brouček to the Moon* has echoes of *La Bohème* (an opera Janáček is not known to have seen in the theatre), and in *Káťa* the music for Káťa and Boris during their final meeting in Act III includes another phrase in octaves (four bars before Fig. 28) that seems to recall, albeit distantly, the Act I love duet in *Butterfly*. *JYL2, TyrInt, VogJan.*

Pupils   See individual entries on: Bakala, Břetislav; Bím, Hynek; Chlubna, Osvald; Firkušný, Rudolf; Haas, Pavel; Hrazdira, Cyril Metoděj; Kunc, Jan; Kvapil, Jaroslav; and Tauský, Vilém

'Putování dušičky'   See Violin Concerto 'The Pilgrimage of a Little Soul' (IX/10)

Radio broadcasts during Janáček's lifetime   Janáček lived into the age of broadcasting, though he did not own a radio himself. His music was broadcast on Prague and Brno Radio from soon after the establishment of Czech Radio. Studios opened in Prague in May 1923 and Brno in September 1924. Two major world premieres were relayed: the *Sinfonietta** conducted by Václav Talich* with the Czech Philharmonic on 26 June 1926, broadcast by Prague Radio, and the *Glagolitic Mass** conducted by Jaroslav Kvapil* on 5 December 1927, broadcast by Brno Radio. The British premiere of the *Sinfonietta*, conducted by Henry Wood* at the Queen's Hall, was broadcast by the BBC (2LO) on 10 February 1928, the first time any music by Janáček had been broadcast in Britain. The listings in *Radio Wien* for 19 December 1927 and 15 January 1928 include the *Sinfonietta* in broadcasts from Munich Radio with no performers specified. These are confirmed by a notice in *Pult und Taktstock* (January/February 1928, p. 16): 'In Munich ... the *Sinfonietta* by Janáček was repeated a few weeks after its first broadcast at the request of the listeners who wanted to hear it a second time.' It is likely that the unnamed conductor was Franz Adam (1885–1954), Kapellmeister of the orchestra of Munich Radio (Deutsche Stunde) from 1924 to 1928. Adam was a fanatical Nazi who in 1931 became conductor of the National Socialist Reich Symphony Orchestra.

The *Lachian Dances** were broadcast at least twice during Janáček's lifetime. On 9 November 1926, *Lidové noviny* listed a performance on Brno Radio the next day (10 November) by the regimental band of the 43rd Infantry Regiment conducted by František Zita (1880–1946), with all six individual dances named in the listing. On 13 January 1927, František Neumann* conducted the *Lachian Dances* for Brno Radio, a performance reported on by Janáček's friends Otto Kretschmer and his wife Marie Luisa: 'Thanks to your letting us know about it, we were able to listen to your delightful *Valachian* [i.e. *Lachian*] *Dances* (VI/17) and we are very grateful for the experience.' Another performance (by unidentified artists) is listed in *Radio Wien* on 13 November 1927, from Brno Radio.

Two of Janáček's operas were broadcast during his lifetime. The Prague premiere of *The Cunning Little Vixen** (conducted by Otakar Ostrčil*) was broadcast on 18 May 1925, the first time an opera by Janáček was transmitted on the radio. *Jenůfa** was relayed by Brno Radio from the Brno NT on 30 August 1927. A year earlier, on 11 May 1926, Leipzig Radio had broadcast *Jenůfa* from the Weimar National Theatre (a production that had opened on 2 May), and on 27 January 1927, Alfred Kalmus at UE informed Janáček that a production in Elberfeld would also receive a radio broadcast 'in the near future'.

Radio listings in the *Wiener Morgenzeitung* and *Radio Wien* (both 3 January 1927) announced a live broadcast on Brno Radio of *The Makropulos Affair** from the Brno NT at 19.15 on 7 January 1927, but this never took place. The world premiere had been given on 18 December 1926, with a second performance on 30 December and a third on 8 January, the day after the listed broadcast. The radio listings in *Lidové noviny* indicate that the opera relay on the evening of 7 January was changed to *Carmen* from the National Theatre in Prague. In the letter from the Kretschmers quoted above (20 January 1927), Janáček's friends wrote that they had been looking forward to the broadcast and were disappointed, adding 'Let's hope it does happen one day.'

The Diary of One Who Disappeared* was broadcast by Brno Radio on 4 December 1926 with Stanislav Tauber* (tenor) and Břetislav Bakala* (piano), and on other occasions. On 20 February 1925, Janáček wrote to Emil Hertzka at UE asking about mechanical performing rights: 'Today I heard that my *Diary of One Who Disappeared*, *Silesian Songs* and *Hukvaldy Folk Poetry in Songs* have been broadcast on the radio from Prague. Does this constitute mechanical-musical exploitation? I ask you to explain this right to me.' Another performance of the *Diary* took place on 4 April 1927 as part of a concert of Moravian music (*Radio Wien* lists the *Diary* as the main work).

On 28 December 1926, Ludvík Kundera* broadcast *1. X. 1905* on Brno Radio. Two performances of the String Quartet No. 1* were given on Vienna Radio (RAVAG): on 8 November 1926, played by the Gottesmann Quartet, and on 15 April 1928 by the Moravian Quartet* (a month before the same ensemble gave Janáček a private preview of his String Quartet No. 2). The *Concertino** was broadcast by Ilona Štěpánová-Kurzová*, who wrote to Janáček on 14 November 1926 that 'in Frankfurt, the *Concertino* was played on the radio'. On 15 April 1927, the Návrat family in Hukvaldy wrote with Easter greetings for Janáček and his wife, adding that 'the day before yesterday we heard your Violin Sonata on the radio'. This is confirmed by a listing in *Radio Wien* for a broadcast on 13 April 1927 (Brno Radio) of a concert from the Brno Conservatory including Janáček's Violin Sonata along with works by Vomáčka and Petrželka (the performers are not identified). Broadcasts of choruses included *The Wreath* (IV/31) and *The Eiderdown* (IV/38) on 30 December 1926 (Prague Radio). *The Seventy Thousand** (IV/36) and *Our Flag** (IV/44) were included in a concert by the PSMU on 5 March 1927 (Brno Radio). On 25 April 1927, the concert given by the KMS including the world premiere of *Nursery Rhymes** (V/17) was broadcast by Brno Radio (Janáček was in Prague and heard the concert on the radio at the home of his friends the Kretschmers). On 29 April, he wrote to Emil Hertzka at UE describing the performance of *Nursery Rhymes* as 'an extraordinary success'.

Josef Charvát (1884–1945) had been a pupil of Janáček's at the Brno Organ School. In 1926 he was working for Radiojournal Prague (Prague Radio). He wrote to Janáček on 15 November 1926, asking if he would be willing to give a broadcast talk during an evening of folk music on 30 November. Charvát requested 'a lecture of about quarter of an hour on folk music'. Janáček evidently declined but, undaunted, Charvát wrote again three days later asking if he might talk instead about the *Lachian Dances**. In the end, Janáček never gave any radio talks. *Anno, JYL2, LN, PatRoz.*

Rákoš Rákoczy, scene from Moravian Slovakia with original dances and songs in one act (I/2). Janáček's only ballet was an anthology of his orchestral arrangements of folk dances and folksongs, several of them previously performed as

Valachian Dances, with choreography by Augustin Berger and a libretto by Jan Herben. The work was composed (or compiled) between January and June 1891. Though the ballet has a plot (see below), Janáček did not know who would be writing the libretto while he was working on the score, but on 21 May 1891, he told the choreographer Augustin Berger that Jan Herben's text – based on the poem *The Girl from the Tatras* by Vítězslav Hálek and written without knowledge of the music – would be ready within two days. As Vogel points out, Janáček and Herben had known each other for years and presumably came to some sort of agreement about what the subject of the ballet would be. When Janáček announced completion of the ballet in *Moravská orlice* (3 June 1891), he gave it the title *The Lord of Nové Zámky* and submitted the work to the Prague NT with this title. It was formally approved on 7 June 1891 by the theatre's dramaturg, Ladislav Stroupežnický. The theatre was usually closed during the summer, but 1891 was the year of the Prague Jubilee Exhibition, a world fair which brought many visitors into the capital. The theatre therefore decided to put on a summer season. (At least two of the buildings constructed for this Exhibition survive: the Petřín Tower – a smaller replica of the Eiffel Tower built for the 1889 Paris Exposition – and the Hanavský Pavilion.)

Rákoš Rákoczy opened at the Prague NT on 24 July 1891, conducted by Mořic Anger, on a double bill with Stroupežnický's play *The Mintmaster's Wife*. There were eight performances in all and the other work on the bill changed (on 27 July it was performed with Mascagni's *Cavalleria rusticana*). In the Brno press it was hailed as a 'splendid success', and even Prague critics were fairly positive, though Janáček's orchestration came in for some criticism. Even so, Janáček was pleased to see one of his works staged for the first time and heartened by a good run of well-received performances.

The score is essentially a patchwork of folk dances, many of them originally intended for orchestral suites, and *Rákoš* includes several tunes that are familiar from Janáček's definitive folk dance suite, the *Lachian Dances** (VI/17). The vocal and choral numbers include plenty of charming music, and *Rákoš Rákoczy* as a whole is a delightful kind of stylised folk pageant. No score has ever been available on sale. A full score was prepared by Dilia, Prague, in 1957 and a vocal score (arranged by Ladislav Matějka) in 1978, both for hire only. *JAWO, JYL1, VogJan.*

SYNOPSIS
The libretto exists primarily to provide a dramatic structure for the dances and songs. Set in about 1815, the outline of the plot is as follows: Rákoš, a swash-buckling impostor, arrives at a village in Moravian Slovakia and pretends to be the Count Rákoczy of Nové Zamký. He wants to marry Katuška, not only the daughter of a wealthy landowner but also the prettiest girl in the village. As Katuška is being led to the altar, Jan, her long-lost sweetheart, arrives. Something of a local hero, he was thought to have lost his life in 1813 at the Battle of Leipzig. Everything turns out happily in the end: Katuška marries Jan, while the disgraced Rákoš beats a hasty retreat.

Rebikov, Vladimir Ivanovich (b. Krasnoyarsk, Siberia, 31 May [OS 19 May] 1866; d. Yalta, Crimea, 1 October 1920), Russian composer. Rebikov is remembered as the composer of charming short piano pieces, but he made a much more significant contribution to opera. Considered one of the fathers of Russian modernism, his use of whole-tone harmony and expressionistic style can be found at its most adventurous in the series of 'musico-psychological dramas' composed between 1894 and 1916. It is likely that Janáček first encountered Rebikov's music through Jan Kunc, who wrote to Janáček in 1906:

> I want to write another article about Rebikov. He is a very interesting composer, not so much in *The Christmas Tree* [1900] ... but in the psychological drama *Thea* [1904]. ... I have never seen so many harmonic novelties. Elevenths and thirteenths are treated as if they were simple consonant chords, and he is unafraid to use rows of parallel semitones. All this seems to me to have grown out of necessity from his harmonic thinking, which is very complex but very logical. He is extremely original.

It's easy to see how music as individual as this might appeal to Janáček (by an odd coincidence, the published score of *Thea* has a dedication to Kovařovic). But it was another of Rebikov's 'musico-psychological dramas' that most aroused Janáček's interest: *Alpha and Omega*, completed in 1911. In an unpublished article from 1915, Janáček described this 30-minute work as 'an opera about the beginning and the end of the world', and he discussed it in detail in courses at the Brno Organ School. In one of his transcribed lectures, he listed it with Smetana's *The Bartered Bride* and Wagner's *Tristan und Isolde* as an example of the current state of opera. His main interest in it was Rebikov's use of extreme (or unexpected) dissonance for expressive purposes. In terms of Janáček's own music, it is intriguing to speculate on whether the increasing astringency of his harmonies might owe something to Rebikov. *KLJ, LJLD2.*

Recordings before 1960 There was a rapid expansion in recordings of Janáček's music from the 1960s onwards, dominated by conductors like Karel Ančerl, Bohumil Gregor, František Jílek, Rafael Kubelík, Václav Neumann and Charles Mackerras. But the work of their pioneering predecessors and (in some cases) their own earliest recordings are of interest in terms of performance style, and the associations they have with the composer or those close to him.

1. Recordings of works by musicians who performed them in Janáček's presence
(a) *Jenůfa* (i): On 10 October 1924, the Prayer from Act II of *Jenůfa* was recorded by Zinaiada Jurjevskaja* for Parlophon, with the Berlin State Opera Orchestra conducted by Max Saal. This was made a few months after Jurjevskaja had sung Jenůfa in the Berlin production, conducted by Erich Kleiber, which was greatly admired by Janáček. It is the earliest recording of any music by Janáček (CD reissue: Preiser 89196).
(b) *Jenůfa* (ii): Gabriela Horvátová*, the Kostelnička in the first Prague production in 1916, recorded 'Co chvíla' (the Kostelnička's aria from Act II) in 1935, with piano accompaniment. Horvátová's voice is still in good shape and the performance is notable for its dramatic engagement. The unnamed pianist is František Maxián. It was published by Radiojournal (CD reissue: Aulos CDGV 0152, 'The Eternal Orpheus of Varaždin').
(c) *Káťa Kabanová*: Antonín Pelc [Pelz], who sang Boris in the 1924 Brno production of *Káťa*, was Kudrjáš in the 1946 Brno Radio broadcast of the opera conducted by Břetislav Bakala*. A short extract from Act II (Fig. 3 to four bars before Fig. 12) is included on CD 1 of Václav Věžník: *Zpívali v Brně II* (track 45). Though Janáček never heard Bakala conduct the work, his close connection

with the opera (as arranger of the vocal score and as rehearsal pianist for the premiere) gives Bakala's performances particular interest. Bakala recorded the Prelude for Ultraphon in 1948, and his complete Brno Radio *Káťa* from 1953 has been rebroadcast (both issued by CRQ Editions).

(d) *The Cunning Little Vixen*: Antonín Pelc was the Schoolmaster in the 1924 world premiere in Brno. For Bakala's 1953 Brno Radio broadcast, he sang the Innkeeper. Bakala arranged the vocal score at Janáček's request, and assisted with preparations for the Brno premiere. This broadcast was published in 1983 by Panton (CD reissue by CRQ Editions).

(e) *The Diary of One Who Disappeared*: Bakala's broadcast of the *Diary* on 11 August 1953 with Josef Válka and Soňa Červená is the only recording of a major work by Janáček made by one of the musicians who had given its world premiere in the composer's presence. It has been published by CRQ Editions.

(f) *Taras Bulba*: In November and December 1924, Václav Talich* conducted two performances of *Taras Bulba* attended by Janáček. He recorded the work for Supraphon in 1954 (CD: Supraphon SU 3823-2).

(g) *Lachian Dances*: In February 1925, Janáček attended a rehearsal of a ballet version of the *Lachian Dances* at the Brno Opera conducted by Bakala, who had very limited conducting experience at the time (see Bakala, Břetislav*). Bakala recorded the *Lachian Dances* on 10 November 1952 with the Brno Radio SO for Supraphon (download: VT 7196-2).

(h) *Sinfonietta*: Otto Klemperer* first conducted the *Sinfonietta* in Wiesbaden on 9 December 1926, and gave the US premiere in New York on 4 March 1927. Janáček described the performance he conducted in Berlin on 29 September 1927 as 'unrivalled by anyone anywhere'. Two Klemperer broadcasts have been published: with the Concertgebouw Orchestra of Amsterdam (11 January 1951, CD: Archiphon ARC 101) and with the Cologne Radio SO (27 February 1956, CD: EMI 575465–2).

(i) String Quartet No. 1: Richard Zika led the Czechoslovak Quartet in the performance of the First String Quartet at the 1925 ISCM Festival in Venice attended by Janáček. He subsequently led the Ondříček Quartet in the first recording of the work, made in November 1941 (Ultraphon H 15140–2).

(j) *Capriccio*: Otakar Hollmann* gave the premiere in Prague on 2 March 1928 in a concert attended by Janáček, who was also present at rehearsals. In May 1956, Hollmann recorded the *Capriccio* with an ensemble conducted by Jarmil Burghauser (Supraphon DV 5478).

(k) Piano works: Rudolf Firkušný* studied with Janáček from 1917 to 1924, then visited him frequently until the composer's death. He often played the piano for Janáček and discussed the solo piano works with him. Firkušný's earliest Janáček recording was the *Concertino* in 1947 (Concert Hall B10), with a group of American instrumentalists. This limited edition was the first Janáček recording to be made in the United States, and pre-dated Ludvík Kundera's first Czech recording by a year. Firkušný made his first recordings of Janáček's solo piano works for Columbia in the early 1950s. Subsequently he recorded the solo works and the *Concertino* and *Capriccio* for Deutsche Grammophon and RCA.

2. Pioneering recordings of Janáček from the 1920s to the 1950s
Apart from Jurjevskaja's recording of Jenůfa's Prayer from 1924, only one other recording was made during Janáček's lifetime: a live performance from 1927 of

the chorus *The Eiderdown* (IV/38) by the male-voice choir Typografia conducted by Vojtěch Borivoj Aim (1886–1972) issued by the German company Homocord (T 5046). It was possibly recorded when the choir visited Frankfurt in August 1927.

Erich Kleiber* recorded the first of the *Lachian Dances* on 13 September 1930 with the Berlin Philharmonic for Ultraphon. Along with Klemperer, Kleiber was one of the first major international conductors to take up Janáček's music, and he led the triumphant Berlin production of *Jenůfa* in 1924. Kleiber conducts with verve but the playing is distinctly rough (CD reissue: Preiser 90311). A year earlier, in October 1929, Otakar Pařík had recorded Nos. 2 and 6 of the *Lachian Dances* with the Radiojournal orchestra, the first records of Janáček's orchestral music (Pathé X 86011). The first recording of all six *Lachian Dances* was made for Esta in 1944, with the Czech Radio SO conducted by Karel Boleslav Jirák; the sixth side of this set included a performance of the *Spring Song* (V/3) by Růžena Hořáková with Josef Páleníček (Esta H 5153–5).

The first of Janáček's chamber works to be recorded was *Youth* in May 1938, played by the Prague Wind Quintet and released by Esta (E 7125–6). The performers were Rudolf Hertl (flute), Václav Smetáček (oboe), Vladimír Říha (clarinet), Otakar Procházka (horn) and Karel Bidlo (bassoon), with Václav Kotas (bass clarinet). This was a distinguished ensemble: Smetáček went on to a major conducting career, and Říha was principal clarinet of the Czech Philharmonic in 1931 (his later records included the Mozart Concerto with Talich). Esta advertised these discs at a special subscription price for orders received by 30 June 1938, announcing the recording as commemorating the tenth anniversary of Janáček's death and the twentieth anniversary of the Czechoslovak Republic.

The String Quartet No. 1 was recorded in 1941 by the Ondříček Quartet (see above). The first recording of the String Quartet No. 2 was made on 5 April 1943 by the Černý Quartet (the name under which the Prague Quartet operated during the war years), published by Ultraphon (G 12968–70). Ladislav Černý was the quartet's violist, and the other players were Alexander Plocek (violin I), Herbert Berger (violin II) and Josef Šimandl (cello). In a pamphlet advertising recordings of Czech music for the 1946 Prague Spring Festival, the performers are called the Prague Quartet. There's a connection to Janáček through Černý, who was the violist in the 1925 ISCM performance of the First Quartet.

The tenor Josef Válka (1904–81) was a Brno native. He studied with Marie Hloušková, the contralto soloist in the world premiere of the *Glagolitic Mass* and a member of the Brno Opera who created the role of the Forester's Wife in *The Cunning Little Vixen*. Válka began his career in the PSMU during the 1920s. He made the first recording of *The Diary of One Who Disappeared* in 1944, with Růžena Hořáková (another Hloušková pupil) and the pianist Josef Páleníček*. (Esta H 5158–61).

Páleníček was involved in several other Janáček recordings in the 1940s. In March 1947, he recorded *Pohádka* with Miloš Sádlo on Ultraphon (G 14897–8), with Sádlo's arrangement of 'Lístek odvanutý' on the fourth side. This was the first complete recording, following a disc of the second movement only made for Ultraphon by Bohuš Heran and Alfred Holeček in 1941. In 1944 Páleníček made the first recording of the Violin Sonata with Alexander Plocek (Esta H 5156–7). Páleníček also made the earliest recordings of three major piano works: *1. X. 1905* and *On the Overgrown Path* (Series I) for Ultraphon in 1943

(H 24211–2; G 12889–91), and *In the Mists* for Esta in 1945 (F 5193–4). Zdeněk Jílek also recorded *1. X. 1905* for Esta in May 1946 (F 5197). There were no standardised English forms of titles at the time, and *On the Overgrown Path* was listed in the March 1946 *Gramophone* as 'By Overgrown Tracks', while an advertisement in the August 1949 *Gramophone* listed it as 'Weedy Sidewalk'.

The first of the large-scale choruses to be recorded were *The Seventy Thousand* by the PSMU under Jan Šoupal on 29 December 1935 (Radiojournal Prague RJ 155) and *Maryčka Magdónova* by the Prague Teachers' Choir under Antonín Bednář in 1936 (Radiojournal Prague RJ 166). A number of choruses were recorded in the 1940s by the PSMU under Jan Šoupal. He had been a member of the choir as a second tenor since 1917 and had sung in the first performances of several choruses under his mentor Ferdinand Vach. Šoupal's pre-1950 recordings with the PSMU for Ultraphon include *The Czech Legion* (C 15093–4), *Kantor Halfar* (C 15103), *Maryčka Magdónova* (G 14952), *The Wandering Madman* (C 15102) and a second recording of *The Seventy Thousand* (C 15092). Šoupal re-recorded the choruses for Supraphon in 1954.

The *Sinfonietta* was recorded for the first time in the Slovanský Hall, Prague on 4–5 October 1946, with the Czech Philharmonic under Rafael Kubelík* for HMV (CD reissue: Testament SBT 1181). This important recording was on a major international label, played by the orchestra that had given the premiere twenty years earlier. Kubelík and the Czech Philharmonic had performed the *Sinfonietta* at his first concert as the orchestra's chief conductor in 1942, and a few months before this recording had played the work in the closing concert of the first Prague Spring Festival (4 June 1946).

The first recording of *Taras Bulba* was made in May 1949 by the Brno Radio SO under Břetislav Bakala for Ultraphon (H 23094–96, reissue on CRQ Editions). A second recording was made in October 1950 by the Vienna SO under the Czech conductor (and Talich pupil) Henry Swoboda for Westminster (WL 5071). Talich's recording (see above) followed in 1954.

Bakala's first Janáček recording was *Kašpar Rucký*, made with the VSMU in November 1946 for Esta, but all his subsequent recordings were for Ultraphon/Supraphon, including a series of discs from 1948. These included the first commercial recordings of music from three of the operas made in November 1948, comprising six 78 r.p.m. sides of extracts from *Káťa Kabanová* (H 24215–7), the Preludes to *Káťa* and *The Makropulos Affair* (G 15209) and the chorus of Fox Cubs and final scene from *The Cunning Little Vixen* (G15210, with Jaroslav Hromádka and Marie Bakalová). Bakala's other Ultraphon records from 1948 included the *Nursery Rhymes* (G 15104–5) and the *Concertino*, with Ludvík Kundera as soloist (G 15106–7). In May 1950, Bakala recorded the *Capriccio* with Kundera in Brno (H 23381–3; download: Supraphon VT 9362-2), and on 16–18 October 1950, he conducted the *Sinfonietta* with the Czech Philharmonic at the Domovina Studio in Prague (H 23508–11; CD: Supraphon SU 3613-2). Bakala conducted the first recording of the *Glagolitic Mass* in March 1951 (Ultraphon H 23791–6; CD: Supraphon SU 3613-2). Reviewing the first international LP release of this recording in *Gramophone* (October 1953), Alec Robertson hailed 'a profoundly original setting of the Ordinary of the Mass'. Bakala's other recordings from the 1950s included the *Lachian Dances* (November 1952), an extract from Act I of *Fate* (October 1954), *The Wolf's Track* and *Hradčany Songs* (December 1955), *The Fiddler's Child* (April 1957), *From the*

House of the Dead (extracts, December 1957) and *The Ballad of Blaník* (March 1958).

Supraphon made the first commercial recordings of three complete Janáček operas in the 1950s: *Jenůfa* conducted by Jaroslav Vogel* (1953), *The Cunning Little Vixen* conducted by Václav Neumann* (1957), and the first Janáček opera to appear in stereo: *Káťa Kabanová* under Jaroslav Krombholc* (1959). All three used inauthentic versions of the scores – Kovařovic's reworking of *Jenůfa* and Talich's retouchings in *Vixen* and *Káťa* – but include some of the finest Czech voices of the time, very well conducted.

The arrival of stereo brought new recordings by established Janáček interpreters and by a younger generation of performers. Perhaps the most auspicious Janáček recording to be released in 1960 was of the *Sinfonietta* coupled with *Jealousy* and the preludes to *Káťa Kabanová*, *Makropulos* and *From the House of the Dead*, played by the Pro Arte Orchestra conducted by Charles Mackerras* – the first of his long series of Janáček recordings. *CurDis, GösŠír, SimBak, SupGen, SupJan.*

Rektorys, Artuš (b. Lovosice, 20 January 1877; d. Prague, 31 August 1973), Czech music critic.   Rektorys served as editor of the Prague music magazine *Dalibor* (1904–10), before founding and editing *Smetana* (1911–20). At the same time he was also working for the Prague Credit Bank, and its address is often used in his correspondence with Janáček. His first contact with Janáček was in 1906, when the interview 'An evening with Leoš Janáček' was published in *Dalibor* (25 May). Rektorys, friendly and supportive towards Janáček, quickly became his most important contact in Prague, offering advice and encouragement in a voluminous correspondence comprising more than two hundred letters between 1906 and 1919. They corresponded at length about the proposed production of *Fate* at the Vinohrady Theatre (an ultimately fruitless campaign that dragged on for six years), then over *The Excursions of Mr Brouček** for which Rektorys helped in securing the rights from the Čech family. It was to Rektorys that Janáček sent his first detailed plan for the *Excursion of Mr Brouček to the Moon*, and to whom he confided about his difficulties with librettists. After Rektorys published Nejedlý's scathing review of *The Fiddler's Child** in December 1917, Janáček assured him that they would 'certainly remain friendly', but in May 1919, Rektorys asked Janáček to confirm a rumour that Kovařovic was claiming part of the royalties for *Jenůfa*. Janáček didn't reply to this gossipy letter, and their friendship cooled. In 1934 Rektorys edited the first volume in the series of letters published by HMUB for the Janáček Archive (comprising Janáček's correspondence with Rektorys himself). Nothing more came of this series until 1948, when a second volume appeared. In all, nine volumes were published by 1953 (see Correspondence*). *JAiv, JYL1, JYL2, JODA, KLJ.*

Reorchestration and Retouching   Janáček worked closely on revisions to the orchestration of his operas with František Neumann* in Brno and Otakar Ostrčil* in Prague. In a report for the Prague NT about *Brouček* (18 November 1919), Ostrčil noted that 'there are many peculiarities and curiosities in Janáček's vocal and orchestral writing. Some will need to be adjusted during rehearsals (the composer has already made adjustments to the vocal parts himself). Others are an integral part of Janáček's individuality and contribute to the original style of this work.' Janáček wrote to Ostrčil on 29 January 1920: 'I would so like to hear the orchestral rehearsals, to fill things out if I feel the need! If you think some colourful retouching would be effective, then don't hesitate to do it!' Janáček attended some *Brouček* rehearsals and made further suggestions (or agreed to Ostrčil's). This became his customary way of working: for *Káťa*, *Vixen* and *Makropulos*, Janáček attended orchestral rehearsals and discussed changes with František Neumann before the premieres (Neumann's marked conducting scores contain many of these late changes).

In short, Janáček was not averse to revising his own orchestration, but Kovařovic's reorchestration of *Jenůfa** (discussed in the entry for Kovařovic, Karel*) and the posthumous reorchestration of four other operas are much more questionable, not least because they failed to recognise what Ostrčil had in 1919 – that idiosyncratic orchestral writing was 'an integral part of Janáček's individuality'. Of the operas to be subjected to posthumous reorchestration, the most drastic was *From the House of the Dead*, prepared for its premiere in 1930 by Osvald Chlubna* and Břetislav Bakala*. Chlubna made his additions in pencil on the authorised copy of the score. The fuller sound Chlubna wanted involved thickening the texture, particularly by adding horn parts (sometimes replacing Janáček's trombones), and by diminishing the impact of the more startling orchestral effects, particularly Janáček's preference for wide spacing between very high and low instruments. More drastic still, Chlubna invented a completely new ending for *From the House of the Dead** (derived from the last prisoners' chorus). Even after Janáček's original ending was restored in the 1960s, many of Chlubna's retouchings persisted, some even lasting into Charles Mackerras's Decca recording. It was not until 2018 that Janáček's original orchestration was heard as he wrote it, when John Tyrrell's edition was first performed at the Royal Opera House, Covent Garden.

The first complete Brno production of *The Excursions of Mr Brouček** was in 1937, conducted by Milan Sachs. Sachs and his assistant Vilém Tauský* subjected the score to extensive orchestral retouching, and it was their version (uncredited) that was used until 2003, when Charles Mackerras* conducted a new production at the Prague NT using Jiří Zahrádka's edition which restored Janáček's original instrumentation.

Václav Talich* conducted a new production of *The Cunning Little Vixen** at the Prague NT in 1937 and set about a fundamental reworking of the orchestration. He told Vladimír Helfert (in a letter of 7 May 1937) that this was required in the interests of clarity, by 'removing some doublings and moving some parts to different instruments. On the other hand, I felt the need to thicken the sound in some places, doubling instruments or transposing them up an octave.' Talich told Helfert that 'these changes were partly made by myself, and I have entrusted their detailed execution to Prof. [Jaroslav] Řídký and staff conductor [František] Škvor. They did this work under my supervision and only to the extent that I approved.' Talich's orchestral suite from the opera shows the effect of some of his changes, but the most far-reaching intervention came in the Act II finale, where Talich added an on-stage band of horns, trumpets, timpani and percussion.

Káťa Kabanová* was published in full score in 1922, and although this edition contained errors, it presented Janáček's original orchestration. When Talich came to perform *Káťa* at the Prague NT in 1938, he once again undertook extensive rescoring, sometimes making musical alterations (most conspicuously, the added off-beat chords in the orchestral epilogue at the end of Act III). He altered many of Janáček's individual orchestral colours, for instance replacing the high solo horn (after Fig. 5 in Act III) with a clarinet. The overall effect is sometimes a softening of the sound by using a more conventional instrumental palette, while elsewhere Talich thickened the sound or added details of his own. Though Talich's version of *Káta* was never published, it was the version by which the opera first became widely known, since Jaroslav Krombholc's 1959 Supraphon recording used Talich's retouchings. At the Prague NT, Bohumil Gregor reverted to Janáček's original orchestration.

Janáček's non-operatic music has not usually been subjected to such radical surgery. One example made during Janáček's lifetime which he almost certainly approved informally with Otto Klemperer* was the addition of the nine fanfare trumpets to the last three bars of the *Sinfonietta*. On 19 September 1927, Klemperer wrote to Janáček: 'Will you permit the closing bars to be played by all 12 trumpets? Is it an oversight that the bassoons do not play at the end?' Janáček's reply has not survived, but he attended Klemperer's Berlin performance ten days later, on 29 September, and was extremely enthusiastic about it. Markings in Klemperer's copy of the full score (Royal Academy of Music, London) suggest that Janáček sanctioned all the trumpets playing at the end, and this has been widely adopted since. The *Sinfonietta* also exists in versions to facilitate performances without the fanfare instruments. The first and most interesting of these was made in 1927 by Erwin Stein, and sent to Janáček for his approval. Though reluctant to rework the piece for a standard orchestra, Janáček sent back detailed instructions which were incorporated into the reduced version, made available by UE (initially as inserts for the score) in October 1927. The 'Stein' reduction was thus made following Janáček's own instructions, albeit under duress. A later version was made by Joseph Keilberth, and in 2018 Heinz Stolba produced a new reduced orchestration. All these are available for hire from UE.

Talich, for whom Josef Suk's orchestral works represented an early twentieth-century ideal, recorded only two pieces by Janáček: the reorchestrated suite from Act I of *The Cunning Little Vixen** and *Taras Bulba**. In *Taras Bulba*, Talich made a number of adjustments to Janáček's orchestration, including the addition of accents, doubling parts and altering a violin solo to be played by a group of violins. Jaroslav Vogel* was among the first musicians to emphasise that such changes were both unnecessary and undesirable. Janáček's music, he wrote, 'must never be adapted according to conventional ideas but its presentation must be as true to its extraordinary style and substance as possible'. *JAWO, JODA, PalPos, PavIns, VogJan, ZahSin.*

Říkadla See *Nursery Rhymes* (V/16 and V/17)

Ritter, William (b. Neuchâtel, Switzerland, 31 May 1867; d. Melide, Switzerland, 19 March 1955), Swiss writer and critic. Ritter was an enthusiastic early champion of Mahler and also had a strong interest in Czech music. In 1923 Otakar Ostrčil introduced Ritter and his companion Janko Cádra to Janáček after a performance of *Káta Kabanová* in Prague. A year later, Ritter tried to interest Janáček in an operatic project: on 22 April 1924, he sent his play *L'Âme et la chair* (The Soul and the Body), suggesting it as a possible libretto (Janáček declined it on 2 May 1924). Ritter attended a rehearsal of the *Glagolitic Mass**

on 29 November 1927 and Janáček wrote to Kamila Stösslová: 'Today I had a glorious day. That French [*recte* Swiss] critic was at the rehearsal for the concert. Such praise from him! It is, he says, my greatest work. After the rehearsal we sat together in the restaurant.' A few months later, on 28 March 1928, the front page of the *Gazette de Lausanne* carried Ritter's review under the headline 'La *Messe Glagolitique* de M. Leos Janacek': 'The premiere in Brno of this passionate and surprising work, truly created from lava and from fire, caused the greatest artistic excitement on our last visit. ... It is a combative and militant mass where one sometimes has the impression of an assault mounted on the celestial citadel, sometimes of naïve prayers, of popular supplications that have frenetic tenderness ... sometimes the convulsions of energy that animate it make one think of Danteesque torment.' Ritter hoped to write a book about Janáček and made arrangements to visit the composer in Hukvaldy in August 1928, but the meeting never took place. On 11 August 1928, Janáček wrote a note to Ritter, scrawled in pencil, from his hospital bed: 'Dear friend, I have fallen ill. I am in the sanatorium of Dr Klein ... Do you want to come here or wait for me in Hukvaldy?' This poignant document was the last letter Janáček wrote. *GazLau, JYL2, WinGla*.

Russia and Russian Literature

1. Visits to Russia

Janáček started to learn Russian in about 1874, and Russian literature was to be a constant source of inspiration throughout his creative life. When his brother František moved to St Petersburg in 1895, he urged Janáček to come and visit. Janáček needed no persuasion and at the earliest opportunity – the summer of 1896 – he set out for Russia. He left on 18 July, taking the train from the small town of Studenká (between Ostrava and Nový Jičín), which lies on the main line between Prague and Warsaw. He arrived in St Petersburg on the evening of 20 July. His visit was the subject of three articles for *Lidové noviny* entitled 'A Few Words from a Holiday Trip' (XV/150). In the first article, Janáček notes that in a working-class area, infants could play safely in a park surrounded by strong railings: 'What rare concern for the security of workers' children!' He admires the police presence that explains 'the phenomenon of feeling as though one is not in a workers' street', draws parallels between St Petersburg and Prague, and takes a boat trip to see the Tsar's summer residence at the Peterhof. In the second article, he goes to Mass and is much impressed by the music: 'It is generally known that Russian choirs are excellent, and it was bliss for a musician to listen to them. ... The choir comes in with admirable agility with the responses, and over the long *pianissimo* with which they finish, the priest continues the prayer, strictly in tune.' The third article opens with a question: 'How do they enjoy themselves in St Petersburg?' Janáček goes to the zoological gardens, where a military band is playing when he arrives at 4.00 p.m., the animals are fed at 5.30, and this is followed by an entertainment in which he couldn't help being impressed by an outdoor ballet with over two hundred dancers that included the ascent of a hot-air balloon to the North Pole. He attended a memorial concert for Anton Rubinstein that ended with the Fourth Symphony played by an 'outstanding orchestra'. Janáček left St Petersburg on 27 July. His journey continued to Moscow. This part of the trip is not described in his articles but noted down in the Russian grammar book that he'd taken with him: 'The Kremlin! God, what a fairy tale! ... All around a beautiful view. From here Moscow is like a sea of domes. I am so glad I spent time here ... the most beautiful part of my journey!!!' After a delay at the Polish border (leading Janáček to jot down an unpleasant tirade against 'Jews – a terrible number of them'), he returned to Hukvaldy on 1 August. Janáček was almost entirely positive about his Russian experience – the only moments of criticism come when he grumbles about too much German music being played.

His next trip to Russia was in March 1902, when he took Olga to visit her uncle and aunt in St Petersburg. It should have been an idyllic trip. In 1896 he had travelled alone, but now he was with the daughter he'd increasingly come to cherish – her love of Russian literature certainly contributing to that. After Janáček returned, Olga fell gravely ill and his third trip, in June, was to accompany Zdenka to St Petersburg, where she would care for Olga (and bring her home).

2. Works inspired by Russia and Russian Literature

Russia or Russian literature provided all or part of the inspiration for several of Janáček's most important works. For detailed discussion of these, see the individual entries on: *Elegy on the Death of my Daughter Olga** (IV/30), *Fairy Tale** (VII/5), *From the House of the Dead** (I/11), *Káta Kabanová** (I/8), *Piano Trio** (X/22), Sonata for Violin and Piano* (VII/7), String Quartet No. 1* (VII/8) and *Taras Bulba** (VI/15).

At least four other works were based on Russian material. On 13 November 1876, at the Brno Beseda, Janáček conducted his melodrama for reciter and orchestra after Lermontov's poem *Death* (X/3), though Janáček set a Czech translation. This piece was already lost by the time of the worklist in Brod's 1924 biography, but the programme for the concert states that only the first part was performed. A review in *Moravská orlice* says the piece as performed consisted of sections of orchestral music alternating with spoken text, rather than the usual model in Czech melodramas of the text being recited over the orchestra. A short *Cossack Dance* (VI/12) arranged for orchestra in 1899 was based on a tune that had been given to him by Marie Nikolayevna Veveritsa, a member of the Brno Russian Circle and Olga's Russian teacher, whose poem Janáček used for the *Elegy* in Olga's memory. Janáček started to sketch an opera on Tolstoy's *Anna Karenina* (IX/4) in January 1907. There are sketches for one scene (between the characters Levin and Kitty) published by Gracian Černušák in *Lidové noviny* (9 August 1936) and reprinted in SKVEJ A/11 (2010). *The Living Corpse* (IX/6), based on Tolstoy's novel, is one of Janáček's more substantial operatic fragments: a scene sketched in full score in 1916 runs to 198 bars before breaking off. It is scored for three voices, Anna Pavlovna, Saša and Naňa (two sopranos and a mezzo-soprano), and orchestra. It is published in SKVEJ A/11 (2010). *Chrono, HelJan, JAWO, JYL1, JYL2, VogJan, ZemEss.*

Šárka, opera in three acts after a libretto by Julius Zeyer* (I/1).   In his diary for January 1885, Janáček jotted down some ideas for an operatic project based on Chateaubriand's *Les Aventures du dernier des Abencérages*. This was the first time he had contemplated an opera. The Brno NT in Veveří Street opened in 1884, and Janáček went to numerous performances, many of which he reviewed in *Hudební listy*. Clearly his thoughts were starting to turn towards an opera of his own. Though the 1885 plans got no further than notes for a scenario,

Janáček soon found inspiration in Julius Zeyer's *Šárka*, originally written as a libretto for Dvořák in 1880. Janáček wrote a first version of the opera in vocal score, completing it by August 1887, when he sent the work to Dvořák for his comments. Janáček had not yet thought to ask for Zeyer's permission: when he did so in November 1887, the response was a swift and unequivocal rejection (see Zeyer, Julius*). Even so, Janáček pressed on, completing a revised version by 18 June 1888 (the date on Stross's copy) and finishing the orchestration of the first two acts soon afterwards. For the next thirty years the work lay untouched. Zeyer died in 1900, and in 1918 Janáček returned to the work. He made revisions, especially to the voice parts, and asked Osvald Chlubna* to orchestrate Act III, which was done in August 1918. Janáček completed his revisions by January 1919. Janáček was happy, perhaps even surprised, with the results: in his autobiography he wrote: '*Šárka*? Everything is so close to my recent work!' In 1919 he tried to interest UE in publishing the score but their response was lukewarm. Vladimír Helfert* reacted very differently. In an article for *Hudební rozhledy* (15 November 1924), he described *Šárka* as resembling 'Smetana's tragic style', and 'uncommonly interesting for Janáček's artistic development'. Early in 1925, the Brno NT approached Janáček about producing the opera, and he made final revisions in June 1925. There was some question about what its title should be, since Fibich's *Šárka* (1897, on a libretto by Anežka Schulzová) had established a secure place in the repertoire. Janáček remained firm, telling František Neumann that he was going to stick to *Šárka*: 'Zeyer wrote the libretto and called it *Šárka* ... I wrote it with a strong image of Šárka in my mind ... when people write about me, they always mention *Šárka* among my works. A short name for a tiny work. That's fitting. So let's print it and say it like this: Fibich's *Šárka*, Janáček's *Šárka*. ... Let's not beat our brains any more over this.'

The premiere took place at the Brno NT on 11 November 1925, conducted by František Neumann* and directed by Ota Zítek*, with a cast that included several of Janáček's regular Brno singers. Šárka was Hana Pírková, Přemysl was Arnold Flögl (who created the role of the Forester in *The Cunning Little Vixen*), Ctirad was Emil Olšovský and Lumír was Valentin Šindler. Janáček quarrelled with Otakar Ostrčil over *Šárka*, unwilling to accept his reservations about a production at the Prague NT. The Prague press reported that Ostrčil had 'turned it down', which wasn't quite true, but he hadn't applied to perform it either. Janáček also nagged Brod to produce a German translation, but Brod declined in a private letter to UE ('I've not found anything in it to attract me'). There were productions in Olomouc (1938), Brno (1958) and Ostrava (1978), broadcasts conducted by Bakala for Brno Radio (one published on CD by Multisonic), and a concert performance in Edinburgh (1993). UE first planned publication of the vocal score in 1926, and told Janáček in February 1927 that it would be issued 'shortly', but it did not appear in print until Jiří Zahrádka edited it for UE/Editio Moravia, the edition recorded by Charles Mackerras* for Supraphon in 2000.

Was Janáček right to have such confidence in *Šárka* in the 1920s? The published scores and recordings suggest that he was. In a review of the 1993 Edinburgh Festival performance (conducted by David Robertson), Raymond Monelle wrote (*Independent*, 27 August 1993) that *Šárka* 'displays a fully digested personal idiom, as different from Suk or Fibich as it is from his own later works. ... *Šárka* is a red-blooded piece based on Czech mythology, with warrior maidens, tomb scenes and a self-immolation. The score is unbelievably rich: majestic, violent, languorous and frenetic by turns.' *HelJan, JAWO, JODA,* *NěmŠár, ZahDiv, ZahŠár.*

SYNOPSIS

Act I: On one side, a castle; on the other, a rock with a door leading to Libuše's tomb. According to legend, after the death of Princess Libuše, women lost their right to choose their own husbands, and led by the warrior-maiden Vlasta, they declared war on men. The leader of the men was Prince Přemysl, now widowed but formerly married to Libuše. A young warrior, Ctirad, arrives at Libuše's castle and explains to Přemysl that he has come for the weapons bequeathed by his ancestors, which are now kept in Libuše's tomb. Ctirad enters the tomb but is disturbed by a group of warriors led by Šárka, who wants to secure Libuše's crown for Vlasta. Ctirad blocks their way, and Šárka and her warriors flee.

Act II: A wild, deserted valley. Šárka wants revenge on Ctirad and sets a trap for him. She orders the other warriors to tie her to a tree and then hide. Ctirad is lured by Šárka's pleas to be set free. She tells him that Vlasta had her bound to the tree for failing to secure Libuše's crown. Ctirad is bewitched by Šárka's beauty and declares his love for her. Šárka is attracted to Ctirad, but she remains resolute. She sounds her hunting horn and her warriors to come out of hiding and kill Ctirad. Šárka instantly regrets this, calling her companions 'monstrous and merciless' and falling on Ctirad's corpse.

Act III. Vyšehrad. A courtyard lined with lime trees. Lumír leads a torchlight procession with four men carrying the covered body of Ctirad to Vyšehrad, where Přemysl is horrified to recognise his friend who was, Lumír tells him, 'killed by Šárka out of spite'. They build a funeral pyre. Šárka arrives and confesses to what she has done. Lumír lights the flames with his torch and Šárka, begging the fire to purify her soul, stabs herself and falls beside Ctirad. With the lovers united in death, the chorus sings of the miracle of love.

Schluck und Jau, incidental music for Gerhart Hauptmann's play (IX/11). On 8 May 1928, Gustav Hartung (1887–1946), director of the Berlin Renaissance Theatre, wrote to Janáček asking him to compose incidental music for a new production of Hauptmann's comedy *Schluck und Jau,* which the author was going to co-direct with Hartung at that year's Heidelberg Festspiele. Since this started on 21 July, Hartung was eager to have a quick response from Janáček. He enlisted Max Brod and Otto Klemperer to encourage the composer; both told Janáček that Hartung was one of the best stage directors in Berlin, and Klemperer added that 'Hauptmann too would be very pleased if this project might interest you.' This campaign did the trick. By 5 June 1928, Janáček had completed two movements and started a third, but then he suddenly abandoned the project. The reason seems to have been a letter from Hertzka in which he told Janáček that the Heidelberg Festspiele 'had not enjoyed great success'. On 5 June, Janáček wrote to Kamila Stösslová: UE 'tells me not to be caught out by that offer from Heidelberg, ... And I've already begun. It will be music and action about two drunken beggars, one of whom shows how he would rule! When he's dead drunk, they persuade him that he's a prince.' These are Janáček's last orchestral pieces and they are of considerable musical interest. Hauptmann's play, loosely based on *The Taming of the Shrew* and with hints of *Waiting for Godot,* evidently appealed to Janáček. In the first piece, there are stylistic similarities with *From the House of the Dead**. Charles Mackerras described the second piece as 'extraordinary, with its 5/8 rhythm with strange, deep trombones so typical of Janáček, and the violins playing in a different rhythm way up at the top of their register'. A score was published by UE in 1978 for hire only, and a critical edition was published in SKVEJ A/11 (2010). Václav Neumann and the Czech Philharmonic gave the first performance on 13 September 1979. *JAWO, MacTyr, VejFra.*

Schmoranz, Gustav (b. Slatiňany, 16 September 1858; d. Prague, 21 December 1930), Czech theatre administrator.   Schmoranz graduated from the Czech Technical School in Prague as an architect and also studied in Paris. From 1900 until 1922, he was the administrative director of the Prague NT, working alongside the dramatist Jaroslav Kvapil and Karel Kovařovic. In 1915 he attempted to persuade Kovařovic to perform *Jenůfa**, but reported to Josef Peška (on 29 September 1915) that he had failed, and included a summary of Kovařovic's critique of the opera. Schmoranz also worked as a stage director at the Prague NT, and he directed the world premiere of *The Excursions of Mr Brouček**, which opened on 23 April 1920. *JAWO, KLJ, NDPrOA.*

Sedláček, Václav (b. Mokrsko, near Nový Knín, 6 July 1879; d. Mokrsko, 20 February 1944), Czech flautist.   Sedláček played flute and piccolo in the Brno NT orchestra from 1910 until 1935, and he taught flute at the Brno Beseda from 1922 to 1938. Sedláček first worked as Janáček's copyist in 1916, when he made the authorised copy of *The Excursion of Mr Brouček to the Moon*, following this a year later with the 'Fifteenth Century' Excursion from *The Excursions of Mr Brouček**. For the next decade, he was Janáček's principal copyist, demonstrating a well-nigh clairvoyant ability to read the composer's increasingly unruly musical handwriting. His last assignment for Janáček was to make the authorised copy of *From the House of the Dead**, with Jaroslav Kulhánek in 1928. His authorised copy of the *Sinfonietta** was used as the printer's copy by UE. Sedláček made authorised copies of several other orchestral works, as well as most of Janáček's later chamber music. He was responsible for one of the authorised copies of the *Glagolitic Mass**, and one of the copies of *The Cunning Little Vixen** (an elusive manuscript that was rediscovered in 1972, only to disappear again a few years later). In 1943 Sedláček collaborated with Ota Zítek* on an orchestration of *The Diary of One Who Disappeared*, performed at Plzeň on 26 June 1943. Janáček dedicated *March of the Bluebirds* (VII/9) to Sedláček. *ČSHS, JAWO, ZahMlá.*

The Seventy Thousand (70,000) [*Sedmdesát tisíc* (70.000)], chorus for male voices (IV/36).   Based on the poem of the same name by Petr Bezruč* published in *Slezské číslo* (Prague, 1903), this is the third of Janáček's Bezruč choruses. It exists in two versions. The first dates from 1909 and was rehearsed in Janáček's presence by Vach's PSMU in 1910, before being withdrawn (it is included in a supplement in SKV C/2). The second version was made by 5 July 1912 (the date on the manuscript copy in the archives of the PSMU) and is a far-reaching revision, considerably shortened and extensively reworked. Janáček sent the chorus to Ferdinand Vach on 16 July 1912, but Vach returned it, declaring it to be unperformable. František Spilka* gave the first performance with his Prague Teachers' Choral Society (PSPU) on 25 March 1914. When HMUB published the chorus in 1923, it had a dedication to Spilka. Vach eventually performed the

18. Václav Sedláček: letter to Janáček on 13 October 1916 about the copying of the score of *The Excursions of Mr Brouček*.

work with the PSMU, taking it on tour to Montpellier in France (earning the PSMU the dedication of *Our Flag* in gratitude).

Bezruč's poem refers to the seventy thousand Czech-speaking inhabitants of the Těšín district, close to the Polish border, who had not abandoned their mother tongue: one hundred thousand had been Germanised, while another hundred thousand chose to speak Polish. Bezruč writes that graves had been symbolically dug for the remaining seventy thousand. Janáček's setting is highly expressive and has a demanding tenor solo as well as solo quartet (TTBB) and divided chorus. The opening is marked by a repeated phrase on the words 'před Těšínem' ('near to Těšín') and eerie interjections with the words 'Smime žít?' ('May we live?') from the solo quartet. The tenor solo sings the words 'Jen žít!' ('Just live!') quietly at first, then with a series of top Cs. The chorus ends with a drinking song offering bitterly ironic praise for 'Marquis Gero', the detested Habsburg Duke of Těšín, Archduke Frederick. At Spilka's request, Janáček provided a note on the work: 'In the evening and through the night, around Těšín the clouds of steam and the fiery glow of the furnaces. ... Beneath the earth, above the earth, coal dust and sulphur fill the air ... devouring the soul. ... Glasses of goralka [slivovic] bang out rhythms on oak tables.' Janáček's description of 'Marquis Gero' in the final section is particularly striking: 'The main culprit continues to wander around here like a poisonous bubble.' Janáček's sketches for the chorus were written in the margins of his copy of *Slezské číslo*, a page of which is illustrated in *JAWO*. *JAWO, JYL1, StrMuž, VogJan, ZemJan*.

Sinfonietta for orchestra (VI/18).   On 27 June 1924, Janáček went to an outdoor concert in Písek with Kamila Stösslová. The music he heard in the park that day included fanfares played by four trumpeters, their ceremonial instruments draped with the flags of the Czechoslovak Republic. This sowed the seeds for an idea that later became the *Sinfonietta* – no doubt helped by the association of the concert with Stösslová. On 29 March 1926, he wrote to her that he had composed 'a beautiful little Sinfonietta with fanfares ... I remember those fanfares in Písek.' The work was commissioned for the Eighth National Sokol Rally, due to take place in Prague in June and July 1926 (see Sokol*). Given his remarks to Stösslová on 29 March, and the discovery of an earlier sketch for some fanfares (scored for horns, trumpets, trombones, timpani and harp, written on the back of the sheets containing sketches for the familiar fanfares), they certainly seem to have been his starting point. At any event, the *Sinfonietta* was composed quickly, with a 'hot pen' as he told the conductor Václav Talich*. Janáček started the work on 2 March 1926 and had finished it a month later. The first performance took place in the Smetana Hall, Prague, on 26 June 1926. This Sokol event was described on the programme as an 'artistic evening for young people'. It began with a speech by Rudolf Medek, a poet who had been a general in the Czech Legion, and this was followed by the first performance of the *Sinfonietta* (listed as 'Rally Sinfonietta'), then three movements from Smetana's *My Country* ('Vyšehrad', 'Tábor' and 'Blaník'), all performed by the Czech Philharmonic conducted by Talich. The concert was broadcast (see Radio Broadcasts during Janáček's Lifetime*). Janáček was present at the rehearsals and was pleased with Talich's preparations. He wrote to Stösslová on 24 June: 'They're playing my *Military Sinfonietta* beautifully! I'll stay here tomorrow for the final rehearsal and in the afternoon I'll go home. Lots of work awaits me there.' Did Janáček really miss this premiere? As Tyrrell puts it, 'it seems extraordinary that with nothing more than "lots of work" awaiting him in Brno Janáček was not prepared to spend the extra day in Prague to be present at the premiere of his finest orchestral work, played by the finest orchestra in Czechoslovakia and directed by one of the finest conductors of his time'. The fact that his first commentary on the work is jotted down on the programme for the first performance suggests that he might have changed his mind and stayed for the concert.

Janáček often called the work 'Military Sinfonietta' ['Vojenská Symfonieta'], and this is the title on the autograph manuscript and authorised copy. It no doubt refers to the military band inspiration, but also suggests that he envisaged the work as a kind of patriotic statement. In an article for the newspaper *Československá republika* (29 June 1926), Jaroslav Vogel reported that Janáček intended a connection with the Czech armed forces (but he had already dedicated *Taras Bulba* 'to our troops'). Janáček's later notes on the work all suggest that it was written to celebrate Brno (see below). When it was published in January 1927, the title had become simply *Sinfonietta*, with a dedication to Mrs Rosa Newmarch*.

The *Sinfonietta* is in five movements. The first – 'Fanfares' – is scored for a spectacular array of brass (nine trumpets in C, two tenor tubas, two bass trumpets) and timpani. Over slow-moving parallel fifths in the tenor tubas, the main idea appears in short phrases (often rhythmic palindromes) that are then extended and developed. This short and resplendent movement was given an outdoor performance in Prague on 6 July 1926. The plan was for it to be played from the top of one of the towers of the Týn Church as the Sokol procession entered the Old Town Square, though how a set of timpani was to be lugged up the stairs is unclear. Still, it was certainly performed somewhere in the Old Town Square that day, at the end of a procession with around eighty thousand participants.

Janáček jotted down titles for the movements on his copy of the programme for the first performance: 'I. Fanfares; II. The Castle; III. The Queen's Monastery; IV. The Street; V. The Town Hall'. Apart from the first movement, all these titles refer to locations in Brno. On 27 December 1927, *Lidové noviny* published Janáček's article 'My Town' (XV/298), in which he amplified this programme, comparing unhappy memories of the Brno of his childhood with the modern independent city it had become: 'The rebirth of 28 October 1918 glorified my native town. Now I looked up to it, I belonged to it. And the blaring of my triumphal trumpets, the solemn silence hovering over the lane leading to the Queen's Monastery [Augustinian Monastery], the night shadows and breezes on the green mountain [the Špilberk, a Habsburg prison in Janáček's childhood], and the vision of the certain rise and greatness of the town – it is from this knowledge that my *Sinfonietta* was born, from my home town of Brno.' In other words, the 'Town Hall' noted as the title of the fifth movement in 1926 stood as a symbol of the city's renewal since the declaration of the Czechoslovak Republic.

The *Sinfonietta* was published by UE in January 1927, in two quite different editions: a full score (72 pp.) reproduced from a copyist's manuscript (UE 8679); and a pocket score (115 pp.) from engraved plates, issued by UE's subsidiary

Wiener Philharmonischer Verlag (UE 8680). Later editions included revised versions of both UE scores by Karl-Heinz Füssl (1978), and a critical edition by Miroslav Barvík and Reiner Zimmermann for Edition Peters, Leipzig (1980). František Jílek made an arrangement for piano duet, published in 1996. A new critical-practical edition by Jiří Zahrádka, including a comprehensive study of the work's history and sources, was published by UE in 2017 (UE 36503).

Following Talich's performance (the only time he ever conducted it), the *Sinfonietta* was next taken up by Otto Klemperer*, who conducted it at Wiesbaden Opera House on 9 December 1926, then gave the US premiere at Carnegie Hall on 4 March 1927. The first performance in Brno, attended by Janáček and given by the Brno NT orchestra under František Neumann*, took place on 4 April 1927, when it was described as 'Military Sinfonietta' on the programme. Klemperer conducted the *Sinfonietta* at the Staatsoper am Platz der Republik (the Krolloper) with the Berlin State Orchestra on 29 September 1927, a performance Janáček attended and which he described as 'unrivalled by anyone anywhere' (see Klemperer, Otto* and Reorchestration and Retouching*). On 10 February 1928, the BBC National Orchestra under Henry Wood* gave the London premiere at the Queen's Hall. The last performance Janáček heard was given by František Neumann and the Brno NT orchestra at 10 a.m. on 27 May 1928 as part of the Exhibition of Contemporary Culture in Brno. Janáček made a note about this miserable occasion: 'A Gala Concert of the *Sinfonietta*. 56 audience members in the theatre! No-one from the exhibition committee, no-one from the theatre management.' *JAWO, JYL2, TyrCh1, TyrInt, VogJan, ZahSin.*

Singing Teaching Manual [*Návod pro vyučování zpěvu*] (V/5). Composed by 25 April 1899 (date of first publication), this is a collection of 104 numbered examples, including vocal exercises (without text) for one and two voices, most with piano accompaniment. It was written when Janáček was teaching music at the Teachers' Institute in Brno, and was published on 25 April 1899 by A. Píša in Brno. According to Milena Duchoňová (in SKV H/2), Janáček used his manual for singing classes at the Institute, and later at the Brno Organ School. The numbered examples range from short exercises to vocalises with piano accompaniment (the longest is No. 35, which runs to 92 bars). Some of the most interesting exercises are those with irregular time signatures or rhythmic complexity: Nos. 71 and 72 are in 5/4, No. 78 has unusual hemiolas, and No. 80 is in 7/4. The final section (Nos. 94–104) comprises exercises for two voices, ending with two substantial vocalises with piano. In the introduction, Janáček sets out his aims, ending with a paragraph encouraging the development of musicianship through singing, adding that 'we must sing *every day* and get to know what the music literature, old and new, for choirs and solo voices, has to offer!' Janáček tried to have his manual officially adopted for schools and teacher-training colleges, but the Ministry of Education in Vienna turned down his request on the grounds that the manual was too short, lacking a theoretical foundation, and too musically demanding for the pupils at which it was aimed. A critical edition appeared as SKV H/2 (1980). *DucNav.*

Six Folksongs sung by Eva Gabel (**26 Folk Ballads** I) [*6 národních písní jež zpívala Gabel Eva* (*26 balad lidových* I)], folksong arrangements for voice and piano (V/9). In October–November 1909, Františka Kyselková* went to a farm at Modřice near Brno to collect folksongs sung by Slovak seasonal workers, including two performed by the solo singer Eva Gabel. As well as making handwritten transcriptions, Kyselková made phonograph* recordings of Gabel's singing. These provide a very rare opportunity to compare Janáček's folksong arrangements with live performances of his source material. He made the arrangements within a few weeks of the recordings being made (one manuscript is dated 10 December 1909). The first performance was given on 5 March 1911 at the Brno Organ School by the singer L. Vytopilová with Marie Dvořáková at the piano. In 1922 these were the first group of songs published by HMUB in the series of *26 Folk Ballads* (see Folk Ballads*), reprinted in 1950 when the *26 Folk Ballads* were issued complete for the first time. *JAWO, ProVza.*

Skuherský, František Zdeněk (b. Opočno, 31 July 1830; d. České Budějovice, 19 August 1892), Czech composer and theoretician. Skuherský was the son of a doctor and went to the Charles University in Prague to study medicine, but did not complete his training. At the Prague Organ School, he studied with Karel František Pitsch. Skuherský became a conductor at the theatre in Innsbruck, was choirmaster of the university church, and enjoyed particular success as conductor of the Musikverein, his repertoire including works such as Beethoven's 'Eroica', Schubert's 'Great' C major Symphony and Haydn's *Die Jahreszeiten*. He married his former pupil Anna von Kofler-Felsheim, but after her early death he moved to Prague, where he was director of the Organ School from 1866 until his retirement in 1890. He taught Janáček in 1874–5 (see Prague Organ School*). His far-reaching reforms of the Organ School curriculum, offering three-year courses including composition, made it the leading institution in Prague for aspiring composers. Skuherský became a member of the State Examination Board for Music in 1875 (and one of the first candidates he examined was Janáček in October 1875). Skuherský's pupils also included Josef Bohuslav Foerster. Skuherský was an important theorist, and his books included *On Musical Form* (Prague, 1873) and a four-volume *Method of Musical Composition* (Prague, 1880–4). Skuherský's compositions include a symphony written to celebrate the wedding of Franz Joseph I and Elisabeth of Bavaria that incorporated the Imperial anthem ('Gott erhalte Franz den Kaiser'), and several operas composed during his time in Innsbruck, but reworked in Czech for performance in Prague. Of these, *Vladimír, God's Chosen One* (originally written for Innsbruck as *Der Apostat*) was performed at the Provisional Theatre in Prague in 1863. Two years later, Bedřich Smetana reviewed a revival in *Národní listy* (3 January 1865), praising some aspects of it but finding the style an uneasy mixture of Wagner and traditional number opera. Even so, he declared it to be 'the first Czech national opera'. *ČHS, TyrCze.*

Smetana, Bedřich (b. Litomyšl, 2 March 1824; d. Prague, 12 May 1884), Czech composer. Janáček's attitude to Smetana was sometimes seen as ambivalent during his lifetime, largely because he was drawn into the highly politicised debate about the merits of Smetana and Dvořák in the years after Dvořák's death. The fanatical support of Smetana (at the expense of Dvořák, Janáček and Suk) by Zdeněk Nejedlý* and his acolytes created a situation in which Janáček, as a friend and supporter of Dvořák, was inevitably viewed as being suspect when it came to his view of Smetana. In 1910 the critic Hubert Doležil, a Nejedlý disciple, accused Janáček of holding 'an anti-Smetana position'. Janáček responded unhesitatingly that 'it is quite unjust to suppose that I was prejudiced against Smetana'. But it suited the posturing of the Smetana faction in Prague to create the illusion that Brno – and Janáček in particular – was promoting a Dvořák 'cult' at Smetana's expense. Nejedlý's view that Smetana represented the One True Way for Czech music would brook no equivocation, though the composers he regarded as worthy guardians of Smetana's spiritual legacy happened to be personal friends (notably Foerster and Ostrčil). Janáček's writings on Smetana reveal a much more positive view of the composer. He never forgot the one time he saw Smetana. His article 'In the Year 1874', published in *Hudební besídka* (March 1925, XV/275), recalled this occasion, a benefit concert for Smetana that took place on 4 April 1875 in the auditorium on Žofín Island, conducted by Adolf Čech. It included *Vyšehrad* and the world premiere of *Vltava*: 'I sneaked right down near the orchestra; it was almost dark with musicians playing and the audience listening. So my memory of Smetana resembles a child's conception of God: in the clouds. When the orchestra finished, the tumultuous applause rose in the name of Smetana ... They led the ailing composer up the stairs. Only his face imprinted itself on my soul and I still have it clearly in my mind. ... A festive day indeed.' Coincidentally, when Janáček was conductor of the Brno Beseda, the only orchestral works by Smetana that he performed were the two that made such an impression in 1875: *Vyšehrad* in 1886 and *Vltava* in 1880 and 1883 (see Conducting, Janáček's*).

Janáček reviewed Smetana's *Dalibor* in *Hudební listy* (1 February 1888). He wrote that 'the effect was powerful, complete – resembling a kind of trance. However, I awakened slowly from this intoxication and the second night allowed me to consider the individual parts more carefully. First of all, islands of charming tunes stand out above the agitated waves, tunes of well thought-out forms, and of Czech character. ... Milada's music anchors itself in the firmly drawn character of Czech song only once, in the duet with Dalibor. ... As with *The Two Widows*, we draw attention again to two different styles of composition.' In *The Bartered Bride*, though, Janáček praised Smetana's characterisation of the roles through their music: 'each of the main characters ... is given a distinctive part to sing', he wrote in *Moravské listy* (8 October 1890), adding that 'this is the merit of the opera, a merit which also distinguishes Mozart's operas'. In the same review, he described *The Secret* as 'simply rapturous', calling it Smetana's 'best opera – by virtue of its outstanding thematic unity'. In 1924 Janáček wrote an article for the Brno NT magazine *Divadelní šepty*, reprinted in *Lidové noviny* on 2 March (XV/250). Its closing paragraph, about Smetana's 'power', sums up Janáček's view of Smetana's influence on Czech music: 'It would be foolish to want another *Bartered Bride* or another *My Country*. Where Smetana stands with his work, there is no room for anyone else. But he casts no smothering shadow. Every composition can grow alongside him, freely and with the same vitality.' *JYL1, JYL2, ZemEss.*

Sokol, Czech gymnastics association. The Sokol ['Falcon'] was founded in Prague in 1862 as a gymnastics association, and branches soon opened in other Czech cities. The aims of the Sokol were much broader than promoting exercise: its founders saw it as offering physical, moral and intellectual training for the Czech nation, and it fostered Czech national consciousness. This broader agenda had an obvious appeal for Janáček, and he joined the Brno I Sokol in 1876. There is no evidence that he participated in any of the physical programmes, but he was an enthusiastic member for the rest of his life. Many other prominent Czechs belonged to the Sokol, including Tomáš Garrigue Masaryk.

Two works by Janáček have specific links with the Sokol: one of them is a minor piano work with few musical features to suggest its composer, while the other is his greatest orchestral work. Aside from the Sokol connection, these two compositions, *Music for Club Swinging* (VIII/13) and the *Sinfonietta* (VI/18), have just one point in common: both begin with fanfares, though in the *Music for Club Swinging* these amount to two-bar introductions for each piece. *Music for Club Swinging* was composed in 1893. In its annual report, the Brno Sokol described the gymnastic display on 16 April 1893 where the pieces were played: 'The music for the gymnastics was composed by one experienced in these matters [of composition], Brother Director Janáček, to whom the Sokol gives renewed thanks.' The title states that the music was for club swinging (using Indian clubs), but it is possible that the pieces were used for exercises without any apparatus. Large Sokol rallies were held outdoors, so Janáček's piano pieces needed scoring appropriately when they were used at the Third National Rally in Prague on 29 June 1895 (two early arrangements for wind band survive, by Josef Kozlík and František Kmoch). The Sokol Gymnastic Association in Brno also published Janáček's piano version in 1895. An edition by HMUB in 1950 included an informative introduction by Bohumír Štědroň. *Music for Club Swinging* was printed in the supplement to SKV F/1 (1978).

After the establishment of the Czechoslovak Republic in 1918, the Sokol grew into a much larger organisation. At the Seventh National Rally held in 1920, there were over 100,000 participants, 78,000 of whom marched through Prague in the parade. The presence of President Masaryk lent lustre to the occasion, and Josef Suk composed the march *Towards a New Life* for the event. For the Eighth National Rally in 1926, the Sokol turned to Janáček for a new piece. Whether he received a formal commission is unclear, and the surviving correspondence with Antonín Krejčí (1884–1955) suggests that the Sokol was uncertain what it had asked for: was it a set of Fanfares, or a 25-minute orchestral work? Janáček had known Krejčí since around 1901, when he was a pupil at the Teachers' Institute. After a career as a teacher and Sokol representative, Krejčí worked for the committee organising the Eighth Sokol Rally in 1926. On 18 May, Krejčí wrote to Janáček to sort out the confusion over what was actually going to be performed. 'I gave your score to the Rally Committee yesterday. The last letter sent to you by the commissioning department was due to a misunderstanding, so the whole work will be played at the concert, the date of which I will confirm shortly.' Four days later, on 22 May, another letter came from the Chairman of the Sokol committee, full of apologies for the confusion, and providing confirmation of the dates:

> Please forgive the unpardonable error in our letter of 5 May suggesting mistakenly that only the fanfares rather than the whole of your *Rally Sinfonietta* would be performed. ... We are pleased to announce that the *Sinfonietta* will be performed in the Smetana Hall of the Obecní dům on 26 June, before Smetana's *My Country*, which will be played by the Czech Philharmonic conducted by Mr Talich. The fanfares will be played on 6 July from the Týn towers in the Old Town Square as the Sokol procession enters this historic location. We will certainly meet your wishes in every way and ask you to arrange rehearsal times directly with Maestro Talich to suit you best.

The performance went ahead as announced (see *Sinfonietta**) and on 1 July, Krejčí wrote to Janáček: 'Dear Maestro, I am very happy with the success of your *Sinfonietta* and am looking forward to your arrival for the final day of the Rally. I would like you to see the display of 14,400 men and 14,400 women performing their physical exercises.' In the end, Janáček couldn't be there, but his niece Věra wrote from Prague on 16 July that 'your fanfares were played after the Sokol procession to the Týn tower, where they were very effective'. This was a magnificent setting for a performance of Janáček's fanfares: a procession of eighty thousand participants watched by a huge crowd, including President Masaryk. It would surely have delighted Janáček as a lifelong supporter of the Sokol. *JAWO, JYL2, KLJ, ŠtěHud, ZahSin.*

Šolc, Emil (b. Kutná Hora, 1 August 1861; d. Prague, 16 August 1931), Czech publisher. Šolc established a Czech bookshop and publishing house in Telč in 1884, with a catalogue that had a strong emphasis on Moravian writers. It was through František Bartoš that Janáček came to be published by Šolc, starting with the *Bouquet of Moravian Folksongs* (XII/1) in 1890, and including the arrangements of songs drawn from this collection for voice and piano, known since 1908 as *Moravian Folk Poetry in Songs**(V/2). Šolc sold his Telč business in 1911 and moved to Prague, where he established the firm of Šolc and Šimáček. *JAWO, KLJ, VesŠol.*

Sonata for Violin and Piano (VII/7). Janáček started composing the Violin Sonata in 1914, in response to the early Russian advances at the start of World War I. The Russian armed forces were mobilised on 30 July, and Janáček's date of '1 August 1914' on one of the sketches confirms that he began the work as soon as this news came through. In 1923, in the article in which he dedicated *Taras Bulba* to the Czechoslovak armed forces (XV/247), Janáček wrote: 'In the *Fairy Tale* for cello and piano a gleam of sharp steel flashed through my mind and in the Sonata for Violin and Piano of 1914 I almost heard its clanging in my troubled mind.'

One movement, the 'Ballada', was completed a little earlier, certainly by May 1914, when Antonín Váňa wrote to Janáček asking to borrow the manuscript for a performance. Since the 'Ballada' is in the same manuscript as the rest of the sonata (and no independent source is known for it), it is possible (as Alena Němcová has argued) that an earlier version of the whole sonata existed by then. The work was certainly finished by October 1915, when Janáček suggested a performance of it in Prague. The violinist Jaroslav Kocian was unenthusiastic, and this prompted Janáček to revise the work extensively. Before then, however, the 'Ballada' was published in 1915 as a stand-alone piece (with no mention of it being part of a larger work) by Adolf Švarc in Kutná Hora, as part of his series *Česká hudba*. Between 1915 and publication in 1922, the work was extensively revised. The original first movement, *Con moto*, was completely rewritten using the same thematic material. The original second movement was the *Adagio* that eventually became the fourth movement. The *Ballada* moved from being the third movement to the second and was replaced by a new *Allegretto*. The finale gave Janáček the most problems: originally a *Con moto*, it was replaced in about 1916 by a new *Allegro*, which in turn was replaced by the *Adagio*. The final order thus became: 1. Con moto; 2. Ballada; 3. Allegretto; 4. Adagio. It was only when Janáček looked at the Sonata again before publication in 1922 that this definitive state of the work was settled.

The first edition was issued by HMUB in March 1922, and the premiere followed a few weeks later on 24 April, at a concert of the KMS performed by František Kudláček* (violin) and Jaroslav Kvapil* (piano). The Prague premiere was on 16 December 1922, when it was played by Karel Hoffmann (first violinist of the Czech Quartet) and Václav Štěpán*. On 5 August 1923, it was given at the ISCM Festival in Salzburg, played by Stanislav Novák and Štěpán. According to Janáček himself, the Violin Sonata was the best-played work in his London concert on 6 May 1926 at the Wigmore Hall, when it was given by Adila Fachiri and Fanny Davies. Janáček heard several other performances, including two more by Hoffmann and Štěpán in Prague (17 and 20 October 1924). A critical edition of the Violin Sonata, edited by Jan Krejčí and Alena Němcová, was published in SKV E/1 (1988). This includes a supplement with the 1916 *Allegro* fourth movement and a complete facsimile of the original version.

Jaroslav Vogel wrote of the 'Russian atmosphere that pervades the work', noting its close motivic connections to *Káťa Kabanová*. In 1915 Janáček was modest about the Sonata, describing it to Maria Calma-Veselá as 'not an exceptional work, but there is some truth in the second and third movements'. His subsequent revisions retained these (as the eventual fourth and second movements), and the two other movements were eventually reworked to his satisfaction. The final result has structural coherence and tension, as well as expressive richness. Hans Hollander summarised its qualities: 'In the Violin Sonata, the glowingly emotional, rhapsodical chamber music style of the composer's middle period appears in full flower.' HolJan, JAWO, LánJan, NěmHou, VogJan.

Šourek, Otakar (b. Prague, 1 October 1883; d. Prague, 15 February 1956), Czech musicologist. Šourek trained as a civil engineer and worked for Prague City Council (1907–39). He was music critic for the newspaper *Venkov* (1918–41). Mainly remembered for his writing on Dvořák (especially the four-volume *Život a dílo Antonína Dvořáka*, 1916–1933), Šourek also wrote on Janáček. On 2 March 1920, he sent Janáček his analysis of the motifs in *The Excursions of Mr Brouček*, to which the composer responded with enthusiasm. It appeared in *Hudební revue* with an introduction by Janáček, and was then published as a pamphlet by HMUB (1920). On 3 December 1927, Šourek asked Janáček if he would write an article for *Venkov*. Following a gentle reminder two weeks later, Janáček duly sent 'Dusk is Falling' (XV/303). Šourek thanked him on 29 January for 'an original insight into the creative workshop of a great artist that contributes significantly to the illumination of some of his most important works' (including *Káťa*, *Vixen*, *Makropulos*, *The Diary of One Who Disappeared* and the influence of Kamila Stösslová). Šourek edited the HMUB series of miniature scores in the 1940s, and produced carefully revised editions of *Taras Bulba*, *Youth*, the *Concertino* and the string quartets. JAWO, KLJ, LJLD1, ŠouBro.

Speech melodies In his article 'The Border between Speech and Song' (XV/185), published in the journal *Hlídka* in 1906, Janáček cautioned his readers: 'Just don't try to sing the speech melodies!' This is a helpful clue in trying to understand how Janáček understood speech melodies (in Czech he called them 'nápěvky mluvy'). In the same article, he argued that there was a need for a dictionary of speech melodies, 'in order to preserve the sound of the Czech language for future generations', which might suggest that Janáček collected speech melodies for much the same reason as he collected folksongs, as a kind of ethnographic and linguistic study. But whereas he worked with a team to collect folksongs, speech melodies represented something much more personal: they were private annotations kept in Janáček's notebooks, often enlivening his articles, and they sometimes included snatches of speech by those to whom he was closest, including Kamila Urválková, Kamila Stösslová and, most movingly, his daughter Olga as she lay dying. For him, speech melodies revealed the psychology and state of mind of the speaker: he called them 'a window into the human soul'.

From 1897 onwards – the year in which he set *Jenůfa* aside after finishing Act I – Janáček took a very serious interest in the subject (and later added a scientific aspect with his use of the Hipp Chronoscope*), but there was always a problem of how to notate speech. It has to be emphasised that these are snatches of speech, not snatches of song, but Janáček's speech melodies are all written down in conventional musical notation. This certainly encourages the notion that Janáček somehow 'used' speech melodies in his compositions. Janáček himself seemed to hint as much in 1903, when he wrote (in 'Melodies of our speech with outstanding dramatic qualities', XV/172) that 'the best way of becoming a good opera composer is to study analytically the melodic curves and contours of human speech. Only in this way can one get to know the true patterns for dramatic speech melodies in the Czech language.' And in his interview with Olin Downes (*New York Times*, 13 July 1924), Janáček declared:

> Song lives by and in speech. The whole spirit of the Czech people is manifested in their speech. To every word they utter is attached a fragment of the national life. Therefore the melody of the people's speech should be studied in every detail.

In the same interview he is quoted saying that

> for individual musical characterisation, especially opera, these melodic fragments from daily life are of the greatest significance. By them we shall hit on the truth; we shall grasp how the human individual utters words of love, with what intensity he expresses his hate. We shall discover the melodic curve of energy; we shall hear how tenderly is rounded off the phrase which comes from the goodness of a woman's heart.

However, as Downes reported, 'Janáček repeated emphatically that he never used these motives [speech melodies] in their literal form, and he never used popular [folk] melodies. "That," he said, "would only be repeating the words of someone else."'

There is no doubt that speech melodies were a vital resource for Janáček: they fuelled his imagination and made him think deeply about how to develop natural and truthful ways of setting words to music, particularly in his operas. Janáček's comments quoted by Downes appear to indicate something more, describing them as 'melodic fragments from daily life'. But he is talking about melodies or patterns of speech, not song, and what formed an essential part of the composer's inner creative process is an entirely different thing from the eventual musical outcome.

Speech melodies were not recycled as musical ideas in his music. They played an essential part in the formation of his mature style and in his thinking about the depiction of characters, but they were not quoted in the finished pieces. If there are hints of speech melodies in Janáček's vocal writing, they

have been stylised to such an extent that they are no longer recognisable as such – above all, because they are sung rather than spoken and now form part of an operatic span. The speech melody 'myth' has been explored in great detail by scholars such as John Tyrrell and Paul Wingfield, and their conclusions are convincing and clear: for Janáček, speech melodies were of the highest significance in his creative development as an opera composer, they had an impact on the rhythmic contours of phrases here and there, but they were not a direct resource for musical ideas and he didn't employ quotations of speech melodies in his music.

This is just as well for Janáček's international reputation. During his own lifetime, several of the opera performances he considered most successful were not sung in Czech at all, but in German. In his correspondence with Max Brod (who made the German translations of all the operas from *Jenůfa* onwards), Janáček's concern was to have a truthful and effective translation, and he was happy for his operas to be sung in a language other than Czech. Similarly, the later success of Janáček in Britain was almost entirely the result of performances given in sympathetic English translations.

It is also just as well for his orchestral and chamber music. John Tyrrell posed the question: 'What happens in Janáček's non-vocal music?' This was an issue Janáček himself had to tackle. On 10 April 1926, he wrote to Rosa Newmarch about his forthcoming London visit: 'An informative article on me was sent from Prague to the Chester [publishing] house in London. By chance, it fell into my hands. My worst enemy could not write a worse comment. ... They say that my principle of the so-called speech melodies is harmful to my instrumental composition, which means that everything in the London concert is worthless!' Jan Mikota at HMUB intervened and requested that the 'informative article' should not be used. In the biographical note on the back of the flyer announcing the Wigmore Hall concert on 6 May 1926, it states that Janáček 'built up his own style as the result of his study of the *napěvky* or melodies of speech. He carried theory into practice in a series of strikingly dramatic male-voice choruses, especially the settings of words by the labour poet, Petr Bezruč.' The first sentence is unarguable (and probably came from Newmarch herself). The comment about 'theory into practice' is much more problematic, but it became the persistent view for many years to come. Outside Czechoslovakia, at least, it did nothing to help dispel the view that Janáček was an eccentric figure, whose music was essentially un-exportable.

Janáček's studies of speech melody enabled him to evolve original ways of portraying character through music with extraordinary skill, but the skill was that of a composer subsuming and then stylising these essential elements of his musical imagination. As John Tyrrell put it, 'they did not ... serve as raw material for Janáček's compositions.' *JYL1, LJLD1, LJLR, TyrSpe, WinSpe.*

Spilka, František (b. Štěkeň, 13 November 1877; d. Prague, 20 October 1960), Czech conductor.   Spilka studied with Dvořák at the Prague Conservatory and became professor of choral singing there in 1906. In 1908 he founded the Prague Teachers' Choral Socety (PSPU) and in 1912 the Prague Women Teachers' Choral Society. After Ferdinand Vach (conductor of the PSMU) had declared *The Seventy Thousand* (IV/36) to be unperformable, Spilka took the work up with his PSPU and gave the first performance on 25 March 1914. When the chorus was published by HMUB in 1923, it was dedicated to Spilka. His correspondence with Janáček included a letter of 21 January 1914 in which he asked the composer for an analysis of *The Seventy Thousand*, which Janáček duly provided (see *The Seventy Thousand**). A verse about Spilka appears in *Muzikantské dušičky* by J. L. Budin, with an accompanying cartoon by Dr Desiderius that depicts Spilka conducting with a thunderbolt. *ČSHS, KLJ.*

Štědroň, Bohumír (b. Vyškov, 30 October 1905; d. Brno, 24 November 1982), Czech musicologist. After studies in Vyškov and graduating from the Brno Teachers' Institute in 1925, Štědroň studied at the Masaryk University with Vladimír Helfert*, whose assistant he was from 1932 to 1938. He taught at the Brno Conservatory and at the Masaryk University (becoming a full professor there in 1963). Štědroň was an accomplished pianist (a pupil of Vilém Kurz), and served as choirmaster of the Brno Sokol. Though Štědroň had wide research interests, it is his work on Janáček that has made the most enduring mark. According to the bibliography in Střelcová (2005), Štědroň's first publication was an obituary for Janáček published on 14 August 1928, and his last – No. 709 in the bibliography – was a study of Janáček and the Brno Russian Circle. As well as a vast output of articles and essays, Štědroň wrote four books that remain cornerstones of the Janáček literature. *Janáček ve vzpomínkách a dopisech* (1946) was translated into English in a slightly abridged version as *Janáček: Letters and Reminiscences* (1955), then revised and expanded as *Vzpomínky, dokumenty, korespondence a studie* (1986). *Dílo Leoše Janáčka* [The Works of Leoš Janáček] (1959) was the most important precursor of *JAWO*. *Zur Genesis von Leoš Janáčeks Oper Jenůfa* (published in German, 1968; enlarged second edition, 1972) is an exhaustive examination of the opera's early history. *Leoš Janáček: k jeho lidskému a uměleckému profilu* [*Leoš Janáček: a profile of the man and artist*] (Prague: Panton, 1976) is a biography that includes thoughtful discussion of the composer's life and works, and has a very useful chronology. Štědroň unearthed Janáček correspondence throughout his career, and he wrote prefaces to more than twenty Janáček editions which often include information not readily available elsewhere. He also edited the first publications of *The Little Queens* (IV/20), *Hukvaldy Songs* (IV/27), *Our Father** (IV/29), *Dumka* (VII/4) and *Moravian Folksongs** (VIII/23). Štědroň was a lexicographer, co-editing the *Československý hudební slovník osob a institucí* (2 vols, Prague, 1963 and 1965) and contributing over three hundred articles. *ČHS, StřŠtě.*

Štědroň, Miloš (b. Brno, 9 February 1942), Czech musicologist and composer, nephew of Bohumír Štědroň. Štědroň's work on Janáček has encompassed musicological research including *Leoš Janáček a hudba 20. Století, paralely, sondy, dokumenty* [*Leoš Janáček and twentieth-century music: parallels, soundings, documents*] (Brno: Masaryk University, 1998), the most comprehensive study of the subject. Štědroň has edited several volumes for SKV (see Editions, Critical and Scholarly*). With Leoš Faltus (b. 1937), he produced completions of Janáček's *Danube** (IX/7) and Violin Concerto* (IX/10), reconstructions based as closely as possible on surviving source material. Both completions have been published: *The Danube* as SKV H/3 (2009) and the Violin Concerto as SKV H/4 (1997).

Steinberg, Hans Wilhelm [later known as William] (b. Cologne, 1 August 1899; d. New York, 16 May 1978), German-born conductor. Steinberg is best remembered for his long tenure as music director of the Pittsburgh SO (1952–76), but before he emigrated to the United States in 1938 he built an impressive career in German opera houses. He worked as Klemperer's assistant in Cologne (where he did the musical preparation for the 1922 production of *Káťa Kabanová*). In 1927 he succeeded Zemlinsky as music director of the Prague German Theatre*. Here he conducted a new production of *Káťa Kabanová** on 21 January 1928, including Janáček's newly extended interludes. On 9 November 1927, Janáček had written to UE: 'The music for the scene changes in Acts 1 and 2 of *Káťa Kabanová* was too short. I have extended the interludes to give more time for setting the stage ... I will send everything to you at the beginning of next week so that the Prague performance can make use of it.' Steinberg incorporated the new interludes and took great care over the preparation of the opera. On 8 January 1928, he wrote to Janáček inviting him to the premiere, informing him that 'rehearsals have been in full swing for a long time' and that he hoped the composer would approve of the performance and of the decision to perform the opera without cuts. Steinberg ended by telling Janáček about his earlier experience of the work: 'I am rehearsing *Káťa Kabanova* for the second time. In Cologne I prepared the first performance in the German language and even conducted the final orchestral rehearsals.' Janáček was delighted with the performance, writing to UE on 25 January 1928: '*Káťa* in Prague under Steinberg was outstanding! His delightful idea: *to play the first two acts in one span, without a break.* Please *promote* this most urgently in my name wherever *Káťa* is given. My insertions [interludes] work marvellously.' To his wife the next day, he wrote: 'You can't imagine how splendidly they performed it ... Brno and the Prague National Theatre were not a patch on it.' *JODA, KLJ, VrbStá.*

Stejskalová, Marie (b. Jamné, 24 August 1873; d. Brno, 2 June 1968), the Janáček family housekeeper from 1894 to 1938. Stejskalová, known as Máňa, attended the Vesna School and studied as a seamstress. She started working for the Janáčeks in 1894 and hit it off with the family straight away. As Zdenka wrote: 'I soon got to like Máňa. With her intelligence she easily got the hang of everything, although she'd never been in service before. Even my husband noticed her honesty and diligence. And to Olga she became her dearest companion and confidante.' Perceptive and clear-headed, Stejskalová was fiercely loyal to Zdenka, becoming her trusted friend and moral supporter when Janáček was pursuing relationships with Gabriela Horvátová* and Kamila Stösslová*. She remained in the household until Mrs Janáčková's death in 1938. Her reminiscences were edited by Marie Trkanová and published as *Ů Janáčků: podle vyprávění Marie Stejskalová* [At the Janáčeks, as told by Marie Stejskalová], (1959). It is a valuable source of information, particularly about the composition of *Jenůfa** and *The Cunning Little Vixen**. *JODA, MLWJ, TrkSte.*

Štěpán, Václav (b. Pečky, 12 December 1889; d. Prague, 24 September 1944), Czech pianist. Štěpán was born into a successful family of brewers. He studied composition with Vítězslav Novák* (1904–9) and musicology at the Charles University with Zdeněk Nejedlý* (1909–13). A severe attack of keratitis left his right eye permanently damaged, and he was declared unfit for war service. Štěpán wore a black eye patch for the rest of his life. His enthusiastic response to Janáček's *Jenůfa* in *Hudební revue* and in letters to the composer set him against his former teacher Nejedlý. On 10 December 1921, he gave an early Prague performance of *The Diary of One Who Disappeared* with the tenor Karel Zavřel. He gave the Prague premieres of *In the Mists** and the Violin Sonata (with Karel Hoffmann) on 16 December 1922. This occasion was attended by Janáček, who also heard the Violin Sonata played by Stanislav Novák and Štěpán at the ISCM Festival in Salzburg (5 August 1923). HMUB published a new edition of *In the Mists* in 1924 and Štěpán was responsible for revising the text, apparently following Janáček's 'verbal instructions'. On 21 June 1924, he married Ilona Kurzová (daughter of the pianist Vilém Kurz), who subsequently became known as Ilona Štěpánová-Kurzová* (their son was the pianist Pavel Štěpán, 1925–98). Štěpán and Janáček were both members of the Czech contingent at the ISCM Festivals in Venice (1925) and Frankfurt (1926). Janáček's *Concertino* was given in Frankfurt on 30 June 1927, with Štěpánová-Kurzová as the soloist, joined – at Janáček's request – by two other players from the Brno premiere: the violinist František Kudláček* and clarinettist Stanislav Krtička. At the rehearsal, Janáček was infuriated by a German viola player and, according to Kudláček, 'he stamped, shouted and sang, showing the way it should be played'. Kudláček recalled that calm was restored by Štěpán, who 'took the opportunity to tell [the German musician] about Janáček and his work. He took over the rehearsal as I, only a youngster at the time, didn't dare to correct my German colleagues. After further peaceful rehearsing, Dr Štěpán showed such a detailed knowledge of Janáček's work ... that the rehearsal became a pleasure.' A friend of the French pianist Blanche Selva, Štěpán gave concerts of Czech music in France, and on 11 February 1923, he played *In the Mists* at one of Léon Vallas's *Petits concerts* in Lyon. Janáček was almost completely unknown in France at the time, and a few months later Štěpán published an article for the *Revue Française de Prague* (July–October 1923): 'Only recently, at the age of 60, Janáček had an extraordinary success with *Jenůfa*. ... When Czech opera is played abroad, it is Janáček's work that will undoubtedly surprise the most, and have the greatest success! Janáček has continued to work and his originality has grown in new works such as *The Diary of One Who Disappeared* and the opera *Káťa Kabanová*.' *ČHS, ColJan, JAWO, JYL2, TauJan.*

Štěpánová-Kurzová, Ilona (b. Lviv, 19 November 1899; d. Prague, 25 September 1975), Czech pianist. Štěpánová-Kurzová was taught by her father Vilém Kurz (1872–1945) and her mother Růžena Kurzová (1880–1938), and made her debut at the age of ten. It was after her marriage to Václav Štěpán* (21 June 1924) that she came to know Janáček, and she became closely associated with the *Concertino**. She gave the world premiere in Brno on 16 February 1926, repeating it in Prague on 20 February (both times with Janáček present), then in Vienna, Berlin, Dresden and at the ISCM Festival in Frankfurt on 30 June 1927 (Janáček was present at the rehearsal and the concert). Štěpánová-Kurzová also gave the first performance of her father's revision of Dvořák's Piano Concerto (9 December 1919), and the Czech premiere of Prokofiev's Third Piano Concerto (21 March 1926), both with Talich and the Czech Philharmonic. Her son, Pavel Štěpán, was born in 1925, and Štěpánová-Kurzová began to reduce her concert activity, retiring altogether in 1937 in order to devote herself to her family and teaching. *ČSHS, KLJ.*

Stösslová, Kamila, née Neumannová (b. Putim, 12 September 1891; d. Písek, 22 June 1935). Janáček first met Stösslová at Luhačovice in July 1917: by 8 July he had already noted down a speech melody of her saying 'please allow me'. Their first exchange was near the Slovácká búda, a wine bar, where Janáček spotted her sitting on the grass. It was a most unpromising start that Janáček recalled it in a letter eight years later: 'I addressed you: "You must be Jewish." You replied, "How do you know?"' A week later, he sent her a bunch of roses (a reminiscence, unconscious or not, of his encounter with Kamila Urválková at Luhačovice in 1903), along with a note in which he declared that 'you will not believe how glad I am to have met you'. For some of the time during this visit, Kamila was with her husband, David Stössel (they had married on 5 May 1912 and had two boys, Rudolf, b. 1913 and Otto, b. 1916), but David was often away on business, giving Janáček the opportunity to go for walks with Kamila.

This was the start of a relationship that was remarkable on several counts. First, it was largely conducted by correspondence: there are 722 surviving letters from Janáček to Kamila written between July 1917 and July 1928. Theirs, however, was a lopsided correspondence: Kamila sent many fewer letters than Janáček, and those that have survived are dry and often dull (Janáček burned a number of them on her instructions, so it is impossible to know if she was ever more effusive). Second, the whole basis of the relationship was curious, since, as Janáček's passion for Kamila increased, it became increasingly clear that most of his feelings were in pursuit of a kind of fantasy: in 1917 Kamila was a happily married young mother in her mid-twenties with no interest in pursuing a grand passion with a man in his sixties. Third, while Janáček's previous affairs had been with performers (Urválková, Horvátová), Stösslová was barely interested in music at all, let alone Janáček's music, and she upset him several times by not replying to invitations to opera premieres and concerts. Fourth, for the vast majority of its span, their relationship was entirely platonic, notwithstanding Janáček's erotic imagination. It was certainly never an affair in the conventional sense of the term. However, although she may have been negligent in answering letters and didn't necessarily care for his music, Kamila never rejected him; she made him laugh and didn't take him too seriously. Fifth, in spite of all this, Janáček's love for Kamila was not only overwhelmingly real, but it also had a profound effect on his composing during the last decade of his life. It's hard to imagine an obsessive fantasy being as spectacularly productive as this one was: the works that were wholly or partly inspired by Kamila include *The Diary of One Who Disappeared**, *Káťa Kabanová**, *The Cunning Little Vixen**, *The Makropulos Affair**, *The Glagolitic Mass**, *The Danube** and the String Quartet No. 2*. To these can be added specific aspects of other works, such as the role of Aljeja in *From the House of the Dead**. Less directly, and despite its programme depicting places in Brno, the *Sinfonietta** is another work with Kamila associations, at least in Janáček's mind: what inspired him to write the piece in the first place were the fanfares he heard at a military band concert that he had attended with Kamila in Písek. In addition to all these works, there were also the series of tiny miniatures that he wrote especially for Kamila in the *Album for Kamila Stösslová** between October 1927 and August 1928.

19. Janáček and Kamila Stösslová in 1926.

When Zdenka Janáčková first met Kamila, she described her as 'a second edition of Horvátová', but they were very different characters. As Zdenka went on to say: Kamila was 'quite nice, young, cheerful, one could have a really good chat with her, she was always laughing. She was of medium height, dark, curly-haired like a gypsy woman, with great black seemingly bulging eyes ... with heavy eyebrows, a sensuous mouth. Her voice was unpleasant, shrill, strident.' Photographs of Kamila in 1917 bear out Zdenka's description: she wasn't glamorous, but she was certainly attractive, engaging the camera with a penetrating gaze and a winning smile. In terms of sheer physical attraction, for Janáček this became ever more intense as she began to put on weight, letting him fantasise about her being pregnant with his children – a fantasy he was only too happy to share with her. There are a number of later photographs of Kamila with Janáček. One of the best was taken in Písek and shows Kamila seated, smiling at the camera from under a hat, with Janáček standing behind her (see plate 19).

In the course of their correspondence, aspects of Janáček's obsessive feelings toward Kamila run like a series of leitmotifs. Kamila loved to sunbathe and probably had naturally olive skin, prompting Janáček to use 'černoška' as a pet name. This is usually translated as 'negress' – undoubtedly what Janáček had in mind, but a problematic word in modern usage. Her 'darkness' was certainly part of her allure in Janáček's imagination. For the first ten years of their correspondence, Janáček usually addressed her as 'Dear Madam' ('Milostivá!') or 'Dear Mrs Kamila' ('Milá paní Kamilo'). After the visit to Písek in April 1927 (see below), recurring forms of address included 'My dear soul', 'My dear little soul' and 'My dear Kamila'. Other terms of endearment included 'devil', 'imp', 'gypsy', 'little dove' and 'dark dove'. By 1928, making their relationship public had become a fixation for him: on 11 January he wrote that 'the world will learn what you are to me! And it will learn we both take pleasure in it.' In his letters, Janáček began increasingly to speak of Kamila as his wife and as the future mother of his children. The idea of marriage was expressed most eloquently in his description of the *Glagolitic Mass* (on 24–25 November 1927), which he envisaged as a Nuptial Mass for the two of them ('Two people enter, they walk ceremonially ... and these two want to be married'), witnessed by the animals of the forest and set in a cathedral of tall trees. The most public declaration of his love for Kamila is the Second String Quartet, and her inspiration was made explicit in the article 'Dusk is falling' (XV/303).

Janáček and Stösslová met frequently, but not as frequently as Janáček wanted. A number of invitations to meet in Brno, Prague, Hukvaldy and Luhačovice were declined by Stösslová. As well as spending time together in Luhačovice, Janáček visited her in Přerov (80 km north-east of Brno), where the Stössels lived until 1919, then in Písek (200 km west of Brno) after 1919. One of the most significant meetings took place in April 1927, and there's an inescapable irony that it had been Zdenka Janáčková's idea to send Janáček off to Písek while the house in Brno was being decorated. She later considered this 'a mistake that I'll always regret'. An unremarkable letter to Zdenka from Janáček reported that he was being looked after by the Stössels, that the weather had improved, and that they'd been on two walks, one of them 'in the company of local artists'. Janáček then had to go to Prague and wrote to Kamila on 25 April 1927, addressing her for the first time as 'Dear soul': 'Believe me, I cannot escape from our two walks. Like a heavy, beautiful dream in which I am bewitched ... something united us in that gale-force wind and heat of the sun. Perhaps something was fated to give us unutterable pleasure? Never in my life have I experienced such an intermingling of myself with you. ... I'd have wished for that walk to be without an end. I waited without tiring for the words that you whispered: what would I have done were you my wife? Well I think of you as if you were my wife.'

This visit marked a change in their relationship, but just what had changed is a mystery. Was it simply that the words Kamila 'whispered' were the ones he wanted to hear? From this time on, Janáček's forms of address in the letters are more intimate. It was their encounter a few months later in Luhačovice that Janáček was to recall in many subsequent letters. This took place on Friday, 19 August 1927, and Janáček wrote, 'I've not experienced more beautiful moments than those this afternoon. ... I can't get to sleep until I tell you that you're more precious to me than my life. Just stay by me, my good angel.' Months later, he revealed that this was the occasion of their first kiss.

On 30 July 1928, Janáček arrived in Hukvaldy with Kamila, her husband David (who left soon afterwards) and their son Otto. Kamila had also brought the Album (see *Album for Kamila Stösslová**) from Písek. This is a touching detail. It suggests she understood her importance to him, and how much he would want to record his innermost thoughts for her eyes only; it also suggests that by this stage in their relationship, she wanted to have those thoughts recorded in her album: after all, it would have been easy for her to have left it at home in Písek. There are moments of the most intimate affection in these last entries. On 4 August he wrote: 'I wait for that moment when I will embrace you and kiss all of you, that moment when the barriers will fall ... when I will see you beautiful as God created you. Come now that moment! My darling Kamilka! I walk around you as around a sacred flame.' Eight bars of music marked 'Passionately' follow this. Kamila, however, was trying to keep things under control, as Janáček wrote: 'Really, after all, [our relationship] is so little, and yet you lecture me to make do with it!' On 5 August (starting on the verso of the leaf containing a codicil to his will) he wrote the loveliest piece in the album: 'I am waiting for you' ('Čekám tě'), a tender song without words in A major. The last piece in the book, written on 7 August, is the joyous *fortissimo* of 'The golden ring' ('Zlatý kroužek'), also in A major – the last seven bars of music Janáček ever wrote.

On 8 August, after a walk, Janáček complained about earache and pains in his throat, and this quickly developed into pneumonia. He summoned the local doctor the next morning but refused the suggestion that he should go to hospital until the following day, Friday, 10 August, when his condition had worsened. He was taken in an ambulance to the sanatorium of Dr Leopold Klein in Moravská Ostrava. Kamila travelled with Janáček, and was given a room next door to his. During the following day his condition worsened and he became delirious. Kamila sat with him and at 8.50 on the morning of Sunday, 12 August she summoned the nurse, who noted that there was 'no pulse'. Janáček was revived briefly with an injection, but between nine and ten o'clock he died, with Kamila at his bedside.

After a difficult meeting with Zdenka Janáčková, who was only summoned after Janáček had died, Kamila returned to Písek (Zdenka would never have tolerated her presence at the funeral). Kamila died young, in her early forties. Her influence on Janáček's last decade was of the most profound significance in terms of what he composed. There is perhaps no more eloquent record of this than the inscription Janáček wrote on 12 February 1928 in Kamila's copy of the vocal score of *Káťa Kabanová*, a few days after she had finally seen the opera that she had inspired:

It was in the summer sun. The slope was warm, the flowers almost fainting bowed towards the earth. At that time the first thoughts about that unhappy Káťa Kabanová – her great love – went through my head. She calls to the flowers, she calls to the birds – the flowers to bow down to her, the birds to sing her the last song of love. 'My friend', I said to Professor [Vilém] Kurz, 'I know a marvellous lady; miraculously she is in my mind all the time. My Káťa grows in her, in her, Mrs Kamila Neumannová! The work will be one of my most tender!' And it happened. I have known no greater love than with her. I dedicate the work to her. Flowers, bow down to her. Birds, never cease your song of eternal love.

JYL2, MLWJ, PřiHad, ProPam, TyrInt.

Straková, Theodora, née Švehlíková (b. Vienna, 21 December 1915; d. Nelepeč-Žernůvka, 27 February 2010), Czech musicologist. Straková studied modern languages (German and French) at the Masaryk University and attended Vladimír Helfert's lectures at the same time. She made a very significant contribution to Janáček scholarship both as a scholar and as the head from 1948 to 1978 of the Department of Music History in the Moravian Museum, including the Janáček Archive, conducting her own research and encouraging many other Janáček scholars. She organised Janáček exhibitions in 1958 and 1978, and lectured at the Masaryk University from 1952 to 1972. Thanks to Straková's efforts, the Janáček Archive moved in 1956 into the former Brno Organ School building, where it remains to this day. As a scholar, Straková ranged widely across Janáček's life and works. Her study of *Fate** (published in 1956–7) was not only an important contribution to Janáček research, but also gave impetus to the first stage production in 1958. In 1974 her *Iconographia Janáčkiána* was published by the Moravian Museum, a valuable collection of paintings, photographs, documents and facsimiles. Over several decades, Straková compiled an annotated list of Janáček's writings, and this was published for the first time in any language as section XV of *JAWO* (1997). *ČHS, EDMB, JAWO.*

String Quartet No. 1, after Tolstoy's *The Kreutzer Sonata* (VII/8). In 1908 Janáček had composed a Piano Trio* (X/22) that used Tolstoy's novella *The Kreutzer Sonata* as its programme. In October 1923, he returned to this story for a String Quartet which also reworked a few ideas from the Trio (Pavel Dědeček*, the violinist in the premiere of the Trio, told Jarmil Burghauser that 'little' of its material was reused in the quartet). On 13 October 1923, during a trip to Prague, Janáček wrote to his wife saying that the Czech Quartet* had asked him to 'write something for them'. This was a request Janáček was delighted to receive, since the Czech Quartet was a long-established ensemble with an international reputation. By 28 October 1923, Janáček had a draft ready, which he revised between 30 October and 7 November, with later revisions made in the summer of 1924. Janáček was present at some of the rehearsals for the premiere, and wrote to Kamila Stösslová on 15 October: 'I have never heard anything so magnificent as the way the Czech Quartet played my work. ... Even I am excited and it's already a year since I composed it ... They're playing it on Friday and again on Monday, and perhaps they'll go on to play it throughout the world.' The Czech Quartet gave the first performance in Prague on 17 October 1924, and repeated it in Brno on 13 December 1924. Janáček heard at least two other quartets playing the work: it was given at the Venice ISCM Festival on 4 September 1925 by the Czechoslovak Quartet (Richard Zika, Herbert Berger,

Ladislav Černý and Ladislav Zika), and was included in Janáček's Wigmore Hall concert on 6 May 1926, played by the Woodhouse Quartet. It was broadcast during Janáček's lifetime on Austrian Radio by the Gottesmann Quartet in 1926 and the Moravian Quartet in 1928 (see Radio Broadcasts during Janáček's Lifetime*). The score and parts were published by HMUB in April 1925, edited (anonymously) by Josef Suk* who, as a member of the Czech Quartet, had played second violin in the work's premiere. A critical edition appeared as SKV E/3 in 2000.

Tolstoy's story was published in 1890. Janáček owned an edition printed in St Petersburg in 1900 which is copiously annotated by the composer. In his letter to Stösslová of 15 October 1924, Janáček wrote about the Tolstoy inspiration of the work: 'I had in mind a poor woman, tormented, beaten, battered to death, as the Russian writer Tolstoy wrote in his work *The Kreutzer Sonata*.' To add to the programmatic context of the work, Janáček makes an allusion to Beethoven's 'Kreutzer' Sonata Op. 47, which had inspired Tolstoy's story in the first place: the main theme of the third movement begins with a motif modelled on the second subject from the first movement of Beethoven's sonata. Robert Smetana (in his introduction to the 1960 reissue of the score) considered that it was explicitly programmatic:

> It is essential that we should try to seek in this work not the traditional principles of chamber music ... but we should endeavour to accept it as a passionate confession of the principle and power of emotions between man and woman in life and art, to grasp the music not as decor, but as an integral part of life ... and to hear in this work about an unhappy and tormented woman the intense personal involvement of the composer.

Jaroslav Vogel wrote that 'while Tolstoy in *The Kreutzer Sonata* ascribes to music "the most immoral effects" ... Janáček in his quartet uses music to the exactly opposite effect as the voice of the conscience of humanity.' Smetana and Vogel both believed that it was a mistake to attempt an analysis of the work 'as pure absolute music', but this is a view that has been challenged (not least by Miloš Štědroň, who pointed out that with appropriate methods it is music that can be analysed in non-programmatic terms). It might be said, for example, that the first movement has a design that resembles a highly compressed sonata form. The work's opening theme (similar to the 'Volga' music for the offstage chorus in *Káťa Kabanová*) returns in the fourth movement (bar 121) and is then subjected to an ecstatic transformation (bar 167) before being inverted and turned into a 'dying fall' in the last three bars. This is not to minimise the importance of the programme in motivating Janáček to write the work in the first place, but this quartet has a highly concentrated structure that makes a forceful impact with or without its programme, analogous, as Štědroň suggests, to contemporary works by composers such as Bartók. Perhaps Otakar Šourek struck a happy medium when he wrote that its form was 'conceived with absolute freedom in pure Janáček fashion'. *JAWO, ŠouSQ1, ŠtěSQ1, TyrInt, VogJan.*

String Quartet No. 2, 'Intimate Letters' ['Listy důvěrné'] (VII/13). Janáček's second string quartet was composed between 29 January and 19 February 1928 and revised by 8 March, with further revisions in May and June after hearing the work performed privately. In a letter to Kamila Stösslová* on 29 January,

Janáček wrote that he had 'started work on a quartet. I'll call it *Love Letters.*' Back in Brno on 1 February, he told her:

Our life will be in it. ... There have already been so many of those dear adventures of ours, haven't there? They'll be little fires in my soul and they'll set it ablaze with the most beautiful melodies. Just think. The first movement I did already in Hukvaldy. The impression when I saw you for the first time! I'm now working on the second movement. I think that it will flare up in the Luhačovice heat. A special instrument will hold the whole thing together. It's called the viola d'amore – the viola of love. Oh how I'm looking forward to it! In this work I'll be always only with you!

Over the next few days, Janáček was visited in Brno by Otakar Hollmann* to play through the *Capriccio*, and on 12 February he was in Písek, the day he inscribed the copy of *Káťa Kabanová* for Kamila (see Stösslová, Kamila*), but he quickly got back to work and on 18 February he wrote: 'Today I was successful with [the third] movement "When the earth trembled". It will be the best. Ah, that was an amazingly beautiful [time], and it was true. Only the most beautiful melodies can find a place in it. I just hope I can bring off the last movement. It will be like my fear about you.' By the next day, that was finished too and he wrote that it 'doesn't sound fearful about my nice little weasel but sounds with great longing – and as if it were fulfilled'. Two months later, on 15 April, he told her that 'it's my first composition whose notes glow with all the dear things that we've experienced together. You stand behind every note, you, living, forceful, loving. The fragrance of your body, the glow of your kisses – no, really of mine. But the softness of your lips. Those notes of mine kiss all of you. They call for you passionately.' The question of the dedication was something he raised at the end of May: should it be, he wondered, to 'Mrs Kamila S', 'Mrs Kamila Stösslová' or 'Mrs Kamila Neumannová S. I'd like to have your maiden name'? Four days later, he confessed that 'I'd most like to dedicate it to Mrs Kamila Janáčková!' By this time he had heard the work played twice at his home by the Moravian Quartet* (18 and 25 May). It was during these performances that he agreed to abandon the idea of using a viola d'amore, admitting that it sounded 'terrible'. Another private performance was given on 27 June 1928.

The 'Intimate Letters' Quartet is the work most directly inspired by Stösslová, and he wanted the premiere to be given in her home town of Písek. He also wanted the Czech Quartet to play it. Neither of these things happened: the Moravian Quartet gave the premiere three weeks after Janáček's death: an invited audience heard it at the Brno Beseda on 7 September 1928, and it was repeated on 11 September as part of the Exhibition of Contemporary Culture in Brno. The Moravian Quartet did, however, play the work in Písek on 1 October 1928, and it would be good to think that Kamila heard it on that occasion. She did not live to see it published: it was not until 1938 that HMUB printed the score and parts, and, on Mrs Janáčková's insistence, it appeared with no dedication. A critical edition by Leoš Faltus and Miloš Štědroň appeared as SKV E/4 (2008), including a supplement with a complete facsimile and transcription of the autograph sketches.

The Second String Quartet is the most intense of musical love letters, a work in which Janáček lays bare his feelings for Kamila in an extended and tautly argued masterpiece. It was the music Milan Kundera chose to have at the funeral of his father Ludvík in 1971. In *Encounter* (2010), Kundera summarised Janáček's musical style in the quartets as a 'dizzyingly tight juxtaposition of highly contrasting themes that follow rapidly one upon another, without transitions and, often, resonating simultaneously; a tension between brutality and tenderness within an extremely short time span.' *JAWO, KunEnc, ŠtěSQ2, TyrInt.*

Stross [Štross], Josef (b. Načeradec, 7 January 1826; d. Brno [?], 1912), Czech oboist. Stross was an oboist who trained at the Prague Conservatory. In a letter to Otakar Nebuška at HMUB dated 22 February 1917, Janáček described Stross as 'in his time an excellent oboist from the Prague Conservatory during the directorship of [Bedřich] D. Weber' (Stross studied there from 1840 to 1846). He moved to Brno and played in the orchestra of the German Theatre. During his time at the Augustinian Monastery, Janáček recalled Stross coming to play the oboe in Masses conducted by Křížkovský. Stross made copies of Janáček's first five stage works, starting with *Šárka** in 1888. In about 1891, he made copies of most of the dances in *Rákoš Rákoczy** and *The Beginning of a Romance**. He made copies of the vocal score and full score of *Jenůfa**, and was one of the main copyists for *Fate** in 1905. He was responsible for the copies of most of Janáček's orchestral dances, the *Adagio* (VI/5), the Suite Op. 3* (VI/6), and the orchestral and piano duet versions of *Jealousy** (VI/10 and VIII/16). Stross also copied several choral works, including *Amarus**, *Our Father** and the *Folk Nocturnes**. The care with which Stross went about making copies may well have determined Janáček's working methods for the rest of his career. Stross signed and dated the authorised score of *Fate* on 6 June 1905. By then he was seventy-nine years old and this was the last work he undertook for Janáček. *JAWO, JYL1, ZahOsu.*

Suite for strings (VI/2). Janáček's first attempt at a work for orchestra was the *Sounds [Zvuky] in memory of Arnošt Förchtgott-Tovačovský (second part)* (VI/1), composed during his study year in Prague and scored originally for 'chromatic' [valve] trumpet and strings, though the trumpet was later replaced with an additional violin part. (A complete facsimile is included in *Sborník skladeb z pražských studií 1874–1875*, Brno, 2001.) Janáček either forgot, or chose to forget, about this piece when compiling the worklists for Veselý and Brod, where the Suite for strings is given as his first orchestral work. It was first performed on 2 December 1877 at a concert of the Brno Beseda conducted by Janáček. His subsequent attitude to the work was ambivalent. Writing about the Suite and the *Idyll** to Zdenka Schulzová in February 1880, he said, 'I think very little of them now', and Janáček commented in Brod's 1924 worklist that the Suite was 'not worth mentioning'. Curiously enough, he was willing for the Suite for strings to be played by the Brno NT orchestra conducted by František Neumann at a concert on 2 December 1924. Whatever reservations Janáček had about this very early work, he allowed a miniature score to be published by Pazdírek in 1926, and even an arrangement of the third movement for three violins (by Josef Gregor), published in *Hudební besídka* (October 1926) with a note that it had been 'reviewed and approved by the composer'. A critical edition of the Suite was published as SKVEJ D/1–1 (2002). *BroJan, JAWO, KnaInt, PřiSui, VohKMS.*

Suite Op. 3, for orchestra (VI/6).   Janáček never described this work as a 'suite'. Originally its only title was 'Op. 3', but in the worklists in his autobiography and in Brod he calls it 'Composition for orchestra'. When the work was first performed on 23 September 1928, at a concert in Brno with the combined orchestras of Radio Prague and Radio Brno conducted by Břetislav Bakala*, it was given as 'Suite' and the title has stuck. The work was completed by 4 January 1891, when the third movement (*Požehnaný*) was performed at the Brno Beseda, conducted by Janáček. Since the only manuscript of this movement is as part of the complete Op. 3, the whole work must have existed by then. On 16 April 1891, Janáček sent the bound volume containing all four movements to František Adolf Šubert at the Prague NT as part of the negotiations that soon led to the composition and performance of *Rákoš Rákoczy**. The invented title (perhaps Bakala's idea, since he gave the first performance) was appropriate, as Op. 3 is partly a kind of opera suite: the first two movements were both incorporated into *The Beginning of a Romance**. A full score and miniature score were published in Prague by SNKLHU in 1958, based on the material used for the 1928 Brno performance. A critical edition was published as SKVEJ D/2 (2011). Despite its ready availability in print since 1958, the Suite is only rarely played and recorded. That it deserves an occasional hearing is clear from recordings such as František Jílek's with the Brno Philharmonic (1991). It is a work of considerable charm and folkish vigour that has many stylistic similarities with the *Lachian Dances*, and rather more than that in the case of the Allegretto (*Požehnaný*), which is almost identical to No. 2 of the dances.   *BroJan, JAWO, ProSui, ŠtěSui, VesJan.*

Suk, Josef (b. Křečovice, 4 January 1874; d. Benešov, 29 May 1935), Czech composer and violinist.   Suk entered the Prague Conservatory in 1885, where his teachers included Antonín Bennewitz (violin) and Josef Bohuslav Foerster (theory). From 1888 he also studied chamber music with Hanuš Wihan. After graduating with his Piano Quartet Op. 1 in 1891, he remained an extra year to study composition with Dvořák. Under Wihan's guidance, Suk played second violin in the group that became the Czech Quartet in 1892 (by the time he retired from the quartet in 1933, the ensemble had given four thousand concerts). Suk graduated from Dvořák's class in 1892. He was Dvořák's favourite pupil, and in 1898 he married Dvořák's daughter Otilie (Otilka). Simrock had published Suk's *Serenade* Op. 6 in 1896 on Brahms's recommendation, and by the turn of the century he was regarded, with Novák, as the leading composer of the modern Czech school. In 1904–5, tragedy struck Suk with the death of Dvořák, followed just over a year later by the death of Otilie. This double loss led to the creation of the *Asrael* Symphony (1905–6).

Suk had little interest in using folk music in his compositions, though he wrote a number of pieces throughout his career using dance forms including the Dumka and Sousedská. He quickly established a bond of friendship with Janáček when they met in Prague at a dress rehearsal for *Jenůfa* in May 1916. Suk recalled that 'I went into the parterre when the lights were already dimmed. Someone tapped me on the shoulder. It was Dr [Jan] Herben and he said: "Janáček is sitting next to you." I looked at the person beside me and saw the silver head.' Suk later recalled that during the Recruits' Chorus he grabbed Janáček by the hand, saying, 'Maestro, thank the good Lord for some burning human blood again!' Janáček was touched by Suk's enthusiasm and soon had reason to be grateful to him: it was Suk who urged Max Brod to go to see *Jenůfa*, thus initiating one of Janáček's most important professional relationships.

It is likely that Suk was behind the request by the Czech Quartet made at a meeting with Janáček in October 1923 to 'write something for them'. When the String Quartet No. 1* was being prepared for publication by HMUB in 1925, Suk edited the score and parts anonymously. Later editions, from Šourek's 1945 HMUB edition onwards, placed Suk's editorial changes in square brackets or suppressed them, but Janáček raised no objections, and it is likely that some of Suk's amendments reflect discussions with Janáček at rehearsals.

When Janáček was awarded the first honorary doctorate to be conferred by the Masaryk University in Brno, Suk attended the ceremony in his capacity as rector of the Prague Conservatory, but he was asked not to read the speech he had prepared on the grounds that there was insufficient time. Undeterred, Suk did read his speech later to a small gathering of Janáček and his friends, and it was printed in *Listy hudební matice* (February 1925). It is one of the most eloquent tributes paid to Janáček by a fellow composer of comparable stature, going far beyond the usual platitudes that tend to be reeled off on such occasions and starting by recalling the impact of *Jenůfa* in 1916:

> I often recall the memorable first performance of *Jenůfa* in Prague. ... After the first act we said to ourselves 'Here is a composer who understands his people.' After the second act it was clear to us that the composer not only understood his people but loved them too, wholeheartedly and compassionately. In the third act, after the breathtaking confession of the Kostelnička, and then when two hearts unite to spend their lives together, we said, 'Lo and behold! A composer who loves all humanity and feels sympathy with it.' It is a miracle that your creative power has continued to shine so brightly since that time, and you have given us works of equal importance, yet each one is new and overwhelming. I immediately associate them with love and compassion whether they are a protest or contain the smile of kindness.

In 1933, on the recommendation of Vladimír Helfert, Suk himself became only the second musician to be awarded an honorary doctorate by the Masaryk University. *JYL1, JYL2, KvěSuk, LHM, LJLR.*

Supraphon, record company (originally Ultraphon) active from the 1930s onwards. In 1927 Gustav Sušický opened a shop in Prague to sell gramophones made by the Ultraphon company, and in 1929 he became the Czech agent for Ultraphon records. After the parent company Deutsche Ultraphon AG went bankrupt in 1931, the Prague firm retained the name for a Czech label. Ultraphon was nationalised on 1 January 1946 to become part of a new company, Gramofonové Závody, which also absorbed the recordings made by Esta (including its 1938 recording of *Youth*). A brochure published for the 1946 Prague Spring Festival lists Ultraphon and Esta recordings of Janáček: a mere eight works. The Supraphon logo appeared for the first time on a record in February 1949 (though the name had been used by Ultraphon since 1932 for its record-players). In 1950 Supraphon issued a brochure listing its Janáček recordings, which now covered three pages, with many works available for the first time, several of them recorded in 1948 by Břetislav Bakala (see Recordings before 1960*), though as yet there were no recordings of the *Glagolitic Mass* or any complete operas. In 1951 Supraphon issued its first long-playing vinyl records and the production of shellac (78 r.p.m.) discs was gradually phased out.

Jaroslav Šeda was director of Supraphon from 1953 to 1974. He was enthusiastic and knowledgeable about Janáček (the author of two books on the composer), and oversaw the company's pioneering recordings of Janáček's operas. Supraphon's *General Catalogue* for 1959 reveals a decade of expansion: it runs to 1,187 pages, and includes six pages devoted to Janáček recordings. These include important additions such as Jaroslav Vogel's *Jenůfa*, Bakala's recordings of the *Glagolitic Mass* and *Sinfonietta*, and Talich's *Taras Bulba*. In 1957 the company recorded *The Cunning Little Vixen*, conducted by Václav Neumann, for which it won a *Grand Prix du Disque* in 1959. One of its earliest stereo recordings, from March 1959, was *Káťa Kabanová* conducted by Jaroslav Krombholc.

The most important Janáček projects of the 1960s and 1970s were the operas recorded at the Prague NT (mostly under Bohumil Gregor), and the *Sinfonietta*, *Taras Bulba* and *Glagolitic Mass* conducted by Karel Ančerl. *Fate* was recorded in 1976, with the Brno NT conducted by František Jílek. In the 1980s Supraphon released a series of Janáček recordings conducted by Charles Mackerras, starting with the *Glagolitic Mass* and *Amarus*. Once the CD was established in the mid-1980s, Supraphon continued to add Janáček recordings, as well as reissuing older material in the new format. There were new recordings of *Jenůfa* and *The Excursions of Mr Brouček* conducted by Jílek; Václav Neumann conducted *The Cunning Little Vixen* (his second recording) and *From the House of the Dead*; and two operas were conducted by Mackerras: his second recording of *Káťa Kabanová* and the only modern recording of *Šárka*. *Janáček Unknown*, a series of four discs, added some very rare repertoire to the catalogue, including fragments of unfinished operas, music from the original versions of *Taras Bulba* and *The Excursion of Mr Brouček to the Moon*, the ballet *Rákoš Rákoczy*, the String Quartet No. 2 with viola d'amore, early Latin motets, and Janáček's piano duet version of *Jealousy*. In 2004 Supraphon issued a two-disc set of Charles Mackerras's Janáček recordings with the Czech Philharmonic. Since then, there have been new Janáček recordings by younger conductors including Jakub Hrůša and Thomas Netopil, and instrumentalists like the Pavel Haas Quartet. Most of Supraphon's back catalogue of Janáček (including discs that were never issued on CD) can be downloaded from its website (www.supraphonline.cz). For the music and book publisher Editio Supraphon, see Hudební matice and its successors*. *SupGen, SupHis, SupJan.*

Sušil, František (b. Rousínov, near Vyškov, 14 June 1804; d. Bystřice pod Hostýnem, 31 May 1868), Czech priest, poet and folklorist. Sušil studied for the priesthood in Brno and was ordained in 1827. He became a professor at the Theological Institute in Brno in 1837. He was a leading figure in the Czech national revival in Moravia with a particular interest in Saints Cyril and Methodius, the ninth-century 'apostles of Moravia' credited with devising the Glagolitic alphabet, and in 1863 he helped arrange the celebrations for the thousandth anniversary of the saints' arrival in Moravia. Sušil began collecting folksongs while still a student, and his first collection was published in 1835. His most substantial achievement was *Moravian Folk Songs*, published complete in 1860. This huge collection included words and tunes for more than 2,300 songs categorised into types (comic songs, wedding songs, ballads and so on) in a similar way to the classification later used by Bartoš and Janáček in *Moravian Songs Newly Collected* (XIII/3). Following the example of Pavel Křížkovský, Janáček used folk poems in Sušil's collection for several choruses. *Take Your Rest* (IV/24) is a setting of one of Sušil's original poems, previously set by Křížkovský for Sušil's own funeral. *ČSHS, JAWO.*

Svatopluk Society Janáček's first conducting experience outside the Augustinian Monastery came in 1873 when he was appointed as an eighteen-year-old to conduct the male-voice choir of the Svatopluk Society, a group of artisans and craftsmen named after Svatopluk I, the ruler of the Great Moravian Empire in the late ninth century. At the Monastery, Janáček was used to working with a small group of boys and young men who were experienced musicians, good sight-readers and quick learners. Svatopluk was a very different proposition: a large group of enthusiastic amateurs whose enthusiasm usually outstripped their musical skills. Janáček and his singers clearly relished the challenge, and the choir was soon being described as one of the best in Brno. Janáček conducted the choir between March 1873 and the start of the academic year 1874–5 (when Janáček studied at the Prague Organ School), and again in 1875–6 after his return to Brno. The importance of this appointment was that Janáček began his composing career by providing new music for the Svatopluk choir to sing. The choruses Svatopluk is known to have performed during these years include *Ploughing* (IV/1), *War Song* (IV/3), *The Fickleness of Love* (IV/4), *Alone Without Comfort* (IV/7) and *True Love* (IV/8). At least two other choruses were written for the choir, but there is no evidence of public performances of *I Wonder at My Beloved* (IV/5) and *The Drowned Wreath* (IV/6). Of all these early choruses, *Ploughing* seems to have been the biggest success. Helfert says it was encored at the first performance on 27 April 1873, and it was included in several later concerts. Janáček was appointed choirmaster of the Brno Beseda in 1876, and his final appearance with Svatopluk that year was at a gala in honour of Dr Josef Illner (1839–94), the chairman of Svatopluk, who had first recognised Janáček's talent. *HelJan, JAWO, JYL1.*

Tagore, Rabindranath (b. Kolkata [Calcutta], India, 7 May 1861; d. Kolkata, 7 August 1941), Bengali writer. Tagore, sometimes known as the 'Bard of Bengal', was already an international celebrity when Janáček heard him give a lecture in Prague in June 1921. Tagore's own English translation of *Gitanjali* was published in 1912 with an introduction by W. B. Yeats, and in 1913 he became the first non-European to win the Nobel Prize for Literature. Tagore's *The Gardener* was published in English in 1913, and a Czech translation by František Balej appeared in 1917. Janáček wrote his impressions of Tagore in an article for *Lidové noviny* (22 June 1921, XV/229):

> He came in quietly. It seemed to me as if a white, sacred flame suddenly burned above the thousands and thousands of those present. He said: 'I'm talking to you here so that you know how to read my poems.' He didn't really talk: it sounded more like a nightingale's song, smooth, shorn of all the harshness of consonants. ... He spoke to us in his own language. Incomprehensible to us, and only from the tones of his voice did we recognise the bitter pain of his soul.

The Gardener inspired one of Janáček's finest choruses, *The Wandering Madman** (1922), as well as Zemlinsky's *Lyric Symphony* (1922–3), which set poems from the same collection. A fragment from *The Wandering Madman* appears on Janáček's tombstone (see Brno Central Cemetery* and The Wandering Madman*). *JYL2.*

Talich, Václav (b. Kroměříž, 28 May 1883; d. Beroun, 16 March 1961), Czech conductor. Talich studied the violin with Otakar Ševčík at the Prague Conservatory (1897–1903), before spending the 1903–4 season as leader of the Berlin Philharmonic Orchestra, where he fell under Arthur Nikisch's spell, going on to study with him in Leipzig. In 1908 he was appointed conductor of the Slovene Philharmonic in Ljubljana, before going on to conduct opera in Plzeň. In 1915 he returned to string playing, becoming a regular guest violist with the Czech Quartet. Talich was appointed principal conductor of the Czech Philharmonic in September 1919, and Janáček first appeared on his programmes in 1924, when Talich conducted *Taras Bulba* on 9 November, and again on 8 December, along with *The Fiddler's Child**, at the composer's seventieth birthday gala concert (see Masaryk, Tomáš Garrigue*). Talich's most important Janáček premiere was on 26 June 1926, when he conducted the *Sinfonietta** for the first and only time in his career.

Talich became chief conductor at the Prague NT in 1935, after the death of Ostrčil. He conducted new productions of *The Cunning Little Vixen** (21 May 1937) and *Káťa Kabanová** (16 September 1938 and 24 April 1947), both heavily reorchestrated (see Reorchestration and Retouching*), and *Jenůfa* (27 February 1941 and 15 March 1946). None of Talich's performances of Janáček operas used the composer's original orchestrations. This is probably the origin of what is sometimes called the 'Prague style' of playing the operas – the orchestral sound is smoother and more blended (thanks to retouchings), while the 'Brno style' used the authentic orchestrations (as had Ostrčil's Prague NT performances). As a result, Talich created a performing tradition that was obstinately enduring, particularly for *Káťa Kabanová*: the 1947 production conducted by Talich and Rudolf Vašata clocked up thirty-two performances by 1950, and Talich's version was used for subsequent Prague productions (until Bohumil Gregor restored Janáček's own orchestration in 1974) and for the Supraphon recording made in 1959, conducted by Jaroslav Krombholc.

It is easy to criticise Talich for his interventionist approach to Janáček's orchestration, but his motives were honourable. *Národní listy* (19 February 1941) published an article by Talich entitled 'Our duty to fight for Janáček', in which he wrote:

I wish to see Janáček established at the National Theatre in the way such a genius deserves, whether we compare him with our dramatic composers of the past or with those of the future; and as far as the future is concerned, I consider it my most important duty to popularise Janáček because he is the gateway to contemporary dramatic music.

Talich made only two Janáček recordings: his own suite from *The Cunning Little Vixen** (April 1954) and *Taras Bulba** (September 1954), both with the Czech Philharmonic. As a teacher, he influenced the next generation of conductors, and two of his pupils became outstanding Janáček interpreters: Karel Ančerl* and Charles Mackerras*. *ČHS, EckJan, JAWO, KunTal, ŠouTal.*

Taras Bulba, rhapsody for orchestra (VI/15). Janáček completed an early version of *Taras Bulba* by 2 July 1915, and the final version, much revised, was dated 29 March 1918. Janáček's interest in Nikolai Gogol's *Taras Bulba* went back a number of years. His annotated copy has notes from March 1905, when the novel was being read by the Brno Russian Circle (though Gogol was Ukrainian, he wrote *Taras Bulba* in Russian). Janáček began work on his 'Slavonic rhapsody' in 1915. The day he finished the first version (2 July), he wrote to Otakar Ostrčil asking him to try out this new work: 'I have written a longish orchestral piece. I would ask if you might play it through for me, without any thought of a public performance, so that I might be sure of where and how to improve it.' This never took place, and nothing was done on *Taras Bulba* for almost three years. During this time, Janáček worked on other projects: *The Excursions of Mr Brouček*, the Violin Sonata and preparations for the Prague premiere of *Jenůfa*. There was also a compelling political reason to set aside *Taras Bulba*: officially, Russia was the enemy, and on 27 February 1915 the Brno Russian Circle, of which Janáček was president, was dissolved by the Moravian authorities. On 25 March 1918, Janáček wrote to Gabriela Horvátová that he had resumed work on *Taras Bulba*: 'Worldwide affairs have developed so terribly that the only thing left is to call out into the void of the future. I have taken up my *musical testament*, my Slavonic rhapsody for orchestra.' The result was a completely revised piece: *Taras Bulba* as we know it today. Large portions of the first (1915) version were published as supplements in SKV D/7, including the whole of the first part. Though it uses some familiar motifs, it's quite different (there is a recording by the Brno Philharmonic under Leoš Svárovský on the Supraphon CD *Janáček Unknown I*).

The first performance did not take place until 1921, but in August that year, within a few days of each other, two conductors expressed an interest in the work. On 1 August 1921, Václav Talich* wrote to say that he was looking to perform it in the next season with the Czech Philharmonic. Janáček replied (2 August) expressing his pleasure at Talich's interest and saying that the orchestral parts needed only a few corrections. By coincidence, on 3 August 1921, František Neumann* wrote to Janáček also asking to give the first performance of the work. Although he had already offered *Taras Bulba* to Talich, Janáček decided to give the premiere to Neumann. Since Neumann planned to give the work in Brno, this would allow Janáček to make corrections at rehearsals. The first performance took place on 9 October 1921, with the Brno NT orchestra under Neumann. Janáček wrote to Neumann the next day, thanking him for performing a work which would otherwise have 'lain in a chest – and I now think that would have been a pity'. On 12 October, Janáček wrote: 'Your conducting encapsulated my conception of the work and the performance was virtuosic.' Neumann conducted it again in Brno on 21 January 1924, at a concert to mark Janáček's seventieth birthday. Talich and the Czech Philharmonic gave the Prague premiere on 9 November 1924, and performed it again on 8 December at the gala concert attended by Janáček and President Masaryk. On 21 September 1922, Janáček had offered *Taras Bulba* to UE, but Hertzka had turned it down. The first published edition of *Taras Bulba* was an arrangement for piano four-hands by Břetislav Bakala issued by HMUB in 1925. The orchestral score followed in 1927. A second edition, scrupulously prepared by Otakar Šourek, was published in 1947. In 1980 *Taras Bulba* appeared as SKV D/7.

Leoš Janáček:

Našemu vojsku.

Byl jsem přesvědčen již dávno, že teplou melodií Smetanovou, mdlou něžností tónů Fibichových, svěžestí rytmů Dvořákových, ba ani věhlasem našich učenců, ani světlou památkou Komenského, ani mučednictvím Husovým — že tím vším svobody národa se nedosáhne.

Kulturní zbraně jsou zářivé, ale tupé.

V „Pohádce" pro cello a klavír kmital mi na mysli svit ostré ocele, v „Sonátě" pro hlousle a klavír z r. 1914 slyšel jsem v podrážděné mysli již — již její třeskot.

V „Rhapsodii" z r. 1915 plesal jsem vidině *našich* pluků vstříc.

Roku 1918 rozhlaholil se její hymnický motiv:

a když branné ochraně našeho národa tuto svou práci připisuji, je to z důvodu, že nechráníte nám jen naše pozemské statky, ale i celý náš myšlenkový svět.

Brno, 15. září 1923.

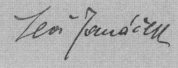

61

20. Janáček's article in *Československé armádě: Pozdravy a vzkazy* (1923) dedicating *Taras Bulba* 'To our troops'.

Once the score was in print, *Taras Bulba* was soon performed more widely. The first overseas performance was given in London by Henry Wood* and the New Queen's Hall Orchestra on 16 October 1928; the German premiere followed a few days later on 25 October 1928, with the Leipzig Gewandhaus

Orchestra conducted by Bruno Walter (who also gave the American premiere on 19 October 1933 with the New York Philharmonic-Symphony Orchestra).

The manuscript sources and first edition have no dedication, but in Janáček's article 'Našemu vojsku' (To our troops) published in 1923 (XV/247), he dedicated *Taras Bulba* 'to the armed forces of our nation, because they defend not only our earthly possessions but also our entire intellectual world'. Jaroslav Vogel wrote that *Taras Bulba* was 'the work in which Janáček expressed himself most significantly and unequivocally on the gigantic struggle of the First World War which was also the struggle for his nation'. Janáček sent some notes on the work for Rosa Newmarch on 8 September 1926: 'The idea: Prophecy and presentiment of the victory of the Slavs. Taras Bulba is the [Cossack] champion of the fight against their enemies. [1. The Death of Andriy]: His son dies – a traitor killed by his own father. [2. The Death of Ostap]: His second son dies, executed by the Polish. [3. The Prophecy and Death of Taras Bulba]: Taras Bulba, burned at the stake by the Polish. Before his death, he prophesies the victory of Christ and his nation.' As Vogel wrote, 'more deeply felt and more authentically national music than this can scarcely be imagined. Janáček maintains the feeling of constant suspense throughout its 25 minutes' duration and the sensation of liberation comes only at the very end.' *JAWO, PřiTar, ŠouTar, VogJan, ZahTar.*

Tauber, Stanislav (b. Blatec, near Olomouc, 28 April 1878; d. Prague, 3 March 1959), Czech singer. As a boy, Tauber sang as a chorister at Olomouc Cathedral under Josef Nešvera, and then attended the Teachers' Institute at Příbor. In 1906 he joined Ferdinand Vach's PSMU, as a first tenor and soloist. He remained closely involved with the PSMU for the rest of his life, and was its president from 1937 to 1946. He had a successful career as a concert singer and became closely associated with Janáček's music. In Brno, he sang the tenor solo in *Amarus** in 1912 (conducted by Vach), as well as on several later occasions, including Brno performances in 1922 and 1924 that were both attended by Janáček. Tauber sang the solo tenor part in *The Eternal Gospel** at Brno in 1919 (attended by Janáček) and at Janáček's seventieth birthday concert with the Czech Philharmonic on 8 December 1924. He also sang tenor solos in the Brno and Prague premieres of the *Glagolitic Mass**. He was one of the first singers to take up *The Diary of One Who Disappeared**, which he broadcast on 4 December 1926 with Břetislav Bakala* at the piano. Tauber wrote about his association with Janáček in his memoirs, *Můj hudební svět* [My musical world] (1949). *ČSHS, JAWO, KLJ, TauMůj.*

Tauský, Vilém (b. Přerov, 20 July 1910; d. London, 16 March 2004), Czech conductor. Tauský became a student in Janáček's composition class in 1927. In his autobiography, he recalled Janáček's 'blazing blue eyes which lent force to all he said'. His speech was 'most alarming, for his words came out in a staccato stream, like a cross between a typewriter and a machine gun'. As for Janáček's teaching, Tauský noted that 'he believed that a sound traditional base must precede progressive ideas in the training of musicians. "First you must know the rules," he used to say, "then sometimes you can afford to discard them."' Tauský's conducting teacher was Zdeněk Chalabala, who found him a post as a repetiteur at the Brno NT. One of Tauský's first tasks was to be a vocal coach for the premiere of *From the House of the Dead** in 1930. From 1932 Tauský worked as a staff conductor under Milan Sachs, and for the first complete

Brno production of *The Excursions of Mr Brouček** in 1937, he revised Janáček's orchestration under Sachs's supervision. These retouchings were only removed when Jiří Zahrádka made a new edition of the opera in 2003. As a Jew, Tauský was forced to flee the Nazis. He volunteered with the Free Czech Army in Paris before settling in England in 1940. He conducted the British premiere of *The Beginning of a Romance* at the Guildhall School of Music (3 December 1974). For the BBC, he conducted broadcasts of *Jenůfa* (25 November 1954) and *Fate* (UK premiere, 22 January 1972). Tauský and his wife Margaret edited *Leoš Janáček: Leaves from his Life* (1982), a collection of Janáček's feuilletons from *Lidové noviny*. PavIns, TauJan, TauTel.

Těsnohlídek, Rudolf (b. Čáslav, 7 June 1882; d. Brno, 12 January 1928), Czech writer. Těsnohlídek attended primary school in Čáslav, where one of his classmates was Jiří Mahen. Těsnohlídek enrolled at the Charles University in Prague to study philosophy and philology, but did not complete the course. He married Jindra (Kaja) Kopecká in May 1905. A few weeks later, when they were on holiday in Norway, she shot herself through the heart in front of Těsnohlídek, who was arrested and accused of her murder (and later cleared). In October 1908, Těsnohlídek joined the staff at *Lidové noviny*, remaining there for the rest of his life. He married Anna Navrátilová in November 1909, but they divorced in 1917. *Lidové noviny* published most of Těsnohlídek's poetry and prose, much of it marked by extreme pessimism. The story for which he is best known is entirely different. His serialised novel *Liška Bystrouška* (*Vixen Bystrouška*), written to accompany a series of drawings by Stanislav Lolek, appeared in *Lidové noviny* between 7 April and 23 June 1920, and Janáček kept the cuttings of each episode. Published in book form in 1921, it has remained popular ever since. Its witty combination of fairy tale and satire charmed Janáček, and he announced his intention to use the story for his next opera in an interview with Adolf Veselý in *Lidové noviny* on 15 May 1921. Těsnohlídek at first thought the report was a joke, and he was anxious about meeting Janáček a year later (May 1922) to discuss the work. His recollection of this occasion appeared in *Lidové noviny* on 3 July 1924:

> Leoš Janáček was waiting for me in the little garden of the Conservatory. He sat among the bushes, with thousands of tiny blossoms about his head; that head of his was just as white, and seemed to be the largest of the flowers. He smiled; and I knew at once that this was the smile which life awards us like a gold medal for bravery in the face of the enemy. For bravery in sorrow, humiliation and anger. At that moment I believed that Vixen Bystrouška was sitting, tamed and quite overcome by the kindliness of the man in the tiny garden, and that unseen she would draw near to sit at our feet and listen to our conspiracy. Janáček made a few remarks about the story and then began talking about his forests in Valachia, which I don't know, about his studies of bird song, and I became aware that he had succeeded in knowing the happiness of that smile.

Janáček's libretto was based closely on Těsnohlídek until the shooting of the Vixen in Act III, which wasn't in the original story (see *The Cunning Little Vixen**). At Janáček's request, Těsnohlídek wrote the words for the song 'Verunko!' in Act II. Otherwise, Janáček got on with the work on his own. Těsnohlídek married Olga Vasická in April 1924. His book *Demänová* (Prague,

1926) is an illustrated guide to the Demänovská caves, which he visited often. Těsnohlídek committed suicide on 12 January 1928 at the offices of *Lidové noviny*, leaving a note on his desk: 'Forgive me for doing this here.' When his wife heard the news, she gassed herself and their joint funeral was held on 16 January 1928. *EDMB, JanLid, JODA.*

Timpani 'That's why I never forget to write a solo for the timpani!' This is how Janáček ended his 1911 feuilleton 'Without Drums' (XV/199), a childhood reminiscence of an Easter Sunday Mass in Hukvaldy: 'The Mass was not triumphant. It was without drums', he explained. Janáček was as good as his word: one of the most remarkable features of his orchestration, especially from *Jenůfa* onwards, is his timpani writing. At the end of Act II of *Jenůfa** the timpani become the instrumental embodiment of the Kostelnička's closing line: 'the icy voice of death, forcing its way in'. Timpani thunder out a five-note rhythm derived from the Kostelnička's last phrase. Initially the rhythm is echoed in the rest of the orchestra before the timpani seems to engulf them in the final bars.

There are notable examples in many later works. At the start of *Káťa Kabanová**, Janáček wrote a prominent solo for timpani (going a tone higher than the upper limit recommended in Rimsky-Korsakov's orchestration treatise): the eight-note motif first heard in bars 5–6 of the Prelude – the leading motif of the whole opera – comprises four Fs and four B flats. Janáček loved the sound of high timpani parts: *Taras Bulba* has many top A flats, and it also requires frequent retuning of the other drums. This indicates that Janáček must have had access to mechanically tuned timpani (the forerunner of modern pedal timpani). According to Wingfield, the Brno NT orchestra had a set of machine timpani, and much of Janáček's later writing would have been unplayable without them. Even with modern pedal timpani, Janáček's parts are often very difficult.

The cut 'Raspet' ('He was crucified') section of the 'Věruju' in the *Glagolitic Mass** is an example of Janáček's writing for multiple timpani: three players, each with their own set of drums, the first part going as high as a B natural. For this, the Brno Beseda had to borrow timpani not only from the orchestra of the Brno NT but also from the Conservatory and the Orchestral Association (Janáček cut this passage before the work's second performance in Prague). In the 'Slava' of the *Glagolitic Mass* there is a timpani solo at bar 83 which is doubled in the definitive version by cellos and basses, but in the earlier (September 1927) version this is for timpani alone – requiring multiple retuning while the drums play what is essentially an unaccompanied melodic line. The final 'Intrada' of the Mass is a rather different case, in which the timpani hammer out a long–short–short rhythm that seems straightforward enough. But there are places where quick retunings present a challenge for players, and, remarkably, what the timpani play throughout the movement is entirely independent of anything else in the orchestra, with no doubling of either the rhythm or the pitch. Independent timpani lines of this kind are a recurrent feature of later operas, for instance at the end of Act I and Act III in *Vixen*, the threatening close of Act II in *Makropulos* and in many places in *From the House of the Dead**.

Perhaps Janáček's most famous timpani writing comes in the first and last movements of the *Sinfonietta**. This is a rare instance when Janáček indicated precisely the sound he wanted from the instrument, adding in his own hand on Sedláček's copy: 'wooden sticks' ('dřevěné paličky'). For some reason this marking was not printed in any early editions, but it has appeared in reprints since Füssl's corrected 1978 edition, in Barvík and Zimmermann's edition, and in the 2017 edition by Zahrádka. The presence of this marking perhaps hints at how Janáček may have envisaged the sound of timpani at similar points in other works. Charles Mackerras certainly believed so and often asked players to use wooden sticks for certain passages in *Taras Bulba**, the *Glagolitic Mass** and the late operas. Not only did Janáček 'never forget to write a solo' for timpani, but when he did so, the results were often startlingly exiting. *WinGla, ZahGla*.

Tonality   See Keys, Janáček's choice of

Tyrrell, John (b. Salisbury, Southern Rhodesia [now Harare, Zimbabwe], 17 August 1942; d. Beeston, Nottingham, 4 October 2018), British musicologist.   Tyrrell studied in Cape Town and Oxford, where his doctoral dissertation (1969) was on Janáček's stylistic development as an opera composer. His books on Janáček and Czech music established him as the pre-eminent English-language Janáček scholar. These include *Káťa Kabanová* (1982), *Czech Opera* (1988), *Janáček's Operas: a Documentary Account* (1992), *Intimate Letters: Leoš Janáček to Kamila Stösslová* (1994), *Janáček's Works: a Catalogue of the Music and Writings of Leoš Janáček* (with Simeone and Němcová, 1997), *My Life with Janáček: the Memoirs of Zdenka Janáčková* (1998) and *Janáček: Years of a Life* (Vol. 1: 2006; Vol. 2: 2007). In collaboration with Mackerras, Tyrrell edited the 1908 version of *Jenůfa** (1996) and *From the House of the Dead** (provisional version, 1990; final version, 2018). In recognition of his work on Janáček, Tyrrell was awarded honorary doctorates by the Masaryk University of Brno (2002) and JAMU (2012).

Ukolébavka   See *Lullaby* (V/14)

Unfinished works   See *The Danube* (IX/7), Mass in E flat (IX/5), *Schluck und Jau* (IX/11), Violin Concerto (IX/10)

Universal Edition (UE), music publisher.   UE was founded in Vienna on 1 June 1901. Its initial aims were described in the *Neue Wiener Tagblatt* on 8 August 1901: 'As well as publishing the classics and significant instructive works, it will also publish compositions by important modern masters.' In 1907 Emil Hertzka* was appointed managing director, with far-reaching consequences: along with senior editor Josef V. von Wöss, Hertzka changed the firm's publishing policy to concentrate on new music and living composers. Janáček's relationship with UE started in 1916, thanks to Max Brod*, who told Hertzka about the success of *Jenůfa** in Prague. Hertzka wrote to Janáček on 22 November 1916: 'You perhaps know that Universal Edition is not only a music publisher but also the largest agent in Germany and Austria-Hungary for musical stage works. I would like to ask you today if you would be prepared to let us handle the promotion of your work [*Jenůfa*] in German theatres.' Janáček signed a contract with UE by 4 December 1916 and began negotiations for a new vocal score with German and Czech text of *Jenůfa* prepared by Wöss. A full score was issued in August 1918. In January 1918, UE published a *Fantasie über Motive der Oper 'Jenůfa'* for solo piano, arranged by Bohumír Morlák (a pseudonym described by UE to Janáček as 'a talented Viennese musician who does not wish to be named'), and in 1927 the firm published a *Fantasie aus der Oper Jenůfa* arranged by Emil Bauer for salon orchestra as part of its *Vindobona Collection*.

UE published all Janáček's later operas: *The Excursions of Mr Brouček** (vocal score in September 1919), *Káťa Kabanová** (vocal score in February 1922; full score in August–September 1922), *The Cunning Little Vixen** (vocal score in July 1924; revised edition in November 1925), *The Makropulos Affair** (vocal score in December 1926) and *From the House of the Dead** (vocal score in August 1930; full score in September 1930). Janáček's non-operatic works contracted to UE during Janáček's lifetime included the *Glagolitic Mass** (vocal score in April 1928; full score in March 1929), *Nursery Rhymes** (vocal score in September 1928, full score in April 1929) and the *Sinfonietta** (miniature score and full score in January 1927). In 1925 the first German edition of Max Brod's *Leoš Janáček: Leben und Werk* was published by UE's subsidiary company, Wiener Philharmonischer Verlag. For more recent editions, see Editions, Critical and Scholarly* *FELJ, HeiErs, HeiMen, HilBri, JAWO, SimTal.*

Urválková, Kamila, née Schillerová, then Houdková after her foster father (b. Dobřichovice, near Prague [?], 1875; d. Poděbrady [?], 1956).   When Janáček met Kamila Urválková at Luhačovice in the summer of 1903, she was married to the head forester in Zahájí, near Dolní Kralovice. In her late twenties, strikingly beautiful, and accompanied by her five-year-old son, Urválková made a deep impression on Janáček. In her memoirs, Zdenka Janáčková recalled a letter from Luhačovice in which he likened Kamila to their daughter Olga, who had died a few months earlier. He wrote that he had 'found an angel, just like the one we had buried'. Zdenka's memoirs continue:

> I thought that the 'angel' was a young girl and wrote back accordingly. But when he returned after the holidays and began telling me about this angel, it turned out that it was the young and beautiful Mrs Kamila Urválková, the wife of a forest ranger from Dolní Kralovice. Apparently she couldn't bear to see him so sad and lonely in Luhačovice. She sent a bunch of red roses to his table. They then got acquainted.

Urválková told Janáček the story of how she fell in love with Ludvík Vítězslav Čelanský*. She regarded his opera *Kamilla* (1897, on his own libretto) as an act of vengeance after their affair ended. Though there is no documentary evidence for their relationship, the description of the characters in Čelanský's libretto leaves little doubt that they were based on Urválková and Čelanský. Janáček was captivated by her story and the young woman telling it, whose voice he likened to a viola d'amore, and he decided to compose an opera in which Kamila would be portrayed more sympathetically (see *Fate**). The evidence suggests that Janáček and Urválková fell in love, and he certainly fell for her. He showed Zdenka Kamila's letters to prove that there was nothing going on between them, but Zdenka discovered another bundle of letters that told a different story. After a furious confrontation, he agreed to end the affair. According to Zdenka's memoirs, this was in December 1903, but Janáček continued to correspond with Kamila. He seems to have had a pet-name for her, since her very few surviving letters to him are signed 'Taťana' or just 'T'.

Soon after the premiere of *Jenůfa* in January 1904, Kamila's husband wrote to Janáček asking him to stop corresponding with his wife, but this did not mark the end of their relationship: Jarmila Procházková has discovered that

21. Kamila Urválková. Photograph by Langhans, signed by Urválková.

Janáček and Urválková stayed in Luhačovice at the same time as each other during the years 1905–9, and on two occasions they stayed in the same hotel. Zdenka had her suspicions too. On 19 August 1907, she wrote to Janáček asking, 'Is she there??', to which he sent a surly reply admitting that she was, 'if that's such an important thing for you to know'. Janáček's passion eventually cooled, and in September 1909 he wrote to Zdenka from Luhačovice that 'Mrs Camilla is somewhat shrivelled.' There is no evidence of any later contact. By 1936–7 (when she corresponded with Vladimír Helfert) Urváklová was widowed and living in Poděbrady. *JODA, JYL1, ProLuh, ZahOsu.*

V mlhách See *In the Mists* (VIII/22)

Vach, Ferdinand (b. Jažlovice, 25 February 1860; d. Brno, 16 February 1939), Czech choirmaster. Vach founded the Moravian Teachers' Choral Society (PSMU) in 1903 and the Vach Choir of Moravian Women Teachers (VSMU) in 1912. From 1886 to 1905 he was director of the Moravan Music School in Kroměříž, and he also taught at the Brno Organ School (1907–9, 1918–19). From 1905 to 1925 he taught music history at the Teachers' Institute in Brno. Vach was an energetic proponent of Janáček's music. On 29 November 1905, with the PSMU, he conducted the premieres of two of the *Four Moravian male-voice choruses* (IV/28). Vach went on to conduct the first performances of Janáček's most demanding choruses for male voices, including *Maryčka Magdónova**, *The Czech Legion**, *The Wandering Madman** and *Our Flag**. Though he didn't give the premiere of *Halfar the Schoolmaster*, he gave many performances of it from 1918 onwards. Vach and the PSMU were tireless advocates of Janáček's choruses on tours abroad, performing his music from 1906 onwards in Germany, Austria, France, the United Kingdom and elsewhere, long before his other music was familiar in these countries. Vach conducted the first complete performance of *Amarus** (Brno, 25 February 1912) and the Brno premiere of *The Eternal Gospel** (18 February 1919). *ČHS, DesLet, JAWO, StoPSM.*

Valachian Dances See *Lachian Dances* (VI/17)

Valašské tance See *Lachian Dances* (VI/17)

Váša, Pavel (b. Čáslav, 23 January 1874; d. Brno, 20 March 1954), Czech philologist. In 1901 Váša was appointed to the Brno Technical College, where he taught until 1925. From 1917 until 1937 he was a Czech-language consultant at *Lidové noviny*, and he was also an authority on folksong. Váša's contribution to Janáček's *Complete Harmony Manual* (XV/202) is acknowledged with a special page: 'Sincere thanks for his painstaking corrections to the text to Mr Pavel Váša, writer and teacher at Czech Technical College in Brno'. In 1918 Janáček asked Váša to proofread the Czech text of the UE vocal and full scores of *Jenůfa*. Váša's contributions to *Lidové noviny* included several on Janáček, among them an article on 'Janáček's study of living speech' (4 July 1914). In an obituary (13 August 1928, afternoon edition), Váša wrote about speech melody in Janáček's operas: 'It would be naïve to think that the great composer created his operas out of notated speech melodies, but they demonstrate how, for him, observing the world meant listening to it, and how speech and music, words and tones, formed an indivisible whole.' Janáček and Váša collaborated on the *Moravian Love Songs* published after Janáček's death (see Folksong Editions*). On 11 May 1928, Váša wrote requesting an article for the special issue of *Lidové noviny* published to celebrate the Exposition of Contemporary Culture. Janáček sent 'My Lachia' (XV/310), his last feuilleton for the paper, published on 27 May 1928. *EDMB, JanLid, KLJ, LN.*

Vašek, Adolf Emil (b. Hrabyně u Opavy, 14 June 1881; d. Brno, 6 June 1948), Czech writer. The author of the first important book on Janáček to appear after his death, Vašek studied at the Charles University in Prague, and taught from 1919 until 1939 at the Gymnasium in Brno, where he lived on Antonínská, round the corner from the Janáčeks' home. His book *Po stopách dra Leoše Janáčka* (1930) was the first to include quotations from Janáček's letters to Stösslová, though he does not mention her by name in the main text. Vašek also spoke to Janáček's brother Josef, and provided a detailed account of the days before the composer's death based on reminiscences by 'local people'. *EDMB, JYL2, VašJan.*

Vávra, Josef (b. Proseč, near Litomyšl, 19 September 1856; d. Ivančice, 8 April 1936), Czech schoolteacher. Vávra was a schoolteacher in Ivančice, a small town south-west of Brno. He wrote to Janáček on 19 January 1897: 'As you have heard from the teacher [Hynek] Bím, I intend shortly to publish a collection of music specially written for harmonium.' He asked Janáček for 'Slavonic melodies harmonised in a simple style accessible to less experienced players'. Janáček did nothing about this immediately, and later in 1897 the first volume of *Slovanské melodie* duly appeared, edited by Emil Kolář* and published by Vávra. The five pieces Janáček eventually sent Vávra (probably in October 1900) were not arrangements of folk tunes, but original works, with the collective title *On the Overgrown Path*. They appeared, as harmonium pieces, in Vol. 5 (1901) and Vol. 6 (1902) of the *Slovanské melodie*, pre-dating the complete edition of Series I of *On the Overgrown Path* by a decade. *FELJ, JAWO, JYL1.*

Věc Makropulos   See *The Makropulos Affair* (I/10)

Věčné evangelium   See *The Eternal Gospel* (III/8)

Veselá, Marie (b. Vienna, 22 November 1892; d. Prague, 20 February 1969), Austrian-born soprano. Veselá trained in Vienna before joining the German Opera in Brno (1914–18). She was a member of the Brno NT (1919–22) and Prague NT (1922–58). She sang the Kostelnička in the 1919 Brno revival of *Jenůfa*, and the title role in the world premiere of *Káťa Kabanová* on 23 November 1921, both conducted by František Neumann. In Prague she sang Káťa in 1923–4 and the Kostelnička in 1926 (conducted by Ostrčil). On 25 May 1937, she sang Mrs Pásek in the new production of *The Cunning Little Vixen* conducted by Talich*, and sang Kabanicha in Talich's 1938 production of *Káťa Kabanová*, taking over the role from Marta Krasová, who had sung the first two performances. After World War II, she continued to sing character roles in Janáček operas at the Prague NT.

Marie Veselá is not to be confused with Marie Calma-Veselá (1881–1966), the singer and writer (see separate entry). *NDPrOA, ZahDiv.*

Veselý, Adolf (b. Lipůvka, near Blansko, 4 January 1886; d. Prague, 7 May 1961), Czech journalist. Janáček and Veselý probably met at the offices of *Lidové noviny*. Veselý compiled and edited *Leoš Janáček: pohled do života i díla* (Prague, 1924), published to celebrate Janáček's seventieth birthday. The text comprises the composer's own reminiscences, usually referred to as 'Janáček's autobiography'. Veselý added a chronology, worklist and bibliography. This lavishly produced book also has some beautiful facsimiles, including the opening of

The Makropulos Affair* (a year before the opera's completion) and a number of photographs. Though the book is dated 1924, Janáček wrote to thank Vesely for it on 27 January 1925, the same day that an announcement appeared in *Lidové noviny* for two different editions: one bound in silk, and the other a deluxe edition in full leather signed by Janáček on the frontispiece (copies bound in silk have a facsimile signature). Vesely interviewed Janáček for *Lidové noviny* about *Káťa Kabanová** (15 May 1921) and *The Cunning Little Vixen** (6 November 1924). His 'Last conversation with Leoš Janáček' was published in *Hudební rozhledy* (Vol. 4, Nos. 4–8, 1928). *JAWO, JYL2, LN, VesJan, VesPos.*

Vesely, František (b. Bystřice nad Pernštejnem, 18 March 1862; d. Prague, 6 January 1923), Czech physician and developer of Luhačovice*. After completing his medical studies at the Charles University in Prague, Vesely worked as a military doctor before becoming a general practitioner at Šaratice, near Brno, in 1894. He first visited Luhačovice in 1898, finding it in a state of neglect but spotting the potential of its healing springs, clean air and beautiful landscape in the foothills of the White Carpathians. Vesely's vision was to build a modern Moravian spa at Luhačovice, its success not only depending on medical efficacy, but also on the creation of an explicitly Slavic cultural environment. In 1902 he established a joint-stock company of Moravian doctors who acquired the spa from Count Otto Serényi. Vesely's vision for Luhačovice became a reality when he asked Dušan Jurkovič* to design a range of buildings and to restore others, giving the spa an entirely individual appearance. Vesely's first wife Anna (née Kašparová) died in 1907, and the following year he married Marie Calma-Veselá*. In due course, the board of management found Vesely's spending plans too risky, and he was dismissed at the end of the 1909 season. He remained on friendly terms with Janáček, becoming chairman of the KPU. Vesely served as an army doctor at the start of World War I, but after refusing to drink a toast on the Emperor's birthday he was dismissed. On hearing about this, the mayor of the spa town of Bohdaneč invited Vesely to become its medical officer, setting in train the circumstances that would lead to the Prague NT putting on *Jenůfa* (another resident of Bohdaneč was Josef Peška*). In December 1915, after a bruising campaign, Vesely, his wife Marie and Peška finally persuaded Kovařovic* to accept *Jenůfa* at the Prague NT. Janáček's failure to invite Vesely and his wife to the Prague premiere in 1916 is inexplicable, especially as Vesely had guaranteed to underwrite the first six performances if they were not sold out. Following Janáček's snub, their friendship cooled. *JAviii, JODA, JYL1, JYL2, ProLuh.*

Vienna Janáček's *Jenůfa* had a triumphant premiere at the Vienna Hofoper in 1918, but his first experience of the city was a dispiriting disaster. After studying at the Leipzig Conservatory (see Leipzig*), he arrived at the Vienna Conservatory at the start of April 1880 for further studies. His teacher was Franz Krenn, and during the two months he spent there he composed four pieces (X/15–18), all of which were described in great detail in his letters to Zdenka Schulzová and all of which are now lost. His early Violin Sonata was entered for the *Vereinsmedaille*, and for the qualifying round only one movement of each work was played. Janáček rehearsed the Adagio of his sonata with the violinist Viktor von Herzfeld, and they performed it to the jury (which didn't include Krenn) on 28 May 1880. The jury rejected the work as too academic.

Furious and hurt, Janáček left Vienna two weeks later, on 12 June. The Violin Sonata was subsequently given on 6 January 1881 at a concert in Brno, played by Gustav Cinke and Janáček. *HelJan, JAWO, JYL1, KnaInt, VogJan*

Viola d'amore   Janáček's enthusiasm for this archaic instrument probably began when he saw *Louise* in May 1903 (see Charpentier, Gustave*), though he had made earlier notes on the instrument during his time in Leipzig (1879). It had become something of an endangered species in instrumental music, but occasionally appeared in the opera house: in Meyerbeer's *Les Huguenots* (1836), in Charpentier's *Louise*, and in Puccini's *Madama Butterfly* (1904), another Janáček favourite. The Humming Chorus in Act II (Fig. 90) is accompanied by a 'viola d'amore, sul palco', marked 'interno ma vicino [off stage but nearby]'.

In 'My Luhačovice' (XV/173), an article published after his summer visit there in 1903, Janáček described the voice of Kamila Urválková* as 'like a viola d'amore', and when he composed *Fate*, the opera inspired by her, he originally included parts for two violas d'amore (removed in his 1907 revision). This was the first time he used the viola d'amore, an instrument he came to associate with his current infatuation: the 'viola of love' was a kind of erotic code. His next use of the instrument was in *Káťa Kabanová*. Inspired by Kamila Stösslová, it has prominent solos in several scenes starting with the Prelude, where it is heard to memorable effect. Janáček used the instrument again in *The Makropulos Affair*, another work in which he associated the heroine with Stösslová. Here its sound enhances the otherworldly effect of Emilia Marty's first entry in Act I, and it has an extended solo at the start of the opera's final scene (Act III, between Figs. 111 and 112). The whole of the viola part in the third movement of the *Sinfonietta** was originally written for viola d'amore. There's no direct association in this movement with Stösslová, but perhaps since the work was initially inspired by the outdoor concert he heard with her in Písek, this was his way of including something of Kamila. In discussion with Talich at rehearsals for the premiere, Janáček changed his mind and gave the part to the whole viola section. His final use of the instrument has clearly erotic associations: the viola part of the String Quartet No. 2, 'Intimate Letters'*, was first written for viola d'amore. After the Moravian Quartet played the work to him privately, he decided to use a conventional viola instead, telling the quartet, 'I've cut it out – it was terrible!' Recent attempts to resuscitate Janáček's original idea of playing it on a viola d'amore – however well played – tend to support his decision. On the whole, Janáček wrote for viola d'amore as if he were writing for a normal viola, with relatively few double stops and a similar compass. But he does seem to have had its distinctive tone quality in mind, especially in *Káťa* and *Makropulos*, and this suggests that his use of it went beyond the purely symbolic. *TyrKat.*

Violin Concerto 'The Pilgrimage of a Little Soul' [Houslový concert: 'Putování dušičky'] for solo violin and orchestra (IX/10).   At the time of the first performance of *From the House of the Dead* in 1930, Osvald Chlubna* wrote that Janáček had started to write a violin concerto in great haste as soon as he returned to Brno on 14 May 1926, after his visit to London. Janáček produced at least two drafts, and then seems to have abandoned it. Rosa Newmarch* had talked to Janáček about his plans for the work when he was in London. In 1931 she wrote that the Prelude to *From the House of the Dead* used 'part of the material intended for a violin concerto which he had in mind during his visit'. In London he had been particularly impressed by Adila Fachiri's performance of the Violin Sonata, and it is possible that he had her playing in mind when he set to work on the concerto. The surviving sketches indicate that the Violin Concerto was intended to be in one movement. By February 1927, Janáček had started the process of transforming some of the material into the Prelude of *From the House of the Dead**, and some pages of the original Violin Concerto manuscript were reused without alteration in the opera. Reuniting those pages with the second draft of the Violin Concerto results in a work that is almost complete, and it was reconstructed by Leoš Faltus and Miloš Štědroň*. The first performance was given on 20 September 1988 by Jan Stanovský with the Brno State Philharmonic conducted by Petr Vronský. The score appeared as SKV H/2 (1997). The title suggests a link with Kamila Stösslová*: Janáček often addressed her as 'soul' or 'little soul'. Quite when Janáček decided that the fate of his Violin Concerto was for it to be recycled as an opera prelude is an intriguing question, prompted in part by the concerto's orchestration. While Janáček had no qualms about including chains (and other implements) in an opera set in a Siberian prison, he would surely have hesitated about writing such a part for a short concert work. Even so, the Violin Concerto has a part for chains similar to that in the Prelude to *From the House of the Dead*. *JAWO, ProPut*.

Violin Sonata   See Sonata for Violin and Piano (VII/7)

Vlčí stopa   See *The Wolf's Trail* (IV/39)

Vogel, Jaroslav (b. Plzeň, 11 January 1894; d. Prague, 2 February 1970), Czech conductor and composer.   Vogel studied the violin with Otakar Ševčík at the Prague Conservatory. He later studied composition with Vítězslav Novák and at the Schola Cantorum in Paris. After World War I he became a staff conductor at the Moravian-Silesian National Theatre in Ostrava. The chief conductor from 1919 to 1927 was Emanuel Bastl, who conducted *Jenůfa* (1 November 1919) and *Káťa Kabanová* (8 January 1924) in Janáček's presence. Vogel was Bastl's successor. He met Janáček on several occasions, corresponded from 1924 onwards and attended his funeral. He conducted several Janáček productions in Ostrava, including *Jenůfa* (1929), *From the House of the Dead* (1932), *The Makropulos Affair* (1935), *The Cunning Little Vixen* (1936) and *Káťa Kabanová* (1938). *Taras Bulba*, the *Glagolitic Mass* and *The Fiddler's Child* were included in his orchestral concerts in Ostrava. Plans to give the stage premiere of *Fate* in 1938 got as far as casting the opera, but were then abandoned. Vogel conducted at the Prague NT from 1949 until 1959, where he led new productions of *Jenůfa* (1950 and 1955), *The Cunning Little Vixen* (1954) and *From the House of the Dead* (1958, the first production to include Janáček's original ending). He conducted the first commercial recording of *Jenůfa* for Supraphon in September 1953. Vogel made a major contribution to Janáček scholarship with *Leoš Janáček Dramatik* (Prague, 1948) and his pioneering biography *Leoš Janáček*, which developed from the earlier book. First published in German (1958), it was followed by editions in English (1962) and Czech (1963). A revised English edition appeared in 1981. It remains a cornerstone of the Janáček literature, above all thanks to Vogel's insightful discussion of the music. *ČerVog, EckJan, StoOst, VogDra, VogJan*.

Vrchlický, Jaroslav [pseud. for Emil Frída] (b. Louny, 17 February 1853; d. Domažlice, 9 February 1912), Czech poet. Janáček set Vrchlický's poems on several occasions. His earliest surviving setting is the *Autumn Song* (IV/14) for mixed chorus completed in 1880. In 1897 Janáček set Vrchlický's *Amarus*, with the poet's approval (see *Amarus**). Vrchlický's poem *The Eternal Gospel** was the text for Janáček's 'Legend' of the same name. In 1916 Janáček set Vrchlický's *The Wolf's Trail** (IV/39), and in 1919 another Vrchlický poem provided the programme for *The Ballad of Blaník** (VI/16). *JAWO, LJLR*.

Dictionary

239

Výlet pana Broučka do měsíce See *The Excursions of Mr Brouček* (I/6 and I/7)

Výlety paně Broučkovy See *The Excursions of Mr Brouček* (I/6 and I/7)

The Wandering Madman [*Potulný silenec*], chorus for male voices with solo soprano (IV/43). According to Janáček's autobiography, he began thinking about setting Tagore's 'Wandering Madman' in July 1922, a year after hearing the poet speaking in Prague (see Tagore, Rabindranath*). The autograph manuscript is dated 12 November 1922, and Janáček made some revisions before publication. *The Wandering Madman* was first performed in Rosice u Brna on 21 September 1924 by the PSMU under Ferdinand Vach*. At the seventieth birthday concert in Prague on 8 December 1924, it was performed by the Prague Teachers' Choir conducted by Metod Doležil* in the presence of both the composer and President Masaryk. Theodora Straková wrote that 'with *The Wandering Madman*, Janáček's choral output reached its pinnacle', a view echoed by Jaroslav Vogel, who called it 'one of the most impressive choral works [Janáček] had ever written'. Tagore's poem is No. 62 of *The Gardener*, in the Czech translation by František Balej. In *The Wandering Madman*, Janáček breaks new ground in the expressive and dramatic possibilities of a work for male-voice chorus, even more so than in the Bezruč choruses: the feverish intensity of the writing, and its moments of repose, evoke the psychological turmoil of Tagore's crazed beachcomber, endlessly seeking stones that will turn ordinary objects into gold. *The Wandering Madman* was published by HMUB in 1925. A critical edition was published in SKV C/2 in 2011. Fragments from the end of the work are reproduced on Janáček's tomb (see Brno Central Cemetery*). *JAWO, JYL2, StrMuž, VogJan*.

The Wolf's Trail [*Vlčí stopa*], chorus for solo soprano, female voices and piano (IV/39). Completed on 25 January 1916, *The Wolf's Trail* is a setting of a poem of the same name by Jaroslav Vrchlický. It was the first of three works for female chorus composed in late January and early February 1916, followed by the *Hradčany Songs** (IV/40) and *Kašpar Rucký** (IV/41). The chorus was sung by the VSMU and Ferdinand Vach*, who gave the first performance in Luhačovice on 23 July 1916. The preparations for this concert were described by Janáček to his wife in a letter on 22 July: 'I'm worried about my *Wolf's Trail*. ... What a horror I've been through! The chorus was completely misunderstood. Sung without feeling, harsh. Bad tempo! Couldn't that person [Vach] have come to Brno for some advice? Pompous fool! I think I could still save it and they could sing it well. But he just sees the notes and nothing of what lies behind them.' The kindest thing Janáček could say about Vach in a letter to Zdenka on 24 July was that he 'is an honest trainer, but he can't rise above himself' (a harsh judgment, given what Vach achieved with Janáček's male choruses). Janáček made some revisions to *The Wolf's Trail* and Vach performed this revised version in Prague on 26 December 1916. Janáček gave the work to HMUB in 1921, and in 1924 the firm wrote to say that it was going to ask Max Brod to provide a German translation. This never materialised, and *The Wolf's Trail* was only published in 1968. A critical edition was published in SKVEJ C/3 (2002). *JAWO, ZahŽen.*

Wood, Henry (b. London, 3 March 1869; d. Hitchin, 19 August 1944), British conductor. At the invitation of his friend Rosa Newmarch* (who wrote programme notes for Wood's Queen's Hall concerts from 1908 onwards), Wood was present at the first London performance of *The Diary of One Who Disappeared* (Wigmore Hall, 27 October 1922). On 3 May 1924, he conducted the British premiere of *The Fiddler's Child** at the Queen's Hall. In 1926 he was a member of the Committee of Welcome for Janáček's visit to London, and members of Wood's Queen's Hall Orchestra formed the ensemble that performed *Youth* at the concert of Janáček's music on 6 May 1926 (see London visit in 1926*). When Janáček visited Wood at his home in Chorleywood on 2 May, Jan Mikota took a series of photographs recording the occasion. Rosa Newmarch informed Janáček on 4 September 1926 that 'Henry Wood is giving *Taras Bulba* in October', though this was postponed and eventually took place on 16 October 1928. On 10 February 1928, Wood gave the first British performance of the *Sinfonietta** (broadcast on the BBC). Wood conducted the *Lachian Dances* at the Promenade Concerts on 19 August 1930, and gave the British premiere of the *Glagolitic Mass** on 23 October 1930 at the Norwich Festival. *FisJan, JacWoo, JAWO, MikJan, PřiZah.*

Writings on Folk Music As well as his anthologies of folk music (see Folksong Editions*), Janáček's writings on the subject range from newspaper articles recalling a visit to a particular area to scholarly essays. About half of them date from the 1890s, when he was collaborating with František Bartoš on *A Bouquet of Moravian Folksongs* (XIII/1) and *Moravian Folksongs Newly Collected* (XIII/3), including the prefaces to both of these collections. 'On the musical aspects of Moravian folksongs', Janáček's introduction to *Moravian Folksongs Newly Collected*, is by far his most substantial work on the subject (136 pages in the original edition). Janáček's shorter writings include reviews of other collections (by Ludvík Kuba, Antonín Vorel, and Bartoš before their collaboration), stylistic studies (for instance, on 'Rhythm in folksong', XV/196), the connection between speech and folksong, and comments on particular songs and dances that he arranged, including the *Lachian Dances** and *Folk Nocturnes**. An edition of Janáček's writings on folksong was published in 1955 as *O lidové písni a lidové hudbě: dokumenty a studie* [*On folk song and folk music: documents and studies*], edited by Jiří Vysloužil. In 2009 the first volume of a critical edition appeared as *Folkloristické dílo I (1886–1927)*, SKVEJ I/3–1. *JYL1, LJFD1, VysJan.*

Writings on Harmony and Rhythm Janáček published a number of articles on harmony in *Hudební listy* between 1884 and 1888, including 'On the Perfect Concept of Two-Note Chords', 'On the Concept of Key', 'On the Scientific Nature of Harmony Treatises' and 'On the Triad' (XV/44, XV/61, XV/68 and XV/76). His book *On the Composition of Chords and Their Connections* was published in 1896, with a second edition in 1897. In 1912 and 1913, the *Complete Harmony Manual* was published (in two volumes) by Píša in Brno, and a revised single-volume edition appeared in 1920. It is Janáček's most extended exploration of the subject. However, as Jaroslav Vogel put it, 'the book is far from easily intelligible and Janáček confuses the reader unnecessarily by his notorious imprecision in terminology, giving different meanings to traditional terms and even inventing his own'. The theoretical basis of Janáček's studies of harmony had its origins in what he learned from František Skuherský in Prague, and on his interpretation of the theories of Helmholtz and (in the revised edition of the *Complete Harmony Manual*) Wilhelm Wundt.

In the *Manual*, Janáček often veers suddenly from hard musical theory to flights of poetic fantasy. He taught this way too: Robert Smetana quoted one exchange in a class: 'How does this chord sound?' – 'Like the crackling of a fire'. For Janáček, the theoretical basis of harmony could only be understood by finding links between acoustics, the psychological impact of sounds, and the emotional effect that progressions of chords could create. Explaining this in a coherent way was always going to be challenging, and Janáček's aphoristic prose style does little to make things clearer. Moreover, as John Tyrrell has written, 'What should be the most interesting question of all, how Janáček's harmonic theory illuminates his own practice, tends to yield rather disappointing results.' In terms of the strictly theoretical passages, this is undoubtedly the case, though perhaps there are more intangible clues in Janáček's comments on the emotional impact of music and, in particular, on the visceral appeal of certain combinations of chords.

Janáček's writings on rhythm shed more light on his own composing processes. His most extended study, which appeared in instalments in *Hlídka* in 1907, is 'My opinion about *sčasování* (rhythm)' (XV/191). Janáček invented '*sčasování*' to describe the organisation of rhythm and metre in music (he makes no distinction between them, and sees rhythm and metre as an entity). His description of rhythmic layers made up of small units that run simultaneously at different speeds is particularly interesting. Unlike Janáček's writing on harmony, this has a much clearer parallel with his own use of ostinatos and his development of short musical ideas by means of rhythmical alteration. The most detailed evaluation of Janáček's theoretical writings is to be found in Michael Beckerman's *Janáček as Theorist* (1994). For a shorter discussion of this complex topic, see Tyrrell's 'Janáček as music theorist' (*JYL1*, chapter 19). *BecJan, JanÚpl, JYL, LJTD1, LJTD2, VogJan.*

Youth [*Mládí*] suite for wind sextet (VII/10).   The initial idea for *Youth* probably occurred to Janáček during his visit to Berlin in March 1924 to hear Erich Kleiber conduct *Jenůfa*. His article 'Berlin' (15 May 1924, XV/253) described his memories of the Prussian troops entering Brno while he was a chorister at the Augustinian Monastery, and was illustrated with a piece for piccolo, bells and drum. A few days after the article appeared, Janáček developed this fragment into *March of the Bluebirds** (VII/9), which was subsequently reworked as the third movement of *Youth*. Janáček went to Hukvaldy on 3 July 1924 (his seventieth birthday), and wrote *Youth* over the next few weeks. His first draft (finished on 19 July) had the title *Youthful Life* [*Mladý život*]. On 24 July, he told Kamila Stösslová that he had 'composed a sort of memoir of youth'. He made some revisions after returning to Brno. At the Brno premiere on 21 October 1924, the players were all musicians familiar with Janáček's music, drawn from the orchestra of the National Theatre: Josef Bok (flute), Matěj Wagner (oboe), Stanislav Krtička (clarinet), František Jánský (horn), František Bříza (bassoon) and Karel Pavlíček (bass clarinet). This should have assured a successful performance, but it was dogged by mechanical problems (Stanislav Krtička's clarinet wouldn't function in the last movement). A repeat performance was scheduled for 27 October, but this was cancelled the day before as only twenty-two tickets had been sold. Finally, Brno heard the work, without mishap, on 2 December 1924 at a concert of the KMS. *Youth* was given in Prague for the first time on 23 November 1924, played by seven members of the Czech Philharmonic (the flute/piccolo part was split between two players), who repeated it on 28 November. It was at the time of these performances that Janáček made his final revisions (the last is dated 25 November), including a change to the end of the fourth movement. HMUB had already expressed an interest in publishing *Youth* in October 1924, and the score appeared in April 1925, with the parts following in June (these contain performance markings that are not in the score by Gustav Nesporý, the flautist in the Prague premiere). HMUB also issued an arrangement for solo piano by Břetislav Bakala*.

Youth was recorded by Esta in May 1938 with the Prague Wind Quintet (including Václav Smetáček as the oboist) and Václav Kotas (bass clarinet). Two critical editions have appeared: SKV E/6 (1990) and an edition by Jiří Zahrádka (Henle, 2015). *JAWO, PřiMlá, ZahMlá.*

Z mrtvého domu   See *From the House of the Dead* (I/11)

Z ulice dne 1. října 1905   See *1. X. 1905* (VIII/19)

Zahrádka, Jiří (b. Brno, 16 May 1970), Czech musicologist and director of the Janáček Archive. Zahrádka has published extensively on Janáček, including numerous articles and the books *Leoš Janáček in Photographs* (with Svatava Přibáňová, 2008) and *Theatre Must not be Comedy for the People: Leoš Janáček and the National Theatre in Brno* (2012). He also wrote chapters for both volumes of John Tyrrell's *Janáček: Years of a Life* (2006 and 2007). Zahrádka has made a major contribution as an editor of Janáček's music, for UE, Bärenreiter, Henle and Editio Janáček, including critical editions of *Šárka, Fate, The Excursions of Mr Brouček, The Cunning Little Vixen, The Makropulos Affair, Glagolitic Mass* ('September 1927' version and definitive version), *The Diary of One Who Disappeared, Sinfonietta, March of the Bluebirds, Youth, In the Mists* and the works for female chorus (SKVEJ C/3). He is preparing further critical editions, including *Jealousy, Káťa Kabanová* and *Taras Bulba*. He is also the editor of *Korespondence Leoše Janáčka* (see Correspondence*).

Žalud, Berthold (b. Ježkovicích u Vyškova, 16 July 1856; d. Drnovicích u Vyškova, 19 July 1886), Czech composer and teacher. Žalud was a friend of Janáček's from childhood in the choir of the Augustinian Monastery and later at the Teachers' Institute. When Janáček was studying in Leipzig and Vienna (1879–80), Žalud took over his conducting duties at the Brno Beseda. An anecdote in Zdenka Janáčková's memoirs recalls an event in about 1880: 'My first ball was the fancy dress ball at the Readers' Club. That was still before my marriage. Not long before, I'd seen [Gounod's] *Faust* in the theatre and I was so taken with Marguerite that I wanted to be her for at least one evening. Leoš had a Faust costume, while his friend and colleague from the Institute, Žalud

... was Mephistopheles.' Janáček and his father-in-law Emilian Schulz were the witnesses at the Žaluds' wedding on 8 August 1882. When the Janáčeks were living apart in 1882–3, the Žaluds acted as intermediaries, arranging for Janáček to visit Olga at their house. Žalud was appointed to teach music at the Czech Gymnasium in 1885, but he died of tuberculosis the following year. After Žalud's death, Janáček took over his teaching at the Czech Gymnasium. *JAWO, MLWJ*.

Zápisník zmizelého See ***The Diary of One Who Disappeared*** (V/12)

Žárlivost See ***Jealousy*** (VI/10)

Zdrávas Maria See ***Hail Mary*** (II/14)

Zemánek, Vilém (b. Prague, 9 May 1875; d. Prague, 8 June 1922), Czech conductor. Zemánek studied medicine in Prague but never practised: after completing his medical training he went to Vienna to pursue his interest in music. He studied conducting with Ferdinand Löwe and Josef Schalk, and musicology with Guido Adler. He conducted at Elberfeld and Riga before appearing with the Czech Philharmonic on 20 November 1902. This was a success and he was appointed the orchestra's chief conductor. He introduced a number of works by young Czech composers, including the first performance of Novák's *Moravian Slovak Suite* Op. 32 on 4 February 1906. Zemánek was friends with Josef Suk, and on 7 January 1912, when the Czech Philharmonic gave its inaugural concert in the Smetana Hall, Zemánek conducted a Suk programme ending with the *Asrael* Symphony. Zemánek asked Janáček to write a new work for the Czech Philharmonic after the Prague premiere of *Amarus* on 6 October 1912, and on 28 April 1913, Janáček sent Zemánek *The Fiddler's Child*. In the end, plans for the performance (to be conducted by Janáček himself) fell through, but when the score of *The Fiddler's Child* was published by the KPU in 1914, it included a dedication 'To Dr Vilém Zemánek' (see *The Fiddler's Child**). Zemánek's relationship with the orchestra deteriorated sharply over the next few years, and on 16 April 1918 he was dismissed from his post. *JAWO, JYL1, JYL2, NouNov, VesČes*.

Zemlinsky, Alexander (b. Vienna, 14 October 1871; d. Larchmont, New York, 15 March 1942), Austrian composer and conductor. Zemlinsky became music director of the Prague German Theatre in September 1911, remaining in the post until the end of the 1926–7 season. His final season included Křenek's *Jonny spielt auf*, Hindemith's *Cardillac*, and *Jenůfa**, which opened on 31 October 1926 (Janáček attended the second performance on 5 November with his wife). *Jenůfa* was the only Janáček opera Zemlinsky conducted, but on 28 February 1929, he conducted the *Glagolitic Mass** in Berlin, the work's first performance outside Czechoslovakia. On 4 November 1938, a month before Zemlinsky fled Hitler's Europe, he saw *Káťa Kabanová** at the Prague NT conducted by Talich. He wrote to Talich the next day: 'It was one of the most beautiful operatic performances I have ever attended. And it seems to me that this was almost entirely of *your doing*. Thank you for the great pleasure. The work numbers among the most inspired in the entire operatic literature.' *Anno, BeaZem*.

Zeyer, Julius (b. Prague, 26 April 1841; d. Prague, 29 January 1901), Czech writer. Zeyer originally wrote the libretto for *Šárka* in about 1880, following a request from Dvořák*. In the end, Dvořák decided not to set it and Zeyer published his libretto in the magazine *Česká Thalie* in three instalments during January and February 1887. Janáček set to work soon afterwards on his own setting, and sent the vocal score to Dvořák in August 1887, asking for his advice. After receiving Dvořák's comments on the opera, Janáček made extensive revisions and then approached Zeyer for permission. Zeyer wrote on 10 November 1887 that Janáček should have done so before writing his opera and 'sending it into the world'. A hurt Janáček later wrote in his autobiography that this was a misunderstanding, as he had only shown it to Dvořák. Zeyer wrote again on 17 November 1887 in emphatic terms: 'I *do not give my consent* for you to use my *Šárka* as the text for your opera.' In spite of this, Janáček got on with *Šárka* anyway, completing the orchestral score of the first two acts in 1888. In 1889 Dvořák again contemplated setting Zeyer's libretto himself, only to abandon it once more. See *Šárka** (I/I). *JAWO, JODA.*

Zítek, Ota [Otakar] (b. Prague, 5 November 1882; d. Bratislava, 28 April 1955), Czech opera director and composer. Zítek studied composition privately with Vítězslav Novák. In 1921 he was appointed stage director at the Brno NT, and worked as dramaturg from 1926. Zítek was responsible for directing the original Brno productions of *The Cunning Little Vixen** (1924), *Šárka** (1925), *The Excursion of Mr Brouček to the Moon** (1926), *The Makropulos Affair** (1926) and *From the House of the Dead** (1930). He also staged revivals of *Jenůfa** (1924 and 1926) and *Káťa Kabanová** (1924 and 1928). He was director of the theatre in Plzeň from 1931 to 1939. That year he was arrested by the Gestapo as a troublesome intellectual and spent two years in Buchenwald Concentration Camp. After his release, the orchestral version of *The Diary of One Who Disappeared** by Václav Sedláček* and Zítek was staged in Plzeň on 26 June 1943. At the Brno NT, Zítek directed new productions of *Jenůfa* (1945), *Káťa Kabanová* (1946), *The Cunning Little Vixen* (1947), *The Makropulos Affair* (1948) and *From the House of the Dead* (1948). *EDMB, HolZít, JODA, NDBrOA, ZahDiv.*

Works

This list includes all of Janáček's completed musical works, with brief information about composition dates, first and early performances, and publication. For further details, see entries on individual works in the Dictionary, and in *JAWO*. For the operas, dates of Brno and Prague premieres are included; for other works, usually only the first performance is listed. For details of unfinished, planned, spurious and lost works, arrangements by Janáček and a complete list of writings, see *JAWO*.

Abbreviations

A	Alto (voice)
B	Bass (voice)
Bar	Baritone (voice)
BB	Beseda brněnská (Brno Beseda)
bcl	bass clarinet
bn	bassoon
Brno NT	Brno National Theatre
cl	clarinet
c.	conductor
Comp.	Date of composition
EM	Editio Moravia, Brno
ES	Editio Supraphon, Prague
facs.	facsimile
fl	flute
FS	Full score
HM	Hudební matice Umělecké besedy, Prague
hn	horn
KPU	Klub přátel umění v Brně (Club of the Friends of Art in Brno)
NTO	National Theatre Orchestra
ob	oboe
org	organ
Perf.	Date(s) of first performance(s)
pf	piano
Prague NT	Prague National Theatre
PSMU	Pěvecké sdružení moravských učitelů (Moravian Teachers' Choral Society)
PSPU	Pěvecké sdružení pražských učitelů (Prague Teachers' Choral Society)
Pub.	Publisher and date of first and other important editions
rev.	revised, revision
S	Soprano (voice)
SHV	Státní hudební vydavatelství
SKV	*Souborné kritické vydání děl Leoše Janáčka* [Complete Critical Edition] (Prague: Editio Supraphon; Kassel: Bärenreiter, 1978–)

SKVEJ	*Souborné kritické vydání děl Leoše Janáčka* (Brno: Editio Janáček, 2001–)
SNKLHU	Státní nakladatelství krásné literatury, hudby a umění
SSPS	*Sborník skladeb z pražských studií 1874–1875* (Brno: Editio Janáček, 2001)
T	Tenor (voice)
UE	Universal Edition, Vienna
va	viola
vc	violoncello
Večery	*Večery*, literary supplement to *Lidové noviny*
vn	violin
VS	Vocal score
VSMU	Vachův sbor moravských učitelek (Vach Choir of Moravian Women Teachers)

I. Stage

I/1: *Šárka*
Opera in three acts after a libretto by Julius Zeyer
Comp.: 1887 version: 1 January–1 February and August 1887; 1888 version: by 18 June 1888; 1919 rev. by 10 January; 1925 rev. by 7 June
Perf.: 11 November 1925, Brno NT, c. František Neumann
Pub.: FS: UE/EM, 2002 (ed. Zahrádka), hire only; VS: UE/EM, 2002 (ed. Zahrádka)

I/2: *Rákoš Rákoczy*
Scene from Moravian Slovakia with original dances and songs
Libretto by Jan Herben
Comp.: by June 1891
Perf.: 24 July 1891, Prague NT, c. Mořic Anger, choreography: Augustin Berger
Pub.: FS: Dilia, 1957, hire only; VS: Dilia, 1978, hire only

I/3: *Počátek románu* [*The Beginning of a Romance*]
'Romantic opera' in one act after the short story by Gabriela Preissová
Libretto by Jaroslav Tichý after Preissová
Comp.: 15 May–2 July 1891; rev. February–March 1892
Perf.: 10 February 1894, Brno NT, c. Leoš Janáček
Pub.: FS: Dilia, 1978, hire only; VS: Dilia, 1978, hire only

I/4: *Její pastorkyňa* [*Her Stepdaughter; Jenůfa*]
Opera in three acts after the play of Moravian life by Gabriela Preissová
Libretto by Janáček after Preissová
Comp.: before 31 December 1894–18 March 1903; rev. October 1903, January 1907 and February 1908
Perf.: 21 January 1904, Brno NT, c. Cyril Metoděj Hrazdira; 26 May 1916, Prague NT, c. Karel Kovařovic (Kovařovic version)
Pub.: FS: UE, 1918 (Kovařovic version); UE, 1969 (Kovařovic); UE, 1996 (Brno 1908 version, ed. Tyrrell and Mackerras); UE, 2009, hire only (1904 version, ed.

Audus); VS: KPU, 1908; UE, 1917 (Kovařovic version); HM, 1934 (ed. Helfert); UE, 1996 (Brno 1908 version, ed. Tyrrell and Mackerras); UE, 2009, hire only (1904 version, ed. Audus)

I/5: *Osud [Fate]*
Three scenes from a novel by Fedora Bartošová on a scenario by Janáček
Comp.: 8 December 1903–12 June 1905; rev. 26 July 1906 and 19 November 1907
Perf: Acts I and III: 13 March 1934; Act II: 2 July 1934; complete: 18 September 1934, Brno Radio, c. Břetislav Bakala; stage premiere: 25 October 1958, Brno NT, c. František Jílek
Pub.: FS: SKV A/5 (ed. Zahrádka); VS: Bärenreiter, 2013 (ed. Zahrádka)

I/6: *Výlet pana Broučka do měsice [The Excursion of Mr Brouček to the Moon]*
Burlesque opera in three acts
Words after Svatopluk Čech arranged by the composer with additions by Viktor Dyk
Comp.: 27 March 1908–5 November 1916; Epilogue: rev. by 29 March 1917
Perf.: 19 November 2010, Brno NT, c. Jaroslav Kyzlink
Pub.: original version: FS: UE, 2003, hire only; VS: UE/EM, 2003 (ed. Zahrádka), hire only; rev. version as part of I/7: FS: UE, 2003 (ed. Zahrádka), hire only; VS: UE, 1919.

I/7: *Výlety paně Broučkovy [The Excursions of Mr Brouček]*
Opera. Part I: The Excursion of Mr Brouček to the Moon. Part II: The Excursion of Mr Brouček to the fifteenth century.
Libretto by Svatopluk Čech, the first part written by Viktor Dyk, the second by F. S. Procházka
Comp.: Part I, see I/6; Part II: 5 May–12 December 1917
Perf.: 23 April 1920, Prague NT, c. Otakar Ostrčil; 15 May 1926, Brno NT, c. František Neumann (Part I only); 27 November 1937, Brno NT, c. Milan Sachs
Pub.: FS: UE, 2003 (ed. Zahrádka), hire only; VS: UE, 1919

I/8: *Káťa Kabanová*
Opera in three acts after A.N. Ostrovsky's *The Thunderstorm* in the Czech translation by Vincenc Červinka
Libretto by Janáček after Ostrovsky, trans. Červinka
Comp.: January 1920–April 1921, rev. after 10 December 1921; interludes by 9 November 1927
Perf.: 23 November 1921, Brno NT, c. František Neumann
Pub.: FS: UE, 1922; UE, 1992 (ed. Mackerras); VS: UE, 1922; UE, 1993 (ed. Mackerras)

I/9: *Příhody lišky Bystroušky [The Cunning Little Vixen]*
Opera in three acts after Rudolf Těsnohlídek's novel *Vixen Bystrouška*
Libretto by Janáček after Těsnohlídek
Comp.: January 1922–October 1923; rev. by 31 October 1924
Perf.: 6 November 1924, Brno NT, c. František Neumann; 18 May 1925, Prague NT, c. Otakar Ostrčil

Pub.: FS: UE, 2009 (ed. Zahrádka); VS: UE, 1924 (with Act III fanfares, 182pp); UE, 1925 (183pp); UE, 2010 (ed. Zahrádka)

I/10: *Věc Makropulos* [*The Makropulos Affair*]
Opera in three acts after Karel Čapek's comedy *The Makropulos Affair*
Libretto by Janáček after Čapek
Comp.: 11 November 1923–3 December 1925
Perf.: 18 December 1926, Brno NT, c. František Neumann; 1 March 1928, Prague NT, c. Otakar Ostrčil
Pub.: FS: UE, 2016 (ed. Zahrádka); VS: UE, 1926; UE, 2016 (ed. Zahrádka)

I/11: *Z mrtvého domu* [*From the House of the Dead*]
Opera in three acts after Feodor Dostoyevsky's *Notes from the House of the Dead*
Libretto by Janáček after Dostoyevsky
Comp.: 18 February 1927–7 May 1928
Perf.: 12 April 1930, Brno NT, c. Břetislav Bakala; 21 February 1931, Prague NT, c. Vincenc Maixner (Chlubna and Bakala version); 17 November 1961, Munich, c. Rafael Kubelík (Kubelík version); 29 September 1974, Brno NT, c. Václav Nosek (Nosek version); 7 March 2018, Royal Opera House, London, c. Mark Wigglesworth (Janáček's definitive version, ed. Tyrrell)
Pub.: FS: UE, 1930 (Chlubna and Bakala version); UE, 1990 (ed. Mackerras and Tyrrell), hire only; UE, 2018 (definitive version, ed. Tyrrell); VS: UE, 1930 (Chlubna and Bakala version); UE, 1964 (with Janáček's original ending); UE, 2019 (definitive version, ed. Tyrrell)

II. Liturgical

II/1: *Graudale 'Speciosus forma'*
Motet for mixed voices and organ
Comp.: 29 December 1874
Pub.: SKVEJ J/1; facs. of autograph: SSPS

II/2: *Introitus in festo Ss. Nominis Jesu*
Motet for mixed voices and organ
Comp.: ?January 1875
Pub.: SKVEJ J/1; facs. of autograph: SSPS

II/3: *Exaudi Deus* (1)
Motet for mixed voices and organ
Comp.: 3 February 1875
Pub.: SKVEJ J/1; facs. of autograph: SSPS

II/4: *Exaudi Deus* (2)
Motet for mixed voices
Comp.: 15 February 1875
Pub.: *Cecilia*, 1877; SKVEJ J/1; facs. of autograph: SSPS

II/5: *Benedictus*
Motet for mixed voices and organ

Comp.: 17 February 1875
Comp.: SKVEJ J/1; facs. of autograph: SSPS

II/6: *Communio 'Fidelis servus'*
Motet for mixed voice
Comp.: 20 June 1875
Pub.: SKVEJ J/1; facs. of autograph: SSPS

II/7: *Regnum mundi*
Motet for mixed voice
Comp: by 21 September 1878
Pub.: SKVEJ J/1

II/8: *Exurge Domine*
Motet for mixed voices
Comp.: ?1875–9
Pub.: SKVEJ J/1

II/9: *Graduale in festo purificationis BVM 'Suscepimus'*
Motet for mixed voices
Comp.: ?1875–9
Pub.: ES/UE, 1971; SKVEJ J/1

II/10: *Deset české církevní zpěvů z Lehnerova mešního kancionálu* [*Ten Czech Hymns from the Lehner Hymnbook for the Mass*]
Organ accompaniments to ten hymns
Comp.: 1881
Pub.: Winkler, 1881; rev. edn (with three additional hymns): Winkler, 1889

II/11: *Svatý Václave* [*Saint Wenceslas*]
Organ accompaniment
Comp.: ?1902, probably as a demonstration of harmonisation
Unpublished

II/12: *Constitues*
Motet for male voices and organ
Comp.: 1903
Perf.: ?29 June 1903, Mass for the Feast of SS Peter and Paul at Brno Cathedral
Pub.: ES/UE, 1971; SKVEJ J/1

II/13: *Veni sancte spiritus*
Motet for male voices
Comp.: by November 1903
Perf.: 13 April 1947, Brno Radio, c. Bohumír Štědroň
Pub.: UE, 1978; ES, 1978; SKVEJ J/1

II/14: *Zdrávas Maria* [*Hail Mary*]
For solo tenor, mixed chorus, violin and organ (Czech trans. of *Hail Mary*)
Comp.: by July 1904

Perf.: 18 October 1943, Brno-Židenice, Church of SS Cyril and Methodius, c. Karel Hradil

Pub.: UE, 1978; ES, 1979 (with cuts marked for version without chorus)

III. Choral-Orchestral

III/1: *Naše píseň* (1) / *Sivý sokol zaletěl* [*Our Song* (1) / *A grey falcon flew away*]
For mixed chorus and orchestra (folk text)
Comp.: 1890
Perf.: ?1890, Brno, Vesna
Unpublished

III/2: *Komáři se ženili* [*The Mosquitoes got Married*]
Folksong arrangement for mixed chorus and orchestra (folk text)
Comp.: 1891
Perf.: 20 November 1892, Brno, choir, Brno NTO, c. Leoš Janáček
Unpublished

III/3: *Zelené sem sela* [*I Have Sown Green*]
Folksong arrangement for mixed chorus and orchestra (folk text)
Comp.: 1892
Perf.: 20 November 1892, Brno, choir, Brno NTO, c. Leoš Janáček
Unpublished

III/4: *Ked' zme šli na hody* [*As we went to the Feast*]
Folksong arrangement for mixed chorus and orchestra (folk text)
Comp.: by March 1893
Unpublished

III/5: *Hospodine!* [*Lord, have mercy!*]
For soloists, mixed double chorus, brass, harp and organ
Comp.: by 19 April 1896
Perf.: 19 April 1896, Brno, Teachers' Institute Choir, c. Leoš Janáček
Pub.: ES/Bärenreiter, 1977

III/6: *Amarus*
Cantata for soloists, mixed chorus and orchestra (Jaroslav Vrchlický)
Comp.: by 21 May 1897; rev. 1901 and 1906
Perf.: Epilogue only: 20 March 1898, Brno, c. Leoš Janáček; without Epilogue: 2 December 1900, Kroměříž, Moravan choir, c. Janáček; complete: 25 February 1912, Brno, c. Ferdinand Vach
Pub.: FS: SKV B/1; VS: HM, 1938

III/7: *Na Soláni čarták* [*Čarták on Soláň*]
Cantata for solo tenor, male chorus and orchestra (Max Kurt)
Comp.: first version by 11 February 1911; rev. version August 1920
Perf.: 23 March 1912, Prostějov, Orlice choir, c. Vilém Steinmann; rev. version: 19 October 1924, Brno, BB, Brno NTO, c. Jaroslav Kvapil
Pub.: FS: SKV B/3; VS: SNKLHU, 1958

III/8: *Věčné evangelium* [*The Eternal Gospel*]
Legend for soloists, mixed chorus and orchestra (Jaroslav Vrchlický)
Comp.: ?1913, certainly by 11 May 1914
Perf.: 5 February 1917, Prague, Hlahol choir, c. Jaroslav Křička
Pub.: FS: SKV B/4; VS: SNKLHU, 1958

III/9: *Mša glagolskaja* [*Glagolitic Mass*]
For soloists, mixed chorus, organ and orchestra
Comp.: 2 August–15 October 1926; rev. by 29 May 1927, 1 September 1927, November–December 1927
Perf.: 5 December 1927, Brno, BB, Brno NTO, c. Jaroslav Kvapil; definitive version: 8 April 1928, Prague, BB, Czech Philharmonic, c. Kvapil
Pub.: FS: UE, 1929; SKV B/5–I; early version ed. Wingfield: UE, 1994; 'September 1927' version ed. Zahrádka: SKV B/5–II; VS: UE, 1928

IV. Choral

IV/1: *Oráni* [*Ploughing*]
Chorus for male voices (folk text)
Comp.: by 27 April 1873
Perf.: 27 April 1873, Brno, Svatopluk, c. Leoš Janáček
Pub.: HM, 1923; SKV C/1

IV/2: *Válečná* (1) [*War Song* (1)]
Chorus for male voices (unknown text)
Comp.: ?by 24 June 1873
Unpublished

IV/3: *Válečná* (2) *k svěcení praporu* [*War Song* (2) *for Dedicating the Banner*]
Chorus for male voices with trumpet, three trombones and piano (unknown text)
Comp.: by 24 June 1873
Perf.: 5 July 1873, Brno, Svatopluk, c. Leoš Janáček
Unpublished

IV/4: *Nestálost lásky* [*The Fickleness of Love*]
Chorus for male voices (folk text)
Comp.: by 23 October 1873
Perf.: 9 November 1873, Brno, Svatopluk, c. Leoš Janáček
Pub.: ES, 1978; UE, 1978; SKV C/1

IV/5: *Divím se milemu* [*I wonder at my Beloved*]
Chorus for male voices (?folk text)
Comp.: 1873–6
Pub.: Melpa, 1937; SKV C/1

IV/6: *Vínek stonulý* [*The Drowned Wreath*]
Chorus for male voices (folk text)
Comp.: 1873–6
Pub.: Melpa, 1937; SKV C/1

IV/7: *Osamělá bez těchy* (I) [*Alone without comfort* (I)]
Chorus for male voices (folk text)
Comp.: by 13 February 1874
Perf.: 14 March 1874, Svatopluk, c. Leoš Janáček
Pub.: UE, 1978; ES, 1978; SKV C/1

IV/8: *Láska opravdivá* [*True Love*]
Chorus for male voices (folk text)
Comp.: by 6 January 1876
Perf.: 23 January 1876, Brno, Svatopluk, c. Leoš Janáček
Pub.: Melpa, 1937; SKV C/1

IV/9: *Osudu neujdeš* [*You cannot escape your fate*]
Chorus for male voices (Czech translation of Serbian folk text)
Comp.: ?by January 1876
Pub.: UE, 1978; ES, 1978; SKV C/1

IV/10: *Zpěvná duma* [*Vocal Elegy*]
Chorus for male voices (František Ladislav Čelakovský)
Comp.: by 23 February 1876
Perf.: 3 April 1876, BB, c. Leoš Janáček
Pub.: Opus, 1934; SKV C/1

IV/11: *Na košatej jedli dva holubi sed'á* [*Two Pigeons are perching on the bushy fir-tree*]
Chorus for male voices (folk text)
Comp.: ?1876
Perf.: 1 December 1957, Prague, Moravan choir, c. Josef Veselka
Pub.: SKV C/1

IV/12: *Slavnostní sbor* [*Festive chorus*]
Chorus for mixed voices (Karel Kučera)
Comp.: by 15 July 1877
Perf.: 15 July 1877, Brno, Teachers' Institute choir, c. Leoš Janáček
Pub.: ES/Bärenreiter, 1972; SKVEJ C/4

IV/13: *Slavnostní sbor ku svěcení nové budovy c.k. slovanského ústava ku vzdělání učitelů v Brně* [*Festive chorus for the consecration of the new building of the Royal Slavonic Teachers' Institute in Brno*]
Chorus for solo baritone, male voices and piano (?Karel Kučera)
Comp.: by 8 July 1878
Perf: 15 September 1878, Brno, Teachers' Institute choir, c. Leoš Janáček
Unpublished

IV/14: *Píseň v jeseni* [*Autumn Song*]
Chorus for mixed voices (Jaroslav Vrchlický)
Comp.: by 18 September 1880
Perf.: 12 December 1880, Brno, BB, c. Leoš Janáček
Pub.: Orbis, 1951; SKVEJ C/4

IV/15: *Na prievoze* [*On the Ferry*]
Chorus for male voices (folk text)
Comp.: ?1880–4
Perf.: 1 December 1957, Prague, Moravan choir, c. Josef Veselka
Pub.: SKV C/1

IV/16: *Ave Maria*
Chorus for male voices (Czech translation of Lord Byron)
Comp.: ?August 1883
Pub.: *Varyto*, 1890; ES, 1979; SKV C/2

IV/17: *Čtveřice mužských sborů* [*Four male-voice choruses*] (folk texts)
Comp.: 1885
Perf.: 2–3: 14 November 1886, BB, c. Leoš Janáček; 1: 23 May 1889, Brno, BB, c.
Josef Kompit; 4: 26 May 1906, Plzeň, Smetana choir, c. Josef Branžovský
Pub.: Winkler, 1886; SKV C/1

IV/18: *Kačena divoká* [*The Wild Duck*]
Chorus for mixed voices (folk text)
Comp.: 1885
Perf.: 19 March 1901, Brno, Czech Gymnasium choir, c. Leoš Janáček
Pub.: Barvič, in *Zpěvník pro školy střední a měšťanské*, 1885; SKVEJ C/4

IV/19: *Tři sbory mužské* [*Three male-voice choruses*] (Eliška Krásnohorská and folk
texts)
Comp.: by 14 May 1888
Perf.: 9 April 1941, Vizovice, PSMU, c. Jan Šoupal
Pub.: SNKLHU, 1959; SKV C/1

IV/20: *Královničky* [*Little Queens*]
Old ritual folk dances with songs (folk texts)
Comp.: by 21 February 1889
Perf.: 21 February 1889, Brno
Pub.: SNKLHU, 1954

IV/21: *Naše píseň* (2) [*Our Song* (2)]
Chorus for mixed voices (Svatopluk Čech)
Comp.: 1880
Perf.: 11 December 1930, Brno Radio, c. Břetislav Bakala
Pub.: Orbis, 1951; SKVEJ C/4

IV/22: *Což ta naše bříza* [*Our Birch Tree*]
Chorus for male voices (Eliška Krásnohorská)
Comp.: by 18 April 1893
Perf.: 21 May 1893, Svatopluk, c. Max Koblížek
Pub.: *Památník Svatopluka*, 1893; SKV C/1

IV/23: *Už je slúnko z téj hory ven* [*The Sun has Risen above that Hill*]
Chorus for mixed voices (folk text)

Comp.: by 19 March 1884
Perf.: 13 May 1894, Brno, BB, c. Leoš Janáček
Pub.: SKVEJ C/4

IV/24: *Odpočiň si* [*Take Your Rest*]
Funeral chorus for male voices (František Sušil)
Comp.: before 7 October 1894
Perf.: 1 November 1894, Old Brno cemetery
Pub.: HM, 1926; SKV C/1

IV/25: *Slavnostní sbor* [*Festival chorus*]
Chorus for male voices (Vladimír Šťastný)
Comp.: by 15 December 1897
Perf.: 24 April 1898, Brno, Teachers' Institute choir, c. Leoš Janáček
Pub.: UE, 1978; ES, 1978; SKV C/1

IV/26: *Osamělá bez těchy* (2) [*Alone without comfort* (2)]
Chorus for male voices (folk text)
Comp.: ?1898
Pub.: UE, 1978; ES, 1978; SKV C/1

IV/27: *Ukvalské písně* [*Hukvaldy Songs*]
Folksong arrangements for mixed voices (folk texts)
Comp.: 11 October 1898
Perf.: Nos. 1, 3, 4, 6: 3 July 1944, Hukvaldy, c. Miloň Dohnal; complete: 25 May 1948, Frýdek-Místek, c. Gabriel Štefánek
Pub.: HM, 1949; SKVEJ C/4

IV/28: *Čtvero mužkých sborů moravských* [*Four Moravian male-voice choruses*] (folk texts)
Comp.: 1 and 3: by 17 July 1900; 2 and 4: 1906
Perf.: 1 and 3: 26 November 1905, Přerov, PSMU, c. Ferdinand Vach; 2: 5 February 1907, Vyškov, PSMU, c. Vach; 4: 23 February 1908, Brno, BB, c. Rudolf Reissig
Pub.: Mojmír Urbánek, 1906; SKV C/2

IV/29: *Otče náš* [*Our Father*]
For tenor solo, mixed voices, harp and organ (Czech translation of Lord's Prayer)
Comp.: by 11 June 1901 (1901 version with piano and harmonium accompaniment); 1906 version: ?July 1906
Perf.: 1901 version: 15 June 1901, Brno, c. Max Koblížek with *tableaux vivants*; 1906 version: 18 November 1906, Prague, Hlahol choir, c. Adolf Piskáček
Pub.: SKV, 1963 (1906 version); 1901 version: unpublished

IV/30: *Elegie na smrt dceri Olgy* [*Elegy on the Death of my Daughter Olga*]
For solo tenor, mixed chorus and piano (Maria Veveritsa)
Comp.: by 28 April 1903
Perf.: 20 December 1930, Brno Radio, c. Břetislav Bakala
Pub.: SNKLHU, 1958

IV/31: *Vínek [The Wreath]*
Chorus for male voices (folk text)
Comp.: ?1904–6
Perf.: 17 October 1925, Brno, PSMU, c. Ferdinand Vach
Pub: HM, 1923; SKV C/2

IV/32: *Lidová nokturna [Folk Nocturnes], 26 balad lidových* II
Folksong arrangements for two-part female voices and piano (folk texts)
Comp.: by 22 May 1906
Perf.: 5 December 1907, Brno, Organ School, performers not known
Pub: HM, 1922; HM, 1950

IV/33: *Kantor Halfar [Halfar the Schoolmaster]*
Chorus for male voices (Petr Bezruč)
Comp.: by 24 October 1906
Perf.: 27 May 1911, Plzeň, Smetana choir, c. Antonín Arnet; 3 August 1918,
Luhačovice, PSMU, c. Ferdinand Vach
Pub.: HM, 1923; SKV C/2

IV/34: *Maryčka Magdónova* (1)
Chorus for male voices (Petr Bezruč)
Comp.: by 11 November 1906
Perf.: 1977, Prague, Prague Philharmonic Choir, c. Josef Veselka (Supraphon
recording)
Pub.: SKV C/2

IV/35: *Maryčka Magdónova* (2)
Chorus for male voices (Petr Bezruč)
Comp.: by 21 March 1907
Perf.: 12 April 1908, Prostějov, PSMU, c. Ferdinand Vach
Pub.: Fr. A. Urbánek, 1909; SKV C/2

IV/36: *Sedmdesát tisíc [The Seventy Thousand]*
Chorus for male voices (Petr Bezruč)
Comp.: by 8 December 1909; rev. 1912
Perf.: 1909 version: Spring 1910, rehearsal, PSMU, c. Ferdinand Vach; 1912
version: 23 March 1914, Benešov u Prahy, PSPU, c. František Spilka
Pub.: 1912 version: HM, 1923; both versions: SKV C/2

IV/37: *5 národních písní [5 folksongs], 26 balad lidových* IV (folk texts)
Comp.: by 9 March 1912
Perf.: 1934, Brno Radio, Moravian Vocal Quartet
Pub.: HM, 1950

IV/38: *Perina [The Eiderdown]*
Chorus for male voices (folk text)
Comp.: ?1914
Perf.: 17 October 1925, PSMU, c. Ferdinand Vach
Pub.: HM, 1923; SKV C/2

IV/39: *Vlčí stopa* [*The Wolf's Trail*]
Chorus for female voices and piano (Jaroslav Vrchlický)
Comp.: by 25 January 1916
Perf.: 18 August 1916, Nová Paka, VSMU, c. Ferdinand Vach
Pub.: ES, 1968; SKV C/3

IV/40: *Hradčanské písničky* [*Hradčany Songs*]
Three choruses for solo soprano, female voices, flute and harp (F. S. Procházka)
Comp.: 1–3 February 1916
Perf.: 1: 26 December 1916, Prague, VSMU, c. Ferdinand Vach; 1–3: 24 November 1918, c. Vach
Pub.: HM, 1923; SKV C/3

IV/41: *Kašpar Rucký*
Chorus for female voices (F. S. Procházka)
Comp.: by 12 February 1916
Perf.: 6 April 1921, Prague, Prague Women Teachers' choir, c. Metod Doležil
Pub.: HM, 1925; SKV C/3

IV/42: *Česká legie* [*The Czech Legion*]
Chorus for male voices (anon., first published 1918)
Comp.: 15–18 November 1918
Perf.: 26 September 1920, Kroměříž, PSMU, c. Ferdinand Vach
Pub.: SKV C/2

IV/43: *Potulný silenec* [*The Wandering Madman*]
Chorus for male voices (Rabindranath Tagore)
Comp.: by 12 November 1922
Perf.: 21 September 1924, Rosice u Brna, PSMU, c. Ferdinand Vach
Pub.: HM, 1925; SKV C/2

IV/44: *Naše vlajka* [*Our Flag*]
Chorus for male voices (F. S. Procházka)
Comp.: by 10 December 1925
Perf.: 16 October 1926, Přerov, PSMU, c. Ferdinand Vach
Pub.: SKV C/2

IV/45: *Sbor při kladení základního kamene Masarykovy university v Brně* [*Chorus for Laying the Foundation Stone of the Masaryk University*]
Chorus for male voices (Antonín Trýb)
Comp.: by 2 April 1928
Perf.: 9 June 1928, Brno, BB, c. Jaroslav Kvapil
Pub.: SKV C/2

V. Vocal

V/1: *Když mě nechceš, což je víc?* [*If you don't want me, so what?*]
Song for tenor and piano
Comp.: ?1871–2, ?1875

Perf.: 23 January 1876, ?solo tenor from Svatopluk, ?Leoš Janáček (pf)
Pub.: EM, 1998; facs. of autograph in *JAWO*

V/2: *Kytice z národních písní moravských* (*Moravská lidová poezie v písních*)
[*Bouquet of Moravian Folksongs* (*Moravian Folk Poetry in Songs*]
Folksong arrangements for voice and piano (folk texts)
Comp.: between 1892 and 1901
Perf.: 4 December 1904, four unspecified songs; see *JAWO* for other early perfs
of unspecified songs
Pub.: Šolc, 1892 and 1901

V/3: *Jarní píseň* [*Spring Song*]
Song for voice and piano (Jaroslav Tichý)
Comp.: 1898, rev. 1905
Perf.: 1898 version: 6 March 1898, Brno, Zdeněk Lev (T), Cyril Metoděj
Hrazdira (pf); 1905 version: 9 April 1905, Brno, L. Vytopilová (voice)
Pub.: Pazdírek, 1944; EM, 1998

V/4: *Ukvalská lidová poezie v písních* [*Hukvaldy Folk Poetry in Songs*]
Folksong arrangements for voice and piano (folk texts)
Comp.: by 18 December 1898
Perf.: 18 December 1898, Brno, Antonín Karas (T), František Vojtěchovský
(Bar), Leoš Janáček (pf)
Pub.: A. Píša, 1899

V/5: *Návod pro vyučování zpěvu* [*Singing Teaching Manual*]
104 examples including vocal exercises with piano accompaniment
Comp.: by 25 April 1899
Pub.: A. Píša, 1899; SKV H/2

V/6: *Pět moravských tanců* [*Five Moravian Dances*]
Folksong arrangements for voice and piano (folk texts)
Comp.: 1908–12
Pub.: 5: facs. of autograph in *Večery*, 17 February 1912; 1–4: Panton, 1978, 1–5:
ES, 1978

V/7: *Čtyři balady* [*Four Ballads*]
Folksong arrangements for voice and piano (folk texts)
Comp.: 1908–12
Pub.: 3: Panton, 1978; 1–4: ES, 1980

V/8: *Dvě balady* [*Two Ballads*]
Folksong arrangements for voice and piano
Comp.: 1908–12
Pub.: 1: Panton, 1978; 2: Unpublished

V/9: *6 národních písní jež zpívala Gabel Eva* [*Six folksongs sung by Eva Gabel*], *26
balad lidových* I
Folksong arrangements for voice and piano (folk texts)

Comp.: by 10 December 1909
Perf.: 5 March 1911, Brno, L. Vytopilová (voice), Marie Dvořáková (pf)
Pub.: HM, 1922; HM, 1950

V/10: *Podme, milá, podme!* [*Let's come, my dear, let's come!*]
Folksong arrangement for voice and piano (folk text)
Comp.: by 23 December 1911
Perf.: 24 February 1949, Brno Radio, Marie Juřenová (voice), Bohumír Štědroň (pf)
Pub.: *Večery*, 23 December 1911

V/11: *Pisně devanské* [*Songs of Detva*], *26 balad lidových* III
Folksong arrangements for voice and piano (folk texts)
Comp.: January 1916
Pub.: HM, 1950

V/12: *Zápisník zmizelého* [*The Diary of One Who Disappeared*]
Song cycle for tenor, alto, three female voices and piano (Ozef Kalda)
Comp.: August 1917–11 November 1919
Perf.: 18 April 1921, Brno, Karel Zavřel (T), Ludmila Kvapilová-Kudláčková (A),
Břetislav Bakala (pf)
Pub.: Pazdírek, 1921; SKVEJ E/4; Bärenreiter, 2016

V/13: *Slezské písně* [*Silesian Songs*]
Folksong arrangements for voice and piano (folk texts)
Comp.: 15–25 January 1918
Perf.: 7 April 1919, Prague, Otto Pacovský (voice)
Pub.: B. Svoboda, 1920; SNKLHU, 1954

V/14: *Ukolébavka* [*Lullaby*]
Arrangement for voice and piano (folk text)
Comp.: by 1920
Pub.: *Kniha Komenského*, 1920; *Hudební besídka*, March–April 1928; without
voice part: UE, 1994

V/15: Folksong arrangements in 'Starosta Smolik'
For voice and unspecified instruments
Comp.: by 18 March 1923
Perf.: 1958, Czech Radio (Nos. 1 and 2 only)
Pub.: *Lidové noviny*, 18 March 1923

V/16: *Říkadla* (1) [*Nursery Rhymes* (1)]
Eight songs for one to three voices, clarinet and piano (folk texts)
Comp.: July–August 1925
Perf.: 26 October 1925, Brno, singers from BB, Stanislav Kritička (cl), Jaroslav
Kvapil (pf)
Pub.: 2 and 6: *La revue musicale*, August 1926; complete: UE/EM, 1993

V/17: *Říkadla* (2) [*Nursery Rhymes* (2)]
Introduction and 18 songs for nine voices and ten instruments (folk texts)

Comp.: 14 November–27 December 1926
Perf.: 25 April 1927, Brno, Moravian Composers' Club
Pub.: FS: UE, 1929; SKVEJ E/5; reduction for voices, viola and piano (Erwin Stein): UE, 1928

VI. Orchestral

VI/1: *Zvuky ku památce Förchtgotta-Tovačovského* (II. oddíl) [*Sounds in Memory of Arnošt Förchtgott-Tovačovský* (Part II)] for strings (and valve trumpet)
Comp.: March–June 1875
Perf.: 9 May 1988, St Louis, Minnesota, members of St Louis SO
Pub.: facs. of autograph is SSPS

VI/2: *Suita* [*Suite*] for strings
Comp.: by 2 December 1877
Perf.: 2 December 1877, Brno, BB, c. Leoš Janáček
Pub.: Pazdírek, 1926; SKVEJ D/1–1

VI/3: *Idyla* [*Idyll*] for strings
Comp.: July–August 1878
Perf.: 15 December 1878, Brno, BB, c. Leoš Janáček
Pub.: Orbis, 1951; SKVEJ D/1–2

VI/4: *Valašské tance* Op. 2 [*Valachian Dances* (*Dances from Valašsko*)]
Two folk dance arrangements for orchestra
Comp.: by 21 February 1889
Perf.: 21 February 1889, Brno, c. Josef Opelt
Pub.: Bursík and Kohout, 1890. For later editions, see VI/17

VI/5: *Adagio* for orchestra
Comp.: ?after 9 November 1890
Perf.: 20 December 1930, Brno Radio, c. Břetislav Bakala
Pub.: SHV, 1964

VI/6: *Suita Op. 3* [*Suite Op. 3*] for orchestra
Comp.: by 4 January 1891
Perf.: 23 September 1928, Brno, Brno and Prague Radio orchestras, c. Břetislav Bakala

VI/7: *Moravské tance* [*Moravian Dances*]
Folk dance arrangements for orchestra
Comp.: by 24 July 1891 and incorporated into *Rákoš Rákoczy* I/2
Perf.: 24 July 1891 (i.e. at perf. of I/2)
Pub.: ES/UE, 1971

VI/8: *Hanácké tance* [*Dances from Haná*]
Folk dance arrangements for orchestra
Comp.: by 24 July 1891 and incorporated into *Rákoš Rákoczy* I/2
Perf.: 24 July 1891 (i.e. at perf. of I/2)

Pub.: 1–3 with VI/7; 1–4 in I/6

VI/9: *České tance, 1. Suita* [*Czech Dances, first suite*]
Folk dance arrangements for orchestra
Comp.: by 22 March 1893
Perf.: Unperformed as this suite
Unpublished as this suite; 1, 2 and 5 in VI/17; 4 in VI/7

VI/10: *Žárlivost (Úvod k Její pastorkyni)* [*Jealousy (Prelude to Jenůfa)*] for orchestra
Comp.: by 16 February 1895
Perf.: 14 November 1906, Prague, Czech Philharmonic, c. František Neumann
Pub.: SHV, 1964; UE, 2019

VI/11: *Požehnaný*
Folk dance arrangement for orchestra
Comp.: 22 November 1899
Perf.: 10 January 1900, Brno, Česká národní kapela, c. Leoš Janáček
Unpublished

VI/12: *Kozáček* [*Cossack Dance*]
Folk dance arrangement for orchestra
Comp.: 9 December 1899
Perf.: 10 January 1900, Brno, Česká národní kapela, c. Leoš Janáček
Pub.: *Dva tance*, No. 1: ES/Bärenreiter, 1977

VI/13: *Srbské kolo* [*Serbian Reel*]
Folk dance arrangement for orchestra
Comp.: by 10 January 1900
Perf.: 10 January 1900, Brno, Česká národní kapela, c. Leoš Janáček
Pub.: *Dva tance*, No. 2: ES/Bärenreiter, 1977

VI/14: *Šumarovo dítě* [*The Fiddler's Child*]
Ballad for orchestra after the poem by Svatopluk Čech
Comp.: by 28 April 1913
Perf.: 14 November 1917, Prague, Czech Philharmonic, c. Otakar Ostrčil
Pub.: KPU, 1914; HM, 1924; SKV D/6

VI/15: *Taras Bulba*
Rhapsody for orchestra after the novel by Nikolay Gogol
Comp.: early version: 1915; final version: by 29 March 1918
Perf.: 9 October 1921, Brno, Brno NTO, c. František Neumann
Pub.: Piano four-hands arr. Bakala: HM, 1925; FS: HM, 1927; HM, 1947; SKV
D/7

VI/16: *Balada blanická* [*The Ballad of Blaník*]
Ballad for orchestra after the poem by Jaroslav Vrchlický
Comp.: ?September–October 1919
Perf.: 21 March 1920, Brno, Brno NTO, c. František Neumann
Pub.: SNKLHU, 1958; SKVEJ D/8

VI/17: *Lašské tance* [*Lachian Dances* (*Dances from Lašsko*)]
Folk dance arrangements for orchestra
Comp.: by 1893; title and definitive order by October 1924
Perf.: 2 December 1924, Brno, Brno NTO, c. František Neumann
Pub.: HM, 1928; SKV D/4

VI/18: *Sinfonietta* for orchestra
Comp.: March–May 1926
Perf.: 26 June 1926, Prague, Czech Philharmonic, c. Václav Talich
Pub.: UE, December 1926/January 1927; Peters, 1980; UE, 2018; facs. of autograph of 'Fanfáry': SHV, 1963

VII. Chamber

VII/1: *Znělka* (1) [*Sonnet* (1)] for four violins
Comp.: by 23 November 1875
Perf.: 5 October 1988, Brno, Jaromír Graffe, Tomáš Hanus, František Krušina, Miloš Vrba (vns)
Pub.: facs. of autograph in SFSS

VII/2: *Znělka* (1) [*Sonnet* (2)] for four violins
Comp.: by 25 November 1875
Perf.: 5 October 1988, Brno, Jaromír Graffe, Tomáš Hanus, František Krušina, Miloš Vrba (vns)
Pub.: facs. of autograph in SFSS

VII/3: *Romance* [Fourth Romance] for violin and piano
Comp.: 16 November 1879
Perf.: 5 July 1904, Ivančice, Rudolf Kratochvíl (vn), Vincenc Šťastný (pf)
Pub.: HM, 1938; SKV E/1

VII/4: *Dumka* for violin and piano
Comp.: ?1879–80
Perf.: 8 March 1885, Brno, A. Sobotka (vn), Leoš Janáček (pf)
Pub.: HM, 1929; SKV E/1

VII/5: *Pohádka* [*Fairy Tale, A Tale*] for cello and piano after Vasily Zhukovský's poem *The Tale of Tsar Berendyey*
Comp.: 1910 version: by 10 February 1910; 1912 version: by 22 September 1912; 1923 version: rev. in 1923 before publication
Perf.: 1910 version: 13 March 1910, Brno, Rudolf Pavlata (vc), Ludmila Prokopová (pf); 1912 version: 22 September 1912, Vyškov, Antonín Váňa (vc), ?Jaroslav Krupka (pf); 1923 version: 7 March 1923, Brno, Julius Junek (vc), Růžena Nebušková (pf)
Pub.: 1923 version: HM, 1924; 1910, 1912, 1923 versions: SKV E/2

VII/6: Presto for cello and piano
Comp.: ?1910, ?1924
Perf.: 15 June 1948, Brno, Karel Krafka (vc), Zdenka Průšová
Pub.: ES/Bärenreiter, 1970; SKV E/2

VII/7: Sonata for Violin and Piano
Comp.: Ballada by May 1914; other movements after 1 August 1914; complete work by 21 October 1915; rev. 1916 and before 1922
Perf.: 24 April 1922, Brno, František Kudláček (vn), Jaroslav Kvapil (pf)
Pub.: Ballada only: A. Švarc, Česká hudba (Kutná Hora), 1915; 1922 version: HM, 1922; 1915 version, discarded Allegro (?1916) and 1922 version: SKV E/1

VII/8: String Quartet No. 1, after Tolstoy's *The Kreutzer Sonata*
Comp.: by 7 November 1923
Perf.: 17 October 1924, Prague, Czech Quartet
Pub.: HM, 1925 (edited anonymously by Josef Suk); SKV E/3

VII/9: *Pochod Modráčků* [*March of the Bluebirds*] for piccolo and piano
Comp.: by 19 May 1924
Perf.: 24 April 1926, V. Pinkava (pic), Vilém Konopka (pf)
Pub.: *Hudební besídka*, March–April 1928; ES, 1970; Henle, 2016

VII/10: *Mládí* [*Youth*] for wind sextet
Comp.: by 24 July 1924
Perf.: 21 October 1924, Brno, Josef Bok (fl/pic), Matěj Wagner (ob), Stalislav Krtička (cl), František Janský (hn), František Bříza (bn), Karel Pavelka (bcl)
Pub.: HM, 1925; SKV E/6

VII/11: *Concertino* for piano, two violins, viola, clarinet, horn and bassoon
Comp.: 1 January–29 April 1925
Perf.: 16 February 1926, Brno, Ilona Štěpánová-Kurzová (pf), František Kudláček (vn 1), Viktor Nopp (vn 2), Josef Trkan (va), Stanislav Krtička (cl), František Janský (hn), František Bříza (bn)
Pub.: HM, 1926; SKVEJ E/7

VII/12: *Capriccio* for piano left hand, flute/piccolo, two trumpets, three trombones and tenor tuba
Comp.: by 30 October 1926
Perf.: 2 March 1928, Prague, Otakar Hollman (pf), c. Jaroslav Řídký
Pub.: SNKLHU, 1953; SKV E/5

VII/13: String Quartet No. 2, 'Listy důvěrné' ['Intimate Letters']
Comp.: by 8 March 1928
Perf.: 18, 25 May, 27 June 1928, Brno, Moravian Quartet, at Janáček's home (private performances); 7 September 1928, Brno, Moravian Quartet
Pub.: HM, 1938; SKV E/4

VIII. Keyboard

VIII/1: Exercises in harmony and counterpoint for keyboard
Comp.: October 1874–June 1875
Pub.: 12 complete and 3 incomplete exercises in Helfert, 1939 (*HelJan*)

VIII/2: *Předehra* [*Prelude*] for organ
Comp.: by 19 June 1875
Perf.: 24 October 1958, Brno, Josef Černocký (org)
Pub.: Panton, 1976; SKV F/2; facs. of autograph in SSPS

VIII/3: *Varyto* for organ
Comp.: by 24 June 1875
Perf.: 24 October 1958, Brno, Josef Černocký (org)
Pub.: Panton, 1976; SKV F/2; facs. of autograph in SSPS

VIII/4: *Chorální fantasie* [*Chorale Fantasia*] for organ
Comp.: by 7 July 1875, later rev. with cuts
Perf.: 23 July 1875, Prague, Organ School, final examination, Leoš Janáček (org)
Pub.: Panton, 1976; SKV F/2; facs. of autograph in SSPS

VIII/5: Exercises in form for keyboard
Comp.: 20 June–13 July 1877
Pub.: two complete and three incomplete exercises in Helfert, 1939 (*HelJan*)

[X/6: Fugues for keyboard]
Three fugues (discovered in 1998) of the 14 composed during Janáček's studies in Leipzig
Comp.: by 14 January 1880
Perf.: 14 February 1880, Leipzig, Leoš Janáček (pf)
Pub.: SKVEJ F/3

VIII/6: *Theme and Variations* for piano
Comp.: 29 January–22 February 1880
Pub.: HM, 1944; SKV F/1

VIII/7: Pieces for Organ, Nos. 1 and 2
Comp.: by 1884
Pub.: Privately printed, Brno, 1884; SKV F/2

VIII/8: *Dymák*, folk dance arrangement for piano
Comp: 1885
Pub.: UE, 1995; SKVEJ G/1

VIII/9: *Na památku* [*In Memoriam*] for piano
Comp.: ?1887
Pub.: ?Brno, c. 1887; SKV F/1

VIII/10: *Národní tance na Moravě* [*Folk Dances in Moravia*], folk dance arrangements for piano two hands and piano four hands
Comp.: mostly 1888–9
Perf.: 1–5 and 7–11: 7 January 1891, Brno, Antonína Nikodemová (pf) and Anna Kumpoštová (pf)

Pub.: Privately printed, Brno, 1891 (Vols. 1–2) and 1893 (Vol. 3); SNKLHU, 1953; SKVEJ G/1

VIII/11: *Srňátko*, folk dance arrangement for piano
Comp.: 1888
Pub.: UE, 1995; SKVEJ G/1

VIII/12: *Ej, danaj!*, folk dance arrangement for piano
Comp. by 2 April 1892
Perf.: 15 June 1948, Brno, Zdenka Průšová (pf)
Pub.: SKV F/1

VIII/13: *Hudba ke kroužení kužely* [*Music for Club Swinging*] for piano
Comp.: by 16 April 1893
Perf.: 16 April 1893, Brno, at the annual display of the Sokol
Pub.: Tělocvičná jednota Sokol v Brně, 1895; HM, 1950; SKV F/1

VIII/14: *Řezníček*, folk dance arrangement for piano
Comp.: 1893
Pub.: UE, 1995; SKVEJ G/1

VIII/15: *Zezulenka*, folk dance arrangement for piano
Comp.: 1893
Pub.: UE, 1995; SKVEJ G/1

VIII/16: *Úvod k Její pastorkyni (Žárlivost)* [*Prelude to Jenůfa (Jealousy)*] for piano four hands
Comp.: by 31 Dec 1894
Pub.: EM/UE, 1995

VIII/17: *Po zarostlém chodníčku* [*On the Overgrown Path*], miniatures for piano
Comp.: seven pieces by 22 October 1900; three pieces by 1908; remaining pieces by September 1911
Perf.: 6 January 1905 (?five pieces); Series I: 3 November 1923, Prague, Jan Heřman (pf)
Pub.: Series I, Nos. 1, 2 and 10: Emil Kolář, 1901; Nos. 4 and 7: Kolář, 1902; Series I, complete: A. Píša, December 1911; Series II, No. 1: *Večery*, 23 September 1911; Series II, complete: HM/Pazdírek, 1942; Series I and II: HM, 1942; SKV F/1

VIII/18: *Moravské tance* [*Moravian Dances*]: *Čeladenský, Pilky*, folk dance arrangements for piano
Comp.: by 22 September 1904
Pub.: A. Píša, 1905; UE, 1995; SKV F/1

VIII/19: *1. X. 1905 (Z ulice dne 1. října 1905)* [*1. X. 1905 (From the Street 1 October 1905)*] for piano
Comp.: between October 1905 and January 1906
Perf.: 27 January 1906, Brno, Ludmila Tučková (pf); 23 November 1924, Prague, Jan Heřman (pf)

VIII/20: *Narodíl se Kristus Pán* [*Christ the Lord is Born*], Bohemian Christmas carol arranged for piano
Comp.: by 24 December 1909
Pub.: *Lidové noviny*, 24 December 1909; UE, 1994

VIII/21: Moderato for piano
Comp.: by April 1911
Pub.: *Hudební revue*, April 1911; UE, 1994

VIII/22: *V mlhách* for piano
Comp.: by 21 April 1912
Perf.: 7 December 1913, Kroměříž, Marie Dvořáková (pf)
Pub.: KPU, 1913; HM, 1924, rev. Václav Štěpán (according to Janáček's 'verbal instructions'); SKV F/1; Henle, 2016; facs. of No. 4: Moravian Museum, 1998

VIII/23: *Moravské lidové písně* [*Moravian Folksongs*], folksong arrangements for piano
Comp.: by 1 January 1922
Pub.: HM, 1950; facs. of autograph as *Patnáct moravských lidových písní*, Panton, 1978

VIII/24: *Ej, duby, duby* [*O, the Oaks, the Oaks*], folksong arrangement for piano
Comp.: by 1 January 1922
Pub.: Panton, 1978

VIII/25: *Budem tady stat* [*We'll Stand Here*], folksong arrangement for piano
Comp.: by 17 March 1922
Pub.: *Lidové noviny*, 17 March 1922

VIII/26: Con moto for piano
Comp.: by 5 July 1923
Pub.: *Lidové noviny*, 5 July 1923; UE, 1994

VIII/27: Untitled piece for piano
Comp.: by 8 January 1924
Pub.: *Lidové noviny*, 8 January 1924

VIII/28: *Bratřím Mrštíkům* [*To the Mrštík Brothers*] for piano
Comp.: 28 February 1925
Pub.: Unpublished; facs. of autograph in *JAWO*, p. 273

VIII/29: Untitled piece for piano
Comp.: ?by 1926
Pub.: UE, 1994

VIII/30: *Na starem hradě Hukvalském* [*At the Old Castle in Hukvaldy*], folk dance arrangement for piano
Comp.: 8 June 1926
Pub.: facs. of autograph in Procházka 1948 (*ProLaš*), p. 187

VIII/31: Andante for piano
Comp.: by 16 January 1927
Pub.: *Lidové noviny*, 16 January 1927; UE, 1994

VIII/32: *Vzpomínka [Reminiscence]* for piano
Comp.: by 8 May 1928
Pub.: *Muzika*, Belgrade, 1928; Melpa, 1936; SKV F/1

VIII/33: *Pieces in Kamila Stösslová's Album* for piano or harmonium
Comp.: 2 October 1927–8 August 1928 (13 pieces in all)
Perf.: 15 December 1994, Brno, Jiří Doležel (pf)
Pub.: Moravian Museum, 1994 (transcriptions and facs. of autograph)

IX. Unfinished

See Dictionary: Mass in E flat*, *The Danube**, Violin Concerto* and *Schluck und Jau**
IX/1: Rondo for piano, 1877
IX/2: *V Oettingenách, 4 VIII 1878 [In Oettingen, 4 August 1878]* for organ, 1878
IX/3: *Paní mincmistrová [The Mintmaster's Wife]*, opera, 1906–7
IX/4: *Anna Karenina*, opera, 1907
IX/5: Mše Es dur [Mass in E flat major], 1908
IX/6: *Živá mrtvola [The Living Corpse]*, opera, 1916
IX/7: *Dunaj [The Danube]*, 1923–28
IX/8: *Sanssouci* for flute and spinet, 1924
IX/9: Allegro for piccolo, glockenspiel and drums, 1924
IX/10: Violin Concerto, 1926
IX/11: *Schluck und Jau*, 1928
IX/12: *Pensistům učitelům po 50 letech maturity [To the Teacher-Pensioners on 50 Years after Matriculation]*, chorus for male voices, 1928
IX/13: untitled fragment for piano, facs. in Smetana 1948, p. 99, captioned 'Hudební myšlenky' [Musical Thought]. A different piece from IX/add., date undetermined
IX/add: *Myšlenky [Thoughts]* for piano, written on verso of the surviving sketchleaf for *Jenůfa* but unrelated to the opera. Not in *JAWO*.

X. Lost

See Dictionary: Leipzig*, Piano Trio*, Vienna* and *JAWO*
X/1: Mše [Mass], ?1872–5
X/2: *Ženich vnucený [The Enforced Bridegroom]*, chorus for male voices, 1873
X/3: *Smrt [Death]*, melodrama for reciter and orchestra, 1876
X/4: *Dumka* for piano, 1879
X/5: Piano Sonata in E flat, 1879
X/6: Fugues for keyboard, 1879–80
X/7: *Die Abendschatten*, song cycle for voice and piano, 1879
X/8: Romances for violin and piano, 1879
X/9: Song for Grill, 1879
X/10: *Sanctus*, 1879
X/11: *Zdenči-menuetto [Zdenka's Minuet]* for piano, 1880

X/12: Violin Sonata [No. 1], 1880
X/13: Scherzo from a symphony, 1880
X/14: Rondos for piano, 1880
X/15: Piece in sonata form for piano, 1880
X/16: Violin Sonata [No. 2], 1880
X/17: *Frühlingslieder*, song cycle for voice and piano, 1880
X/18: String Quartet, 1880
X/19: Minuet and Scherzo for clarinet and piano, 1881
X/20: *Valašské tance* [*Valachian Dances*], 'idyllic scene in one act', 1889
X/21: Piece for *Po zarostlém chodníčku* [*On the Overgrown Path*] for piano, 1908
X/22: Piano Trio, 1908
X/23: *Komár* [*The Mosquito*] for violin and piano, ?1922–8

XI. Planned

For details, see *JAWO*

XI/1: *Poslední Abencerage* [*The Last of the Abencerages*], planned opera, 1884–5
XI/2: *Pod Rahoštém* [*At the foot of Radhošt*], planned ballet, 1889–9
XI/3: Organ Sonata, planned 1895–6
XI/4: *Písně otroka* [*Songs of a Slave*], planned cantata, between 1895 and 1903
XI/5: *Život* [*Life*], unspecified work, planned ?1901
XI/6: *Andělská sonáta* [*Angel Sonata*], planned opera, 1902–3
XI/7: *Maryša*, planned opera, 1904
XI/8: *Gazdina roba* [*The Farm Mistress*], planned opera, 1904, ?1907
XI/9: *Dítě* [*The Child*], planned opera, 1923

XII. Arrangements and Transcriptions

See Dictionary: *Gott erhalte den Kaiser!** and *JAWO*

XII/1: Joseph Haydn: *Gott erhalte den Kaiser!*, ?1872–1903
XII/2: Antonín Dvořák: *Šest moravských dvojzpěvů* [*Six Moravian duets*], 1877 and 1884
XII/3: Edvard Grieg: *Landkjending*, 1901
XII/4: Mass after Liszt's *Messe pour orgue*, 1901
XII/5: *Církevní zpěvy české vícehlasné z příborského kancionálu* [*Czech hymns for several voices from the Příbor hymnbook*], ?1904

XIII. Folk-Music Editions

See Dictionary: Folksong Editions*

XIII/1: *Kytice z národních písní moravských*, 1890
XIII/2: *Kytice z národních písní moravskýchm slovenských a českých*, 1901
XIII/3: *Národní písně moravské v nově nasbírané*, 1901
XIII/4: *Z nově sbírky národních písní moravských*, 1911–12
XIII/5: *Moravské písně milostné*, 1930–6

XIV. Spurious

For details, see *JAWO*

XIV/1: Nocturne, 1873

XIV/2: *Trauermarsch*, 1879

XIV/3: *Toni orationum*, ?1880s

XIV/4: *Oříšek léskový* [*The Hazelnut*], ?1899

XIV/5: Songs with piano accompaniment, 1899

XIV/6: *Jarní píseň* [*Spring Song*], opera, 1904

XIV/7: Moderato for orchestra, ?1904

XIV/8: *Honza hrdina* [*Honza the Hero*], 1905

XIV/9: *Duše zvonů* [*The Soul of the Bell*], 1905

XIV/10: *Jarní píseň* [*Spring Song*] (for piano), 1912

XIV/11: *Ondráš*, 1918

XIV/12: *Divoška* [*The Tomboy*] 1920

XIV/13: *Pluh* [*The Plough*], ?1920

XIV/14: *L'Âme et la chair*, 1924

XIV/15: Piece about the dog Čipera, 1925–8

XIV/16: *Hymna míru* [*Hymn of Peace*], 1928

XV. Writings

See Dictionary: *Hudební besídka**, *Hudební listy**, *Lidové noviny**, Writings on Folk Music* and Writings on Harmony and Rhythm*. For the complete list of Janáček's writings by Theodora Straková, see *JAWO* section XV, pp. 357–445.

Bibliography

Anno   *ANNO: Austrian Newspapers Online.* Website: anno.onb.ac.at

AudJen   Mark Audus, *The 1904 version of Leoš Janáček's Jenůfa: sources,
          reconstruction, commentary*, diss., (University of Nottingham, 2007).

BajHud   Jitka Bajgarová, *Hudební spolky v Brně a jejich role při utváření
          'hudebního obrazu' města 1860–1918* [Music societies in Brno and
          their role in the formation of the 'musical picture' of the city
          1860–1918] (Brno: Centrum pro studium demokracie a kultury,
          2005).

BalMor   Milan Balódy, *Smíšený pěvecký sbor Moravan v Kroměříži v letech
          1862–1918* [The Moravan mixed choir in Kroměříž in the years
          1862–1918], diss. (Olomouc: Palacký University, 2014).

BarJíl   Jindřiška Bartová, *František Jílek: Osobnost dirigenta* [František Jílek:
          the personality of the conductor] (Brno: JAMU, 2014).

BarLaš   Miroslav Barvík, Introduction to *Lašske tance* (SKV D/4, 1982).

BeaZem   Antony Beaumont, *Zemlinsky* (London: Faber, 2000).

BecBau   Michael Beckerman and Glen Bauer (eds.), Janáček *and Czech
          Music* (Stuyvesant, NY: Pendragon Press, 1995).

BecJan   Michael Beckerman, *Janáček as Theorist* (Stuyvesant, NY:
          Pendragon, 1994).

BecWor   Michael Beckerman (ed.), *Janáček and his World* (Princeton, NJ:
          Princeton University Press, 2003).

BekSch   Josef Bek, *Erwin Schulhoff: Leben und Werk* (Hamburg: Von Bockel,
          1994).

BesDům   Miloš Štědron, Lea Frimlová and Zdeněk Geist (eds.), *Besední dům:
          Architektura, společnost, kultura* [The Beseda House: Architecture,
          society, culture] (Brno: Státní Filharmonie, 1995).

BMI   *Bohuslav Martinů Institute: Database of Sources.* Website: database.
          martinu.cz

BroJan   Max Brod, *Leoš Janáček: Život a dílo* [Leoš Janáček: life and work],
          Czech trans. by Alfred Fuchs (Prague: Hudební matice, 1924;
          original German version, Vienna: Wiener Philharmonischer Verlag,
          1925).

BroSte   Max Brod, *Sternenhimmel: Musik- und Theatererlebnisse* (Prague:
          Orbis; Munich: Kurt Wolff, 1923).

BudMuz   J. L. Budin, *Muzikanské dušičky: epitafy. S osmi kresbami Dr Desideria*
          [Musical Souls: Epitaphs. With eight drawings by Dr Desiderius]
          (Prague: A. Srdce, 1922).

ČapMas   Karel Čapek, *President Masaryk Tells his Story* (London: George
          Allen & Unwin, 1934).

ČapMoj   Helena Čapková, *Moji milí bratři* [My dear Brothers] (Prague:
          Československý spisovatel, 1962).

ČerVog	Lenka Černíková, *Jaroslav Vogel 1884–1970: interpret hudebního prostoru* [Jaroslav Vogel 1884–1970: interpreter of musical space] (Ostrava: Ostrava Museum, 2014).
ChlJan	Osvald Chlubna, 'Janáček: učitel' [Janáček: teacher], *Musikologie* 3 (1955), 51–8.
Chrono	Eva Drlíková, *Leoš Janáček: Život a dílo v datech a obrazech. Chronology of his Life and Work* (Brno: Opus musicum, 2004, 2/2010), text in Czech and English.
ČHS	*Český hudební slovník osob a institucí* [Czech music dictionary of people and institutions], ed. Petr Macek, Petr Kalina, Karel Steinmetz and Šárka Zahrádková. Website: www.ceskyhudebnislovnik.cz/slovnik
CobCyc	Walter Willson Cobbett (ed.), *Cobbett's Cyclopedic Survey of Chamber Music*, second edition (London: Oxford University Press, 1963).
ColJan	Joseph Colomb, *Janáček en France: de l'indifférence à la reconnaissance. La réception française de la musique de Janáček* (Clichy: Les éditions de l'île bleue, 2014).
ČSHS	*Československý hudební slovník osob a institucí*, ed. Gracian Černušák, Bohumír Štědroň and Zdenko Nováček. Vol. I, A–L (Prague: Státní hudení vydavatelství, 1963); Vol. II, M–Z (Prague: Státní hudení vydavatelství, 1965).
CurDis	William D. Curtis, *Leoš Janáček. Discography series XVIII* (Utica, NY: J. F. Weber, 1978).
DesLet	*Deset let Pěveckého sdružení moravských učitelů 1903–1913* [Ten Years of the Moravian Teachers' Choral Society 1903–1913] (Brno: privately printed, 1913).
DLJ	Bohumír Štědroň, *Dílo Leoše Janáčka* [The work of Leoš Janáček] (Prague: Hudební rozhledy, 1959).
DrlCon	Eva Drlíková, Introduction to *Concertino* (SKVEJ E/7, 2001).
DrlCow	Eva Drlíková, 'Henry Cowell, Leoš Janáček and Who were the Others?', in Michael Beckerman and Glen Bauer (eds.), *Janáček and Czech Music* (Stuyvesant, NY: Pendragon Press, 1995).
DucBak	Katarína Duchoňová, *Břetislav Bakala jako janáčkovský dirigent* [Břetislav Bakala as a Janáček conductor] (Brno: JAMU, 2016).
DucNav	Milena Duchoňová, Introduction to *Návod pro vyučování zpěvu* (SKV H/2, 1980).
DušJur	*Dušan Jurkovič* (Pardubice: Východčeská galerie, 1988), exhibition catalogue.
EckJan	Pavel Eckstein, *Leoš Janáček a Národní divadlo* [Leoš Janáček and the National Theatre] (Prague: Národní divadlo, 1978).
EDMB	*Encyklopedie dějin města Brna* [Encyclopedia of the History of Brno]. Website: encyklopedie.brna.cz
FELJ	Nigel Simeone, *The First Editions of Leoš Janáček: A bibliographical catalogue with illustrations of the title pages* (Tutzing: Schneider, 1991).

FilSpo *Filharmonický spolek 'Beseda brněnská' v letech 1911–1930* [The Philharmonic Society of the Brno Beseda in the years 1911–1930] (Brno: Beseda brněnská, 1931).

FisCze Zdenka Fischmann, *Essays on Czech Music* (New York: Columbia University Press, 2002).

FisJan Zdenka Fischmann (ed.), *Janáček–Newmarch Correspondence* (Rockville, MD: Kabel Publishers, 1986).

FLN Leos Janáček, *Fejetony z Lidových novin* [Feuilletons from *Lidové noviny*], ed. Jan Racek (Brno: Krajské nakladatelství, 1958).

FraBar *František Bartoš.* Website: www.frantisekbartos.cz

Fronek Josef Fronek, *Velky česko-anglický slovník. Comprehensive Czech-English Dictionary* (Prague: Leda, 2000).

FukVio Jiří Fukač, Introduction to *Skladby pro violoncello a klavír* (SKV E/2, 1988).

GazLau *Gazette de Lausanne,* online archives. Website: www.letempsarchives.ch

GolMax Hugo Gold (ed.), *Max Brod: Ein Gedenkbuch 1884–1968* (Tel Aviv: Olamenu, 1969), esp. Yehuda Cohen: 'Max Brod, der Musiker', pp. 277–87.

GösŠír Gabriel Gössel and Filip Šír, *Český katalog nahrávek gramofonové firmy Esta 1930–1946* [Czech Catalogue of Recordings by Esta 1930–1946] (Brno: Moravská zemská knihovna, 2014).

GryKPU Kristýna Grycová, *Klub přátel umění v Brně a Leoš Janáček* [The Club of the Friends of Art in Brno and Leoš Janáček], diss. (Brno: Masaryk University, 2008).

HeiErs Hans Heinsheimer, *UE: die ersten 37½ Jahre: eine Chronik des Verlags* (Vienna: Universal Edition, 2017).

HeiMen Hans Heinsheimer, *Menagerie in F sharp* (Garden City, NY: Doubleday, 1947).

HelEle Vladimír Helfert, Introduction to *Elegie na smrt dceri Olgy* (Prague: SNKLHU, 1958).

HelJan Vladimír Helfert, *Leoš Janáček: I. V poutech tradice* [Leoš Janáček: I. the bonds of tradition] (Brno: Pazdírek, 1939).

HelMod Vladimír Helfert, *Česká moderní hudba* [Czech modern music] (Olomouc: Index, 1936).

HelNeu Vladimír Helfert, *František Neumann* (Prostějov, published for the Neumann family, 1936).

HelŠtě Vladimír Helfert, *O Janáčkovi* [On Janáček], ed. Bohumír Štědroň (Prague: Hudební matice, 1949).

HeyKle Peter Heyworth, *Otto Klemperer: His Life and Times. Vol. 1: 1885–1933* (Cambridge: Cambridge University Press, 1983).

HilBri Ernst Hilmar (ed.), *Leoš Janáček: Briefe an die Universal Edition* (Tutzing: Schneider, 1988).

HnáNěm Kateřina Hnátová and Alena Němcová: Introduction to *Liturgické skladby* (SKVEJ J/1, 2007).

HolČes	Vladimír Holzknecht, *Česká filharmonie: příběh orchestru* [The Czech Philharmonic: the story of the orchestra] (Prague: SHV, 1963).
HolJan	Hans Hollander, *Leoš Janáček: his Life and Work*, trans. Paul Hamburger (London: John Calder, 1963).
HolZít	Moníka Holá, *Ota Zítek v dokumentech a vzpomínkách* [Ota Zítek in documents and reminiscences] (Brno: JAMU, 2011).
HorPet	Ladislava Horňáková and Blanka Petráková, *Jurkovičovy Luhačovice (sny a skutečnost)* [Jurkovič's Luhacoviče (Dreams and Reality)] (Luhačovice: Prameny, 2007).
HraHud	František Miťa Hradil, *Hudebníci a pěvci kraji Leoše Janáčka: paměti a dokumentace* [Musicians and singers in the countryside of Leoš Janáček: reminiscences and documents] (Ostrava: Profil, 1981).
IcoJan	Theodora Straková, *Icongraphia Janáčkiána* [Janacek Iconography] (Brno: Moravian Museum, 1975).
JAi	*Korespondence Leoše Janáčka s Artušem Rektorysem* [Correspondence of Leoš Janáček with Artuš Rektorys], ed. Artuš Rektorys (Prague: Hudební matice, 1934), Janáčkův archiv Vol. 1.
JAii	*Korespondence Leoše Janáčka s Otakarem Ostrčilem* [Correspondence of Leoš Janáček with Otakar Ostrčil], ed. Artuš Rektorys (Prague: Hudební matice, 1948), Janáčkův archiv Vol. 2.
JAiii	*Korespondence Leoše Janáčka s F. S. Procházkou* [Correspondence of Leoš Janáček with F. S. Procházka], ed. Artuš Rektorys (Prague: Hudební matice, 1949), Janáčkův archiv Vol. 3.
JAiv	*Korespondence Leoše Janáčka s Artušem Rektorysem* [Correspondence of Leoš Janáček with Artuš Rektorys], second enlarged edition, ed. Artuš Rektorys (Prague: Hudební matice, 1949), Janáčkův archiv Vol. 4.
JAv	*Korespondence Leoše Janáčka s libretisty Výlety Broučkových* [Correspondence of Leoš Janáček with the librettists of *The Excursions of Mr Brouček*], ed. Artuš Rektorys (Prague: Hudební matice, 1950), Janáčkův archiv Vol. 5.
JAvi	*Korespondence Leoše Janáčka s Gabrielou Horvátovou* [Correspondence of Leoš Janáček with Gabriela Horvátová], ed. Artuš Rektorys (Prague: Hudební matice, 1950), Janáčkův archiv Vol. 6.
JAvii	*Korespondence Leoše Janáčka s Karlem Kovařovicem a ředitelstvím Národního divadla* [Correspondence of Leoš Janáček with Karel Kovařovic and the directors of the National Theatre], ed. Artuš Rektorys (Prague: Hudební matice, 1950), Janáčkův archiv Vol. 7.
JAviii	*Korespondence Leoše Janáčka s Marií Calmou a MUDr. Františkem Veselým* [Correspondence of Leoš Janáček with Marie Calma and Dr František Veselý], ed. Jan Racek and Artuš Rektorys (Prague: Orbis, 1951), Janáčkův archiv Vol. 8.
JAix	*Korespondence Leoše Janáčka s Maxem Brodem* [Correspondence of Leoš Janáček with Max Brod], ed. Jan Racek and Artuš Rektorys (Prague: SNKLHU, 1953), Janáčkův archiv Vol. 9

JacWoo	Arthur Jacobs, *Henry Wood: Maker of the Proms* (London: Methuen, 1994).
JanBak	Libuše Janáčková, *Leoš Janáček a Břetislav Bakala: Edice vzájemné korespondence* [Leoš Janáček and Břetislav Bakala: correspondence], diss. (Brno: Masaryk University, 2007).
JANGES	Leoš Janáček Gesellschaft website, including online Janáček encyclopedia by Jakob Knaus: www.leos-janacek.org
JanLid	Libuše Janáčková, *Leoš Janáček a Lidové noviny. Leoš Janáček and Lidové noviny* (Brno: Moravian Museum, 2014), text in Czech and English.
JanMas	*Slavnostní promoce Leoše Janáčka čestního doktora fil. fakulty Masarykovy university v Brně, 25. I. 1925.* [Festive Graduation of Dr Leoš Janáček as an Honorary Doctor of the Philosophy Faculty of Masaryk University in Brno, 25. I. 1925] (Brno: Pazdírek, 1925).
JanSkl	Leoš Janáček, *O skladbě souzvukův a jejich spojův* [On the composition of chords and their connection] (Prague: Fr. A. Urbánek, 1897).
JanÚpl	Leoš Janáček, *Úplná nauka o harmonii. II. vydání* [Complete Harmony Manual, Second edition] (Brno: Píša, 1920).
JAWO	Nigel Simeone, John Tyrrell and Alena Němcová, *Janáček's Works: A Catalogue of the Music and Writings* (Oxford: Clarendon Press, 1997).
JODA	John Tyrrell, *Janáček's Operas: A documentary account* (London: Faber, 1992).
JosLad	*Josef Lada.* Website: www.joseflada.cz
JožUpr	*Galerie Joži Uprky v Uherském Hradišti.* Website: web.jozauprka.cz
JurDům	*Dušan Jurkovič: Architekt a jeho dům* [Dušan Jurkovič: the architect and his house] (Brno: Moravská galerie], exhibition catalogue.
JYL1	John Tyrrell, *Janáček: Years of a Life. Vol. I (1854–1914): The lonely blackbird* (London: Faber, 2006).
JYL2	John Tyrrell, *Janáček: Years of a Life. Vol. II (1914–1928): Tsar of the Forests* (London: Faber, 2007).
KarAnč	*Karel Ančerl.* Website: www.karel-ancerl.com
KleBez	Martina Klezlová, *Guide to the Petr Bezruč Memorial and Chalet* (Opava: Silesian Museum, 2012).
KLJ	Jiří Zahrádka et al. (eds.), *Korespondence Leoše Janáčka* [Leoš Janáček's Correspondence]. Website: www.musicologica.cz/ korespondencejanacek
KnaFug	Jakob Knaus, Introduction to *Fugy* (SKVEJ F/3, 2008).
KnaInt	Jakob Knaus (ed.), *Leoš Janáček: Intime Briefe: 1879/80 aus Leipzig und Wien* (Zurich: Leoš Janáček Gesellschaft, 1985).
KnaMat	Jakob Knaus (ed.), *Leoš Janáček: Materialien* (Zurich: Leoš Janáček Gesellschaft, 1987).
KobExp	Ilse Kobán, 'Expressing the Unsaid', disc notes for *Das schlaue*

Füchlein dir. Walter Felsenstein, cond. Václav Neumanm, Arthaus DVD 101297.

KonČte   Hana Konečná et al., *Čtení o Národím divadle* [Essays on the National Theatre] (Prague: Odeon, 1983).

KroNem   *Kroměřížská nemocince*, 'Historie chirurgie' [History of surgery]. Website: www.nem-km.cz/historie-chirurgie

KuncHR   Jan Kunc, 'Leoš Janáček', *Hudební revue*, Vol. 4, No. 3 (March 1911), 121–34; No. 4 (April 1911), 185–9.

KunEnc   Milan Kundera, *Encounter*, trans. Linda Asher (New York: Harper, 2010).

KunJan   Ludvík Kundera, *Janáček a Klub přátel umění* [Janáček and the Club of the Friends of Art in Brno] (Olomouc: Velehrad, 1948).

KunKva   Ludvík Kundera, *Jaroslav Kvapil: život a dílo* [Jaroslav Kvapil: life and work] (Prague: Hudební matice, 1944).

KunMůj   Milan Kundera, *Můj Janáček* [My Janáček] (Brno: Atlantis, 2004).

KunTal   Milan Kuna, *Václav Talich 1883–1961. Šťastný i hořký úděl dirigenta* [Václav Talich 1883–1961: the happy and bitter fate of the conductor] (Prague: Academia, 2009).

KunVar   Ludvík Kundera, *Janáčková varhanická škola* [Janáček's Organ School] (Olomouc: Velehrad, 1948).

KvěSuk   J. M. Květ, *Živá slova Josefa Suka* [Living Words by Josef Suk] (Prague: Topičova, 1946).

LamMas   Patrick Lambert, 'Leoš Janáček and T. G. Masaryk', in Harry Hanak (ed.), *T. G. Masaryk (1850–1937), Volume 3: Statesman and Cultural Force* (London: Macmillan, 1989).

LánJan   Oldřich Lána: *Leoš Janáček a Umělecká beseda (1920–1928)* [Leoš Janáček and The Society of Artists (i.e. Hudební matice) (1920–1928)], diss. (Brno: Masaryk University, 2017).

LázLuh   *Lázně Luhačovice 1902–1927* [The Spa of Luhačovice] (Luhačovice: Ruda Kubíček, 1927).

LEOJAN   *Leoš Janáček*. Website (in Czech and English): www.leosjanacek.eu

LHN   *Listy Hudební matice*

LidUpr   'Joža Uprka: svébytný umělec nebo folklorista?' [Joža Uprka: individual artist or folklorist?], unsigned article, 23 October 2011, published online in www.lidovky.cz

LJFD1   *Leoš Janáček: Folkoristické dílo I* [Leoš Janáček: Folkloric Studies I], ed. Jarmila Procházková, Marta Toncrová and Jiří Vysloužil (Brno: Editio Janáček, 2009), SKVEJ I/3–1.

LJLD1   *Leoš Janáček: Literární dílo I* [Leoš Janáček: Literary Works], ed. Theodora Straková and Eva Drlíková (Brno: Editio Janáček, 2003), SKVEJ I/1–1.

LJLD2   *Leoš Janáček: Literární dílo II* [Leoš Janáček: Literary Works II], ed. Theodora Straková and Eva Drlíková (Brno: Editio Janáček, 2003), SKVEJ I/1–2.

LJLR   Bohumír Štědroň, *Leos Janáček: Letters and Reminiscences*, trans. Geraldine Thomsen (Prague: Artia, 1955).

LJTR1   *Leoš Janáček: Teoretické dílo I* [Leoš Janáček: Theoretical Works I], ed. Eva Drlíková, Leoš Faltus, Svatava Přibáňová and Jiří Zahrádka (Brno: Editio Janáček, 2007), SKVEJ I/2–1.

LJTR2   *Leoš Janáček: Teoretické dílo II* [Leoš Janáček: Theoretical Works II], ed. Eva Drlíková, Leoš Faltus, Svatava Přibáňová and Jiří Zahrádka (Brno: Editio Janáček, 2008), SKVEJ I/2–2.

LN   *Lidové noviny* online archive (1893–1945). Website: www.digitalniknihovna.cz/mzk

MacPia   Elyse Mach, *Great pianists speak for themselves*, new edition (Mineola, NY: Dover, 1991).

MacTyr   Charles Mackerras, interviewed by John Tyrrell, 'My Life with Janáček's Music', disc notes for Supraphon SU 3739-2 032.

MarRob   Ivan Margolius, 'The Robot of Prague', in *Newsletter*, issue 17 (Autumn 2017) of the Friends of Czech Heritage, 3–6.

MetArc   *Metopera Database: The Metropolitan Opera Archives*. Website: archives.metoperafamily.org

MetDol   *Metod Doležil k šedesátým narozeninám vydalo Pěvecké sdružení pražských učitelů* [Metod Doležil on his sixtieth birthday] (Prague: Pěvecké sdružení pražských učitelů, 1945).

MikJan   Jan Mikota, 'Leoš Janáček v Anglii' [Leoš Janáček in England], *Listy Hudební matice*, Vol. 5 (1926), 257–68.

MikTaj   Jan Mikeska: *Tajemství P.S. aneb odhalení autora textu Janáčkova Zápisníku zmizelého* [The Secret P.S. or the revelation of the author of the text of Janáček's *The Diary of One Who Disappeared*] (Vizovice: Lípa, 1998).

MLWJ   John Tyrrell, ed. and trans., *My Life with Janáček: The Memoirs of Zdenka Janáčková* (London: Faber, 1998).

MooVzp   Karel Moor, *V dlani osudu: Vzpomínky českého hudebníka* [In the hand of fate: Memoirs of a Czech Musician] (Nový Bydžov: Janata, 1947).

MucMuc   Jiří Mucha, *Alphonse Mucha: His Life and Art by his Son* (London: Heinemann, 1966).

MülJan   Daniel Müller, *Janáček* (Paris: Rieder, 1930).

NDBrOA   *Národní divaldo Brno Online Archive*. Website: www.ndbrno.cz/modules/theaterarchive

NDPrOA   *Národní divadlo Prague* [online archive]. Website: archiv.narodni-divadlo.cz

NejČes   Zdeněk Nejedlý, *České moderní zpěvohra po Smetanovi* [Czech modern opera since Smetana] (n.p., [1911]).

NejJej   Zdeněk Nejedlý, *Leoše Janáčka 'Její pastorkyňa'* [Leoš Janáček's *Jenůfa*] (Prague: Hudební knihovna časopisu Smetana, XXII, 1916).

NěmHou   Alena Němcová, Introduction to *Skladby pro housle a klavír* (SKV E/1, 1988).

NěmŘík   Alena Němcová, Introduction to *Říkadla* (SKVEJ E/5, 2006).

NěmŠár   Alena Němcová, Disc notes for *Šárka*, Supraphon SU 3485-2 631.

NěmZap   Alena Němcová, Introduction to *Zápisník zmizelého* (SKVEJ E/4, 2004).

NeuPam   Alois Augustin Neumann, *Z pamětí rodiny Neumannovy z Olešnice na Moravě* [Memoirs of the Neumann family from Olešnice na Moravě] (Brno: privately printed, 1940).

NewMus   Rosa Newmarch, *The Music of Czechoslovakia* (London: Oxford University Press, 1942).

NosOpe   Václav Nosek (ed.), *Opery Leoše Janáčka na brněnske scéně* [The Operas of Leoš Janáček on the Brno Stage] (Brno: State Theatre, 1958).

NouNov   Zdeněk Nouza and Miroslav Nový, *Josef Suk: Tematický katalog skladeb, Thematic catalogue of the works* (Prague: Bärenreiter, 2005), text in Czech and English.

NovSob   Vítězslav Novák, *O sobě a o jiných* [About himself and others] (Prague: Editio Supraphon, 1970).

NYT   *New York Times*

ÖBL   *Österreichisches biographisches Lexikon*. Website: www.biographien. ac.at

OreMen   Vítězslav Orel, *Gregor Mendel: The First Geneticist* (Oxford: Oxford University Press, 1996).

PalJan   Josef Páleníček, 'Páleníček on Leoš Janáček', disc notes for Supraphon SU 3812-2.

PalJev   František Pala, 'Jevištní dílo Leoše Janáčka' [The stage works of Leoš Janáček], *Musikologie*, Vol. 3 (1955), 61–210.

PalPos   František Pala [Vols. 1–4] and Vilém Pospíšil [Vol. 5], *Opera Národního divadla v období Otakara Ostrčila* [Opera at the National Theatre in the era of Otakar Ostrčil] (Prague: Divadelní ústav, 1962, 1964, 1965, 1970, 1983).

PatRoz   A. J. Patzaková, *Prvních deset let Československého rozhlasu* [The first ten years of Czech Radio] (Prague: Radiojournal, 1935).

PavIns   Gabriela Pavlátová, *Instrumentační úpravy partitur oper Leoše Janáčka českými dirigenty* [Instrumental adaptations of the works by Leoš Janáček by Czech conductors], diss. (Brno: Masaryk University, 2012).

PazHud   Gracian Černušák and Vladimír Helfert (eds.), *Pazdirkův hudební slovník naučný. II: Část osobní. Svazek prvý A–K* [Pazdírek's music dictionary. II: biographical section, A–K] (Brno: Pazdírek, 1937).

PečHel   Rudolf Pečman, *Vladimír Helfert* (Brno: Nadace Universitas Masarykiana, Edice Osobnosti, 2003).

PedHaa   Lubomír Peduzzi, *Pavel Haas: Leben und Werk des Komponisten* (Hamburg: Von Bockel, 1996).

PetFir   Ivan Petrželka, *Leoš Firkušný o Janáčkovi a české hudbě* [Leoš Firkušný on Janáček and Czech music] (Brno: Šimon Ryšavý 2007).

PetKov   Jan Petr (ed.), *Vzpomínáme Karla Kovařovice* [In Memory of Karel Kovařovic] (Prague: Korber, 1940).

PetMaj   Ivan Petrželka and Jiří Majer, *Konservatoř Brno: Sborník k padesátému výročí trvání první moravské odborně umělecké školy* [The Brno Conservatory: Festschrift for the fiftieth anniversary of the first Moravian music school] (Brno: Blok, 1969).

PisVeč   [Adolf Piskáček], 'Večer s Leošem Janáčkem' [An Evening with Leoš Janáček], *Dalibor*, Vol. 28 (1906), 227.

PlaKat   Dragan Plamenac, 'Nepoznati komentari Leoše Janáčka opera *Katja Kabanova*' [An unknown commentary on Leoš Janáček's opera *Káťa Kabanová*], *Muzikološki zbornik* [Ljubljana], Vol. 17 (1981), 122–31.

PohRud   Richard Pohl, *Rudolf Firkušný* (Brno: JAMU, 2016).

PosFes   Klára Pospíšilová, *Historie Brněnských festival věnovaných odkazu Leoše Janáčka* [The History of the Brno Festival dedicated to Leoš Janáček's legacy], diss. (Brno: Masaryk University, 2016).

Přildy   Svatava Přibaňová, Introduction to *Idyla* (SKVEJ D/1–2, 2003).

PřiKat   Svatava Přibáňová, *Káťa Kabanová na brněnském jevišti* [*Káťa Kabanová* on the Brno Stage] (Brno: Janáček Opera et al., 2003).

PřiLed   Svatava Přibáňová and Zuzana Lederová-Protivová, *Svět Janáčkových oper. World of Janáček's Operas* (Brno: Moravian Museum et al., 1998), text in Czech and English.

PřiMlá   Svatava Přibáňová, Introdiction to *Mládí* (SKV E/6, 1990).

PřiPam   Svatava Přibáňová, *Památník Leoše Janáčka* [The Leoš Janáček Memorial] (Brno: Moravian Museum, 1983).

PřiSui   Svatava Přibáňová, Introduction to *Suita pro smyčce* (SKVEJ D/1–1, 2002).

PřiTar   Svatava Přibáňová, Introduction to *Taras Bulba* (SKV D/7, 1980).

PřiThe   Svatava Přibáňová (ed.), *Thema con variazioni. Leoš Janáček korespondence s manželkou Zdeňkou a dcerou Olgou* [Theme and Variations: Leoš Janáček correspondence with his wife Zdenka and daughter Olga] (Prague: Bärenreiter, 2007).

PřiZah   Svatava Přibáňová and Jiří Zahrádka, *Leoš Janáček ve fotografiích. Leoš Janáček in Photographs* (Brno: Moravian Museum, 2008), text in Czech and English.

ProBal   Jarmila Procházková, Introduction to *Balada blanická* (SKVEJ D/8, 2003).

ProCap   Jarmila Procházková, Introduction to *Capriccio* (SKV E/5, 2001).

ProDun   Jarmila Procházková, Introduction to *Dunaj* (SKV H/3, 2009).

ProHud   Jaroslav Procházka, *Hudební dílo Leoše Janáčka* [The musical works of Leoš Janáček] (Frýdek-Místek: Okresní vlastivědé muzeum, 1979).

ProKaf   Jaroslav Procházka, 'Brods Uebersetzung des Librettos der *Jenůfa* und die Korrekturen Franz Kafkas', in Jakob Knaus (ed.), *Leoš*

	Janáček: Materialien (Zurich: Leoš Janáček Gesellschaft, 1987), 30–80.
ProLaš	Jaroslav Procházka, *Lašské kořeny života i díla Leoše Janáčka* [The Lachian roots in the life and work of Leoš Janáček] (Prague: Hudební matice, 1948).
ProLeo	Jarmila Procházková, 'Leoš Janáček jako organizátor orchestrálních koncertů v Brně 1889–1914' [Leoš Janáček as organizer of orchestral concerts in Brno 1889–1914], *Opus musicum*, Vol. 30 (1998), No. 2, 50–9.
ProLuh	Jarmila Procházková, *Janáčkovy Luhačovice: genius loci et genius musicae* [Janáček's Luhačovice: the spirit of place and the spirit of music] (Luhačovice: Prameny, 2009).
ProMil	Jarmila Procházková, 'Janáček and Military Music', *Sborník prací filozofické fakulty brněnské university, řada hudebněvědná (H)*, Vol. 47 (1998), No. 33, 43–53.
ProNar	Jaroslava Procházková, Introduction to *Národní tance na Moravě* (SKVEJ G/2, 2005).
ProPam	Jarmila Procházková (ed.), *Památník pro Kamilu Stösslovou* [Album for Kamila Stösslová] (Brno: Moravian Museum, 1994; English edition trans. John Tyrrell, 1996).
ProPut	Jarmila Procházková, Introduction to *Putování dušičky: Houslový concert* (SKV H/4, 1997).
ProSui	Jarmila Procházková, Introduction to *Suita Op. 3* (SKVEJ B/2, 2011).
ProVol	Jarmila Procházková and Bohumír Volný, *Born in Hukvaldy* (Brno: Moravian Museum, 1995).
ProVza	Jarmila Procházková et al., *Vzaty do fonografu* [Recorded by phonograph] (Brno: Etnologický ústav, 2012).
ProZáz	Jarmila Procházková, *Janáčkovy záznamy hudebního a tanečního folkloru. I. Komentáře* [Janáček's Records of Folk Music and Dance. I. Commentary] (Brno: Etnologický ústav, 2006).
PulTak	*Pult und Taktstock*, CD-Rom (Vienna: Universal Edition, UE 45015).
RacBra	Jan Racek, *Bratří Mrštíkové a jejich citový vstah k Leoši Janáčkovi a Vítězslavu Novákovi* [The Mrštík brothers and their relationship with Leoš Janáček and Vítězslav Novák] (Brno: Moravské kolo spisovatelů, 1940).
RacObr	Jan Racek, *Leoš Janáček: obraz života a díla* [Leoš Janáček: a picture of his life and work] (Brno: Výbor pro pořádání Leoše Janáčka, 1948).
RacSou	Jan Racek, *Leoš Janáček a současní moravští skladatelé* [Leoš Janáček and contemporary Moravian composers] (Brno: Unie, 1940).
RakVýs	Jan Racek, *Katalog výstavy Leoš Janáček, osobnost a dílo* [Catalogue of the Exhibition Leoš Janáček, personality and work] (Brno: Výbor pro pořádání Leoše Janáčka, 1948).
SelKap	Lubomír Selinger, *Václav Kaprál v Rovnosti 1920–1922* [Václav Kaprál

in *Rovnost* 1920–1922] (Brno: Vydavatelství Československý novinář, 1968).

SimBak   Nigel Simeone, *Břetislav Bakala conducts Janáček* [booklet to accompany CRQ Editions CDR] ([Sheffield]: CRQ Editions, 2017).

SimBro   Nigel Simeone, Disc notes for *The Excursions of Mr Brouček*, Deutsche Grammophon 477 7387.

SimHyp   Nigel Simeone, Disc notes for *The Eternal Gospel*, *The Ballad of Blaník* and *The Fiddler's Child*, Hyperion CDA 67517.

SimMor   Nigel Simeone, 'Janáček's Moravian publishers', in Paul Wingfield (ed.), *Janáček Studies* (Cambridge: Cambridge University Press, 1999), 170–82.

SimTal   Nigel Simeone, 'A Tale of Two Vixens: Janáček's relationship with Universal Edition and the 1924 and 1925 editions of *The Cunning Little Vixen*', in *Sundry Sorts of Music Books: Essays on the British Library Collections presented to O. W. Neighbour on his 70th birthday* (London: British Library, 1993).

SimTyr   Nigel Simeone and John Tyrrell (eds.), *Charles Mackerras* (Woodbridge: Boydell Press, 2015).

SimZam   Nigel Simeone, 'Zamýšlené uvedení Janáčkovy Věci Makropulos v Berlíně roku 1928 [The proposed Berlin production of Janáček's *The Makropulos Affair* in 1928], *Opus musicum*, xxv (1993), 245–8.

SkaSed   František Skacelík (ed.), *Sedmdesát let Umělecké besedy 1863–1933* [Seventy years of the Society of Artists] (Prague: Umělecká beseda, 1933), incl. Václav Mikota, 'Leoš Janáček a Hudební matice' [Leoš Janáček and Hudební matice], 190–4.

SKV   *Soubourne kritické vydání děl Leoše Janáčka* [Complete critical edition of the works of Leoš Janáček] (Kassel: Bäreneiter; Prague: Bärenreiter, 1978–).

SKVEJ   *Soubourne kritické vydání děl Leoše Janáčka* [Complete critical edition of the works of Leoš Janáček] (Brno: Editio Janáček, 2002–).

SmeVyp   *Robert Smetana: Vyprávění o Leoši Janáčkovi* [Stories about Janáček] (Olomouc: Velehrad, 1948).

ŠmoSbo   Jan Šmolík, 'Sbory Leoše Janáčka na texty Petra Beruče' [Leoš Janáček's choruses on texts by Petr Berzruč], *Leoš Janáček: sborník statií a studií* (Prague: Hudební rozhledy, 1959).

ŠouBro   Otakar Šourek, *Leoš Janáček: Výlety paně Broučkovy. Úvodní slovo skladatelovo. Rozbor Otakara Šourka* [Leoš Janáček: The Excursions of Mr Brouček. Foreword by the composer. Analysis by Otakar Šourek] (Prague: Hudební matice, 1920).

ŠouSQ1   Otakar Šourek, Introduction to String Quartet No. 1 (Hudební matice, 1945).

ŠouTal   Otakar Šourek (ed.), *Václav Talich: život a práce* [Václav Talich: life and work] (Prague: Hudební matice, 1943).

ŠouTar   Otakar Šourek, Introduction to *Taras Bulba* (Prague: Hudební matice, 1947).

SpuHaa	Lubomír Spurný, 'Pavel Haas: "Janáček's most talented student"', *Muzikolški zbornik*, Vol. 60 (2015), 119–25.
ŠtěHud	Bohumír Štědroň, Introduction to *Hudba ke kroužení kužely* (Prague: Hudební matice, 1950).
SteJan	Benjamin Steege, 'Janáček's Chronoscope', *Journal of the American Musicological Society*, Vol. 64 (2011), No. 3, 647–87.
SteNew	Lewis Stevens, *An Unforgettable Woman: The Life and Times of Rosa Newmarch* (Kibworth Beauchamp: Matador, 2011).
ŠtěObr	Bohumír Štědroň, *Leoš Janáček v obrazech* [Leoš Janáček in pictures] (Prague: Státní pedagogické nakadaltelství, 1958).
ŠtěOtč	Bohumír Štědroň, Introduction to *Otče náš* (Prague: SHV, 1963).
ŠtěSQ1	Miloš Štědron, Introduction to String Quartet No. 1 (SKV E/3, 2000).
ŠtěSQ2	Miloš Štědron, Introduction to String Quartet No. 2 (SKV E/4, 2008).
ŠtěSui	Bohumír Štědroň, Introduction to *Suita Op. 3* (Prague: SNKLHU, 1958).
ŠtěZur	Bohumír Štědroň, *Zur Genesis von Leoš Janáčeks Oper Jenůfa* (Brno: University J. E. Purkyně, 1968).
StoLöw	Ivo Stolařík, *Jan Löwenbach a Leoš Janáček: Vzájemna korespondence* [Jan Löwenbach and Leoš Janáček: Correspondence] (Opava: Slezský studijní ústav, 1958).
StoOst	Ivo Stolařík, *Umělecká hudba v Ostravě 1918–1938* [Art Music in Ostrava 1918–1938] (Ostrava: Tilia, 1997).
StoPSM	Ivo Stolařík (ed.), *60 let PSMU* (Ostrava: Krajské nakladatelství, 1963).
StrČár	Theodora Straková, Introduction to *Na Soláni Čarták* (SKV B/3, 1981).
StrMuž	Theodora Straková, Introduction to *Mužské sbory II* (SKV C/2, 2011).
StrSbo	Theodora Straková, Introduction to *Sborník skladeb z pražských studií* (Brno: Editio Janáček, 2001).
StřŠtě	Stanislava Střelcová (ed.), *Bohumír Štědroň: hudební historik, kritik, umělec, učitel* [Bohumír Štědroň: music historian, critic, artist, teacher] (Brno, Editio Moravia, 2005).
StrŽár	Theodora Straková, Introduction to *Žárlivost* and *Adagio* (Prague: SHV, 1963).
SupGen	*Generální katalog čs. gramofonových desek Supraphon 1959* [General Catalogue of Supraphon Czech Gramophone Records 1959] (Prague: Gramofonové zavody, 1959).
SupHis	'History of Supraphon' on Supraphon website: www.supraphon.com/about-us
SupJan	*Leoš Janáček: Supraphon* [list of available Janáček recordings] (Prague: Gramofonové zavody, 1950).

SusJan   Charles Susskind, *Janáček and Brod* (London: Yale University Press, 1985).

TauJan   Vilém Tauský and Margaret Tauský, *Leoš Janáček: Leaves from his Life* (London: Kahn & Averill, 1982).

TauTel   Vilém Tauský, *Vilém Tauský tells his story* (London: Stainer and Bell, 1979).

TauMůj   Stanislav Tauber, *Můj hudební svět* [My Musical World] (Brno: Hapala, 1949).

TelJan   Vladimír Telec, *Leoš Janáček 1854–1928: výběrová bibliografie* [Leoš Janáček: select bibliography] (Brno: Universitní knihovna, 1958).

TěsDem   Rudolf Těsnohlídek, *Demänová* (Prague: Vydavatelstvo Družstevní práce v Praze, 1926).

TrkSte   Marie Trkanová, *U Janáčků podle vyprávění Marie Stejskalové* [At the Janáčeks after the account of Marie Stejskalová] (Prague: Panton: 1959, second edition 1964).

TroVěč   Jan Trojan, Introduction to *Věčně evangelium* (SKV B/4, 2002).

TygIlu   Jozef Męcina-Krzesz, 'Ojce Nasz', *Tygodnik Ilustrowany*, 1899, No. 48 (28 October 1899), 946–7. Illustrations for *Our Father* (IV/29).

TyrCh1   John Tyrrell, Disc notes for Janáček Orchestral Works Vol. 1, Chandos CHSA 5142, incl. *Sinfonietta*.

TyrCh2   John Tyrrell, Disc notes for Janáček Orchestral Works Vol. 2, Chandos CHSA 5156, incl. *The Danube*.

TyrCze   John Tyrrell, *Czech Opera* (Cambridge: Cambridge University Press, 1988).

TyrInt   John Tyrrell (ed. and trans.), *Intimate Letters: Leoš Janáček to Kamila Stösslová* (London: Faber, 1993), edited translation of *PřiHad*.

TyrKat   John Tyrrell, *Leoš Janáček: Káťa Kabanová* (Cambridge: Cambridge University Press, 1982).

TyrNej   John Tyrrell, 'Janáček, Nejedlý and the Future of Czech National Opera', in *Art and Ideology in European Opera: Essays in Honour of Julian Rushton*, ed. Rachel Cowgill, David Cooper and Clive Brown (Woodbridge: Boydell Press, 2010), 103–21, incl. substantial extracts in English from *NejČes* and *NejJej*.

TyrSim   'A Spark of God: John Tyrrell and Nigel Simeone discuss Janáček's last opera', *Opera*, Vol. 69, No. 3 (March 2018), pp. 268–76.

TyrSpe   John Tyrrell, 'Janáček and the *Speech-Melody Myth*', *Musical Times*, Vol. 111 (1970), 793–6.

UEAn   *Die Musikblätter des Anbruch 1919 bis 1937*, CD-Rom (Universal Edition, UE 45014).

VašJan   Adolf Vašek, *Po stopách Dra Leoše Janáčka* [In the Footsteps of Dr Leoš Janáček] (Brno: Brněnské knižní, 1930).

VDKS   Bohumír Štědroň, *Leoš Janáček: Vzpomínky, dokumenty, korespondence a studie* [Leoš Janáček: Reminiscences, documents, letters and studies] (Prague: Editio Supraphon, 1986).

VejFra   Veronika Vejvodová, Introduction for *Musiche per drammi: Frammenti (1906–1928)* (SKVEJ A/11, 2010).

VesČes   Richard Veselý, *Dějiny České filharmonie v letech 1901–1924* [History of the Czech Philharmonic in the years 1901–1924] (Prague: [no publisher], 1935).

VesJan   Adolf Veselý (ed.), *Leoš Janáček: Pohled do života i díla* [Leoš Janáček: a view of the life and works] (Prague: Fr. Borový, 1924), generally referred to as 'Janáček's autobiography'.

VesPos   Adolf Veselý, 'Poslední rozhovor s Leošem Janáčkem' [The last interview with Leoš Janáček], *Hudební Rozhledy*, Vol. 4, Nos. 4–8 (1928).

VesŠol   Terezie Veselá, 'Emil Šolc', online article on Telč official website: www.telc.eu/turista_a_volny_cas/historie/osobnosti/solc_emil

VěžZpí   Václav Věžník, *Zpívali v Brně II: Kronika české opery v Brně* [They Sang in Brno II: Chronicle of Czech Opera in Brno] (Brno: JAMU, 2014).

VogDra   Jaroslav Vogel, *Leoš Janáček: dramatik* [Leoš Janáček: dramatist] (Prague: Hudební matice, 1948).

VogJan   Jaroslav Vogel, *Leoš Janáček: A biography* [rev. edition by Karel Janovický] (London: Orbis Publishing, 1981).

VohKMS   Suzanne Vohnoutová El Roumhainová, *Počátky Klubu moravských skladatelů (1919–1928)* [The Beginnings of the Moravian Composers' Club (1919–1928)], Master's thesis (Brno: Masaryk University, 2012).

VokLuh   Vlastimil Vokurka, *Luhačovice a Leoš Janáček* [Luhačovice and Leoš Janáček] (Luhačovice: Lázně Luhačovice et al., 1996).

VrbRus   Přemysl Vrba, 'Ruský kroužek v Brně a Leoš Janáček' [The Brno Russian Circle and Leoš Janáček], *Slezský sborník*, Vol. 57 (1960), 71–85.

VrbStá   Tomáš Vrbka, *Státní opera Praha: Historie divadla v obrazech a datech 1888–2003 / The Prague State Opera: Theatre History in Pictures and Dates 1888–2003* (Prague: Slovart, 2004), text in Czech and English.

VycVěč   Ladislav Vycpálek, *Věčně Evangelium* [review], *Hudební revue*, February 1917, 231–2.

VysAma   Jiří Vysloužil, Introduction to *Amarus* (SKV B/1, 2000).

VysJan   Jiří Vysloužil (ed.), *Leoš Janáček: O lidové písni a lidové hudbě* [Leoš Janáček: on folk song and folk music] (Prague: SNKLHU, 1955).

VysŠum   Jiří Vysloužil, Introduction to *Šumařovo dítě* (SKV D/6, 1984).

WieArc   *Wiener Staatsoper Spielplanarchiv*. Website: archiv.wiener-staatsoper.at

WinGla   Paul Wingfield, *Janáček: Glagolitic Mass* (Cambridge: Cambridge University Press, 1992).

WinJan   Paul Wingfield, 'Janáček's "Lost" Kreutzer Sonata', *Journal of the Royal Musical Association*, Vol. 112, No. 2 (1986–7), 229–56.

WinMlh   Paul Wingfield, 'Janáček's V mlhách: towards a new chronology', *Časopis Moravského Muzea*, Vol. 52 (1987), 189–204.

WinSpe   Paul Wingfield, 'Janáček's speech-melody theory in concept and practice', *Cambridge Opera Journal*, Vol. 3 (1991), No. 4, 281–301.

WinStu   Paul Wingfield (ed.), *Janáček Studies* (Cambridge: Cambridge University Press, 1999).

ZahCow   Jiří Zahrádka, 'Henry Cowell a Brno. Příspěvek k brněnským meziválečným kontaktům s představiteli světové avantgardy' [Henry Cowell and Brno. Contribution to the Brno inter-war contacts with the international avant-garde], *Musicologia brunensia*, Vol. 44 (2009), 217–23.

ZahDiv   Jiří Zahrádka, *'Divadlo nesmí býti lidu komedií': Leoš Janáček a Národní divadlo v Brně. 'Theatre must not be comedy for the people': Leoš Janáček and the National Theatre in Brno* (Brno: Moravian Museum, 2012), text in Czech and English.

ZahFoo   Jiří Zahrádka, *In the Footsteps of Leoš Janáček* (Brno: Moravian Museum et al., 2017).

ZahGla   Jiří Zahrádka, Introduction to *Glagolská mše* (SKV B/5–I, 2011).

ZahMak   Jiří Zahrádka, Introduction to *Věc Makropulos* (Vienna: Universal Edition, 2016).

ZahMlá   Jiří Zahrádka, Introduction to *Mládí* (Munich: Henle, 2015).

ZahMlh   Jiří Zahrádka, Introduction to *V mlhách* (Munich: Henle, 2016).

ZahOsu   Jiří Zahrádka, Introduction to *Osud* (SKV A/5, 2016).

ZahPoc   Jiří Zahrádka, Introduction to *Marsch der Blaukehlchen* [*Pochod Modráčků*] (Munich: Henle, 2016).

ZahŠár   Jiří Zahrádka, Introduction to *Šárka*, vocal score (Vienna and Brno: Universal Edition and Editio Moravia, 2002).

ZahSin   Jiří Zahrádka, Introduction to *Sinfonietta* (Vienna: Universal Edition, 2018).

ZahTar   Jiří Zahrádka, Introduction to *Taras Bulba* (Kassel: Bärenreiter, 2015).

ZahVix   Jiří Zahrádka, Introduction to *Příhody lišky Bystroušky* (Vienna: Universal Edition, 2009).

ZahZap   Jiří Zahrádka, Introduction to *Zápisník zmizelého* (Prague: Bärenreiter, 2016).

ZahŽen   Jiří Zahrádka, Introduction to *Ženské sbory* (SKVEJ C/3, 2002).

ZávPre   Artur Závodský, *Gabriela Preissová* (Prague: Státní pedagogické nakladatelství, 1962).

ZemEss   Mirka Zemanová (ed. and trans.), *Janáček's Uncollected Essays on Music* (London: Marion Boyars, 1989).

ZemJan   Mirka Zemanová, *Janáček: A Composer's Life* (London: John Murray, 2002).

ŽeňHud   Ladislav Liška and Emilian Hörbinger, *Žeň Hudební matice: Soupis vydaných publikací k 31. prosinci 1949* [The Harvest of Hudební matice. A list of editions published to 31 December 1949] (Prague: Hudební matice, 1949).

ZouMar   Vít Zouhar, 'Bohuslav Martinů's notes on Janáček's introduction to the *Moravian Folksongs Newly Collected* (*Národní písně v nově nasbírané*)', *Musicologica Brunensia*, Vol. 48 (2013), 191–9